Proverbs Are the Best Policy

Proverbs Are the Best Policy

Folk Wisdom and American Politics

Wolfgang Mieder

Utah State University Press
Logan, Utah

Utah State University Press
Logan, Utah 84322–7800
www.usu.edu/usupress/

Manufactured in the United States of America
Printed on acid-free paper

Library of Congress Cataloging-in-Publication Data

Mieder, Wolfgang.
    Proverbs are the best policy : folk wisdom and American politics /
Wolfgang Mieder.
        p. cm.
    Includes bibliographical references (p.) and indexes.
    ISBN-13: 978-0-87421-622-6 (pbk. : alk. paper)
    ISBN-10: 0-87421-622-2 (pbk. : alk. paper)
    1. United States--Politics and government--Miscellanea. 2. United
States--Politics and government--Quotations, maxims, etc. 3. Proverbs,
American. 4. Proverbs--Political aspects--United States. 5. Rhetoric
--Political aspects--United States. 6. Politicians--United States
--Language.   I. Title.
E183.M54 2005
398.9'21'0973--dc22

                                                        2005018275

Dedicated to

PATRICK LEAHY and JIM JEFFORDS
U.S. Senators from Vermont

and

BERNIE SANDERS
U.S. Representative from Vermont

Contents

Acknowledgments

While the eight chapters of this book are based on my own scholarly work, I certainly want to acknowledge that no serious scholarship ever takes place in an absolute vacuum. Thus many of the statements and observations in this study were informed by primary and secondary sources, by discussions with colleagues at conferences, and by the invaluable talks with my students. My departmental colleagues and friends Gideon Bavly, Maggie Gordon, Theresia Hoeck, Dennis Mahoney, Kevin McKenna, Kenneth Nalibow, Susanna Nazarova, Helga Schreckenberger, David Scrase, Janet Sobieski, and Beatrice Wood have been incredibly supportive, and my work-study students Valentina Griffin, Courtney Maguire, Maida Omerović, Benjamin Perkins, and Erin Regan have provided much-appreciated help. I am also deeply indebted to Lisa Brooks, Barbara Lamonda, Daryl Purvee, and Nancy Rosedale of the Interlibrary Loan Department of the Bailey-Howe Library at the University of Vermont for obtaining important secondary sources. I also benefitted from the expertise of the two reference librarians Jake Barickman and Karl Bridges. As I express my appreciation to all of these kind people, I also want to thank my fellow folklorists and proverb scholars Shirley L. Arora, Ronald Baker, Dan Ben-Amos, Simon Bronner, Jan Harold Brunvand, Charles Clay Doyle, Alan Dundes, Kimberly J. Lau, Isaac Jack Lévy and Rosemary Lévy Zumwalt, Jay Mechling, Elliott Oring, Anand Prahlad, Barry Toelken, Peter Tokofsky, Olga Trokhimenko, and Stephen D. Winick for their work and insights that continue to inform my own research. Finally, thanks are also due to the journal editors for permitting me to include five previously published chapters in this book.

Introduction

Several years ago my book on *The Politics of Proverbs: From Traditional Wisdom to Proverbial Stereotypes* (1997) appeared in print, and I was deeply honored when it was selected for the Giuseppe Pitrè International Folklore Prize. This award most assuredly encouraged me to continue my work on the use and function of proverbial wisdom in political rhetoric, resulting in such books as *The Proverbial Abraham Lincoln* (2000) and *"Call a Spade a Spade": From Classical Phrase to Racial Slur* (2002). It is indeed with much pleasure that I can now present eight additional studies on various aspects of the political employment of proverbial language under the collective title of *Proverbs Are the Best Policy: Folk Wisdom and American Politics*. While my earlier book contained chapters on Adolf Hitler's, Winston S. Churchill's, and Harry S. Truman's authoritative and effective manipulation of proverbs, the proverbial discourse of the Cold War, and the origin, history, and meaning of the two proverbial slurs "The only good Indian is a dead Indian" and "No tickee, no washee," the present volume is focused on the American political scene ranging from early revolutionary times to the present day. It thus represents a survey of the obvious predominance of proverbs in American political discourse.

The first chapter on "'Different Strokes for Different Folks': American Proverbs as an International, National, and Global Phenomenon" serves as an introductory analysis of what characterizes American proverbs. It is shown that many of the proverbs current in the United States have their origin in classical times, the Bible, and the Middle Ages. As such, they were translated into many languages over the centuries, making up a common stock of proverbial wisdom in large parts of the world. Of course, new proverbs were also coined in the United States with some of them having only a regional distribution while others belong to the basic set of commonly known American proverbs with a national dissemination. With the important political and cultural role of the United States and its version of the English language in the world today, both sets of proverbs, the international and national texts, have now a significant global influence. With English being the *lingua franca* of the modern age, Anglo-American proverbs are being disseminated throughout the world in English or as loan translations. There is thus no doubt that English-language proverbs are now playing the role that Latin proverbs did in former times. In addition, the new American proverbs with their worldview of a democratic and future-oriented society also have a considerable influence on the sociopolitical discourse on the globe.

The second chapter on "Government of the People, by the People, for the People': The Making and Meaning of an American Proverb about Democracy" investigates when this triadic statement originated and how it became an American proverb defining the entire concept of democracy in a most succinct manner. The various sections of this detailed survey deal with the early beginnings with John Adams and John Marshall, with Daniel Webster's significant speech of January 26, 1830, with Theodore Parker's important abolitionist speeches and writings, and with Abraham Lincoln as the catalyst and phrase-forger with his use of the proverbial triad at the end of his famous Gettysburg Address of November 19, 1863. From there I move on to Frederick Douglass's repetitive use of the proverb, taking it far beyond its white-male connotation to include African Americans and women by speaking of "all people." All of this is followed by further sections on the appearance and meaning of the proverb after Lincoln and Douglass in the latter part of the nineteenth century, the first half of the twentieth century, its use by Churchill and Truman in their attempt to defend democracy during the beginning of the Cold War, and the survival of the "people" proverb in the modern age, both during recent presidential campaigns and in the sociopolitical struggles as they are presented in the mass media. While Abraham Lincoln's name remains attached to this verbal sign of democracy, the proverb is also often cited as an anonymous piece of wisdom that encompasses the fundamental principles of a democratic government.

Considerable work has been done on the use of proverbs by such major political figures as Otto von Bismarck, Vladimir Ilych Lenin, Mao Tse-tung, and those mentioned above, but there is no reason why female politicians like Indira Gandhi or Margaret Thatcher should not be investigated as well. As a start, my third chapter on "'God Helps Them Who Help Themselves': Proverbial Resolve in the Letters of Abigail Adams" looks at how this remarkable woman influenced her husband John Adams, her family, and numerous politicians of the day with her epistolary missives rich in proverbial wisdom. She never held a political office and never gave a public speech, but her strong character and keen intellect had much influence during the revolutionary years and the subsequent period of building a democratic

American nation. Her employment of proverbs indicates her resolve, her eagerness to give advice, her debating abilities, her role as an independent matriarch, her struggle for the proper treatment of women, her unbending morality, her skill as a political strategist, her insightful observations on human nature, and her incredible optimism regarding the future of her new country. In all of her vast correspondence, be it in the form of letters to family members or to important political leaders, she made ample use of proverbial language to underscore her arguments with the common sense expressed in folk metaphors.

In the fourth chapter on "'A House Divided Against Itself Cannot Stand': From Biblical Proverb to Abraham Lincoln and Beyond" I look at the role that the divided house proverb (see Mark 3:25) has played in American politics, starting with Thomas Paine's remarkable essay on *Common Sense Addressed to the Inhabitants of America* (1776). Abigail Adams made good use of it during the War of 1812, followed by such major political figures as Sam Houston and Daniel Webster. By the time Abraham Lincoln gave his famous "House Divided" speech on June 16, 1858, the proverb had become a metaphor for the division in the American nation over the issue of slavery. The proverb developed into a proverbial slogan during the famous Lincoln-Douglas debates of that same year, with Lincoln losing the Senate election to Stephen A. Douglas. Once the Civil War started, Lincoln stopped using the Bible proverb, as its prophetic wisdom had already proven itself to be true. But the proverb had become attached to Lincoln's name as can be seen from a multitude of contextualized occurrences to this day. In fact, the proverb or allusions to it has repeatedly been used in the titles of historical or political studies regarding divisive issues ranging from the Civil War to the Vietnam War. Former German chancellor Willy Brandt introduced the proverb with reference to Lincoln during the time of Germany's reunification as a powerful political slogan, showing how this American symbol of unity can be deployed anywhere in the world.

Frederick Douglass, former slave and abolitionist spokesman, shared the proverbial prowess of his friend Abraham Lincoln, as I demonstrate in my fifth chapter on "'Do Unto Others as You Would Have Them Do Unto You': Frederick Douglass's Proverbial Struggle for Civil Rights." As a deeply religious person, Douglass relied heavily on biblical proverbs to strengthen the social and moral statements in his debates, lectures, and writings. But while this wisdom from the Bible provided religious authority to Douglass's rhetoric, he was also very much aware of the social significance of folk proverbs in his fight against slavery and for civil rights. He employs proverbs as collective wisdom and social strategies to bring across his important social and moral messages that included the struggle for his own race after the

Civil War and the expansion of women's rights. As such, proverbs show themselves to be traditional wisdom well suited to become verbal weapons in his untiring fight for freedom, democracy, and civil rights for all people. Douglass fought with words and deeds for his egalitarian beliefs, with his own proverbial motto "If there is no struggle, there is no progress" expressing his moral commitment to uphold the so-called Golden Rule of doing unto others as you would have them do unto you as the ultimate wisdom for human life.

Such American presidents as John Adams, Abraham Lincoln, and Harry S. Truman were masterful "proverbialists," but this could certainly be shown to be true for a number of additional presidents. In order to get at least an idea of how proverbial some of our other leaders have been, I looked at a certain speech that every president delivers in my sixth chapter on "'It's Not a President's Business to Catch Flies': Proverbial Rhetoric in Presidential Inaugural Addresses." I carefully investigated all fifty-five ceremonial speeches by American presidents, dividing my findings into seven convenient sections from George Washington to John Quincy Adams, from Andrew Jackson to James Buchanan, from Abraham Lincoln to William McKinley, from Theodore Roosevelt to Herbert Hoover, from Franklin Delano Roosevelt to Dwight D. Eisenhower, from John F. Kennedy to Jimmy Carter, and from Ronald Reagan to George W. Bush. There is no doubt that the inaugural speeches by Lincoln, FDR, and Kennedy stand out in rhetorical quality, and their speeches also contain some of the most often quoted phrases that have found their way into dictionaries of quotations and proverbs. The use of quotable phrases or proverbs adds significantly to the communicative and emotional quality of such presidential rhetoric to millions of people. As presidents struggle to find the right words to relate to people of different cultural, ethnic, and intellectual backgrounds, they will do well in citing at least some proverbs as sapiential expressions of common sense.

Both Franklin Delano Roosevelt and Winston S. Churchill were magnificent public speakers and masters of the English language, frequently relying on proverbs and proverbial expressions to add metaphorical expressiveness to their statements. The seventh chapter on "'We Are All in the Same Boat Now': Proverbial Discourse in the Churchill-Roosevelt Correspondence" demonstrates this by way of a detailed analysis of the 1161 and 788 messages sent by Churchill and Roosevelt respectively to each other during the turbulent war years between 1939 and 1945. As both world leaders rallied their people through word and deed to fight as allies against the dictatorial powers during the Second World War, they relied heavily on proverbial language for effective communication. This is also true for their private and secretive letters, messages, memoranda, and telegrams. The proverbial language, especially metaphorical texts referring to the body, animals, and the military, gives their important communications a lively and humane flavor that illustrates their deep friendship, trust, and support of each other. Frequently used as colloquial arguments, these proverbial interjections into an otherwise factual epistolary exchange bear witness to the determination of these two leaders of the free world to win the struggle against the Axis powers. There is no doubt that the use of proverbs helped these two friends to cope with life and death matters by adding some traditional common sense to a complex situation.

Finally, the eighth chapter on "'Good Fences Make Good Neighbors': The Sociopolitical Significance of an Ambiguous Proverb" looks once again at the origin, history, dissemination, function, and meaning of an American proverb by interpreting a large number of contextualized examples from the middle of the nineteenth century to the present day. This time I have divided my inclusive investigation into fourteen sections on international proverbs about fences, two English antecedents to the proverb, other proverbs of the structure "Good X make(s) good Y," the Irish variant "Good mearings make good neighbors," the history of the proverb before 1914, the proverb in dictionaries of quotations and proverbs, and Robert Frost's celebrated poem "Mending Wall" (1914) that helped to spread the hitherto rather infrequently found proverb throughout the nation and beyond. Then I look at the proverb in literary works and in the mass media, dividing the rich references into those dealing with fences as positive and aesthetic structures, housing feuds over fences, metaphorical fences, the proverb and the law, international politics and the proverb, and the need for fences in the modern world. As such, this chapter becomes a survey in culture, folklore, history, language, psychology, and worldview, showing that the proverb "Good fences make good neighbors" is by no means a "simple" piece of folk wisdom. The proverb certainly takes on a very ambiguous role as it is applied to the political ramifications of building walls at the borders between Mexico and the United States or between Israel and the Palestinians. This chapter is thus a unique example of the many layers of meaning that one and the same proverb can take on in different contexts.

As can be seen from these short paragraphs summarizing the eight individual chapters, there is considerable overlap among them to justify bringing them together under the heading of *Proverbs Are the Best Policy: Folk Wisdom and American Politics*. They represent part of my work on proverbs during the past five years, with five chapters having previously been published. The additional three chapters help to round out the picture of how proverbs play a major role in the American political scene throughout the history of the United States and ranging from everyday political issues to presidential politics. Proverbs permeate our sociopolitical life everywhere and at all times, and they are significant signs of the wisdom and worldview of an entire nation trying to uphold the inalienable rights of life, liberty, and the pursuit of happiness for all its citizens, and, with the help of the United Nations, for all humankind. It is my hope then that this book might be a small contribution to a better understanding of how proverbs as strategically used folk wisdom continue to be important communicative devices that deserve close scrutiny.

1

"Different Strokes for Different Folks"

American Proverbs as an International, National, and Global Phenomenon

Proverbs as one of the smallest ubiquitous folklore genres have been collected and studied since the beginning of written records. Both paremiographers and paremiologists have been hard at work at publishing collections and treatises throughout the world. In fact, proverb scholarship has reached such a phenomenal level of accomplishment that it is difficult for the fledgling proverb scholar to deal with the plethora of valuable information.[1] And yet, as is true for most intellectual endeavors, there still remains much work to be done in both areas of proverb studies. The varied use and function of proverbs as cultural signs and strategically placed rhetorical devices need to be investigated in much more detail by paying attention to different historical periods.[2] Much can also still be learned by socio- and psycholinguistic approaches that look at proverbs from the point of view of cognition, comprehension, and communication.[3] Above all, much more attention should be paid to the continued employment of proverbs in the modern age of technology, the mass media, the internet, and general globalization.[4] But additional proverb collections based on serious lexicographical principles are also a definite desideratum, including regional, national, and international compilations. While much is known about common European proverbs, it is high time to assemble comprehensive and comparative African as well as Near and Far Eastern proverb collections. Such compendia will eventually enable paremiographers to isolate fundamental proverb types that connect peoples through common wisdom all over the world.[5] Proverbs have always played a major role in human communication, be it in oral or written form, and there is no doubt that proverbs as traditional expressions of human wisdom are here to stay for generations to come. Antiquated proverbs might in fact drop out of usage, but there are those proverbs that will forever be applicable to the human condition, with new proverbs constantly being added to this treasure trove of folk wisdom.

The International Base of American Proverbs

The subfield of comparative paremiography can indeed look back on a strong tradition with several hundred polyglot collections having been assembled during the past centuries. This is especially the case for European proverbs with their common classical, biblical, and medieval Latin origins. However, many of these collections are mere enumerations of texts without any scholarly apparatus revealing the origin and historical dissemination of such common proverbs. It is for this reason that the Lithuanian paremiographer and paremiologist Kazys Grigas some thirty years ago was justified to begin the introduction to his significant comparative proverb collection *Lietuvių patarlės* (1976) with the statement that "the correlation between national and international elements in proverbs of different nations has received very little attention."[6] And the following paragraph from these introductory remarks holds as true today as when they were composed by Kazys Grigas:

> What are the laws of interrelation between the linguistic and extralinguistic factors which govern the origin, evolution, dissemination, longevity and death of proverbs and, finally, the penetration of their imagery into different languages? What are the levers which direct the movement of proverbs into one or another channel? What is the correlation of qualitative linguistic differences and similarities in proverbial texts? What elements reflect individual cultures—ethnic traditions and the mode of spiritual life,—and what has to be ascribed to phenomena typical of many cultures? What facts of language, linguistic stylistics and history of culture must be summoned up to investigate the national sources of proverbs and proverbial phrases of one's own people? And, finally, what is the ratio of internationally disseminated proverbs to proverbs of restricted distribution within the lore of one nation?[7]

These questions occupied Kazys Grigas throughout his long and active life, and he has provided many answers regarding especially the national corpus of Lithuanian proverbs and its relationship to European proverbs in such superb publications as his comparative proverb collection *Patarlių paralelės* (1987), his magisterial national collection of *Lietuvių patarlės ir priežodžiai* (2000) that will eventually comprise five massive volumes, as well as numerous essays tracing the origin and international distribution of individual proverbs.[8]

Cognizant of the importance of the English language and culture, Kazys Grigas has, of course, included many English equivalents or variants in his polyglot collections. The same is true for the many other modern paremiographers with comparative interests, as can be seen from such invaluable collections as Jerzy Gluski's *Proverbs: A Comparative Book of English, French, German, Italian, Spanish and Russian Proverbs with a Latin Appendix* (1971); Jens Aa. Stabell Bilgrav's *20,000 Proverbs and Their Equivalents in German, French, Swedish, Danish* (1985); Matti Kuusi's *Proverbia septentrionalia: 900 Balto-Finnic Proverb Types with Russian, Baltic, German and Scandinavian Parallels* (1985); Emanuel Strauss' *Dictionary of European Proverbs* (1994); Luis Iscla's *English Proverbs and Their Near Equivalents in Spanish, French, Italian and Latin* (1995); and Teodor Flonta's *A Dictionary of English and Romance Languages Equivalent Proverbs* (2001). In fact, these comparative collections are based on the English language as a recognized world language, and this is also the case with Gyula Paczolay's unrivaled polyglot collection of *European Proverbs in 55 Languages with Equivalents in Arabic, Persian, Sanskrit, Chinese and Japanese* (1997), one of the finest paremiographical accomplishments of all times.

The proverbs listed as "English" in these collections are indeed current in Great Britain, but for the most part they are also very much in use in the other parts of the world where English is spoken. After all, these polyglot collections with their limited number of entries deal with the most common European proverbs, with almost all of them having classical, biblical, or medieval Latin origins, in other words, they are to a considerable degree not really indigenous to Great Britain at all. And there is another problem with these polyglot compendia, useful as they are for comparative purposes and for translators as well as students of foreign languages. They basically contain a certain European paremiological minimum shared by most European languages or at least by such linguistically related languages as the Baltic, Germanic, Romance, or Slavic languages.[9] What they include to a much lesser extent are nationally distinct variants or various degrees of equivalents. And regarding the English language, no distinction is being made to proverbs particular to Canadian, American, Australian and any of the other "Englishes" spoken on the globe. In addition, modern English-language proverbs, no matter what their origin might be, are not listed, even though some of them have entered other languages through loan translations.

But in any case, there is no doubt that the English-language proverbs in use in the world in general and in Great Britain as well as the United States in particular are a proverbial mixed bag and certainly represent quite an international phenomenon. Such proverbs as "One swallow does not make a summer," "One hand washes the other," "Big fish eat little fish,"[10] and "Love is blind" go back to classical times and were loan translated into English. Biblical proverbs like "He who digs a pit for another, will fall into it himself" (Proverbs 26:27), "Man does not live by bread alone" (Deuteronomy 8:3 and Matthew 4:4), "As you sow, so will you reap" (Galatians 6:7–8), and "He that will not work, shall not eat" (2 Thessalonians 3:10) have entered the English language through skillful Bible translations, and many medieval Latin proverbs have also been anglicized, among them "The pitcher goes so long to the well until at last it breaks," "Strike while the iron is hot," "All that glitters is not gold," and "New brooms sweep clean."[11] Nevertheless, the English language of Great Britain has its own rich proverb tradition with thousands of well-known texts, as for example "Beauty is only skin deep," "A penny saved is a penny earned," "A friend in need is a friend indeed," and "The proof of the pudding is in the eating." British settlers brought this international and national proverb repertoire with them to the United States, and other immigrant groups carried their foreign language proverbs with them as well, of which some have been translated into English as well. A couple of German proverbs that were translated into English and which have become very popular in the United States over time are "Don't throw the baby out with the bath water" and "The apple does not fall far from the tree."[12] But proverbs from immigrants of other nationalities have also been translated, notably from Italian and ever more from Spanish because of the millions of bilingual Spanish/English speakers. The rich Yiddish proverb tradition has also had a considerable influence on proverbs current in American English, but paremiologists need to investigate more individual proverbs to illustrate these fascinating linguistic and cultural processes. Most collections and studies of proverbs have looked only at the texts in their native languages without paying any attention to their loan translations gaining currency in the United States.[13] Much important work still needs to be done to study the proverb lore that has become part of the American language by means of translating foreign language proverbs of the thousands of immigrants.

It also needs to be pointed out that the Native Americans have had a minuscule influence on the American proverb corpus. This is not due to the terrible treatment that the Indian tribes received from the immigrants and the eliminationist policies of various government agencies. The reason lies in the yet unsolved conundrum of the incredible dearth of proverbs among the Native Americans. Anthropologists have recorded only very few proverbs from a number of tribes, and the total of recorded indigenous Indian proverbs is at best two hundred! This is a truly astonishing phenomenon when one considers, for example, the wealth of African proverbs that have been collected from oral tradition. It appears that Indians have less metaphorical language, and wisdom was handed down orally more through folk narratives than such proverbs as "The deer, though toothless, may accomplish something" (don't judge by appearances), "When the fox walks lame, old rabbit jumps," and "The moon is not shamed by the barking of dogs."[14] Basically then, the majority of proverbs in general use in America was imported, and just as this large country represents an international melting pot, so the proverbs, with a preponderance of British texts, are a smorgasbord of traditional wisdom. This also includes African proverbs brought to America with the unfortunate slaves and resulting in a very rich African American proverb tradition.[15] And yet, this international basis of proverbs also contains national American proverbs that were coined in the United States and which spread regionally as well as throughout the entire land.

Turning to the specific case of American proverbs, i.e., proverbs that can be proven to have originated in the United States, matters become quite complex if not chaotic. Actually, some comparative paremiographers have paid some lip service to the obvious importance of American proverbs in the modern world. Thus Selwyn Gurney Champion in his still valuable collection of *Racial Proverbs. A Selection of the World's Proverbs arranged Linguistically* (1938) did in fact include a small list of 73 "American— USA" proverbs, among them "Don't sell America short," "Put up or shut up," "Life is just one damned thing after another," and "Every man must skin his own skunk."[16] Other examples, however, can be traced back at least to British origins, pointing clearly to the difficulty of establishing the national American identity of a particular proverb. The same is the case for the section of 56 proverbs from the "United States" in Gerd de Ley's *International Dictionary of Proverbs* (1998), where one finds proverbs like "Ignorance is bliss" and "Love laughs at locksmiths" that are determinately not of American origin. My own *Encyclopedia of World Proverbs* (1986) and Harold V. Cordry's *The Multicultural Dictionary of Proverbs* (1997) list considerably more American proverbs throughout their many pages. However, both Cordry and I have clearly made errors in labelling some proverbs too quickly as "American." Upon closer scrutiny one quite often finds that such texts had been in use in Great Britain long before they became established as folk wisdom in the United States.

AMERICAN PROVERBS AS A DISTINCT NATIONAL CORPUS

Fortunately, however, paremiographers have at least several excellent historical proverb dictionaries at their disposal that help to establish the origin and distribution of English language proverbs in Great Britain and the United States (in part also Canada). There is no need to review the long and impressive history of British paremiography here. Suffice it to mention F. P. Wilson's third edition of *The Oxford Dictionary of English Proverbs* (1970) and the third edition of John Simpson's and Jennifer Speake's *The Concise Oxford Dictionary of Proverbs* (1998). Regarding the issue of American proverbs at hand, four major historical dictionaries based on sound scholarly practices are available to the paremiographer, including thousands of proverbs and variants recorded from written sources that span all four centuries of the development of the United States: Bartlett Jere Whiting, *Early American Proverbs and Proverbial Phrases* (1977), Archer Taylor and Bartlett Jere Whiting, *A Dictionary of American Proverbs and Proverbial Phrases, 1820–1880* (1958), Bartlett Jere Whiting, *Modern Proverbs and Proverbial Sayings* (1989), and Wolfgang Mieder, Stewart A. Kingsbury, and Kelsie B. Harder, *A Dictionary of American Proverbs* (1992). There is, however, one major problem with these collections in that they are an international hodgepodge of proverbs from many sources and only in part comprised of national American texts. Their titles are thus somewhat misleading in that the word "American" merely signifies that the registered proverbs in these volumes are in common use in North America. They are "American" proverbs in that the general population makes use of them frequently as concisely expressed traditional bits of wisdom. As such, they certainly belong in a general dictionary of so-called American proverbs, albeit that many of them are not of American origin.

The complexity of all of this was demonstrated by the American paremiologist Richard Jente in the early 1930s. He was able to show that of a collection of 199 supposedly American proverbs only 10 or a mere 5% were in fact coined in the United States, among them "Don't kick a fellow when he is down," "It pays to advertise," and "Great minds run in the same channels."[17] About the same time, the American poet Carl Sandburg (1878–1967) with his ear close to the ground of proverbial folk speech, composed his long poem *Good Morning, America* (1928) as well as his epic poem *The People, Yes* (1936).[18] They are replete with hundreds of proverbs and proverbial expressions from all walks of life and ethnic minorities of the United States. He saw himself as the voice of the cross section of American life, being very well aware of the fact that proverbs, despite their conciseness and simplicity, make up the worldview or mentality of practical life.[19] As he put it in section eleven of *Good Morning, America,* it behooves lay people and scholars alike to "behold the proverbs of a people, a nation," for they are verbal and cultural signs of their mores and attitudes:

> A code arrives; language; lingo; slang;
> behold the proverbs of a people, a nation:
> Give 'em the works. Fix it, there's always

a way. Be hard boiled. The good die young.
[...]
Business is business.
What you don't know won't hurt you.
Courtesy pays.
Fair enough.
The voice with a smile.
Say it with flowers.
Let one hand wash the other.
The customer is always right.
[...]
There are lies, damn lies and statistics.
Figures don't lie but liars can figure.
There's more truth than poetry in that.
You don't know the half of it, dearie.

It's the roving bee that gathers the honey.
A big man is a big man whether he's a president or a prizefighter.
[...]
It pays to look well.
Be yourself.
Speak softly and carry a big stick.
War is hell.
Honesty is the best policy.
It's all in the way you look at it.
Get the money—honestly if you can.
It's hell to be poor.
Well, money isn't everything.
Well, life is what you make it.
[...]
There must be pioneers and some of them get killed.
The grass is longer in the backyard.
[...]
Can you unscramble eggs?
Early to bed and early to rise and you never meet any prominent
    people.
Let's go. Watch our smoke. Excuse our dust.
Keep your shirt on.[20]

This is a revealing composite of slang and proverbial speech to
characterize American society, integrating phrasal elements almost at

random from all segments of the American people. What a daunting task it would be to trace the origin of each expression of this collage, be they from other lands or actually of American coinage.[21] While it is difficult to prove a general American origin, the problem of establishing what proverbs might have been coined in a particular state or region of the United States is an even more vexing proposition. In fact, the question of the origin of any particular proverb becomes a major research project in itself. It is thus extremely difficult to speak of American proverbs, New England proverbs,[22] or even Vermont proverbs.[23] Such designations are to a large degree mere constructs. However, the issue is, in any case, not so much one of origin but rather the fact that a particular proverb or a set of proverbs have been in use or are presently in common employment somewhere in the United States in general or in certain regions.

But there is no reason to despair, even though it is high time that paremiographers put together a scholarly collection of *bona fide* American proverbs. The four hybrid collections contain, after all, numerous proverbs that have been proven to be of a purely American origin. They do represent a national stock of American proverbs, expressing to a certain degree also the American worldview that has developed over a period of four centuries. Benjamin Franklin, who for the most part copied the proverbs for his *Poor Richard's Alamacks* during the first half of the eighteenth century out of British proverb collections, was nevertheless the originator of a number of proverbs: "Three removes is (are) as bad as a fire," "Laziness travels so slowly, that poverty soon overtakes him," "Industry pays debts, while despair increases them," and "There will be sleeping enough in the grave."[24] They certainly helped to establish the American ideal of Puritan ethics that included the idea of the "self-made man," giving hope to thousands of immigrants as they looked forward to make their fortune in this thriving country.[25] The pragmatically oriented transcendentalist Ralph Waldo Emerson added the ever-popular proverb "Hitch your wagon to a star" in 1870 as an expression of high hopes for a good life to the optimistic American worldview.[26] But Emerson was also an early American paremiologist, reflecting deeply on the purpose of proverbs in the expanding American society. In his first lecture on "Shakspear" [*sic*] (1835) he speaks of proverbs as "pictures" and of "the value of their analogical import." These comments foreshadow the modern theoretical interpretation of proverbs as signs.[27] One could indeed speak of Emerson as a precursor to paremiological semiotics:

> The memorable words of history and the proverbs of nations consist usually of a natural fact selected as a picture or parable of moral truth. Thus, "A rolling stone gathers no moss;" "A bird in the hand is worth

two in the bush;" "A cripple in the right way will beat a racer in the wrong;" "'Tis hard to carry a full cup even;" "Vinegar is the son of wine;" "The last ounce broke the camel's back;" "Long lived trees make roots first;" and the like. In their primary sense these are trivial facts but we repeat them for the value of their analogical import.[28]

With the addition of the proverb "Make hay whilst the sun shines," Emerson also included this paragraph in his significant chapter on "Language" in his book *Nature* (1836), explaining that "the world is emblematic. Parts of speech are metaphors because the whole of nature is a metaphor of the human mind."[29] Clearly then Emerson looks at proverbs as emblematic or analogic signs for nature in general and humanity in particular.

It is also a known fact that at the beginning of the twentieth century President Theodore Roosevelt declared that American international politics ought to follow the wisdom of "Speak softly and carry a big stick" (1901), and this utterance has long since become an often quoted American proverb. But most of the American proverbs are, of course, anonymous, or nobody thinks of their individual originators any longer, as can be seen from such proverbs as "Paddle your own canoe" (expressing the spirit of independence), "The best defense is a good offense" (being proactive), "You can't unscramble eggs" (impossibilities), "Figures don't lie" (reliance on facts), "Banks have no heart" (economics), "What is good for General Motors, is good for America" (big business), "Life begins at forty" (youthfulness), "Garbage in, garbage out" (world of computers), and even the scatological "Shit happens" (acceptance of fate). Some of these examples clearly show that proverbs are still being coined today, while others drop out since they do not fit modern attitudes and mores any longer. Older English proverbs like "A woman's tongue wags like a lamb's tail" or "Spare the rod and spoil the child" have disappeared or are on their way out, while such proverbs as "A woman without a man is like a fish without a bicycle" or "There is no free lunch" are steadily gaining in currency and popularity.

Other modern truly American proverbs originated among the Black population and have entered general American folk speech, for example "What goes around comes around" and, of course, the truly liberating and quintessential American proverb "Different strokes for different folks" from the 1950s.[30] But just as certain ethnic groups have their own proverbs, the different professions have also formulated proverbs that fit their interests. Proverbs like "An ounce of prevention is worth a pound of cure" and "An apple a day keeps the doctor away" are old British health rules that continue to be in frequent use in America, while "If you hear hoofbeats, think horses, not zebras" is a modern American piece of advice to young physicians who might be looking too hard for rare diseases rather than common ailments.[31] Just as medical doctors have their proverbial maxims, so lawyers possess legal rules to fall back on that have been in use in Latin and the vernacular since the Middle Ages, such as "A man's home is his castle" and "First come, first served." But there is also that infamous proverbial statement "If the glove doesn't fit, you must acquit" that was coined by the defense lawyer Johnnie Cochran during the O. J. Simpson murder trial in 1995. Other indigenous American proverbs that have gained general currency especially during the twentieth century are among many others "The grass is always greener on the other side of the fence,"[32] "Hindsight is twenty-twenty," "Life is just a bowl of cherries," "Shit or get off the pot," "It takes two to tango," and "You're only young once." Popular culture, films, and the entire mass media play a major role in spreading such new proverbs. While proverbs continue to be cited in their standard wording in the modern age, they quite often get changed into so-called anti-proverbs that intentionally vary the wisdom of the traditional wording, as for example "No body is perfect" (Nobody is perfect) or "Home is where the computer is" (Home is where the heart is). In fact, these two anti-proverbs are presently well on their way of becoming new American proverbs in their own right.[33] They reflect Americans' preoccupation with the appearance and health of their bodies, and Americans certainly feel the need to be connected to a computer and the internet most of the time.

But here are a few additional relatively new American proverbs that have gained much popularity throughout the country during the past half century. While many are contained in *A Dictionary of American Proverbs* (1992), others are part of a fascinating annotated list that the American paremiologist Charles C. Doyle has put together after detailed analysis as to their origin. He entitled his list quite appropriately "On 'New' Proverbs and the Conservativeness of Proverb Dictionaries" (1996), thereby pointing out that paremiographers everywhere must pay much more attention to modern proverbs.[34] Not doing this gives people the absolutely false impression that proverbs are not created any longer, while actually quite the opposite is true. Modern people, even of a highly technological society as that of the United States, are still very much in need to couch their observations and experiences into concise proverbs expressing the wisdom of their age in modern metaphors, as for example:

> Been there, done that.
> The buck stops here.
> The camera doesn't lie.

You can't beat (fight) city hall.
Crime doesn't pay.
Another day, another dollar.
No guts, no glory.
Nice guys finish last.
Last hired, first fired.
You only live once.
It's better to be pissed off than to be pissed on.
If you can't say something nice (good), don't say anything at all.
You can prove anything with statistics.
Three strikes and you're out.
Don't sweat the small stuff.
It takes one to know one.
If you want to talk the talk, you got to walk the walk.
Things are tough all over.
It's the thought that counts.
Two can live as cheaply as one.
That's the way the ball bounces.
Winning isn't everything.

The various American oriented proverb collections mentioned earlier contain hundreds more proverbs that were coined in the United States, indicating clearly that this immigrant nation has had and continues to have its own history of proverb making.

American Proverbs as a Global Phenomenon

These texts are but a small sample of American proverbs that are in common usage in the United States and that have been spread to a large degree also throughout the rest of the English-speaking world. They express modern thoughts regarding individuals in their relationship with social issues, ranging from a claim of personal freedom to the submission to outside forces, from optimism to pessimism, and from the humorous to the sublime.[35] Many of them are not particularly metaphorical, stating their proverbial wisdom instead in rather direct language and thus reflecting a rather matter-of-fact attitude towards modern mass society. As such they are easily transferable from one English-speaking culture to another, except for such proverbs as "Three strikes and you're out" or "Another day, another dollar" with their specifically American references to the game of baseball and the standard currency.

But this constantly increasing global influence of American as well as earlier British proverbs is by no means limited to those countries where

English is the national language. While much more research is needed to illustrate the acceptance of American proverbs either in their English wording or as loan translations in other national languages and cultures, I have been able to show by some detailed studies that this is most certainly the case in Germany, a country where the population perhaps has been too quick at times to take over thousands of American words and to a lesser degree also phraseologisms.[36] The takeover of proverbs is by no means always positive, as in the case of the American stereotypical proverb "The only good Indian is a dead Indian" that gained currency in the United States after the Civil War. It is a terribly prejudicial invective against Native Americans, summarizing the inhumane view and brutal treatment of these indigenous peoples. Regrettably, the proverb can still be heard today, and its applicability has been expanded by replacing the "Indians" by any despised group of people. Variants like "The only good German (Jew, Nigger, Serb, etc.) is a dead German (Jew, Nigger, Serb. etc.)" have all been recorded.[37] But while it is a national shame that this negative proverb continues to linger in American rhetoric, it is indeed highly suspect that the loan translation "Nur ein toter Indianer ist ein guter Indianer" has gained currency in Germany, once again including variants dehumanizing other ethnic and national groups.[38]

While this is a disturbing example of the powerful influence of American culture as expressed in proverbs, there is also a rather innocuous but surprising development taking place with the English proverb "The early bird catches the worm" that has long been very popular in the United States as well. The German proverb "Morgenstunde hat Gold im Munde" (The morning hour has gold in its mouth; i.e., The early bird gets the worm), according to empirical paremiological research the most popular German proverb, has been considered the perfect equivalent for the English text by native speakers and translators, although the metaphors of both texts are strikingly different.[39] Since the sixteenth century both proverbs have lived side by side, without one or the other having been loan translated into the other language. But this has now changed during the past two decades due to the tremendous influence of the American mass media and popular culture. Translators of books, magazine articles, film scripts, comic strips, etc. have repeatedly rendered the proverb in German as "Der frühe Vogel fängt den Wurm" rather than replacing it by the customary "Morgenstunde hat Gold im Munde." There are occasions where this literal translation of the English metaphor does in fact make sense in a particular context, but more often than not the "Morgenstunde" proverb would have been a perfectly meaningful rendering. And yet, my international proverb archive contains numerous references to the new loan translation, and a computer search of large electronic data bases brought to light so many additional texts that there can be no doubt that "Der frühe Vogel fängt den Wurm" is a new loan proverb in the German language.[40] It has not and will not replace the "Morgenstunde" proverb, but it certainly has entered the German language and culture and is bound to gain even more in popularity.

If this new "Vogel" loan proverb can give the "Morgenstunde" proverb a bit of competition, as it were, it should not be surprising that some old as well as new American proverbs for which no German equivalents exist are gaining acceptance in Germany. At times they are cited in the English language to add a certain worldly appeal to a statement. When such proverbs begin to be quoted as loan translations, they are usually introduced by such formulas as "an English proverb says" or "according to an English proverb" to draw attention to the unusual piece of wisdom. Once in a while the designation "American" is used, but for the most part the generic term "English" appears, perhaps because people are simply not aware whether a proverb is of British or American origin. In any case, once a loan translation has gained some familiarity because of frequent use, the new "German" proverb begins to stand alone and loses its American identity. In a number of individual studies I have been able to illustrate this phenomenon by means of numerous contextualized examples for the following American/German proverb pairs:

It takes two to tango.
Zum Tango gehören zwei.[41]

A (one) picture is worth a thousand words.
Ein Bild sagt mehr als tausend Worte.[42]

An apple a day keeps the doctor away.
Ein Apfel pro Tag hält den Arzt fern.[43]

Good fences make good neighbors.
Gute Zäune machen gute Nachbarn.[44]

The grass is always greener on the other side of the fence.
Das Gras auf der anderen Seite des Zaunes ist immer grüner.[45]

Don't put all your eggs into one basket.
Man soll nicht alle Eier in einen Korb legen.[46]

The proverb "Don't put all your eggs into one basket" is actually of British origin, dating back to the seventeenth century. However, it never jumped across the Channel to Germany. This only happened in the early

1980s by way of the incredible American influence on the German language. The German "Eier" proverb is thus technically speaking a loan translation of an Angloamerican rather than an American proverb *per se*. But there is no need to split hairs over the matter. There is no doubt that English language proverbs are entering the German linguistic and cultural scene both in their original language or as loan translations primarily by way of the United States. This phenomenon has taken place especially since the 1950s with America's influential role in Germany in particular. Since the 1980s a number of American proverbs have become new German proverbs through loan translations, but obviously this fascinating development is by no means as wide spread as with individual words and idioms. Proverbs are structurally too rigid and metaphorically too demanding to be accepted in large quantities, but the process might well intensify and accelerate in the future.

It also remains to be shown whether such loan translations are occurring in other countries of the world as well. The global influence of American proverbs in English speaking countries is certainly considerable with American English playing a dominant role in all spheres of international communication. But the distribution of American proverbs by way of loan translations is definitely part of this intriguing process. It is a modern phenomenon reminiscent of the role that the Latin language once played as a *lingua franca,* and it definitely merits the close attention of paremiographers and paremiologists everywhere.

2

"Government of the People, by the People, for the People"
The Making and Meaning of an American Proverb about Democracy

Abraham Lincoln's closing remarks of his short yet famous Gettysburg Address of November 19, 1863, have become proverbial as "Government of the people, by the people, for the people." Yet, as is the case with some other famous utterances of Lincoln, he relied on the wisdom and insights of others to create his memorable phrase that provides a most succinct definition of democracy. Already on May 9, 1901, Samuel A. Green made the following observation on the widespread distribution and currency of this American credo:

> One short clause at the very end of this speech has been quoted on various occasions so often that it is now as familiar as a household word. I refer to the expression: "That this nation, under God, shall have a new birth of freedom, and that government of the people, by the people, for the people, shall not perish from the earth." The sentiment here contained is so simple, and defines a democracy so clearly and tersely, that it seems somewhat singular that the same idea has never been fully expressed before; as the Preacher says: "There is no new thing under the sun."[1]

Green then proceeds to refer to somewhat similar statements by Thomas Cooper (1794), an address presented to President John Adams (1798), Chief Justice John Marshall (1819), Daniel Webster (1830), Alphonse de Lamartine (1850), and Theodore Parker (1850), and there is, as expected, a whole series of subsequent attempts to find precursors to Lincoln's profound statement. It will be the task of this chapter to trace this history of the phrase in much more detail by citing references in context. But the story does not end there, since Lincoln's unique formulation turned from a quotable definition of democracy to a generally known democratic proverb. As such it has survived in numerous and very different contexts to this day, and this development needs to be told as well.

Lexicographical Accounts of the "People" Triad

The British journal *Notes & Queries* included several short paragraphs between 1908 and 1916 on the phrase, starting with the question whether anybody could verify the claim that John Wycliffe included the following declaration in the preface to his Bible translation of 1384: "This Bible is for the government of the people, by the people, and for the people."[2] This matter came up again in 1916, but once again nobody was able to find the statement in the various editions of the Wycliffe Bible.[3] Instead, the scholars drew attention to John Marshall (1819), Daniel Webster (1830), Theodore Parker (1850 and 1854), and, of course, Abraham Lincoln as the last link in this chain.

More modern lexicographers followed suit in their various dictionaries of quotations. Of special importance is Kate Louise Roberts' completely revised and enlarged *Hoyt's New Cyclopedia of Practical Quotations* (1922) with references to Thomas Cooper (1794), John Adams (1798), John Marshall (1819), Benjamin Disraeli (1827), Daniel Webster (1830), Lamartine (1850), Theodore Parker (1850, 1854, and 1858), and Abraham Lincoln (1863).[4] Of major significance is also the reliable *Home Book of Proverbs, Maxims, and Famous Phrases* (1948) by Burton Stevenson, which adds the names of Lord John Russell (1831), J. R. Lowell (1884), Oscar Wilde (1895), and Michael Arlen (1939) to the list of references, thus actually taking the recorded history of the phrase beyond Lincoln for once.[5] Subsequent compilers of quotation dictionaries do not equal the number of references of these two early standard works,[6] and it is a definite disservice when editors continue to refer to Wycliffe's Bible as the first occurrence of the phrase under discussion.[7] While Gregory Titelman also maintains the erroneous reference to Wycliffe in his *Dictionary of Popular Proverbs and Sayings* (1996), he ascribes a correct proverbial character to the well-known phrase and mentions Daniel Webster, Theodore Parker, and Abraham Lincoln, while at the same time also referring to the modern use of the phrase by Bel Kaufman (1964), Walter Mondale (1984), and Rudolph Giuliani (1994).[8]

Clearly scholars tracing the history and dissemination of a particular expression must not only look for its possible sources but should also investigate how the particular quotation-turned-proverb lives on in various contexts. One thing is for certain, E. D. Hirsch and his co-authors were correct when they included the following statement in *The Dictionary of Cultural Literacy* (1988): "government of the people, by the people, and for the people Words from the GETTYSBURG ADDRESS of Abraham LINCOLN, often quoted as a definition of DEMOCRACY."[9] Because of space constraints, this says very little, of course, and the same is true for the minimal contextual information given in the many dictionaries of phrases, proverbs, and quotations. Better or more voluminous such compilations might cite longer passages, but most often the references are unsatisfactory and at times simply copied from an earlier compilation. What follows is an attempt to show a much more inclusive history of this proverbial definition of democracy, showing its somewhat different verbalization before Lincoln by John Marshall, Daniel Webster, Theodore Parker and others, then Lincoln's unique reformulation of it, and eventually its survival through a century and a half until the present day, noting especially the powerful employment of the statement by Frederick Douglass, Winston S. Churchill, Harry S. Truman, and many other political and literary figures as well as journalists and copy writers of advertisements. The dictionaries already mentioned have provided a solid start for this study, but my own voluminous readings in American history, literature, and the mass media added many additional references. Also, the modern electronic search abilities yielded fascinating additional materials that would not have been located without this new world of databases.[10] The result is a detailed chronological investigation of one of the most famous phrases of American history that expresses not only for this nation but for the entire world in a proverbial nutshell the underlying principle of a democracy.

Early Beginnings with John Adams and John Marshall

The earliest statement that has at least some resemblance with Abraham Lincoln's powerful triad is contained in an epistolary description of the new American government and society for a British friend that Thomas Cooper includes in his book entitled *Some Information Respecting America* (1794):

> You ask what appear to me to be the general inducements to people to quit England for America? In my mind, the first and principal feature is, The total absence of anxiety respecting the future success of a family. There is little fault to find with the government of America, either in principle or in practice: we have very few taxes to pay, and those are of acknowledged necessity, and moderate in amount: we have no animosities about religion; it is a subject about which no questions are asked: we have few respecting political men or political measures: the present

irritation of men's minds in Great Britain, and the discordant state of society on political accounts, is not known there. The government is the government of the people, and for the people.[11]

Even though Cooper uses but two elements of the triadic structure, he is already expressing the fundamental idea that a democratic government consists of the members of that society and exists for their benefit. Four years later, in early July of 1798, the citizens of the County of Westmoreland in Virginia sent a declaration of support to President John Adams which included this passage:

> The Declaration that our People are hostile to a Government made by themselves, for themselves and conducted by themselves is an Insult malignant in its Nature, and extensive in its Mischief. [...] That Freemen should differ in Opinion concerning the Measures of their Government is not only to be expected but is even to be desir'd when Obedient to Law and Guided by Love of Country. [...] Where is the Nation that can coerce United Columbia into Submission? The Sun has not yet shone upon it.[12]

Adams clearly was appreciative of this statement at a time when he was struggling with the possibility of having to go to war in Europe. On July 11, 1798, he took the time to respond to this supportive address by quoting the governmental triad from it, showing that he took an immediate liking to this definition of democracy about whose nature he had given so much thought in written and oral form:

> An address so replete with sentiments purely American and so respectful to me, subscribed with the Names of four hundred respectable Citizens of Virginia is to me of inestimable Value. The declaration that our People are hostile to a Government, made by themselves, for themselves, and conducted by themselves, if it were true, would be a demonstration that the people despise and hate themselves; this inference unnatural and shocking as it seems, is however, always literally true of a corrupted people.[13]

It should be noted, however, that Adams is merely quoting the Virginia declaration and that he did not originate this particular formulation. It also gained no currency in the public sphere but serves as an indication that the underlying idea of the phrase is in the air at this time. This is very well shown by a comment that Chief Justice John Marshall made in his

"McCulloch v. Maryland" opinion of March 6, 1819: "The government of the Union, then, [...], is, emphatically and truly, a government of the people. In form and in substance it emanates from them. Its powers are granted by them, and are to be exercised directly on them, and for their benefit."[14] This is not to say that some thoughts along these lines were not going on in Europe. The British statesman and novelist Benjamin Disraeli included these reflections on governmental power in his first novel *Vivian Grey* (1827), long before he became Prime Minister in the second half of the nineteenth century:

> We must not forget [...] that it is the business of those to whom Providence has allotted the responsible possession of power and influence—that it is their duty—[...] to become guardians of our weaker fellow-creatures—that all power is a trust—that we are accountable for its exercise—that, from the people, and for the people, all springs, and all must exist; and that, unless we conduct ourselves with the requisite wisdom, prudence, and propriety, the whole system of society will be disorganised; and this country, in particular, fall a victim to that system of corruption and misgovernment which has already occasioned the destruction of the great kingdoms mentioned in the Bible; and many other States besides—Greece, Rome, Carthage, etc.[15]

Yet another masterful British statesman, Earl John Russell, followed suit on March 1, 1831, when he rose in Parliament in support of the Reform Bill (1832) for the House of Commons, once again showing that thoughts regarding the political future of the people were expressed in triads:

> To establish the Constitution on a firm basis, you must show that you are determined not to be the representatives of a small class, or of a particular interest; but to form a body [of government], who, representing the people, springing from the people, and sympathising with the people, can fairly call on the people to support the future burthens of the country, and to struggle with the future difficulties which it may have to encounter; confident that those who call upon them are ready to join them heart and hand: and are only looking, like themselves, to the glory and welfare of England.[16]

Sixteen years later, in France, Alphonse de Lamartine expressed similar views in his comprehensive study of the French Revolution with the title *Histoire des Girondins* (1847): "Ce but, c'était la souveraineté représentative de tous les citoyens. puisée dans une élection aussi large que le peuple lui-même, et agissant par le peuple et pour le peuple dans un conseill électif qui serait tout le gouvernement. L'ambition de Robespierre, si souvent calomniée alors et depuis, n'allait pas au-delà."[17] An English translation of this analysis appeared in 1847, the year of its original publication: "This end was the representative sovereignty of all the citizens, concentrated in an election as extensive as the people themselves, and acting by the people, and for the people, in an elective council, which should be all the government. The ambition of Robespierre, so often calumniated then and since, went not beyond this."[18] There might not have been much if any influence of the Disraeli or Lamartine formulations on the American scene, but they do show a definite preoccupation with the attempt to express in a succinct fashion the basic ideas of a democratic government.

DANIEL WEBSTER'S SPEECH OF JANUARY 26, 1830

There is no doubt that Abraham Lincoln was aware of Daniel Webster's definition and characterization of the American government which he included in a famous speech in the Senate of January 26, 1830, that dealt with the so-called Missouri Compromise of 1820, which admitted Missouri as a slave state and Maine as a free state while prohibiting slavery in territories that later became Kansas and Nebraska:

> It is the people's Constitution, the people's government, made for the people, made by the people, and answerable to the people. The people of the United States have declared that this Constitution shall be the supreme law. We must either admit the proposition, or dispute their authority. The States are, unquestionably, sovereign, so far as their sovereignty is not affected by this supreme law. But the State legislatures, as political bodies, however sovereign, are yet not sovereign over the people. [...] I hold it [the government] to be a popular government, erected by the people; those who administer it, responsible to the people; and itself capable of being amended and modified, just as the people may choose it should be. It is as popular, just as truly emanating from the people, as the State governments. [...] The people, then, erected this government. They gave it a Constitution, and in that Constitution they have enumerated the powers which they bestow on it. They have made it a limited government. They have defined its authority.[19]

This is an extremely important argument for the singleness of the nation that is governed by laws that go beyond those of individual states.

His argument for a national "people's government, made for the people, made by the people, and answerable to the people" is quite close to Lincoln's statement at the end of the Gettysburg Address some thirty years later, but it does not yet have the "proverbial ring" to it which Lincoln, the masterful rhetorical craftsman, was able to give to it.

This is also true for a similar description of the American form of government which Asher Robbins presents in his essay on "The American Revolution" (1841), namely "that the most powerful, the most prosperous, and the most happy of all governments, is the government of the people, by the people."[20] This short binary formula of "government of the people, by the people" rings well in the ear, and it is slowly but surely becoming a rhetorical standard and will be picked up by Lincoln in due time. It is, however, not known and perhaps doubtful that he knew this particular essay, although he was an avid reader in such matters.

MAJOR IMPORTANCE OF THEODORE PARKER'S SPEECHES AND WRITINGS

In a speech of May 25, 1850, at a meeting of the citizens of Boston in Faneuil Hall, the clergyman, social reformer, and abolitionist Theodore Parker addressed the vexing problem that slavery presented to the nation, and his words mark the beginning of a constant flow of attempts by him to find the best wording for a short definition of the nature of the American government. In these early remarks, he has not yet found a concise triadic structure:

> It is a great question, comprising many smaller ones:—Shall we extend and foster Slavery, or shall we extend and foster Freedom? Slavery, with its consequences, material, political, intellectual, moral; or Freedom, with the consequences thereof? A question so important seldom comes to be decided before any generation of men. This age is full of great questions, but this of Freedom is the chief. It is the same question which in other forms comes up in Europe [revolutions of 1848]. This is presently to be decided here in the United States by the servants of the people, I mean, by the Congress of the nation; in the name of the people; for the people, if justly decided; against them, if unjustly. If it were to be left tomorrow to the naked votes of the majority, I should have no fear. But the public servants of the people may decide otherwise.[21]

But then, two months later on May 29, 1850, Parker found truly compelling words in his speech on "Slave Power in America" at a New

England anti-slavery convention in Boston. Here he defines the American government in exactly the same way that Abraham Lincoln would do it thirteen years later, but there is one considerable difference in that Parker adds the inclusive adjective "all" three times before the noun "people," clearly signalling that he means to include the hopefully soon to be freed slaves of the nation as well. His remarks belong to the most impressive statements of that period in American history, and they certainly deserve to stand next to those of Lincoln whose important utterances could obtain wider currency due to his leadership position:

> There is what I call the American idea. I so name it, because it seems to me to lie at the basis of all our truly original, distinctive and American institutions. It is itself a complex idea, composed of three subordinate and more simple ideas, namely: The idea that all men have unalienable rights; that in respect thereof, all men are created equal; and that government is to be established and sustained for the purpose of giving every man an opportunity for the enjoyment and development of all these unalienable rights. This idea demands, as the proximate organization thereof, a democracy, that is, a government of all the people, by all the people, for all the people; of course, a government after the principles of eternal justice, the unchanging law of God; for shortness' sake, I will call it the idea of Freedom.[22]

This speech had its influence on Lincoln in many ways, notably on his repeated use of the statement that "all men are created equal; that they are endowed by their creator with certain unalienable rights; that among these are life, liberty, and the pursuit of happiness" from the Declaration of Independence,[23] to which Parker is obviously alluding as well. Quite certainly Lincoln was influenced by Theodore Parker's use of the triadic structure of his government definition. When Lincoln concluded his Gettysburg Address on November 19, 1863, with the claim that the "government of the people, by the people, for the people, shall not perish from the earth,"[24] he gave it the concise and perfect form in which it survives. He can hardly be called the originator of this phrasal definition, but it was he who implanted it in the minds and worldview of his contemporaries and generations of Americans to come. Interestingly, Lincoln dropped out the inclusive word "all," and that is exactly where the historical, cultural, social, and political problem arises with Lincoln's proverb. Did he even include the African-American population in his thoughts when he spoke of a "government of the people, by the people, for the people?" After all, Lincoln's Emancipation Proclamation of January 1, 1863, had not yet brought suffrage to the former slaves, and women's right to vote was also not established yet. Thus the proverb appears as a privileged statement for white males, with Theodore Parker's more liberal statement proving the exception to the rule.

Half a year later, Parker returned to his inclusive definition of a true democracy, but in his Thanksgiving sermon of November 28, 1850, he reduced his triad to an absolute minimum, dropping the noun "people" and using instead the nominalization of "all" to bring his point across that he does mean everybody:

> This democratic idea is founded in human nature, and comes from the nature of God who made human nature. To carry it out politically is to execute justice, which is the will of God. This idea, in its realization, leads to a democracy, a government of all, for all, by all. Such a government aims to give every man all his natural rights; it desires to have political power in all hands, property in all hands, wisdom in all heads, goodness in all hearts, religion in all souls.[25]

It is hard to say whether Parker at this early date in American history thought of women in his claim that "every man" deserves the fair treatment of a democratic government, but be that as it may, he certainly includes the slaves as such. Linguistically it should be noted, however, that he has not yet found a repeatable formula for his triadic definition. Not only has he deleted the noun "people," he also changed the order of the prepositions of "of, by, for" (which Lincoln will use as well) to "of, for, by."

In any case, Lincoln might also have known Parker's address "Some Thoughts on the Progress of America," which he delivered at an anti-slavery convention in Boston on May 31, 1854. Here Parker returned to his original triad with the same sequence of prepositions:

> First there is the Democratic Idea: that all men are endowed by their Creator with certain natural rights; that these rights are alienable only by the possessor thereof; that they are equal in all men; that government is to organize these natural, unalienable, and equal rights into institutions designed for the good of the governed; and therefore government is to be of all the people, by all the people, and for all the people. Here government is development, not exploitation.[26]

Another four years later, on May 26, 1858, Parker delivered a speech at yet another New England anti-slavery convention on "The Relation of Slavery to a Republican Form of Government." This time he defines three

forms of government, returning more or less to his truncated triad but
changing the preposition "of" to the interesting variant "over":

> All society must have its government, that is, Rules of Conduct, and
> Conductors to see that they are kept.—Abstract Rules, Concrete Rulers.
> The substance of government consists in these two, and is always the
> same: but the forms thereof vary much from land to land, and age to age;
> yet may they be thus grossly summed in three:
> I. Monarchy—The One-Man Power; government over all, but by
> one, and often in practice it turns out to be chiefly for the sake of that
> one.
> II. Oligarchy—The Few-Men Power; government over all, but by
> a few, and often in practice it turns out to be chiefly for the sake of that
> few.
> III. Democracy—The All-Men Power; government over all, by all,
> and for the sake of all. Yet, practically, it must be government by the
> Majority, and in fact, it often turns out to be chiefly for the advantage
> of that majority. As a general rule, no majority, no small body of men,
> no individual man, is ever trusted with unlimited power over others, but
> he abuses it—for his gain, to their loss. Such is the friction in all social
> machinery.[27]

A little more than a month later, in his last great anti-slavery address
on July 4, 1858, entitled "The Effect of Slavery on the American People,"
Parker uttered the following words in the Music Hall at Boston:

> Theocracy, the priest power; monarchy, the one-man power; and
> oligarchy, the few-men power—are three forms of vicarious government
> over the people, perhaps for them, not by them. Democracy is direct
> self-government, over all the people, by all the people, for all the people.
> Our institutions are democratic: theocratic, monarchic, oligarchic
> vicariousness is all gone.[28]

We know for a fact that Abraham Lincoln was aware of Parker's work at
that time. His friend and early biographer William H. Herndon reports that
he brought with him "additional sermons and lectures by Theodore Parker,
who was warm in his commendation of Lincoln. One of these lectures was
a lecture on 'The Effect of Slavery on the American People,' which was
delivered in the Music Hall in Boston, and which I gave to Lincoln, who
read and returned it. He liked especially the following expression, which
he marked with a pencil, and which he in substance afterwards used in

his Gettysburg address: 'Democracy is direct self-government, over all the people, for all the people, by all the people.'"[29]

There is one more reference from the influential writings and opinions by Theodore Parker that deserves to be cited here in conclusion. In his significant essay on "Transcendentalism" (published posthumously in 1876), Parker shows how much the ideal of a democratic government is not based on experience and precedents alone but that it starts from a consciousness of human nature, appealing to a natural justice and a harmonious and progressive development:

> The great political idea of America, the idea of the Declaration of Independence, is a composite idea made up of three simple ones: 1. Each man is endowed with certain unalienable rights. 2. In respect of these rights all men are equal. 3. A government is to protect each man in the entire and actual employment of all the unalienable rights. Now the first two ideas represent ontological facts, facts of human consciousness; they are facts of necessity. The third is an idea derived from the two others, is a synthetic judgment *a priori;* it was not learned from sensational experience; there never was a government which did this, nor is there now. Each of the other ideas transcended history: every unalienable right has been alienated, still is; no two men have been actually equal in actual rights. Yet the idea is true, capable of proof by human nature, not of verification by experience; as true as the proposition that three angles of a triangle are equal to two right angles; but no more capable of a sensational proof than that. The American Revolution, with American history since, is an attempt to prove by experience this transcendental proposition, to organize the transcendental idea of politics. The idea demands for its organization, a democracy—a government of all, for all, and by all; a government by natural justice, by legislation that is divine as much as true astronomy is divine, legislation which enacts law representing a fact of the universe, a resolution of God.[30]

Not meaning to take anything away from Parker's philosophical and religious thoughts, he simply can't get his triple formula straight! This time it is "a government of all, for all, and by all," and this new variant is proof that the formula as such has not been solidified into a proverbial quotation by Parker himself let alone the general American population. It took Abraham Lincoln in his public role as President of the United States to accomplish this feat. But never could it be denied that Theodore Parker had a major influence on the political and social thought of Lincoln, including the definitive formulation of "government of the people, by the people, for the people" in his Gettysburg Address of 1863.

Abraham Lincoln as Catalyst and Phrase Forger

Before turning to Lincoln's Gettysburg Address, it might do well to cite one more paragraph that includes the spirit albeit not the precise linguistic form of the triadic phrase. In 1857, W. Alfred Jones reflected on the American government in his essay on "Titles," chastising his fellow citizens for placing too much value on pomp and circumstance in the form of honors, ceremonies, titles, etc. This ought not to be so in a true democracy which he defines as follows:

> Democracy is a principle (political, not social), and does not depend upon the dress or pursuits or accomplishments of the individual professing it. It is a philanthropic and philosophic system of polity, wholly irrespective of personal habits or prejudices. It is the government of the people by themselves. Of this great body, the leaders (for the mass cannot act as one man, and must delegate duties and assign powers) are expected to be in advance, socially and intellectually, if not also morally and politically of their fellows, else why leaders? And we find as a matter of history, the staunchest advocates of liberal views and free government at all times, and especially in the most excited times, to have been able men, good patriots and gentlemen—to look at Lafayette in France; Sidney and Russell and Hampden in England; and all of our own great Revolutionary characters without exception.[31]

Admittedly, the phrasal segment "government of the people by themselves" is perhaps a mere allusion to the actual tripartite formula that is gaining in currency in the mid 1850s. But Lincoln had the same problem in his "Message to Congress in Special Session" of July 4, 1861, where he is justifying his decision to go to war with the rebelling Southern states:

> And this issue [the beginning of open hostilities and the possible break-up of the country over slavery] embraces more than the fate of these United States. It presents to the whole family of man, the question, whether a constitutional republic, or a democracy—a government of the people, by the same people—can, or cannot, maintain its territorial integrity, against its own domestic foes. It presents the question, whether discontented individuals, too few in numbers to control administration,

according to organic law, in any case, can always, upon the pretences made in this case, or on any other pretences, or arbitrarily, without any pretence, break up their Government, and thus practically put an end to free government upon the earth. It forces us to ask: "Is there, in all republics, this inherent, and fatal weakness?" "Must a government, of necessity, be too *strong* for the liberties of its own people, or too *weak* to maintain its own existence?" So viewing the issue, no choice was left but to call out the war power of the Government; and so to resist force, employed for its destruction, by force, for its preservation.[32]

It is a bit surprising that Lincoln only used the bipartite phrase of "government of the people, by the same people" in this extremely important speech at the outset of the Civil War. Obviously the reading of speeches and essays by Webster and Parker had not ingrained the triadic phrase to such a degree that it flowed as a prefabricated formula into his political rhetoric at this time.

Since not even Webster or Parker had this obvious influence on Lincoln, it is very doubtful indeed that the remarks which Louis Kossuth (1802–1894), the Governor of Revolutionary Hungary in 1849, made on February 7, 1852, before the Ohio Legislature at Columbus during a fund-raising trip to the United States, had any direct link to Lincoln's Gettysburg Address. At that time Kossuth observed that "The spirit of our age is Democracy. All for the people, and all by the people. Nothing *about* the people *without* the people. That is Democracy, and that is the ruling tendency of the spirit of our age."[33] The somewhat patriotic argument by Steven Béla Várdy in an article on "Louis Kossuth's Words in Abraham Lincoln's Gettysburg Address" (1999) goes too far in its claim that Kossuth's speech "was more than likely the source of inspiration for Abraham Lincoln's oft-recited masterpiece, the 'Gettysburg Address.'" His arguments become even more questionable when one considers the errors in the concluding paragraph of the article:

> There is no doubt that Kossuth's and Lincoln's phrases *by the people, for the people,* are philologically identical. The question, however, remains whether the American President in 1864 knowingly and deliberately quoted the Kossuthian phrase or only accidently used the same words as Kossuth. If the identical phrasing is accidental, we can suppose that "by the people for the people" may have been a stereotype of American liberal journalism of the 50s and 60s in the last century. A comprehensive data collection on the phrase from the contemporary media could help to answer this puzzling question.[34]

First of all, the phrases by Kossuth and Lincoln are not philologically identical: Kossuth in 1852 has "all for the people, and all by the people," while Lincoln in 1863 (not 1864!) says "of the people, by the people, for the people." And who is to say that Lincoln came across the Kossuth speech in the *Ohio State Journal* of February 7, 1852? This is all but conjecture, and Várdy appears to be not at all aware of any of the references mentioned thus far in this chapter. He is, however, correct, that a comprehensive collection of data on the phrase will shed light on all of this, as the numerous references of this very chapter illustrate.

There is no doubt that Lincoln "conned the texts of speeches made by Webster,"[35] Parker, and others, and it is only natural that such careful studies led to rhetorical borrowings ranging from direct quotations to paraphrases and indirect allusions. As Lincoln prepared his numerous speeches, he would gather material from many sources and spend days "reading, listening, rephrasing, refocusing, and strengthening his arguments."[36] Clearly no person works in absolute isolation, and as Byron D. Murray aptly and not at all defensively has pointed out, "it detracts nothing from Lincoln to say that he appears not to have written always out of the loneliness of his own mind, but to have reflected upon and given his own savour to some of the best expression of his time."[37] To suggest even the thought of plagiarism is utterly absurd, and the interrogatively phrased title of a journalistic essay "Lincoln: Rhetorical Copycat?" not only misses the point but intimates a *modus operandi* on the part of Lincoln which does not hold water. One might, however, be inclined to agree with its author Thoburn V. Barker that in certain instances, including some of his famed utterances, "what he [Lincoln] said was customary rather than original, universal rather than unique."[38] But it was he, Lincoln, who said what he said, when he said it, and how he said it. That cannot possibly be argued away or diminished in any way.

These considerations lead quite naturally to one of the most famous phrases attributed to Lincoln, namely that included in the closing remarks of his short yet famous Gettysburg Address of November 19, 1863:

> Four score and seven years ago our fathers brought forth on this continent, a new nation, conceived in Liberty, and dedicated to the proposition that all men are created equal.
>
> Now we are engaged in a great civil war, testing whether that nation, or any nation so conceived and so dedicated, can long endure. We are met on a great battlefield of that war. We have come to dedicate a portion of that field, as a final meeting place for those who here gave their lives that that nation might live. It is altogether fitting and proper that we should do this.

But in a larger sense, we can not dedicate—we can not consecrate—
we can not hallow—this ground. The brave men, living and dead, who
struggled here, have consecrated it, far above our poor power to add or
detract. The world will little note, nor long remember what we say here,
but it can never forget what they did here. It is for us the living, rather,
to be dedicated here to the unfinished work which they who fought here
have thus far so nobly advanced. It is rather for us to be here dedicated
to the great task remaining before us—that from these honored dead we
take increased devotion to that cause for which they gave their last full
measure of devotion—that we here highly resolve that these dead shall
not have died in vain—that this nation, under God, shall have a new
birth of freedom—and that government of the people, by the people, for
the people, shall not perish from the earth.[39]

When Lincoln added at the very end that a democratic government
"shall not perish from the earth," he might well have had a passage from
the Bible in mind: "Where there is no vision, the people perish: but he that
keepeth the law, happy is he" (Proverbs 29:18). But regarding the precise
wording of "government of the people, by the people, for the people," the
phrase is indeed Lincoln's! Bi- and tripartite variants of it were in considerable
oral and written circulation. But if there was any direct influence, it most
likely was by Daniel Webster or even more obviously by Theodore Parker.
As will be recalled, the admired Daniel Webster, on January 26, 1830, had
spoken about the origin of the government of the United States and its true
character: "It is the people's Constitution, the people's government, made
for the people, made by the people, and answerable to the people."[40] While
Lincoln had almost certainly read this speech, he might also have come
across Theodore Parker's anti-slavery speech (or a number of others by this
prolific reformer) of May 29, 1850: "[...] a democracy, that is, a government
of all the people, by all the people, for all the people."[41] Except for the word
"all," Parker's phrase is absolutely identical with that of Lincoln, and the
latter can hardly be considered the originator of this triadic formulation. For
the "people" triad at least, Thoburn Barker's observation that what Lincoln
said at Gettysburg "was customary rather than original, universal rather
than unique"[42] holds true. That does not mean, of course, that Lincoln
did not popularize his version through his masterful Gettysburg Address
so that it now has become a proverbial definition of a free and democratic
government. In the precise wording of "Government of the people, by the
people, [and] for the people" this statement-turned-memorable-quotation
and eventually having become a well-known proverb belongs to Abraham
Lincoln—no doubt about it.

FREDERICK DOUGLASS AND HIS REPETITIVE USE OF THE PROVERB

In all of his work for the steady improvement of the Black race, Lincoln's contemporary and friend, the former slave and subsequent abolitionist and sociopolitical reformer Frederick Douglass, never lost sight of his goal to fight for civil rights of all the people. In a bitter speech on January 17, 1850, in Syracuse, New York, he made this point very clearly, but this time still primarily from the point of view of the abolitionist: "Talk to me of the love of liberty of your Washingtons, Jeffersons, Henrys. They were strangers to any just idea of Liberty! He who does not love Justice and Liberty for all, does not love Liberty and Justice. They wrote of Liberty in the Declaration of Independence with one hand, and with the other clutched their brother by the throat! These are the men who formed the union! I cannot enter into it. Give me NO UNION WITH SLAVEHOLDERS!"[43] About six years later, on May 28, 1856, by chance in the same city of Syracuse, his message sounded much more inclusive: "It [the Constitution] does not know anything of Irishmen, Englishmen, or Germans, of white men or black men; but of men. It knows nothing of a north, south, east or west; but *the people.*"[44] And another year later, on May 11, 1857, in New York, he speaks of "the people" and the Constitution by directly alluding to its preamble: "'We, the people'—not we, the white people—not we, the citizens, or the legal voters—not we, the privileged class, and excluding all other classes but we, the people; not we, the horses and cattle, but we the people—the men and women, the human inhabitants of the United States, do ordain and establish this Constitution, etc."[45] Douglass obviously delighted in this explication of the preamble of the Constitution, as can be seen from this somewhat expanded paragraph from his speech on "The Constitution of the United States: Is It Pro-Slavery or Anti-Slavery?" that he gave on March 26, 1860, at Glasgow, Scotland:

> But it has been said that negroes are not included in the benefits sought under the declaration of purposes. Whatever slaveholders may say, I think it comes with ill grace from abolitionists to say the negroes in America are not included in this declaration of purposes. The negroes are not included! Who says this? The constitution does not say they are not included, and how dare any other person, speaking for the constitution, say so? The constitution says "We the people;" the language is "we the people;" not we the white people, not we the citizens, not we the privileged class, not we the high, not we the low, not we of English extraction, not we of French or of Scotch extraction, but "we the people;" not we the horses, sheep, and swine, and wheelbarrows, but we the human inhabitants;

and unless you deny that negroes are people, they are included within the purposes of this government. They are there, and if we the people are included, negroes are included; they have a right, in the name of the constitution of the United States, to demand their liberty.[46]

It is always the integrity of the people that Douglass champions. When it comes to governing this nation, then all the people must count: "The beauty and perfection of government in our eyes will be attained when all the people under it, men and women, black and white, shall be conceded the right of equal participation in wielding its power and enjoying its benefits. Equality is even a more important word with us than liberty" (Aug. 24, 1871).[47] In his essay on "The Work of the Future" that appeared in November 1862 in *Douglass' Monthly,* he put all of this quite succinctly into the formulaic statement: "The Government is not enthroned above the people but is of, by and through the people."[48]

This almost proverbial statement precedes Lincoln's quite similar conclusion "government of the people, by the people, for the people" of the Gettysburg Address (November 19, 1863) by about a year. But once Douglass learned of Lincoln's formulation in the Gettysburg Address, he too started using it in that precise wording in numerous speeches, thus in fact adding to its popularity which resulted in its eventual proverbial status. In his major speech on the "Sources of Danger to the Republic," delivered on February 7, 1867, in St. Louis, he used it for the first time, starting the paragraph with a bit of folk humor by including the proverbial expression "dyed in the wool" to refer to himself as a true democrat, and not as a member of the Democratic but rather the Republican Party:

> In fact, I am here tonight as a democrat, a genuine democrat dyed in the wool. I am here to advocate a genuine democratic republic; to make this a republican form of government, purely a republic, a genuine republic; free it from everything that looks toward monarchy; eliminate all foreign elements, all alien elements from it; blot out from it everything antagonistic of republicanism declared by the fathers—that idea was that all governments derived their first powers from the consent of the governed; make it a government of the people, by the people and for the people, and for all the people, each for all and all for each; blot out all discrimination against any person, theoretically or practically, and make it conform to the great truths laid down by the fathers; keep no man from the ballot box or jury box or the cartridge box, because of his color—exclude no woman from the ballot box because of her sex. Let the government of the country rest securely down upon the shoulders

of the whole nation; let there be no shoulder that does not bear up its proportion of the burdens of the government. Let there [be] no conscience, no intellect in the land not directly responsible for the moral character of the government—for the honor of the government. Let it be a genuine Republic, in which every man subject to it is represented in it, and I see no reason why a Republic may not stand while the world stands.[49]

What a statement barely two years after the Civil War! What a vision for a positive Reconstruction of the nation "for all the people, each for all and all for each," without any discrimination by race or gender! He is clearly years ahead of major constitutional amendments in this ideal view of a new republic. It must never be forgotten that "next to Abolition and the battle for equal rights for the Negro people, the cause closest to Douglass' heart was woman's rights."[50] Looking back on his life's work, Douglass stated with much linguistic insight: "In the old days, of slavery I began all my speeches with the saying, 'Every man is himself.' He lives and dies and is responsible for himself. What is true of man is true of woman. I affirm the individuality and self-ownership of women" (Dec. 3, 1884).[51] In its more explicit contextualization, Douglass's use of Lincoln's famous phrase-turned-proverb goes further than what Lincoln had said in his Gettysburg Address. So why should Douglass's statement not stand next to Lincoln's and bear witness to the life of a man equal in stature to this great president? Pray that one of the next presidents of this nation might include this powerful statement in his or her inaugural address to give credit to a great champion of civil rights.

Fifteen years later, in an address on May 30, 1882, in Rochester, New York, Douglass incorporated the proverb into a global vision, indicating that he went far beyond the purely American interpretation of its wisdom. The breadth and depth of Douglass's thoughts on race, gender, and politics are indeed astounding in such statements that are as fitting today as they were in the nineteenth century:

> If the existence of society is more than the lives of individual men; if all history proves that no great addition has ever been made to the liberties of mankind, except through war; if progress of the human race has been disputed by force and it has only succeeded by opposing force with force; if nations are most effectively taught righteousness by affliction and suffering; if the eternal laws of rectitude are essential to the preservation, happiness and perfection of the human race; if there is anything in the world worth living for, fighting for and dying for, the suppression of our rebellion by force was not only a thing right and proper in itself but an

immense and immeasurable gain to our country and the world. Had that rebellion succeeded with all its malign purposes, what then would have become of our grand example of free institutions, of what value then would have been our government of the people by the people and for the people? What ray of light would have been left above the horizon, to kindle the first hope for the toiling millions in Europe? Every despot in the Old World would have seen in our manifest instability of government, a new and powerful argument in favor of despotic power.[52]

While Douglass has the entire "human race" of the "world" in mind, he obviously knew his American political and social history and its famous documents the best. This becomes evident in yet another speech on September 24, 1883, in Louisville, Kentucky, in which he blends segments of the Declaration of Independence with the Gettysburg Address, to stress once again his deep-rooted belief in equality of all people, in a concise oratorical masterpiece: "We hold it to be self-evident that no class or color should be the exclusive rulers of this country. If there is such a ruling class, there must of course be a subject class, and when this condition is once established this Government of the people, by the people and for the people, will have perished from the earth."[53] Two and a half years later, on April 16, 1886, in the nation's capital, Douglass uses the proverb once again with specific reference to Abraham Lincoln: "We may affirm what must be admitted by all, that under this form of government so happily described, and so faithfully upheld by the great and lamented Abraham Lincoln, as 'government of the people, by the people, and for the people,' this nation has become rich, great, progressive and strong."[54] How happy indeed would Lincoln have been had he lived to hear the leading spokesman of African Americans make this pronouncement.

Yet exactly two years later, on April 16, 1888, Douglass uses the same democratic proverb to illustrate that Reconstruction is not going all so well:

> Let us see what are the relations subsisting between the negro and the state and national governments. What support, what assistance he has received from either of them. Take his relation to the national government and we shall find him a deserted, a defrauded, a swindled, and an outcast man. In law, free; in fact, a slave. In law, a citizen; in fact, an alien; in law, a voter; in fact, a disfranchised man. In law his color is no crime; in fact, his color exposes him to be treated as a criminal. Toward him every attribute of a just government is contradicted. For him, it is not a government of the people, by the people, and for the people. Toward

him, it abandons the beneficent character of a government, and all that gives a government the right to exist.[55]

All of these citations show that Douglass's work as agitator and reformer was never done, and he dedicated much of his energy in his later life to the cause of women's suffrage. Once again Lincoln's proverb served him extremely well to agitate for this basic right: "And now I ask, What right have I, what right have you, what right has anybody who believes in a government of the people, by the people, and for the people, to deny to woman this full and complete citizenship? What right have I, what right have you, what right has anybody, thus to humiliate one-half of the human family? There is no such right outside of the right of the robber and the usurper!" (Sept. 22, 1887).[56] Seven years later on January 9, 1894, Douglass picked up his proverbial *leitmotif* again in front of an audience in Washington, D.C., arguing vehemently against restricting the right of "uneducated" Blacks to vote and for women's suffrage: "I cannot follow these gentlemen in their proposition to limit suffrage to the educated alone. I would not make suffrage more exclusive, but more inclusive. I would not have it embrace merely the elite, but would include the lowly. I would not only include the men, I would gladly include the women, and make our government in reality as in name a government of the people and of the whole people."[57] As is generally known, the nineteenth amendment giving women the right to vote was not passed until 1920, but Douglass deserves much credit for having supported women of all races in the struggle for universal suffrage.

It is well known that Lincoln and Douglass had their differences, but there was deep mutual respect and admiration that grew in Douglass, as he reflected and spoke on Lincoln on various occasions after the assassination. Both great men had many obstacles to overcome on their path to become servants of others. Slavery and poverty characterize their respective youths, but then came that drive towards self-education by all means. To this were added hard work and fundamental moral principles that made "self-made men" *par excellence* out of them. Little wonder then that their ideals and dreams became joint in the extended proverb "Government of the people, by the people, and for the people, and for all the people!"

Beyond Lincoln and Douglass—Last Third of the Nineteenth Century

Despite Douglass's repeated use of the phrase, even he got the order of the prepositions wrong once in his revised biography *Life and Times of Frederick*

Douglass (1893). As a resident of greater Washington D.C., he certainly was well aware of its peculiar political situation:

> The District of Columbia is the one spot where there is no government for the people, of the people, and by the people. Its citizens submit to rulers whom they have had no choice in selecting. They obey laws which they had no voice in making. They have a plenty of taxation, but no representation. In the great questions of politics in the country they can march with neither army, but are relegated to the position of neuters.[58]

Perhaps Douglass altered the structure of the triad on purpose, but be that as it may, the following definition of a "popular government" that John Cordner attempted on December 22, 1864, shows that he might not have Lincoln's passage in his repertoire of ready-made phrases as yet: "Popular government, I define as a government of the people, by the people. Now this is what we have in Canada. With us, however, it is administered under the form of limited monarchy. But the difference here, as compared with the government of the United States, is formal, rather than substantial."[59] But by the 1870s, the triad from Lincoln's Gettysburg Address appears well established among writers, as the following contextualized references show. In indirect reverence to Lincoln, authors often place the well-known phrase into quotation marks, or they mention Lincoln directly:

> [1872:] No American can look over the history of this country without being devoutly thankful for the blessings of that freedom and unrestrained liberty which is ours, or fail to experience a growth in that noblest form of patriotism which declares that this Government of the people, by the people and for the people, *shall be maintained!*[60]
>
> [1874:] So far as churches are concerned, they undeniably promote that public intelligence, conscientiousness, and moral purity, without which society would utterly perish in its own corruption, and democratic government "of the people, by the people, for the people," would be impossible.[61]
>
> [1876:] When, in the economy of providence, this land was to be purged of human slavery, and when the strength of government of the people by the people for the people was to be demonstrated, the Republican party came into power.[62]
>
> [1879:] The American idea of a republic, as "a government of the people, by the people, and for the people," has been consistently developed and ceased to be a mere experiment.[63]

[1879:] The Volunteer Soldiers of the Union, whose Valor and
Patriotism saved to the world a "Government of the People, by the
People, and for the People [a toast]."[64]

[1884:] President Lincoln defined democracy to be "the government
of the people by the people for the people." This is a sufficiently compact
statement of it as a political arrangement.[65]

[1890:] Let us hold fast to the sublime declaration of Lincoln. Let
us insist that this, the Republic, is "A government of the people, by the
people, and for the people."[66]

[1894:] Between the political institutions of the several nations
which compose the civilized world there is no gap so great as that which
separates those of Russia from those of the United States. Our civil war
was fought that "government of the people, by the people, for the people
should not perish from the earth." In this country there is universal
suffrage.[67]

These texts in contexts are all precise citations of the proverbial utterance
by Abraham Lincoln. But there are, of course, also other references which are
not quite so sacrosanct. For example, Charles Dickens made the following
statement during a speech on April 10, 1869, at Liverpool: "It appeared to me
[...] that literature was a dignified profession, by which any man might stand
or fall. I made a compact with myself that in my person literature should stand,
and by itself, of itself, and for itself; and there is no consideration on earth
which would induce me to break that bargain."[68] It would be difficult to prove
that Dickens is playing here with Lincoln's triad, but the addition of "there is
no consideration on earth" also brings to mind Lincoln's "shall not perish from
this earth," and thus Dickens might well be aware of the formula.

Oscar Wilde on the other hand, in his essay on "The Soul of Man
Under Socialism" (1895) very obviously negates the meaning of Lincoln's
phrase, while he keeps its wording and structure intact:

> *All modes of government are failures.* Despotism is unjust to everybody,
> including the despot, who was probably made for better things.
> Oligarchies are unjust to the many, and ochlocracies are unjust to the
> few. High hopes were once formed of democracy; but democracy means
> simply the bludgeoning of the people by the people for the people. It
> has been found out. I must say that it was high time, for all authority is
> quite degrading.[69]

Neither Lincoln nor Douglass would have shared this cynicism about
the American experiment in a democratic government. But how pleased

would they have been by the following remarks which the civil war soldier, lawyer, orator, and writer Robert G. Ingersoll included in his lecture "Eight to Seven Address" (1877) that dealt with electoral reforms: "We are equals. We are all fellow-citizens. In a Government of the people, by the people and for the people, there shall not be an outcast class, whether white or black."[70]

But the last words of this review of nineteenth-century appearances of Lincoln's proverb belongs to the women's suffrage leader and social reformer Elizabeth Cady Stanton, who included the following remarks in her "Address of Welcome to the International Council of Women" on March 25, 1888, at Washington, D.C. There is a good chance that Frederick Douglass might have been there for this memorable event, and if so, he would have been most pleased to hear his friend Abraham's proverbial words used in this fashion and context:

> Here, under the very shadow of the Capitol of this great nation, whose dome is crowned with the Goddess of Liberty, the women from many lands have assembled at last to claim their rightful place, as equal factors, in the great movements of the nineteenth century, so we bid our distinguished guests welcome, thrice welcome, to our triumphant democracy. I hope they will be able to stay long enough to take a bird's eye view of our vast possessions, to see what can be done in a moral as well as material point of view in a government of the people. In the Old World they have governments and people; here we have a government of the people, by the people, for the people—that is, we soon shall have when that important half, called women, are enfranchised, and the laboring masses know how to use the power they possess.[71]

This is indeed effective rhetoric, quoting a well-known Lincoln phrase-turned-proverb in a most positive way and then adding an unexpected twist to it that places it right in the middle of women's rights and the whole problem of voting by women and the masses in general. Abraham Lincoln's proverbial definition of a democratic government has established itself well, and it will be made use of in whatever way to comment on the positive and negative sides of the American government.

THE FIRST HALF OF THE TWENTIETH CENTURY AND THE "AMERICAN'S CREED"

The revealing contextualized texts of the proverb during the nineteenth century recount the struggle of the American society towards a meaningful

and sincere interpretation of this democratic wisdom. By the beginning of
the twentieth century, the proverb has lost its limited male orientation and
can in fact be understood as a piece of folk wisdom describing democratic
principles where race and gender should not make a difference. This is clearly
indicated by a lecture on "The Country's Path to Duty" which Archbishop
Ireland of Chicago delivered on February 13, 1903, to commemorate the
ninety-fourth anniversary of the birth of Abraham Lincoln:

> The Republic is what she is because she has vitally remained what Wash-
> ington intended her to be, what Lincoln bade her to be—a government
> of the people, by the people, for the people. This is what she must remain,
> if she is still to live and to reign. The vital principles of democracy must
> animate her. Every man under the flag must be equal before the law in
> civil and political rights; it matters not what his place of birth, what his
> religious creed, what the color of his face; if he is an American citizen,
> the laws of the land must shield him, the favors of the land must flow
> upon him.[72]

In the same year, on October 31, 1903, President Theodore Roosevelt
made the following Thanksgiving Proclamation, proudly quoting the words
of Lincoln without having to name the former president. His fellow citizens
knew very well whom he was citing: "In no other place and at no other time
has the experiment of government of the people, by the people, for the people
been tried on so vast a scale as here in our own country in the opening years
of the twentieth century. Failure would not only be a dreadful thing for us,
but a dreadful thing for all mankind, because it would mean loss of hope for
all who believe in the power and righteousness of liberty."[73] Roosevelt urged
the American people "to war steadfastly for good and against all the forces
of evil, public and private," so that it might never come to the collapse of
the democratic government, as Ambrose Bierce expressed it in his satirical
text of October 17, 1904, "Opposition, *n*. In politics the party that prevents
the Government from running amuck by hamstringing it," which became
part of his infamous *Devil's Dictionary* (1906): "One day a bill imposing a
tax on warts was defeated—the members of the Government party had not
been nailed to their seats! This so enraged the King that the Prime Minister
was put to death, the parliament was dissolved with a battery of artillery,
and government of the people, by the people, for the people perished from
[the fictional] Ghargaroo."[74] With World War I raging in Europe and
endangering democratic governments, *The New York Times* published a list
of demands on December 24, 1916, "which Americans of Anglo-Saxon
blood would like to see made by England to Germany." As expected, one

of the requests included the basic proverb of democracy: "England believes in the principle that the government of a nation rests on the consent of the governed: that government of the many by the few must come to an end, and that government of the people by the people for the people must take its place."[75]

Of course, the United States eventually was drawn into this war that ended with the armistice day of November 11, 1918. In the political fervor of the day, an interesting occurrence took place in the United States House of Representatives on April 6, 1918, when its members adopted the little-known *The American's Creed,* formulated by William Tyler Page, a veteran House of Representatives employee from Friendship Heights, Maryland.[76] In March, 1917, the city of Baltimore had offered a prize of $1000 in a contest of formulating a national creed. Several thousand creeds were submitted, and no. 384 by Page was selected:

> *The American's Creed*
>
> I believe in the United States of America as a Government of the people, by the people, for the people, whose just powers are derived from the consent of the governed; a democracy in a Republic; a sovereign Nation of many sovereign States; a perfect Union, one and inseparable; established upon those principles of freedom, equality, justice, and humanity for which American patriots sacrificed their lives and fortunes.
>
> I therefore believe it is my duty to my country to love it, to support its Constitution, to obey its laws, to respect its flag, and to defend it against all enemies.[77]

While the text and report concerning the creed occupies about a third of a column in the *Congressional Record—House,* much more space was allotted to it (five large columns) in the *Appendix to the Congressional Record.*[78] There is a detailed discussion by Dr. Claxton, United States Commissioner of Education, of the various quotations of important historical American documents which Page assembled into his collage, including "that the second clause—'A government of the people, by the people, for the people'—is from the preamble to the Constitution of the United States [incorrect!], Daniel Webster's speech in the Senate of January 26, 1830, and Abraham Lincoln's Gettysburg speech."[79] There is also this somewhat longer comment: "The power of condensation of language is one of the most valuable in writing or speaking. That is the reason why this creed that he [Page] has written will be popular. It contains everything that is necessary, and there are no wasted words in it. He has Lincoln's most famous phrase, one that will live forever, that can not be amended. And it is strange to remember how close Daniel Webster came to getting that phrase. Two other [i.e., different] men expressed the same idea, but Webster said this was a government of all the people, by all the people, for all the people, and all that Lincoln did to it was to leave out the superfluous word 'all,' thereby making it immortal."[80] Speaker Clark of the House, who made these remarks, is, of course mistaken in his quotation of Daniel Webster, who, on January 26, 1830, had said (as discussed above): "It is the people's Constitution, the people's government, made for the people, made by the people, and answerable to the people." It was in fact Theodore Parker, who (as pointed out above) on May 29, 1850, had spoken of "[...] a democracy, that is, a government of all the people, by all the people, for all the people." As the record stands, the *Congressional Record* is wrong, and in regards to the discussion of Frederick Douglass's use of the phrase above, it should also be added that the adjective "all" is perhaps not as superfluous as Speaker Clark might have thought. It behooves us even today to stress that we do indeed mean government of each and every citizen when we quote Lincoln's version of the definition of democracy. At the end of the proceedings, Commissioner of Education Claxton made this final comment that was greeted with applause: "With the consent of those who have these proceedings in charge, I consider it my duty to see that every schoolhouse in the United States is furnished with a copy of this creed, to be learned by the 20,000,000 people now in these schoolhouses and the scores and hundreds of millions who will follow."[81] At the very end of this report, *The American's Creed* was read aloud as Tyler Page was presented to the entire House that cheered him with applause.[82] However, these emotions with all their patriotism also reflect war times, and the fate of the creed was not as favorable as these proceedings might suggest. I don't know whether the creed was ever mailed to the schools and whether millions of students did learn it by heart. In any case, *The American's Creed* has not become part and parcel of American cultural literacy and has vanished from the landscape. It must be remembered that today the practice at schools to have students memorize the preamble to the Constitution or at least parts of the Declaration of Independence or Gettysburg Address is also waning, a cultural process that carries definite problems with it. These national treasures should well remain in the minds and hearts of all American citizens as symbols of a free society.

This problem of memory was part of a column on the "Topics of the Times" in *The New York Times* of December 4, 1936, where a commentator thought it well to remember Lincoln's famous words on the basics of democracy as the dictatorial Nazi regime in Germany was gaining ever more threatening momentum:

The new Nazi critic will conclude with a few words about an American literary masterpiece, the Gettysburg Address. This is approximately 250 words long and was delivered on Nov. 19, 1863, on the site of the battlefield of Gettysburg, a borough and the county seat of Adams County, Pa., thirty-five miles southwest of Harrisburg. The speech was delivered by ABRAHAM LINCOLN, who was then 54 years old and 6 feet 4 inches in height. He was the sixteenth President of the United States.

The reason why the Gettysburg Address is so close to the hearts of all Americans is that they can never remember whether it is of the people, for the people, by the people, or by the people, of the people, for the people, or for the people, by the people, of the people. This compels them to look up the original text and has made the speech near and dear to them.[83]

The author of this satirical paragraph never gets the triad "of the people, by the people, for the people" quite right, but that is, quite surely, the point of the exercise. The indirect message of these comments is clearly that Americans ought to recall their impressive history of valiant struggles for freedom and liberty at a time when a serious menace is threatening Europe and the world.

In the same year the American poet and renowned Lincoln biographer Carl Sandburg stepped forth with his epic poem *The People, Yes* (1936), celebrating America as a country of immigrants, diversity, and nevertheless national unity. The impressive section on Abraham Lincoln, quoting freely from his works, includes the following lines:

> Lincoln?
> He was a mystery in smoke and flags
> saying yes to the smoke, yes to the flags,
> yes to the paradoxes of democracy,
> yes to the hopes of government
> of the people by the people for the people,
> no to debauchery of the public mind,
> no to personal malice nursed and fed,
> yes to the Constitution when a help,
> no to the Constitution when a hindrance,
> yes to man as a struggler amid illusions,
> each man fated to answer for himself:
> Which of the faiths and illusions of mankind
> must I choose for my own sustaining light
> to bring me beyond the present wilderness?[84]

And yet, not every literary appearance of Lincoln's proverb is cast in a positive light. In Michael Arlen's novel *The Flying Dutchman* (1939), for example, things are seen in a rather cynical way: "We say that those dictatorships [Mussolini, Stalin, and Hitler] make free people servile. But the fact remains that the enormous wealth of people like ourselves [leaders of industry] is due to that servile rottenness inherent in the democratic system which we call the government of the people, for the people, by the people, and to hell with the people.[85] In light of modern concerns along these lines, it is surprising that the addition of "to hell with the people" does not appear more frequently in oral and written communication.

Lincoln's words also reappeared in the mass media of the turbulent years of the first half of the twentieth century with its two world wars, prohibition, stock market crash, and many social problems. At times, the famed proverb is parodied to add satirical bite to the critical comments:

> [1924:] They [the two major political parties] have fallen under control of a single dominant power which uses them to further its own interests. Instead of a government of the people, by the people, for the people, we have a government of Wall Street, by Wall Street and for Wall Street. I [Senator Wheeler of Montana, Vice Presidential candidate on the La Follette ticket] use the term "Wall Street" to designate the industrial and commercial interests centering in that crooked line in lower New York City.[86]
>
> [1928:] Voters of the U.S.A.—Wanted all 100 per cent. citizens to support the Progressive Party, advocating the wisdom of a non-political Government of the people, by the people, for the people; the initiative, the referendum and the recall is the answer to the prohibition problem and business and social unrest, with equity and justice purges of bigotry.[87]
>
> [1939:] One specific service which a program of education for democracy can render is to bring back into common use an old synonym for democracy, and that is the word "freedom." The connotations of democracy are precious, and the issues between the democratic nations and their avowed enemies in the world today are sufficiently clear. Yet there is a warmth about the thing called freedom that makes the heart beat faster. Democracy is technically a way of government, but freedom is a way of life. American pulses respond easily to the ideal of government of the people, by the people, for the people. But a free people comes even closer to us than a self-governing people, except as the mind automatically translates a self-governing people into a nation of freemen.[88]

[1940:] Since the Declaration of Independence the United States has adhered to some form of democracy, which Lincoln said meant "government of the people, by the people, for the people." Such government has always been characteristic of this country. Whether it "can long endure" is being challenged. If it cannot, it will because the American Way has been discarded.[89]

[1943:] How do Abraham Lincoln's three [the other two are "You can fool some of the people ..." and "The Lord must love the plain people ..."] best-known discoveries stand up on his 134th birthday? Only a year ago we would have had to say that the outlook was grim. Government of the people, by the people, for the people had ceased to exist on the continent of Europe. The world's two great democracies, Britain and ourselves, were fighting for survival, with the prospect of victory none too bright. If the English-speaking peoples went down it would be all over with free government. The test which had been successfully met at Gettysburg would have been annulled eighty years later. Now that we are sure of victory for the United Nations we are justified in saying that when the present job is finished Abraham Lincoln will be more than vindicated.[90]

The last few paragraphs show how Abraham Lincoln's words became a rallying cry in America's war with Nazi Germany. It was indeed a very positive propagandistic use of the proverb, one that helped to convince the American population that the menace and horror of the Hitler regime had to be eliminated. To this end, President Roosevelt proclaimed that May 21, 1944, be "I Am an American Day." For the special celebration of this day, the Immigration and Naturalization Service of the Department of Justice issued a manual for "The Gateway to Citizenship" which included various documents in the form of speeches, songs, prayers, etc. for a better understanding of the democratic principles of the United States. *The New York Times* printed a page of excerpts,[91] among them in the first position *The American's Credo* by William Tyler Page discussed above, thus giving this patriotic statement an important public forum after all.

THE RHETORIC OF TWO WORLD LEADERS—CHURCHILL AND TRUMAN

Both Winston S. Churchill and Harry S. Truman made repeated use of Abraham Lincoln's proverbial triad, with Churchill even having a bit of fun with it in the House of Commons on April 28, 1927, when he was accused of wrong appropriations for the road fund. Rejecting such accusations, he stated that he was tired of having to deal with such problems as "Government

of the motorists, by the motorists, for the motorists"[92] and that he was not
going to fight this battle any longer. He also alluded to the phrase in the
satirical title of the essay "Government of the by the for the Dole-Drawers"
(1931), restating it more fully in the text itself: "'Government of the dole-
drawers, by the dole-drawers, for the dole-drawers.'"[93] This varied triad
was directed against the financial and unemployment policies by the Labor
Government in England, but things became much more serious for this
masterful orator as Hitler's regime grew in power. In his essay "I Ask You—
What Price Freedom?" (1936) he states straightforwardly what the task at
hand is:

> These are not the days when the ordinary citizen can afford to neglect
> any precaution or withhold any labour or sacrifice which is necessary
> to preserve the health and strength of Parliamentary institutions or to
> uphold, in the famous American expression, "government of the people,
> by the people, for the people." We will not surrender these title deeds
> of individual rights for which uncounted generations of illustrious men
> and women have fought and conquered to the morbid regimentation of
> a totalitarian State, whether it be pressed upon us by force from without
> or by conspiracy from within.[94]

When as Prime Minister he travelled to the United States to deliver
his speech on "A Long and Hard War" to a Joint Session of Congress on
December 26, 1941, he included the following personal remarks in the
second paragraph of this memorable address:

> I have been in full harmony all my life with the tides which have flowed
> on both sides of the Atlantic against privilege and monopoly, and I have
> steered confidently towards the Gettysburg ideal of "government of the
> people by the people for the people." I owe my advancement entirely
> to the House of Commons, whose servant I am. In my country, as in
> yours, public men are proud to be the servants of the State and would
> be ashamed to be its masters. On any day, if they thought the people
> wanted it, the House of Commons could by a simple vote remove me
> from my office. But I am not worrying about it at all. As a matter of
> fact, I am sure they will approve very highly of my journey here, for
> which I obtained the King's permission in order to meet the President of
> the United States and to arrange with him all that mapping-out of our
> military plans, and for all those intimate meetings of the high officers
> of the armed services of both countries, which are indispensable to the
> successful prosecution of the war.[95]

Americans obviously were pleased with this nod to Lincoln and the ideal of a democratic government. And Churchill was not merely doing lip service, he meant what he said and repeated this political maxim in his "Review of the War" on January 18, 1945, in the House of Commons in London when the war was slowly but surely drawing to an end:

> We have one principle about the liberated countries or the repentant satellite countries which we strive for according to the best of our ability and resources. Here is the principle. I will state it in the broadest and most familiar terms: Government of the people, by the people, for the people, set up on a basis of election by free and universal suffrage, with secrecy of the ballot and no intimidation. That is and has always been the policy of this Government in all countries. This is our only aim, our only interest, and our only care. It is to that goal that we try to make our way across all the difficulties, obstacles and perils of the long road.[96]

Lincoln would surely have been proud of this policy of "malice towards none" based on democratic principles. Two days after the end of World War II, Churchill rose again on August 16, 1945, in the House of Commons to deliver his prophetic speech on "The Iron Curtain Begins to Fall (Final Review of the War)" that looked into the future of a Europe divided into East and West. With clear understanding of the political challenges that were facing western Europe, he returned one more time to the proverbial triad that had served him so well before:

> We must know where we stand, and we must make clear where we stand, in these affairs of the Balkans and of Eastern Europe [with Russia taking control], and indeed of any country which comes into this field. Our ideal is government of the people, by the people, for the people—the people being free without duress to express, by secret ballot without intimidation, their deep-seated wish as to the form and conditions of the Government under which they are to live.[97]

It is, of course, an impressive tribute to American values for Winston S. Churchill, as Prime Minister of Great Britain and Americanophile, to cite this special proverb in his key speeches regarding world politics. On the American side of the struggle of World War II and its aftermath, it was Harry S. Truman who repeatedly drew on Lincoln's wisdom to underscore the ideals of a democratic government. On March 29, 1941, he stated the abbreviated form of the proverb during a "Speech on 'Jackson Day'" in Louisville, Kentucky: "He [President Andrew Jackson] did not set up a government of, by, and for the people but he did force a government to respond to the voice of the people. He did not solve all of the problems of his age, but he did and does inspire us to believe that problems can and must be solved."[98] The same formulation was repeated in an undelivered draft speech of October 1946 dealing with the vexing problem of price control after the war. He was, in fact, venting his frustration in the following comments: "You've deserted your President for a mess of pottage, a piece of beef—a side of bacon. My fellow citizens, you are the government. This is a government of, by and for the people. If you the people insist on following Mammon instead of Almighty God—your President can't stop you all by himself. He can only lead you to peace and happiness with your consent and your willing cooperation."[99] This is a fine example of Truman as President scolding his people for not seeing the right path towards economic improvement—"giving them hell,"[100] as it were.

During his presidential campaign in the fall of 1948, President Truman crisscrossed the country by train and made dozens of so-called "whistle-stops" in small towns. He would stand on the rear platform of a railroad car and do a few minutes worth of plain talking with the country people, referring again and again to Lincoln's proverbial definition of a democratic government. As will become obvious from the following five excerpts, Truman once in a while got the order of the prepositions mixed up in the heat of the campaign rhetoric:

> I am fighting for the education of the people of this country. When you have the proper education, you can't help but believe that our system of Government [in opposition to that of the Communists] is the best that's ever been conceived in the history of the world. It's a Government of the people [Truman did not complete the triad in this case]. In fact, you are the Government. You are the Government, and you are the Government because you have a right of free franchise, and when you don't exercise that right of free franchise, you are not doing the right thing by your country. You are a shirker, and when things don't go right in your Government and you don't vote, you're to blame for it.[101] (Provo, Utah; September 21, 1848)
>
> Now they're [the Republicans] trying to get out of that [raising money to deal with cattle diseases]. They go around telling you just exactly how they feel toward the people and what they'll do for the people. I wish you'd go back over the list of things that they did to the people in the 80th [so-called "do-nothing"] Congress. You wouldn't have one bit of trouble making up your mind. I know the people of Texas are going to make up their minds the right way because they know what's

what when it comes to Government of the people, for the people, and by the people. I'm asking you to turn out at election day and give us the biggest majority we've ever had in the history of the country.[102] (Marfa, Texas; September 25, 1848)

I want all of you to vote this time, and then I know that the country will be in safe hands, because when the people are aroused and when the people know what the issues are we have never had any difficulty making this Government run in the interests of the people, for the people, and by the people. I am going all up and down this country telling you that your interests and my interests and the interests of all the people are at stake in this campaign.[103] (Oneida, New York; October 8, 1848)

I want you to think just how out of place Lincoln would be with present day Republicans. Republicans don't charge low fees [as Lincoln did as a lawyer] any longer. The higher the better is their motto. They don't think any longer about "of the people, by the people, and for the people." The record of the Republican 80th Congress is proof of that.[104] (Danville, Illinois; October 12, 1848)

Now I want to say this to you, that if you believe in government of, by, and for the people, if you believe in your own self-interest, the best thing for you to do on November the 2nd is to go to the polls early and vote the straight democratic ticket, and then the country will be safe for another 4 years.[105] (New York City, New York; October 28, 1948)

Truman did well in relying on the democratic proverb for his reelection campaign. Lincoln's words served him well to spread his grass-root message, and he continued citing the words of his revered Abraham Lincoln during the next four years in office. In his "Remarks to Officers of the Veterans of Foreign Wars" on February 18, 1949, he employed it once again: "I am counting on you for help and support to carry out those policies which will make the country a better place in which to live and one which will give the rest of the world an example of how a government, of and by and for the people, can function."[106] He made similar "Remarks to Members of Reserve Officers Association" on June 28, 1950: "I believe that this is a Government of and by and for the people, as Abraham Lincoln said. And as far as I can, as President of the United States, I am trying to implement that theory, not only in the United States but in the world at large."[107]

These comments, albeit indirectly, indicate Truman's vexing problem with European politics after the war in particular. The so-called "Iron Curtain" had come down to separate Democracy from Communism, and the Cold War also had its start. Truman dealt with these problems more directly in his "Remarks to Members of the Associated Church

Press" on March 28, 1951, challenging the other side to be open and forthcoming:

> Our Government is a government of the people, for the people, and by the people, and we are trying to make it work as best we can. And we are making it work. What we want to do is to convince the people behind the Iron Curtain that we do not, under any circumstances, want to control or tell them what to do. All we want is for them—for their own welfare and benefit—to do the things that are necessary for the welfare of their own people, and to do it in their own way. Raise the curtain, and let us see how they do it. Maybe they can teach us something. I know we can teach them something, if they will come and look at us. But they won't come and make the effort to implement the mobilization of the moral forces of the world—all of them—against the unmoral forces. Then we will have peace in the world. And that's all we are striving for. That's all in the world we are striving for.[108]

While Truman once again mixed up his prepositions in this significant passage—one is reminded of President Ronald Reagan's remark some forty years later on June 12, 1987 at the Berlin Wall: "Mr. Gorbachev, open this gate! Mr. Gorbachev, tear down this wall!"[109]—he certainly gets them straight in an "Address at the Ceremonies Commemorating the 175th Anniversary of the Declaration of Independence" on July 4, 1951, at the Washington Monument. Praising the soldiers who have died in the service for their country, he stated: "They died in order that 'government of the people, by the people, for the people, shall not perish from the earth.' They have died in order that other men might have peace."[110] Truman is employing a direct quotation from the Gettysburg Address in this case, and as a well-informed historian, having written essays on numerous U.S. presidents,[111] he checked his source or paid special attention to get it right at this occasion.

This is, however, not the case in a private diary entry written down in Paris on June 6, 1956: "We drove out of Paris at 10 A.M. and arrived at Versailles to see the palace and the gardens. It is the extravaganza of King Louis XIV, the 'Grand Monarque,' whose statement 'I am the State' is one of the historical sentences expressing the Bourbon attitude toward government. It is the exact opposite of 'Government of the people, for the people and by the people,' the statement of Abraham Lincoln."[112] And finally, there is this short paragraph in a letter of January 31, 1960, that Truman never mailed to Joseph Clark. It shows that the aging former President is still very much involved with party politics, relying one more time on the shortened but correctly cited triad by his idol Abraham Lincoln: "The democratic Party has been the only political party since 1808 that has had the ordinary man's interest in its concept of what government is for. That has been true through Jackson, Lincoln (who coined the phrase 'Of, by and for the people'), Grover Cleveland in his first term, Teddy Roosevelt, to some extent, Woodrow Wilson and Franklin Roosevelt (without reservation)."[113] All of this is "plain talk" in its best sense, and Abraham Lincoln most assuredly would have approved of the way Harry S. Truman as well as Winston S. Churchill used his proverb to advance democratic "government[s] of the people, by the people, for the people" throughout the world.

Survival of the "People-Proverb" in the Modern Age

During the past five decades, Lincoln's proverb has found continued use as a well-known verbal symbol of democracy. At times the name of Abraham Lincoln is mentioned in order to add his authoritative voice to an argument or observation, but perhaps more often than not it suffices to state the entire phrase by itself or even just to allude to it. While the triad is often employed to comment on governmental issues, it is also called upon to deal with other political and social matters. This is the case, for example, with its effective employment in an article on "Our Faith Is Mightier Than Our Atom Bomb" (1949) by David E. Lilienthal, member of the Atomic Energy Commission:

> We should boast, as Whitman would, that the song of America is a song of great horizons; of a "new order of the ages"; of a new way of life under the sun. We should boast that in the United States we have created the most luminous concepts of the objectives of human society that any people has ever dedicated itself to: "life, liberty and the pursuit of happiness"; "government of the people, by the people, for the people"; "We hold these truths to be self-evident, that all men are created equal … one nation, indivisible, with liberty and justice for all." We in America have no need for slogans of other lands when on our banner are inscribed such imperishable cries of the human spirit as these.[114]

With the Cold War in full swing, weapons of mass destruction were very much under discussion, especially in the aftermath of the employment of the atomic bomb. The Soviet Union and the United States started to throw aggressive slogans at each other, and the arms race was well on its way. But what Lilienthal is saying here by way of a number of famous American proverbial quotations is that no such military rhetoric is necessary if the faith of the American people remains strongly embedded in democratic principles. But there were also those voices that questioned the claim of the universality of such American quotations, as was done by E. L. Woodward in his article "Words Loom Large in the World Struggle: Their Meanings Can be Dangerously Elusive" in *The New York Times* of March 16, 1952: "Examine the best known definition of democracy: government of the people, by the people, for the people. Government by what people? Those 'chosen by election'?"[115] Such a question may serve as a fitting transition to the following contextualized references from the modern mass media:

> [1959:] Nearly one hundred years ago Abraham Lincoln in his memorable address spoke of the sacrifices made so that in his words "Government of the people, by the people, for the people shall not perish from the earth." That was the question he posed to our nation in his generation. In our lives and actions, the people of America, in private and public sectors, daily face millions of choices with this continuing question always in the background.[116] (President Dwight D. Eisenhower)
>
> [1960:] By democratic values, the right to vote is fundamental, for the very existence of government dedicated to the concept "of the people, by the people, for the people," to use Lincoln's words, depends on the franchise.[117] (Justice Douglas)
>
> [1961:] Now he (U.N. Secretary General Dag Hammarskjold) is gone, but the cause of liberty and justice is not dead. Out of this day's shadow, facing uncertain events, we must look forward. [...] The words Lincoln spoke on a great battlefield where the dead were hardly yet buried, in the midst of a war whose outcome was not yet certain, may come to mind. We too lament the dead, of two world wars, of fighting in Korea and of U.N. soldiers other than the Secretary General who have fallen in line of duty. We too must highly resolve "that government of the people, by the people, for the people shall not perish from the earth."[118]

Again and again one observes how sacrosanct Lincoln's words can become in serious sociopolitical matters. The Gettysburg Address is, of course, a national treasure, and the entire text or parts of it are often recited. In fact, on November 19, 1963, *The New York Times* republished it on the 100th anniversary of the short but pregnant speech.[119] And the last sentence, long proverbial in American parlance, once again reminded readers of this unique and memorable definition of democracy. Three days later, President John F. Kennedy was assassinated on November 22, 1963. The citizens of Hyannis Port, Massachusetts, where the Kennedy family has a home, passed the following resolution that paraphrased Lincoln's solemn address to honor the slain Kennedy: "We hereby highly resolve that John F. Kennedy shall not have died in vain, that each one of us, under God, shall do everything possible to eliminate any ideas of hatred, intolerance or revenge in our own hearts to the end that government of the people, by the people and for the people, shall not perish from the earth."[120] During those sad times, this short statement, spoken by the people, was most appropriate to pay tribute to John F. Kennedy and to proclaim the survival of the American democracy.

Of course, not every use of Lincoln's phrase appears in such sublime surroundings. There was also the poster at Calvin Coolidge High School proclaiming that "Government of the Students, by the Students, for the Students, shall not perish from Calvin Coolidge" (1964).[121]And then came the corruption of the Nixon presidency with its Watergate scandal. Adlai E. Stevenson, Jr., Democratic Senator from Illinois, made effective use of the proverb in his Senate speech of October 2, 1972, by expanding it to show how President Richard Nixon negated its accepted truth: "The people are left to conclude what they will. And they will conclude that Mr. Nixon's Administration, because it will not permit an impartial investigation of the charges against it, has a great deal to hide. They are left to conclude that government of the people, by the people, for the people has given way, in Mr. Nixon's Washington, to the politics of wealth and stealth. And they are left to conclude that the era of the New Deal and the era of the Fair Deal have given way to Mr. Nixon's era: the Era of the Deal."[122] All of this led the Rev. Theodore M. Hesburgh, president of the University of Notre Dame, to ask the following question: "Have we become so inured to unethical behavior on the part of those who govern us that we are beyond surprise or indignation whatever the crime? How did we come to such a sorry pass, we who pride ourselves on government of the people, by the people, for the people, with liberty and justice for all?"[123] As will be remembered, Vice President Gerald Ford took over the reigns after Nixon's disgraceful fall from the highest office of the land. The new president did his best to heal the political and moral wounds, and in his State of the Union Message of January 12, 1977, he began his remarks by reassuring the American people that the United States will carry on: "We can be confident, however, that 100 years from now a freely elected President will come before a freely elected Congress, chosen to renew our great republic's pledge to government of the people, by the people and for the people."[124] This was an effective way to begin this speech as the American nation was beginning its third century with new hope for a more perfect people's government.

By the time of the national election of 1980, however, there was once again the worry that not enough people would take advantage of that great privilege and right of voting for their national government. The journalist

Laurin Hall Healy commented on this malaise in an article in the *Christian Science Monitor* of November 3, 1980, effectively concluding it with Lincoln's phrase:

> American democracy cannot survive unless it has an informed, educated, and concerned citizenry actively involved in the political process. Apathy must be overcome. The idea must be eliminated that "what difference does it make who is elected?"—that "politicians are all crooked, and no matter which party wins the people always lose." [...] Tomorrow there will be more than 157 million Americans of voting age. If past experience holds true only 84 million of them will bother to go to the polls on election day. Will the other 73 million remain in the huge third party—the No-Vote Party? Or will an enhanced sense of these perilous times arouse the silent ones to stand up and be counted in defense of that unique experiment in government of the people, by the people, and for the people?[125]

This is all true, but voter apathy is at least to some degree understandable when one considers the modern ways of campaigns: "Those TV spots, that no politician can run for office without, have all but turned 'government of the people, by the people and for the people' into government of the lobbyists, by the lobbyists and for the lobbyists. And you can blame television for that."[126] What is needed, of course, is a broad educational process in politics. *The New York Times* certainly tries its best at it, giving people a chance to voice their opinions as well, as a self-advertisement of May 3, 1981, demonstrates. The headline reads: "Of the people, by the people, for the people." This is followed by a picture of Congress with two people reading the *Times*. Underneath is the slogan: "The Op-Ed Page. Every morning. The place to look for interesting ideas. *The New York Times.*"[127] And there was also the advertisement by WOR Radio of New York with the headline and caption containing the following message: "RADIO OF THE PEOPLE, BY THE PEOPLE, FOR THE PEOPLE. Beginning tomorrow and continuing through 1983, WOR Radio will bring you a contemporary essay on America. It will be a revelation to anyone who wants to understand the American Spirit. We'll explore the country from Boston Harbor to San Francisco Bay: We'll meet and talk with teachers, truck drivers, factory workers and mayors [...]."[128] And why not also high government officials, who hopefully are mindful that they represent a government of the people, by the people, for the people!

Presidential candidates are also quite aware of the emotional power of Lincoln's democratic proverb that resonates so well in the minds of Americans. Democrat Walter Mondale, for example, made the following remarks on the political stomp in February of 1984: "Most Americans are never going to make a lot of money. They're going to live on modest incomes. But in America, we don't measure people by money. We measure people by what they really are. And when we talk about government of the people, by the people and for the people, that's what we mean. But what we've got today is a government of the rich, by the rich, and for the rich."[129] He liked his substitution of "rich" for "people" so much that he repeated this variant in his address accepting the Democratic Party nomination for President on July 19, 1984: "Four years ago, many of you voted for Mr. Reagan because he promised that you'd be better off. And today, the rich are better off. But working Americans are worse off, and the middle class is standing on a trap door. Lincoln once said that ours is to be a government of the people, by the people, and for the people. But what we have today is a government of the rich, by the rich, and for the rich and we're going to make a change in November."[130] Mondale was not elected, voter turnout was once again not impressive, and when three years later the country celebrated two hundred years of the Constitution, the question was raised: "Is this still 'government of the people, by the people, and for the people'? Are 'We the people' turned off politics?"[131] Such are the perils of a democracy, but in typical American fashion of looking forward,[132] hope springs eternal that citizens will make it their responsibility that their government is based on the free choices of the people themselves.

Here is a telling example of a time in Germany when this was not at all the case: "The words 'Dem Deutschen Volke' ('to the German people') on the Reichstag were quite different from the notion of 'government of the people, by the people, for the people.' They were to demonstrate that the Reichstag was a gift to the people from the higher powers who legally continued to hold sovereignty: the heads of the 15 monarchies and 3 cities that established the German empire in 1871. [...] It is not surprising that for lack of tradition and experience, and in the face of traumatic changes after World War I, Germany's first attempt at a genuine democracy [Weimarer Republik] did not succeed."[133] One is reminded in this respect and regarding all governmental experiments of a two-line stanza of William Matthews' poem "Frazzle" (1998) with its intentional variation of the traditional preposition sequence:

> By the people. For the people. Of the people. Grammar—
> but politics is an incomplete sentence, after all.[134]

But speaking of politics, Lincoln's proverb was even utilized during the national crisis of September 11, 2001, when the American democracy was shaken by dreadful terrorist attacks. The reaction to this tragedy took many forms, but here is the comment by Kathryn L. van Heyningen from Palm Harbor, Florida, who as a citizen had this to say in the *St. Petersburg Times:* "Though the World Trade Center was demolished, the Pentagon damaged, we must remember that this country is more than glass, steel and concrete. The terrorists struck at symbols of our nation, but it is the people who make a country great. We cannot and will not live in fear. We will not surrender, and as Lincoln said: 'The government of the people, by the people and for the people shall not perish from this earth.'"[135]

This short paragraph was indeed a rhetorically and emotionally appropriate reaction to this terrible tragedy. For several days and even weeks similar heartfelt and patriotic comments appeared in print or were expressed orally in the mass media. The same was true, of course, around the days of the first anniversary of the attack on America. And yet, everyday life has once again engulfed the country, and there is no lack of mundane phrases and slogans to mark a modern existence devoid of the depth of the wisdom expressed by Abraham Lincoln and some of the other great presidents before and after him. Today's political rhetoric does not seem to measure up any longer to the lofty heights of the remarks by some of these national leaders. The journalist Tim Cuprisin made this point on January 2, 2002, in his satirical article "'Dead Body' Phrase May Mark Bush's Political Life" by contrasting Lincoln's proverb and two of Franklin D. Roosevelt's memorable phrases with the inane utterances of recent presidents:

> It's still too early to tell, but we just may have witnessed one of those landmark presidential sound bites over the weekend. It wasn't one of the stately phrases that presidents once uttered, like Abraham Lincoln's "government of the people, by the people and for the people" or Franklin D. Roosevelt's "we have nothing to fear but fear itself," or "a date which will live in infamy." We're talking about the TV age, when a short burst of simple, almost trivial, words caught on videotape, like Richard Nixon's "I'm not a crook," can characterize an entire presidency. For George Bush the elder, it was, of course, "read my lips, no new taxes." He, of course, went on to ignore those lips. And no one can dispute that Bill Clinton's "I did not have sexual relations with that woman" is likely the most famous lie ever uttered on camera from behind a straight face. For George W. Bush, there's a good chance that Saturday's "not over my dead body will they raise your taxes" will enter that pantheon of presidential sound bites, although he meant what he said. He's just as sincere as his dad was back in 1988.[136]

These are clearly different times for presidents, when every word is recorded and together with pictures is broadcast instantly around the world. That being the case, it behooves modern presidents to pay close attention to their rhetoric once again as their predecessors most assuredly practiced it. The words and phrases of spontaneous utterances as well as of formal addresses or speeches need to be chosen with considerable care, and a good dose of pride in the English language ought to be added to it. With such proper respect for the power of words, modern presidents as well can formulate statements that will be entered into the annals of American political and social history. In the meantime Americans have Abraham Lincoln's proverb "Government of the people, by the people, for the people" to guide them in their attempt to make democracy work. It certainly is a piece of wisdom that might lead humankind with the assistance of the United Nations to a free and democratic world.

3

"God Helps Them Who Help Themselves"

Proverbial Resolve in the Letters of Abigail Adams

American patriarchs like John Adams, Aaron Burr, Benjamin Franklin, Alexander Hamilton, Thomas Jefferson, James Madison, George Washington, and others are deservedly revered as the founding fathers of the American nation,[1] but behind all of these political heroes stood their wives and other women, who helped or enabled these great men to construct a republican government based on sound democratic principles. While the glory of these men continues to shine, there is also a female star that has received universal acclaim. This person is Abigail Adams (1744–1818), wife of President John Adams (1735–1826) and mother of President John Quincy Adams (1767–1848), who as the matriarch during revolutionary and nation-building times could most assuredly hold the proverbial candle to her male compatriots. While she as a woman could not participate publicly in the revolution or political debates, she nevertheless worked in the background and made her views on sociopolitical issues known. To be sure, she did not write pamphlets or a book, she never gave a public speech, she did not keep a diary, and as a woman, she never had the opportunity to vote despite her keen interest in women's issues.[2] However, she was her husband's most astute political adviser and confidante, telling him her ideas when he happened to be home or expressing them to him in hundreds of letters when he was separated from her for periods of several years at a time. But there are countless other letters to family members and political leaders of her time by this barely five-feet tall woman, with "the epistolary network knit[ting] together women and men with widely differing social, economic, and religious positions."[3] Throughout her invaluable epistles, Abigail Adams shows herself to be a person of the highest moral standards with a sincere commitment to do her part as a public servant next to and not in the shadow of John Adams.

Judging by the steady stream of letters that she composed throughout her life, one might well talk of an epistolary "addiction"[4] to familial, instructional, didactic, political, moralizing, descriptive, impressionistic, analytical, judgmental, opinionated, reflective, and at times also gossipy missives. Ten years after their marriage, John Adams wrote to his wife on July 2, 1774, that she should "put them [their letters] up safe, and preserve them. They may exhibit to our Posterity a kind of Picture of the Manners, Opinions, and Principles of these Times of Perplexity, Danger and Distress" (I,121).[5] Abigail herself did not always have such high opinion of the potential importance of her letters which, as she expressed to her sister Mary Cranch on May 26, 1798, she considered nothing but "first thoughts, without correction [including unorthodox spelling, random capitalization, and almost nonexistent punctuation; all of which have faithfully been maintained throughout this chapter]" (NL,182).[6] As spontaneously formulated impressions, observations, and reflections her letters are indeed literary documents of invaluable authenticity, containing the view of a revolutionary world seen through the eyes of one of the keenest minds of the American eighteenth century. To be sure, Abigail Adams was "the quintessential Puritan—purposeful, pietistic, passionate, prudish, frugal, diligent, courageous, well-educated, and self-righteous," but just like her husband, Thomas Jefferson, and others, Abigail also embraced the "Enlightenment confidence in freedom and openness."[7]

Little wonder that this female intellectual giant in the world of male domination is a complex figure of ambivalent contradictions. In a fascinating review article on "The Abigail Industry" (1988) of the many studies and biographies on this unique American woman of wit and emotions, Edith B. Gelles speaks of the multifaceted interpretations of her life and character: the saintly Abigail, the romantic Abigail, the flirtatious Abigail,[8] the feminist Abigail, the Freudian Abigail, the political Abigail, and the hidden (manipulative) Abigail.[9] One thing is for certain, Abigail Adams was part of "what was legally, economically, and politically a man's world,"[10] She thus had no choice but to excel in the realm of domesticity while letting her intelligence on worldly affairs shine in her letters that she often signed with the penname of Portia, the "loving and faithful wife of Brutus, liberator of Rome, who is said to have shared the physical weakness of women, but whose patriotism was as steadfast as any man's."[11] Abigail did not only stand by her husband through all of his political life, she very much stood solidly on her own two feet as an independent thinker and accomplished farmeress and wife of a revolutionary, diplomat, and Vice(President). As a female participant and observer of the pre- to post-revolutionary period in America, Abigail Adams' exquisite mind, forceful determination, strong opinions, political ambition, and powerful rhetoric had much to do with her husband's career, who in turn acknowledged her intellectual prowess and supportive love throughout their long fifty-four year marriage as spirited and committed soul mates.

"Out of the Abundance of the Heart, the Mouth Speaketh"—Epistolary Floods

This deep love for each other is already expressed proverbially in an early courtship letter of September 12, 1763, by then Abigail Smith to John Adams:

> You was pleas'd to say that the receipt of a letter from your Diana [Abigail's earlier penname] always gave you pleasure. Whether this was designed for a complement (a commodity I acknowledg that you very seldom deal in) or as a real truth, you best know. Yet if I was to judge of a certain persons Heart, by what upon the like occasion passes through a cabinet of my own, I should be apt to suspect it as a truth. And why may I not? when I have often been tempted to believe; that they were both cast in the same mould, only with this difference, that yours was made, with a harder mettle, and therefore is less liable to an impression. Whether they have both an eaquil quantity of Steel, I have not yet been able to discover, but do not imagine they are either of them deficient. Supposing only this difference, I do not see, why the same cause may not produce the same Effect in both, tho perhaps not eaquil in degree. (I,8–9)

This is indeed a bit of playful epistolary indirection, with the proverbial expression of "to be cast in the same mold" with plenty of steel in it indicating that here might just be two lovers made for each other.[12] But true to her determined disposition, Abigail does not stop with this metaphor. Instead, she continues with a clear allusion to the Bible proverb "It is better to give than to receive" (Acts 20:35), now quite directly telling John that she expects him to be more forthcoming with his expression of love to her: "But after all, notwithstanding we are told that the giver is more blessed than the receiver I must confess that I am not of so generous a disposition, in this case, as to give without wishing for a return" (I,9). Some thirteen years later, Abigail returned to this proverb in her letter of April 21, 1776, to John at Philadelphia, reprimanding him for the rarity and shortness of his letters: "I have to acknowledg the Recept of a *very few* lines dated the 12 of April. You make no mention of the whole sheets I have wrote to you, by which I judge you either never Received them, or that they were so lengthy as to be troublesome; and in return you have set me an example of being very concise. I believe I shall not take the Hint, but give as I love to Receive" (I,389). This is the independent and witty wife, who is quite capable of giving her husband, albeit with a good dose of irony, a bit of her mind.

When one considers the lengthy periods of separation that Abigail had to endure, she had every reason to scold her husband from time to time for not being as prolific a correspondent with her as she was forever with him.

It is not surprising, then, that Abigail also favored the Bible proverb "Out of the abundance of the heart the mouth speaketh" (Matthew 12:34) as a psychological explanation for her epistolary profuseness as an expression of her loneliness. This was already the case when on April 12, 1764, she wrote the following lines from her parental home in Weymouth to her fiancé John in not at all faraway Braintree: "Here am I all alone, in my Chamber, a mere Nun I assure you, after professing myself thus will it not be out of Character to confess that my thoughts are often employ'd about Lysander (John's penname), 'out of the abundance of the Heart, the mouth speaketh,' and why Not the Mind thinketh" (I,25). What an absolutely delightful use of the traditional proverb with that splendid addition to it, indicating that her nunlike seclusion does by no means prevent her from having amorous thoughts. In a second allusive use of the proverb in a letter of October 25, 1778, Abigail vents her frustrations at being alone in Braintree with the children while John is conducting his diplomatic services in distant France:

> In the very few lines I have received from you not the least mention is made that you have ever received a line from me. I have not been so parsimonious as my Friend, perhaps I am not so prudent but I cannot take my pen with my Heart overflowing and not give utterance to some of the abundance which is in it. Could you after a thousand fears and anxieties, long expectation and painful suspences be satisfied with my telling you that I was well, that I wished you were with me, that my daughter sent her duty, that I had ordered some articles for you which I hoped would arrive &. &.—By Heaven if you could have changed Hearts with some frozen Lapplander or made a voyage to a region that has chilld every Drop of our Blood.—But I will restrain a pen already I fear too rash, nor shall it tell you how much I have sufferd from the appearance of—inattention. (III,110–111)

Abigail knew very well how much John loved her, how much he hated their long separations, and she also knew that many of their letters were lost at sea. But at this moment she wanted to let John know that she needed and deserved more attention from him, as she managed the domestic life at home. About twenty years later, her love for John unaltered, she writes on April 26, 1797, from Quincy (formerly Braintree) to the new President in Philadelphia: "I am ready and willing to follow my husband wherever he chooses; but the hand of Heaven has arrested me. Adieu, my dear friend. Excuse the melancholy strain of my letter. From the abundance of the heart the stream flows" (LA,377). It was difficult for Abigail to say her goodbyes to her relatives and friends in Massachusetts, as she prepared to leave for the capital to take on her more urban role as the second "first lady" of the United States. Her heart and mind were always filled with emotions and thoughts, and their abundance resulted in a steady stream of letters, with the Bible proverb, even if it is merely alluded to, becoming an explanatory *leitmotif* of sorts for her obsessive letter writing.

"There is a Tide in the Affairs of Men"—Seizing the Moment

One is reminded of an early letter that Abigail wrote to John on April 16, 1764, telling him before their marriage "I write to you with so little restraint," for after all, as she states proverbially, "what is bred in the bone will never be out of the flesh" (I,32). Three days later, she shows an incredible strength of character when she literally invites John to inform her of her faults before they speak their marriage vows, for as the proverb claims, there is "No time as proper as the present":

> But altho it is vastly disagreeable to be accused of faults, yet no person
> ought to be offended when such accusations are deliverd in the Spirit of
> Friendship.—I now call upon you to fullfill your promise, and tell me all
> my faults, both of omission and commission, and all the Evil you either
> know, or think of me, be to me a second conscience, nor put me off to
> a more convenient Season. There can be no time more proper than the
> present, it will be harder to erase them when habit has strengthned and
> confirmd them. (I,37)

But never mind, John Adams was a man who liked his strong, courageous, and intelligent bride just the way she was, accepting her as his intellectual equal, a stance that put him far above most men of his time. Abigail continued to live up to the wisdom of this proverb, always speaking her mind at the time she saw fit.

In fact, there is another proverb that encouraged her to act in word and deed according to her principles. Quoting several lines from William Shakespeare's *Julius Caesar* on March 7, 1776, Abigail's revolutionary spirit is eager to push John into deliberate action towards independence from Great Britain: "I cannot Bear to think of your continuing in a State of Supineness this winter. 'There is a tide in the affairs of Men / Which taken, at the flood leads on to fortune; [...]'" (I,354). About fifteen years later she used this piece of wisdom again without a direct reference to Shakespeare in a letter of January 9, 1791, to her sister Mary Cranch, this time to express her view that the younger generation must be active participants in the construction of the new American nation: "'There is a tide in the affairs of men.' Our young folks must watch for it" (NL,69). By putting the statement in quotation marks, Abigail signals that she is in fact quoting her beloved Shakespeare. However, his statement from the year 1599 had long become proverbial both in England and the United States.[13]

But with all of her proactive determination in her personal and social affairs, Abigail Adams was also well aware of mankind's limitations and the transitoriness of life. She expresses this predicament with typical humility by quoting a couplet out of Oliver Goldsmith's (1728–1774) *The Vicar of Wakefield* (1764) which had quickly become proverbial: "In what so ever state I am I will endeavour to be therewith content. 'Man wants but Little here below / Nor wants that Little long'" (I,355).[14] This statement is part of the letter of March 7, 1776, in which Abigail had encouraged John to take time by the forelock, so to speak. But here, in a mood shift in the same letter, the deeply religious Abigail reminds herself and John of the frailty of human life. This proverb became a comforting device of rationalizing for Abigail as she faced various toils, challenges, and frustrations, as can be seen from two additional occurrences in letters to John:

> If I have neither Sugar, molasses, coffe nor Tea I have no right to complain. I can live without any of them and if what I enjoy I can share with my partner and with Liberty, I can sing o be joyfull and sit down content—
> "Man wants but little here below
> Nor wants that little long."
> (II,324; August 22, 1777)

> Were we less Luxurious we should be better able to support our Independance with becomeing dignity, but having habituated ourselves to the delicacies of Life, we consider them as necessary, and are unwilling to tread back the path of Simplicity, or reflect that
> "Man wants but little here below
> Nor wants that little long."
> (IV,344; July 17, 1782)

From revolutionary times to her life on the stage of world politics, Abigail Adams seems to have remembered this wisdom concerning a life of satisfaction and simplicity based on Puritan ethics.

"God Helps Them Who Help Themselves"—
Undoubting Resolve

Her favorite proverb, however, was the internationally disseminated proverb
"God helps them who help themselves" that has been traced back to classical
antiquity.[15]Abigail used it as a leitmotif of resolve and determination four
times, with John Adams quoting it back to her, accepting it as a principle
of taking fate into one's own hands: "As to Politicks, We have nothing to
expect but the Whole Wrath and Force of G. Britain. But your Words are as
true as an oracle 'God helps them, who help them selves, and if We obtain
the divine Aid by our own Virtue, Fortitude and Perseverance, We may be
sure of Relief" (I,290; October 1, 1775). But while John Adams cites the
anonymous folk proverb as an oracular truth, his wife connects the proverb
with King Richard by using such introductory formulas as "as King Richard
said," "that saying of king Richard," "King Richards [observation]," and "it
was a saying of king Richards." Clearly she associated the popular proverb
with an historical figure, but who might this have been? She often quotes
Shakespeare in her letters, and she might have had a passage out of his *King
Richard II* (1596) in mind that can be read as an allusion to the proverb:

> The means that heavens yield must be embrac'd,
> And not neglected. Else if heaven would
> And we will not, heaven's offer we refuse,
> The proffer'd means of succors and redress. (III,2,29–32)

Two paremiographers and Shakespeare scholars have identified this
passage as a reminiscence of the proverb "God helps them (those) who (that)
help themselves,"[16] and there is no reason why Abigail might not have made
the same connection upon her reading of the play. But the editors of the
Adams Family Correspondence, at a loss who this King Richard might be,
came up with the idea that "this might be AA's joke, since one source of this
saying, which appears as early as Æsop's fables, is Benjamin Franklin's *Maxims
Prefixed to Poor Richard's Almanac* [1757]" (V,177, note 3 to Abigail's letter of
June 14, 1783). Benjamin Franklin actually cited the proverb as "God helps
them that help themselves" already in June 1736 in one of the twenty-five
celebrated and extremely popular *Poor Richard's Alamacks* that he edited from
1733 to 1758.[17] And indeed, he repeated it in the preface to his famous essay
The Way to Wealth (1758) that served as an introduction to the last almanac,
summarizing the entire proverbial wisdom of the previous issues, as it were:
"Let us hearken to good advice, and something may be done for us; *God*

helps them that help themselves, as Poor Richard says."[18] Obviously Abigail Adams knew this reference, but upon reading the following four occurrences of the proverb in her letters, it seems doubtful that she is referring jokingly to Franklin's "Poor Richard" as "King Richard." Had she wanted to allude to the almanac, she would have used the formula "as poor Richard says" that had long become proverbial at her time. But perhaps her knowledge of both Shakespeare's and Franklin's passages became intermingled in her insistence on the association of the proverb with the name of Richard in some way, with more credit most likely going to Shakespeare. In any case, the actual contextualized occurrences of the proverb in her four letters have nothing humorous about them. Instead they speak of such solid values as virtue, fortitude, perseverance, determination, independence, justice, and confidence that should be the basis of all Americans as they construct a government founded on democratic principles:

> God helps them that help themselves as King Richard said and if we can obtain the divine aid [for the revolutionary cause] by our own virtue, fortitude and perseverance we may be sure of releaf. (I,280; September 16, 1775)
>
> Heaven grant us success at the Southard [against the British]. That saying of king Richard often occurs to my mind "God helps those who help themselves" but if Men turn their backs and run from an Enemy they cannot surely expect to conquer them. (II,358; October 25, 1777)
>
> [...] but King Richards [observation] was a more independant one. God says, he helps those who help themselves. Advise is of little avail unless it is reduced to practise nor ought we implicitly to give up [on] our judgement to any one what ever may be our regard or esteem for them untill we have weighed and canvassed that advise with our reason and judgment—then if it is right agreable to virtue expedient and prudent we ought strictly to adhere to it—a mutability of temper and inconsistency with ourselves is the greatest weakness of Humane Nature, and will render us little and contemtable in the Eyes of the World. There are certain principal which ought to become unchangeable in us justice temperance fortitude hold the first rank—he who possesses these will soon have all others added unto them. (V,176; June 14, 1783; letter to Royall Tyler)
>
> It was a saying of king Richards "that God helps those who help themselves." I should think our Countrymen have too often experienced this doctrine not to see their path plain before them. (VI,298; August 25, 1785; letter to Thomas Welsh)

Of course, these references also show once again Abigail's deep faith in God looking out for her young nation. Never mind how much sacrifice will be needed by its citizens as long as there is the willpower and hope to establish a society based on freedom and democracy.

And there is another proverb that lends plenty of hope and confidence for the future: "God tempers the wind to the shorn lamb." Abigail employs this sixteenth-century French proverb that had become current in English as a loan translation during the seventeenth century in a letter of October 31, 1799, to her sister Mary Cranch. But again, instead of citing it as an anonymous folk proverb, she refers to Laurence Sterne's (1713–1768) use of it in his *A Sentimental Journey through France and Italy* (1768),[19] a clear indication of her literary prowess:

> Where is the situation in Life which exempts us from trouble? Who of us pass through the world with our path strewed with flowers, without encountering the thorns? In what ever state we are, we shall find a mixture of good and evil, and we must learn to receive these vicissitudes of life, so as not to be unduly exalted by the one, or depressed by the other. No cup so bitter, but what some cordial drops are mingled by a kind Providence, who knows how as Sterne says, to "temper the wind to the Shorn Lamb."—But I shall insensibly run into moralizing. (NL,212)

Convinced that God will look out for her and her compatriots, Abigail Adams can face life's challenges and provide a bit of moral support to her sister and others by citing a most appropriate proverb.

"If It Is Worth Doing at All, It Is Worth Doing Well"— Free Advice

Her dedication to particular truths from the realm of religion, politics, and social intercourse in general frequently led Abigail to speak with a moralizing and judgmental voice of authority, addressing family members, friends, and acquaintances of all ages and both genders. Her oldest son John Quincy Adams received numerous such missives from his mother, and more often than not they include solid proverbial advice, as can be seen in this letter to him of March 2, 1780:

> You have great reason for thankfulness to your kind preserver, who hath again carried you through many dangers, preserved your Life and given you an opportunity of making further improvements in virtue and knowledge. You must consider that every Moment of your time is

precious, if trifled away never to be recalled. Do not spend too much of it in recreation, it will never afford you that permanant satisfaction which the acquisition of one Art or Science will give you, and whatever you undertake aim to make yourself perfect in it, for if it is worth doing at all, it is worth doing well. (III,293)

The proverb "If it is worth doing at all, it is worth doing well" was one of the favorite proverbs of Lord Chesterfield (Philip Dormer Stanhope, 1694–1773), who used it repeatedly in his many prescriptive letters to his son Philip Stanhope as a guiding principle for success in life.[20] Abigail had just read Chesterfield's famous *Letters to His Son* (1774), and it might well be that she remembered the proverb from Chesterfield's instructional letters. But both John and Abigail found Chesterfield's letters much too worldly and unprincipled, "inculcating the most immoral, pernicious and Libertine principals," as Abigail opined. Add to this "his abuse of our sex," i.e., Chesterfield's chauvinistic and anti-feministic statements, and it is not surprising that they rejected the popular letters as a book of social conduct and etiquette. Abigail even began to refer "to a breach of morality as Chesterfieldian."[21] And yet, she is willing to grant "his Lordship the merrit of an Elegant pen, a knowledge of *Mankind* and a compiler of many Excellent maxims and rules for the conduct of youth" (III,289; February 28, 1780; letter to Mercy Otis Warren).

But to be sure, Abigail herself was somewhat of a female Chesterfield, never in lack of words to give advice of proper social conduct. This certainly is the case in a letter of July 14, 1784, to Royall Tyler, the unsuccessful suitor of Abigail's and John's daughter Abigail (Nabby):

Upon all occasions I have deliverd my sentiments to you with freedom; *(and shall continue to do;)* but it remains with you to give them energy and force. Your favorite Rochefoucault observes we may give advice, but we cannot give conduct. If I could I would kindle in your Breast a spirit, of emulation, and ambition, that should enable you to shine with distinguished Brightness as a deep thinker a close reasoner and eloquent Speaker, but above all a Man of the strickest honour and integrity, for without these, the former would be only of temporary duration and the fame acquired by them would be like a faint meteor gliding through the Sky, shedding only a trancient light, whilst the latter like the fixed stars never change their place but shine on to endless duration. (V,391)

Again Abigail decides to show her literary knowledge by mentioning that François de La Rochefoucauld (1613–1680) had included the wisdom of "We may give advice, but we cannot give conduct" among his *Maxims* (1665), of which John Adams had bought a Paris 1777 edition in 1780 (V,393, note 2). However, the text had long become proverbial in the English language, with Benjamin Franklin including it in his 1751 (June) *Poor Richard's Almanack* and at the end of *The Way to Wealth* (1758). The anonymous folk proverb could have sufficed, but clearly Abigail's epistolary style is informed by the literary elegance of eighteenth-century correspondence.

But here are a few additional instructive and didactic passages from Abigail's letters to various people, where well-known proverbs conclude a paragraph or an entire letter as a concise summary of the intended message:

> There are entanglingments [...] from which Time the great solacer of Humane woe only can relieve us. And Time I dare say will extricate those I Love from any unapproved Step, into which inexperience and youth may have involved them. But untill that period may arrive Honour, Honour, is at Stake—a word to the wise is sufficient. (VI,366; September 18, 1785; letter to William Stephens Smith)

> Pray let me hear from you. The season is plentifull. Let us rejoice & be glad. Cheer up my good Sister. A merry Heart does good like a medicine. (NL,22; August 9, 1789; letter to Mary Cranch)

> But you know there are cases where silence is prudence [varied: golden], and I think without flattering myself I have attained to some share of that virtue. We live in a world where having Eyes we must not see, and Ears we must not hear. (NL,36; January 5, 1790; letter to Mary Cranch)

> But such are the visisitudes of Life and the Transitory fleeting state of all sublinary things; of all pride that which persons discover from Riches is the weakest. If we look over our acquaintance, how many do we find who were a few years ago in affluence, now reduced to real want, but there is no Family amongst them all whose schemes have proved so visionary, and so abortive as the unhappy one we are now commisirating. Better is a little with contentment than great Treasure; and trouble therewith. (NL,37; February 20, 1790; letter to Mary Cranch)

> What is past cannot be remedied. We seldom learn from experience untill we get too old to use it, or we grow callous to the misfortunes of the world by Reiterated abuse. (NL,142; March 13, 1798; letter to Mary Cranch)

> I do not regreet that my Nephew is disappointed, if so he is. I am sure the family connexion could never have proved happy, however

amiable Ann was, or is. She will be better the wife of any other Man. I
never thought it a judicious connexion. Oil & water might as well mix,
as the Fathers harmonize. (NL,239; March 15, 1800; letter to Mary
Cranch)

The last text shows that Abigail feels free to break the normal structure of
the proverb "Oil and water do not mix" in order to get her point across that
a young couple and their families were simply not made for each other.

But here is yet another advisory letter by a caring mother to her studious
son John Quincy that is in some way reminiscent of the way Lord Chesterfield
"pestered" his son with a constant barrage of proverbial wisdom:

> Your friends are not anxious that you will be in any danger through want
> of sufficient application, but that a too ardent pursuit of your studies [at
> Harvard] will impair your health, and injure those bodily powers and
> faculties upon which the vigor of the mind depends. Moderation in all
> things is conducive to human happiness, though this is a maxim little
> heeded by youth whether their pursuits are of a sensual or a more refined
> and elevated kind.
>
> It is an old adage, that a man at thirty must be either a fool or a
> physician. Though you have not arrived at that age, you would do well
> to trust to the advice and experience of those who have. Our bodies are
> framed of such materials as to require constant exercise to keep them in
> repair, to brace the nerves, and give vigor to the animal functions. Thus
> do I give you "line upon line, and precept upon precept." (LA,341)

Abigail even uses introductory formulas as "this is a maxim" and "it is
an old adage" to draw her son's attention to the generational wisdom that
is contained in her advice couched in traditional folk proverbs. And John
Quincy adhered well to her counsel, for he did indeed excel as ambassador
to England and Russian and eventually as President of the United States.

Reading such passages makes it difficult to understand why scholars
have repeatedly argued that proverbs were not in high esteem during the
eighteenth century, that so-called Age of Reason and Enlightenment that
could not possibly be positively disposed towards folk wisdom. Paremiologist
Richard Jente observed in 1945 that the literature of that time "with its
enlightenment and sophistication made less use of the proverb than the
preceding centuries,"[22] and social historian James Obelkevich in 1987
drew the overstated conclusion that "by the early decades of the eighteenth
century opinion was turning sharply against them [the proverbs]. Though
evidently still widely used in conversation, there too they came under attack;

Swift pillories them, along with trite witticisms and banal small talk of the day; other critics found them ostentatious, competitive [i.e., contradictory], insincere—to use them was a 'sign of a cox-comb.' Having dropped out of polite literature (and the manuals of rhetoric), they were then banished from polite conversation; by the 1740s, when Lord Chesterfield advised his son that 'a man of fashion never has recourse to proverbs or vulgar aphorisms,' the process was complete."[23] But closer scrutiny of written sources of various types has by now shown that there was no general collapse of proverbiality, and the infamous Lord Chesterfield himself made ample use of proverbs in his didactic letters while at the same time arguing against their use. There simply was no major hiatus in the literary or oral appearance of proverbs in the eighteenth century! Renowned European authors such as William Blake, Louis Carmontelle, Denis Diderot, Henry Fielding, Johann Wolfgang von Goethe, Johann Gottfried Herder, Gotthold Ephraim Lessing, Georg Christoph Lichtenberg, Johann Friedrich Schiller, Tobias George Smollett, Laurence Sterne, Jonathan Swift, and François-Marie Voltaire have all proven to be quite proverbial in detailed studies on their literary style.[24] And in the United States, the writings of Benjamin Franklin, Cotton Mather, and such major figures as George Washington and Thomas Jefferson are replete with proverbs as well. For the American stage, paremiographer Bartlett Jere Whiting has illustrated the high frequency of folk proverbs during the eighteenth century in his invaluable collection of *Early American Proverbs and Proverbial Phrases* (1977), stating quite correctly in the introduction that "of the Founding Fathers—and now we must include a mother—John Adams, amply seconded by his redoubtable wife Abigail, bears away the bell as user of proverbs. It is no accident that the Harvard College Library possesses a copy of John Ray's *Collection of English Proverbs* (1670) with John Adams' autograph scrawled on the title page."[25]

And yet, the extensive scholarship on both John and Abigail Adams has almost completely ignored this, with my article on "Narrative History as Proverbial Narrative: David McCullough's Best-Selling *John Adams* [2001] Biography" (2002) being the only study having picked up on Whiting's observation concerning the propensity towards employing proverbs by these two major figures of the eighteenth century.[26] Otherwise only Kathleen Ann Lawrence has referred to Abigail's partiality for folk wisdom in passing: "When lost for the words of her own, Abigail made use of proverbs, maxims and prose [i.e., quotations] to write what she could not utter,"[27] But as the examples cited thus far have shown and what numerous additional contextualized proverb references will clearly substantiate, Abigail Adams is a most conscious, deliberate, and effective user of proverbs which serve her as major rhetorical and argumentative devices. Her employment of proverbs has nothing to do with lacking the words to express herself, but their traditional wisdom is part and parcel of her epistolary style and wit.

"I Feel the Absence of My Better Half"—Love and Separation

This is also true for the numerous passages in Abigail's letters where she expresses her deep love for John and her almost unbearable loneliness during their long separations. In fact, "letters were their only consolation. They were a poor substitute for conversation, but Abigail had nothing else. She wrote often, with an ease and grace that made her letters as close to conversation as the written word could be. She poured out her worries about everything from planting corn to the possibility of war with Great Britain. Just putting her thoughts on paper helped relieve her mind, but it could take weeks for John's answers to come—when they came at all."[28] Again and again Abigail cites the proverbial expression "to be one's better half" to state how much she missed her beloved husband: "I feel the absence of my better half, in this Day of Distress" (I,190; May 2, 1775; letter to Mercy Otis Warren); "[...] in the Education of my little flock [the children] I stand in need of the constant assistance of my Better half" (I,377; April 13, 1776; letter to Mercy Otis Warren); "[...] my Heart was too full to bear the weight of affliction which I thought just ready to overtake us, and my body too weak almost to bear the shock unsupported by my better Half" (II,301; August 5, 1777; letter to John); and "[...] cannot you immagine me seated by my fire side Bereft of my better Half, and added to that a Limb lopt of to heighten the anguish" (II,390; February 15, 1778; letter to John Thaxter). The last reference refers to the extreme anxiety that Abigail experienced after John and their son John Quincy had left on their transatlantic voyage for France during the hazardous winter and the dangerous wartime with Great Britain.

It is not surprising that Abigail often used somatic "heart" expressions to vent her emotional ups and downs during the long periods of separation from John. They add a great deal of emotive expressiveness to her letters that are filled with love and tenderness as well as anxiety:

> I want very much to hear from you, how you stood your journey, and in what state you find yourself now. I felt very anxious about you tho I endeavourd to be very insensible and heroick, yet my heart felt like a heart of Led. (I,193; May 4, 1775)
>
> I set down with a heavy Heart to write to you. I have had no other since you left me. Woe follows Woe and one affliction treads upon the heal of an other. (I,284; September 25, 1775)

My Heart is as light as a feather and my Spirits are dancing. I received this afternoon a fine parcel of Letters and papers [from you], it was a feast to me. I shall rest in quiet I hope this Night. (I,416; May 27, 1776)

I am sometimes quite discouraged from writing. So many vessels are taken, that there is Little chance of Letters reaching your Hands. That I meet with so few returns is a circumstance that lies heavy at my Heart. (III,140; December 27, 1778)

I recollect the untitled Man to whom I gave my Heart, and in the agony of recollection when time and distance present themselves together—wish we had never been any other. Who shall give me back Time? Who shall compensate to me those *years* I cannot recall? How dearly have I paid for a titled Husband; should I wish you less wise that I might enjoy more happiness!" (*Adams Papers,* October 25, 1782)[29]

Of course, Abigail was way too much a realist and pragmatist not to support her husband in his political role as a servant of the American cause. No matter how much she lamented and complained, she actually shared John's ambitions and thus was willing to endure loneliness while she trusted him to be faithful to her during his long absences. This is beautifully expressed with the proverb "The falling out of Lovers is the renewal of Love" in her letter of November 13, 1780, to John at Paris. In that epistle, Abigail is taking issue with John's earlier statement that he likes her letters especially when they do not include any complaints:

I am wholy unconscious of giving you pain in this way since your late absence. If any thing of the kind formerly escaped my pen, had I not ample retaliation, and did we not Balance accounts tho the sum was rather in your favour even after having distroyed some of the proof. In the most Intimate of Friendships, there must not be any recrimination. If I complaind, it was from the ardour of affection which could not endure the least apprehension of neglect, and you who was conscious that I had no cause would not endure the supposition. We however wanted no mediating power to adjust the difference, we no sooner understood each other properly, but as the poet says, "The falling out of Lovers is the renewal of Love."

Be to my faults a little Blind

Be to my virtues ever kind

and you are sure of a Heart all your own, which no other Earthly object ever possessd. Sure I am that not a syllable of complaint has ever stained my paper, in any Letter I have ever written since you left me. I should have been ungratefull indeed, when I have not had the shadow of a cause;

but on the contrary, continual proofs of your attention to me. You well know I never doubted your Honour. Virtue and principal confirm the indissoluable Bond which affection first began and my security depends not upon your passion, which other objects might more easily excite, but upon the sober and setled dictates of Religion and Honour. It is these that cement, at the same time that they ensure the affections. (IV,13–14; November 13, 1780)

It is interesting to note once again that the educated Abigail introduces the proverb with the introductory formula "as the poet says." Its wisdom goes back to classical antiquity, and it has appeared in variations in Terence, Shakespeare, Robert Burton, Jonathan Swift, Samuel Richardson, and others,[30] and Abigail might have had almost any of these "poets" in mind. And yet, she really is citing an insight that had long become a folk proverb.

Be that as it may, she is well aware of the fact that the proverb "Time erases all sorrows" is commonly known among her compatriots, as is indicated by her use of the introductory formula "which is said to" in yet another epistle to John: "Time which is said to soften and alleviate Sorrow, encreases anxiety when connected with expectation. This I hourly experience" (IV,229; October 21, 1781). This summarizes Abigail's situation for most of her life, and she never stopped declaring her love for John in her lonesome letters. She has herself described her predicament the best in a letter to John of September 23, 1776: "There are perticuliar times when I feel such an uneasiness, such a restlessness, as neither company, Books, family Cares or any other thing will remove, my Pen is my only pleasure, and writing to you the composure of my mind" (II,133). And she even calls on the Bible proverb "No man liveth for himself" (Romans 14:7) for authoritative support in venting her anxieties to John:

> I feel a disposition to Quarrel with a race of Beings who have cut me of, in the midst of my days from the only Society [i.e., John] I delighted in. Yet No Man liveth for himself, says an authority I will not dispute. Let me draw satisfaction from this Source and instead of murmuring and repineing at my Lot consider it in a more pleasing view. Let me suppose that the same Gracious Being [God] who first smiled upon our union and Blessed us in each other, endowed my Friend with powers and talents for the Benifit of Mankind and gave him a willing mind, to improve them for the service of his Country. (V,22; October 25, 1782)

Such letters are indeed "a revealing source of self-analysis"[31] that place her love for John in the greater realm of service to society, but Abigail is not always the keen intellectual in her epistles to John. There are numerous passages in these letters that abound with love and emotion,[32] as for example "My Dearest Friend—How much is comprised in that short sentence? How fondly can I call you mine, bound by every tie, which consecrates the most inviolable Friendship, yet seperated by a cruel destiny, I feel the pangs of absence sometimes too sensibly for my own repose" (IV,50; December 25, 1780) or "Adieu and believe me most affectionately, most tenderly yours and only yours and wholly yours. A Adams" (V,409; July 30, 1784). These are emotional outbursts that have sexual undertones. This is as far as Abigail dared to go, and in the case of such intimate allusions proverbs most understandably have no place because of their rigid structure and "folksy" formulation.

"Nothing Venture Nothing Have"—A Castle in the Air in Vermont

Vacillating between a public life on the center stage and the domestic tranquility of rural life, the enlightened and rational Abigail was also perfectly capable of a Rousseauistic desire of returning to nature. To this end she contemplated buying land in remote Vermont in the spring of 1781, with "Vermont becoming a dream, a hope, for a future free from war and politics."[33] Already on May 1, 1780, Abigail had hinted to John: "I have a Castle in the air which I shall write to you upon by the next opportunity, either for you to laugh at and reject, or to think of if practicable" (III,335). The editors of the letters indicate in a footnote that it is not clear what Abigail might have had in mind with this proverbial castle in the air (III,336, note 4). But I am quite convinced that this "castle" is a reference to a haven in Vermont, where the couple could retire from the politics of Massachusetts and the federal government, to wit her letter of December 9, 1781: "Two years my dearest Friend have passd since you left your Native land. Will you not return e'er the close of an other year? I will purchase you a retreat in the woods of Virmont and retire with you from the vexations, toils and hazards of publick Life. Do you not sometimes sigh for such a Seclusion—publick peace and domestick happiness" (IV,257). About three months later, on March 17, 1782, Abigail has much to say about Vermont, and it is here where in my opinion it becomes clear that a possible life in Vermont is the longed-for castle in the air for her. Here she repeats the proverbial expression, albeit referring to a farm close to their homestead that they cannot afford to buy:

> Most sincerely can she [Portia=Abigail] unite with you in the wish of
> a sequestered Life, the shades of Virmont, the uncultivated Heath are

preferable in her mind to the servility of a [French] court. [...] I mean a Lot of Land of 300 acres for each of our children in the New State of Virmont, for which I have been very assiduously collecting all I could spair from taxes. [...] Land here [in Massachusetts] is so high taxed that people are for selling their Farms and retireing back. [...] Mr. Alleyne has Burried his Mother and sister. He now wishes to sell his Farm and has accordingly put it upon sale. It is a place I should be fond of, but know it must still be my castle in the air" (IV, 293,295,296)

Abigail did not know that the Alleyne farm would come up for sale when she used the "castle" phrase about a year earlier. Having told John about her desire to buy land in Vermont, her castle in the air about to become reality, she is now simply transferring the proverbial phrase to the Alleyne farm which is beyond their means. And sure enough, this strong lady purchased the land, writing her husband on July 18, 1782: "My favorite Virmont is a delightfull Grain Country. I cannot tell why, but I feel a great fondness for the prosperity of that State. [...] I recollected the old adage Nothing venture nothing have; and I took all the Lots 5 in number 4 of which I paid for, and the other obligated myself to discharge in a few months" (IV,345). The use of the folk proverb is indeed a shrewd way for Abigail to justify her purchase to John, who was, however, not interested in the venture as a brief statement in his letter of June 17, 1782, to James Warren indicates: "God willing, I will not go to Vermont. I must be within the scent of the sea."[34] And they didn't go, even though they now owned some 1500 acres of beautiful and natural Vermont. John wanted and needed to be in the public sector, becoming a two-term first Vice President and then a one-term second President of the young nation. And Abigail, certainly not because she was a subservient wife, moved with him through all three capitals, from New York to Philadelphia, and on to Washington. They were public servants *par excellence,* and their commitment to making a success of the United States kept them from secluding themselves in quiet Vermont that remained a mere castle in the air after all.

"NECESSITY HAS NO LAW"—DOMESTIC CONCERNS OF A MATRIARCH

As this Vermont venture amply shows, Abigail Adams was perfectly capable of handling her multifaceted domestic obligations while John was away on various colonial, European, and (vice)presidential missions. She "remained dogmatically domestic in her own self-image, her consciousness, and her ideology," and despite of her interest in women's issues, "she continued to believe in the primacy, the propriety, and the dignity of women's domestic role."[35] In her life and letters, Abigail tried "to balance international, political, and domestic concerns, but always tended toward the latter. Familial and personal concerns were mingled easily with discussions of politics, economics, and international affairs."[36] As she became ever more the matriarch of the growing Adams clan, she excelled in what has been called "kinkeeping" or "kin work," i.e., the conscious attempt by women of "holding together and exercising guardianship for an extended family."[37] In an early letter of April 11, 1776, to her husband, busy with his legal affairs and revolutionary politics, Abigail described her situation and aspirations the best: "I hope in time to have the Reputation of being as good a *Farmeress* as my partner has of being a good Statesmen" (I,375). Some six years later, as she thought more seriously of crossing the Atlantic to join John in Europe, she wrote to John Thaxter on October 26, 1782: "I love the peacefull Rural Retirement and pleasures of domestick Life" (V,26). In talking about her role at home with her children and extended family, Abigail quite frequently finds proverbs to be the perfect traditional phrases to describe her concerns and tribulations. As but a few contextualized references show, proverbs helped her to put some common-sense wisdom into her epistles that give them much metaphorical vividness:

> We talked of keeping Thanksgiving with you [her sister Mary Cranch and family], but farming and the Courts come so thick upon us, that we cannot bring that to bear, for next week the Superior Court sets, the inferiour is adjournd to the week after. So that there is no opportunity till the week after that, and then I hope there will not any more Mountains arise to hinder me. Mole hills I always Expect to find, but them I can easily surmount. (I,54; July 15, 1766; letter to Mary Cranch)
>
> As to applying to some of the Members of the General Court for Horses, I remember the old proverb, he who waits for dead mens schooes may go barefoot. It would only lengthen out the time, and we should be no better of, than before I askd. (II,105–106; August 22, 1776; letter to John Adams)
>
> Necessity is the Mother of invention. There is a Manufactory of Molasses set up in several Towns. Green corn Storks ground and boild down to Molasses, tis said an acre will produce a Barrel. I have seen some of it, it both tastes and looks like Sugar Bakers molasses. (II,340; September 10, 1777; letter to John Adams)
>
> The door opens into the Cabbin [of the ship that carried Abigail to Europe to join John in France] where the Gentlemen all Sleep; and wh[ere] we sit dine &. We can only live with our door Shut, whilst we dress and undress. Necessity has no law, but what should I have thought

on shore; to have layed myself down to sleep, in common with half a dozen Gentlemen? We have curtains it is true, and we only in part undress [...]. (V,361; July 6, 1784; letter written on board the ship to her sister Mary Cranch)

My Family has been so large for this year past, that we shall not make both ends meet, as they say. The expenses of Removing a Family, Furniture & was a heavy burden, and the wages of servants is very high here [in New York city], especially for such misirables as one is obliged to put up with—but I hate to complain. No one is without their difficulties, whether in High, or low Life, & every person knows best where their own shoe pinches. (NL,43; March 21, 1790; letter to Mary Cranch)

I wrote to the Dr. [Cotton Tufts] and proposed having the outside of the house [at Braintree] new painted, and the Garden fence also which never was more than primed, but I would not put too many Irons at once in the fire. (NL,166; April 26, 1798; letter to Mary Cranch)

The lower class of whites are a grade below the Negroes in point of intelligence, and ten below them in point of civility [she is speaking of servants in the newly built White House in Washington]. I shall bear and forebear. (*Adams Papers,* November 28, 1800; letter to Cotton Tufts)[38]

This [White] House [in Washington] is twice as large as our meeting House [in Braintree]. I believe the great Hall is as Bigg. I am sure tis twice as long. Cut your coat according to your Cloth. But this House is built for ages to come. The establishment necessary is a tax which cannot be born by the present sallery: No body can form an Idea of it but those who come into it. I had much rather live in the house at Philadelphia. (NL,259; November 21, 1800; letter to Mary Cranch)

One really gets the feeling that Abigail and John lived in "splendid misery" (NL,90; May 16, 1797; letter to Mary Cranch) in the three capitals of the young nation, but they bore and forbore, as Abigail put it proverbially in one of her letters just cited. While the proverbs in the letters dealing with domestic matters are used to describe, explain, and deal with various problems, Abigail can also employ them with a certain sense of humor or irony, as when she comments on the newest fashion in Philadelphia in a letter to her sister Mary Cranch of November 15, 1799: "I have heard of once a Man & twice a child, and the Ladies caps are an exact copy of the baby caps—those which are made with drawings, and drawn with a bobbin to a point, a quarter and Nail deep, a lace upon the border, a bow upon the point, three bows behind and one before, the Hair a little drest at the side & a few curls upon the forehead, the cap to lie flat upon the head" (NL,215). And there is also this touching paragraph in a letter to her granddaughter

Caroline A. Smith of February 26, 1811: "As if you love me, proverbially, you must love my dog, you will be glad to learn that Juno [the family dog] yet lives, although like her mistress she is gray with age. She appears to enjoy life and to be grateful for the attention paid her. She wags her tail and announces a visiter whenever one appears" (LA,404). Such passages show Abigail as a woman of practicality, common sense, wisdom, understanding, and compassion, and the proverbs contained in them serve her well to comment on all aspects of life.

"ALL MEN WOULD BE TYRANTS IF THEY COULD"— "REMEMBER THE LADIES"

While Abigail might have had a bit of fun describing the fashionable caps of the ladies of Philadelphia, she had much more urgent concerns for women, especially during the early revolutionary years. In fact, as John and other male revolutionaries contemplated the proper form of a new American government, she wrote her most famous letter to him that is commonly referred to as the "Remember the Ladies" epistle of March 31, 1776. The letter deals primarily with issues of independence and the question of political power, quoting a Bible proverb in its second paragraph that has been overlooked by scholars thus far:

> I have sometimes been ready to think that the passion for Liberty cannot be Eaquelly Strong in the Breasts of those who have been accustomed to deprive their fellow Creatures of theirs. Of this I am certain that it is not founded upon that generous and christian principal of doing to others as we would that others should do unto us. (I,369)

This is, albeit somewhat indirectly expressed, a strong condemnation of slavery in the original colonies, with Abigail and John having the distinction among the founding families of never having owned a slave. The proverbial golden rule of "Do unto others as you would have them do unto you" (Matthew 7:12)[39] was the perfect proverb to cite in this context, even though Abigail does not go on to argue openly against slavery. It took another six and a half decades until Frederick Douglass (1818–1895), himself a former slave turned abolitionist, made this proverb his *leitmotif* in 1842, arguing with its wisdom for the next fifty years against slavery and for equal rights for African Americans and women as well, and making him one of the greatest champions for civil rights in the United States.[40]

The thought of treating other people fairly and equally as one would wish to be treated must have led Abigail to think of the lot and role of women, causing her to make a truly remarkable statement to her husband who was working on new laws of independence and rights:

> I long to hear that you have declared an independancy—and by the way in the new Code of Laws which I suppose it will be necessary for you to make I desire you would Remember the Ladies, and be more generous and favourable to them than your ancestors. Do not put such unlimited power into the hands of the Husbands. Remember all Men would be tyrants if they could. If perticuliar care and attention is not paid to the Ladies we are determined to foment a Rebelion, and will not hold ourselves bound by any Laws in which we have no voice, or Representation.
>
> That your Sex are Naturally Tyrannical is a Truth so thoroughly established as to admit of no dispute, but such of you as wish to be happy willingly give up the harsh title of Master for the more tender and endearing one of Friend. Why then, not put it out of the power of the vicious and the Lawless to use us with cruelty and indignity with impunity. Men of Sense in all Ages abhor those customs which treat us only as the vassals of your Sex. Regard us then as Beings placed by providence under your protection and in immitation of the Supreem Being make use of that power only for our happiness. (I,370)[41]

A few weeks later, Abigail returned to this theme in her letter of May 7, 1776, reproaching John that not enough consideration was being given to the women of the revolution:

> I can not say that I think you very generous to the Ladies, for whilst you are proclaiming peace and good will to Men, Emancipating all Nations, you insist upon retaining an absolute power over Wives. But you must remember that Arbitary power is like most other things which are very hard, very liable to be broken—and notwithstanding all your wise Laws and Maxims we have it in our power not only to free ourselves but to subdue our Masters, and without voilence throw both your natural at legal authority at our feet. (I,402)

Rebellious as these statements sound, it must be remembered that Abigail voiced them primarily in the privacy of her letters. She cannot be considered a feminist revolutionary in the modern sense, and "these bold paragraphs were not a declaration of the principle of sexual equality for which nineteenth- and twentieth-century feminists would contend. Abigail Adams did not call for a revolution in the roles of men and women. She hoped rather for a legal system under which women could find maximum fulfillment in their ascribed roles as wives and mothers, as domestic beings deferential to, but not abused by, fathers and husbands."[42] Abigail expressed all of this quite clearly in a much later letter of June 5, 1809, to her sister Elizabeth Shaw that illustrates her basic social conservatism: "I consider it as an indispensable requisite, that every American wife should herself know how to order and regulate her family; how to govern her domestics, and train up her children. For this purpose, the all-wise Creator made woman an help-meet [mate] for man, and she who fails in these duties does not answer the end of her creation" (LA,402).

Nevertheless, all of these comments show the strength and resolve of Abigail Adams in a world governed by men. The unfortunately too often true phrase that "All men would be tyrants if they could" is, however, not original with her. Even though she does not place quotation marks around it, she might well be quoting the second line of Daniel Defoe's (1660–1731) couplet "Nature has left this tincture in the blood, / That all men would be tyrants if they could" from his *Kentish Petition* (1712).[43] But she might also have recalled the fact that John had used this quotation about a year before their marriage in 1763 as the title for an essay on man's lust for power.[44] But be that as it may, it is Abigail's use of this apparent truth that has become proverbial today, especially in feminist circles. Since 1980 it has been entered under her name in editions of John Bartlett's *Familiar Quotations*,[45] and as part of Abigail's rallying cry "Remember the Ladies"[46] it is approaching proverbial status in a world where modern women fight valiantly against male supremacy in all social, political, and economic spheres. Clearly Abigail did not only influence her well-meaning husband with her astonishing gender awareness. Her bold statement lives on and still has an impact on the continuous fight against the proverbial truth that "All men would be tyrants if they could."

"RIGHTEOUSNESS EXALTETH A NATION"—BIBLICAL MORALITY

Abigail might not have been successful with John as an early feminist, but she certainly had much influence on him ethically. Being a minister's daughter, she often used Bible proverbs to give her husband moral support and advice. She did the same with their children, relatives, and friends, citing biblical wisdom to add authority to her explanatory comments. There was no need for her to identify these sayings as stemming from the Bible, although references to "the best Authority" or "the greatest Authority" are, of course, indirect allusions to the Bible. Her Puritan compatriots were for the most part equally well versed in this wisdom literature, and the frequent use of Bible proverbs had turned them into anonymous folk proverbs in any case.[47] For Abigail "religion [...] was most important in providing a set of moral standards for behavior and a source of hope in troubled times,"[48] and as the following epistolary passages show, Bible proverbs represented readymade phrases to be used to support arguments, give advice, and express resolve and hope:

> The race is not to the swift, nor the battle to the strong [Ecclesiastes 9:11], but the God of Israel is he that giveth strength and power unto his people. Trust in him at all times, ye people pour out your hearts before him. God is a refuge for us. (I,222; June 18, 1775; letter to John Adams)
>
> But alass our virtues are not of the first Magnitude; we are told by the best Authority that the Love of Money is the Root of all Evil [1. Timothy 6:10], we want a Solon and Licurgus to restrain the ruling passion of the present day. (III,6; April 9, 1778; letter to John Thaxter)
>
> Yet there is envy and jealousy sufficient in the world to seek to lessen a character however beneficial to the Country or useful to the State. Nor are these passions Local. They are the Low, Mean and Sordid inhabitants of all countries and climates, an Instance of which I can give you, with regard to Mr. Adams. [...] A prophet is not without honour save in his own country [Matthew 13:57]. (III,298; March 13, 1789; letter to Elbridge Gerry)[49]
>
> The two most important Lessons in life for a young person to acquire, is a knowledge of themselves, and of the connections they form. As the latter determines and establishes the character, too much attention cannot be paid to this important matter. Who can touch pitch and not be defiled? [Ecclesiasticus 13:1]. Tho Merrit alone seldom obtains the distinction that is its due, yet when united with a knowledge of the world and those Graces which happily for Mr. Warren he has not now to acquire, they will not fail obtaining favour with every character whose acquaintance he would be ambitious to cultivate. (III,353; May 19, 1780; letter to Winslow Warren)
>
> Yet such is the unhappy lot of our native land, too, too many of our chief Actors *have been and are unprincipled wretches,* or we could not have suffered as we have done. It is Righteousness, not Iniquity, that exalteth a Nation [Proverbs 14:34]. There are so many and so loud complaints against some persons in office that I am apt to think neither *age* nor *Fame* will screen them. (IV,2; October 8, 1780; letter to John Adams)
>
> Heaven has yet in store for you some sweet female companion to smooth the Rugged road of Life, and sweeten the bitter cup—indeed

you shall not live single. The greatest Authority pronounced that it was not good for Man to be alone [Genesis 2:18]. (V,149; April 29, 1783; letter to John Thaxter)

It ought to be a warning to every man not to contract habits of sloth, and inaction, to consider that no Man liveth for himself [Romans 14:7]. (NL,249; May 3, 1800; letter to Mary Cranch)

This letter is written in confidence. Faithful are the wounds of a friend [Proverbs 27:6]. Often have I wished to have seen a different course pursued by you. I bear no malice. I cherish no enmity. I would not retaliate if it was in my power; nay more, in the true spirit of Christian charity, I would forgive as I hope to be forgiven. (LA,393–394; July 1, 1804; letter to Thomas Jefferson)

The cited Bible proverbs do not so much refer to a mystical faith, but rather they function as pragmatic statements to reflect upon and to deal with everyday occurrences, problems, and challenges. The advice given by Abigail is always meant well, as can be seen by one final example of an internationally disseminated proverb in an early letter of October 6, 1766, to Mary Cranch. It is not a Bible proverb, and it advocates nothing more than pure pragmatism in its epistolary context:

Methinks your Salem acquaintance have a very odd kind of politeness. By what I have heard of them, they have well learnd the lesson of Iago, to Rodorigo, "put money in thy purse." It is the Character of the whole people I find, get what you can, and keep what you have got. My advice to you is among the Romans, do as the romans do. This is a selfish world you know. Interest governs it, there are but a very few, who are moved by any other Spring. They are Generous, Benevolent and Friendly when it is for their interest, when any thing is to be got by it, but touch that tender part, their Interest, and you will immediately find the reverse, the greater half [of] the World are mere Janases. (I,55–56)

These proverbial passages show Abigail as a careful observer of social behavior who takes much interest in the world around her. Her insights into human nature are invaluable, and the same is true for her sociopolitical thoughts that she was ever willing to share with her politician husband.

"The Die Is Cast"—Political Strategies

Abigail Adams was thirty years old when the political situation in the colonies became increasingly tense and an uprising against the British appeared unavoidable. Abigail was part of the revolutionary spirit, writing to her husband on September 22, 1774: "I will not despair, but will believe that our cause being good we shall finally prevail. The Maxim in time of peace prepair for war, (if this may be call'd a time of peace) resounds throughout the Country. Next tuesday they are warned at Braintree all above 15 and under 60 to attend with their arms, and to train once a fortnight from that time, is a Scheme which lays much at heart with many" (I,161). And then, four and a half months later on February 3, 1774, Abigail begins a letter to her friend Mercy Otis Warren with a proverb and a powerful paragraph that express the unavoidability of the revolution:

> The die is cast. Yesterday brought such a Speach from the Throne as will stain with everlasting infamy the reign of G[e]orge the 3 determined to carry into Execution "the acts passd by the late parliment, and to Mantain the authority of the Legislature over all his dominions." The reply of the house of commons and the house of Lords shew us the most wicked and hostile measures will be pursued against us—even without giving us an opportunity to be heard in our defence. Infatuated Brittain! poor distressed America. Heaven only knows what is next to take place but it seems to me the Sword is now our only, yet dreadful alternative, and the fate of Rome will be renued in Brittain. (I,183)

Abigail did well in choosing the classical proverb "The die is cast" to refer to the inescapableness of war with Britain, just as Julius Caesar had used it on crossing the Rubicon after coming from Gaul and advancing into Italy against Pompey (49 B.C.) and as Winston S. Churchill would employ it repeatedly in his struggle against Nazi Germany.[50] She repeated the proverb in her letter of August 15, 1785, to her sister Mary Cranch to signal her acceptance of a family matter: "[...], but the die is cast" (VI,277). And when George Washington in September of 1796 announced that he would not accept a third term as President, she used it again in a letter to her son Thomas Boylston Adams of September 25, 1796: "The die is cast! All America is or ought to be in mourning."[51] Of course, this also meant that John would most likely become the second president of the country.

As the revolutionary skirmishes with the British increased in 1775, Abigail tells John that the men of Braintree do not "[...] tremble at the frowns of power." Slightly varying the proverb "Danger makes men bold," she touchingly describes how even a quiet physician plays his part: "Our good Friend the Doctor is in a very misirable state of Health, has the jaundice to a very great degree, is a mere Skelliton and hardly able to ride from his own house to my fathers. Danger you know sometimes makes timid men bold.

He stood that day very well, and generously attended with drink, Bisquit, flints &c. 5 hundred men without taking any pay" (I,225; June 22, 1775). Two weeks later she employs the proverb again to assure John that she is doing fine and that she has plenty of courage to carry on the fight: "I would not have you be distressed about me. Danger they say makes people valient. Hitherto I have been distress'd, but not dismayed. I have felt for my Country and her Sons, I have bled with them, and for them" (I,239; July 5, 1775). Here Abigail relies on a proverb to deal with a dangerous situation, taking solace in the traditional wisdom that she too can muster up the strength and courage to be a responsible part of the revolution. And when things don't go so well, she is quick to remind John proverbially that "Rome was not Built in a day" (II,47; July 13, 1776), that "Experienced Birds are not to be caught with chaff" (II,172; March 8, 1777), and that "Affliction is the good mans shining time" (III,371; July 5, 1780), thus keeping up her resolve that the insurgents will prevail and build an independent America in due time.

Clearly Abigail could count on John's recognition and appreciation of her proverbial statements and allusions. As quite the proverbial stylist himself, he must have enjoyed her description of an upcoming election in Massachusetts in which she prophecies the eventual demise of a bad politician by a mere hint at the proverb "Give a man rope enough and he will hang himself":

> This is a Great and important day in the political System of this State. Mr. Bowdoin has merrit and integrity, all the judicious people will vote for him, but popular Clamour will elect an other [John Hancock], who ought to forfeit every vote, by the low mean Arts he has taken to procure them. I could tell you many, if prudence did not restrain me, yet nothing that would surprize you, for you know every Avenu of his vain Heart. Give an extensive cord, and you know the adage. (III,406; September 3, 1780)

Little wonder that two weeks later Abigail wrote to her friend James Lovell on September 17, 1780: "O my dear Sir I am Sick[,] Sick of politicks. How can you exist so long in the midst of them? There is such mad ambition, such unbounded avarice, such insufferable vanity, such wicked peculation of publick property. Yet Hosana to these wretches" (III,415).

And yet, Abigail could not and surely also did not want to stay out of politics, defending, advising, and supporting her husband in all of his trials as he rose ever more towards national prominence. As she expressed her views in letter after letter to John and others, proverbs served her well to underscore her points, adding traditional wisdom to her revealing missives:

Time was you know Sir, when an amicable treaty might have been made with England very favourable to America, and you know to what intrigues it was oweing that the Commercial powers were taken from the person in whom they were first invested [Abigail is referring to Congress' decision, in July 1781, to revoke John's sole power to negotiate a commercial treaty with England]; but Time past, can not be recalled, as our Country Men now feel, and as was then predicted. (VI,77–78; March 8, 1785; letter to Cotton Tufts)

Mr. [Oliver] Wolcott [John's Secretary of the Treasury] seemd anxious at the Idea of the Presidents going so far from the Seat of Government [to his home in Braintree] at so critical a period. I know he will not leave here [Philadelphia] for any time if the Ministers think his presence necessary. We may truly say, we know not what a day will bring forth. From every side we are in Danger. We are in perils by Land, and we are in perils by sea, and in perils from false Breathern [with Wolcott being one of them, conspiring with Alexander Hamilton against John Adams]. (NL,101; July 6, 1797; letter to Mary Cranch)

The President [John Adams] has said, and he still says, he will appoint to office merit, virtue & Talents, and when Jacobins possess these, they stand a chance, but it will ever be an additional recommendation that they are friends to order and Government. [...] But the Ethiopen [*sic*] [Abigail speaks of the conspiring Tench Coxe, whom Adams had not appointed as Secretary of the Treasury after Alexander Hamilton resigned, placing Oliver Wolcott in the position instead] could not Change his Skin, and the Spots of the Leopard have been constantly visible, tho sometimes shaded [Jeremiah 13:23]. (NL,127; February 1, 1798; letter to Mary Cranch)[52]

This is reminiscent of modern politics as well, and Abigail's warning "Hear before you blame, is a good maxim" (NL,178, May 21, 1798; letter to Mary Cranch) would be a fitting proverb to recall in today's political acrimony. This is also true for her proverbial observation that "On such occasions as the present, every hand should be put to the plough" (Nl,178) in the same letter, and every politician would certainly want to keep in mind what Abigail wrote to their son Thomas Boylston on November 13, 1800, after his father had been defeated in his attempt at a second presidential term by Thomas Jefferson: "The triumph of the Jacobins is immoderate, and the Federalists deserve it. It is an old and just proverb, 'Never halloo until you are out of the woods'" (LA,381; November 13, 1800). And how touching her philosophical view regarding John's defeat and the change that will bring for them in the same letter:

The consequence to us, personally, is, that we retire from public life. For myself and family, I have few regrets. At my age, and with my bodily infirmities, I shall be happier at Quincy [formerly Braintree]. Neither my habits, nor my education or inclinations have led me to an expensive style of living, so that on that score I have little to mourn over. If I did not rise with dignity, I can at least fall with ease, which is the more difficult task. I wish your father's circumstances were not so limited and circumscribed, as they must be, because he cannot indulge himself in those improvements upon his farm, which his inclination leads him to, and which would serve to amuse him, and contribute to his health. I feel not any resentment against those who are coming into power, and only wish the future administration of the government may be as productive of the peace, happiness, and prosperity of the nation, as the two former ones have been. I leave to time the unfolding of the drama. I leave to posterity to reflect upon the times past; and I leave them characters to contemplate. (LA,380)

Such self-analytical philosophical thoughts are, perhaps, not in need of proverbs, but when Abigail reflects on human nature in general, she often cites the traditional wisdom of Bible and folk proverbs to underscore her general observations.

"The Great Fish Swallow Up the Small"—Reflections on Human Nature

Throughout her massive correspondence, Abigail shows herself as a socio-psychological analyst, reflecting on common traits of human nature.[53] When one considers that proverbs are in fact generalized truths of the human condition that have been appropriately defined as "monumenta humana,"[54] it is not surprising that the more philosophical passages of Abigail's epistles abound with proverbs from the Bible or traditional folk proverbs. Thus she turned to the Bible proverb "Love thy neighbor as thyself" (Leviticus 19:18; Matthew 19:19) to reflect upon the ambivalent value of human ambition that in its negative effects has factionalized the country and has undermined the moral values of its people:

The passion of Ambition when it centers in an honest mind possess'd of great Abilities may and often has done imminent Service to the World. There are but few minds if any wholly destitute of it and tho in itself it is Laudable yet there is nothing in Nature so amiable but the passions and intrest of Men will pervert to very base purposes. When I consider the Spirit which at present prevails throughout this continent I really detest that restless ambition of those artfull and designing men which has thus broken this people into factions—and I every day see more and more cause to deprecate the growing Evil. This party Spirit ruins good Neighbourhood, eradicates all the Seeds of good nature and humanity—it sours the temper and has a fatal tendancy upon the Morals and understanding and is contrary to that precept of christianity thou shallt Love thy Neighbour as thy self. (I,98; February 27, 1774; letter to Mercy Otis Warren)

About six years later, Abigail refers to this proverb again in one of the many letters of advice to her son John Quincy, reminding him that "The only sure and permanant foundation of virtue is Religion. Let this important truth be engraven upon your Heart [...]. Man is bound to the performance of certain duties which all tend to the happiness and welfare of Society and are comprised in one short sentence expressive of universal Benevolence, 'Thou shalt Love thy Neighbour as thyself'" (III,310–311; March 20, 1780). But again, when Abigail speaks of religion, she has in mind not merely faith but above all the moral code of Christianity, i.e., the Puritan ethic with which she grew up in the parsonage of her parents.

Turning to more worldly matters, it is her letter to John of November 27, 1775, that contains one of her most powerful statements about human nature written at the time of American revolutionary reactions against the British abuse of power. The proverb "Big fish eat little fish" has served to describe human power struggles since classical times,[55] and it most assuredly is also a befitting metaphor for eighteenth-century politics, showing that human nature in the Age of Reason and Enlightenment has barely evolved from that of the fish world:

I am more and more convinced that Man is a dangerous creature, and that power whether vested in many or a few is ever grasping, and like the grave cries give, give. The great fish swallow up the small, and he who is most strenuous for the Rights of the people, when vested with power, is as eager after the perogatives of Government. You tell me of degrees of perfection to which Humane Nature is capable of arriving, and I believe it, but at the same time lament that our admiration should arise from the scarcity of the instances. (I,329)

This is a devastating indictment of humanity bordering on a fatalistic worldview regarding the corruptness of power and government. Not even a year later in another letter to John of August 29, 1776, Abigail cites the proverb "Man is the only animal who is hungry with His Belly full" (II,113) as describing "Humane Nature," but she is quick to state more positively and more befitting her resolute nature of struggling for success that "Pure and disintrested Virtue must ever be its own reward" II,113).

Abigail and John Adams certainly tried to live by the proverb that "Virtue is its own reward," while adding a bit of positive ambition to it. They believed in the Puritan ethic and, proverbially speaking, that "Experience is the mother of wisdom" and that "Great necessities call out great virtues," as can be seen from yet another letter by mother Adams to her son John Quincy:

> These are times in which a Genious would wish to live. It is not in the still calm of life, or the repose of a pacific station, that great characters are formed. Would Cicero have shone so distinguished an orator, if he had not been roused, kindled and enflamed by the Tyranny of Catiline, Millo [Abigail is mistaken here, since Cicero was n ardent supporter of Millo], Verres and Mark Anthony. The Habits of a vigorous mind are formed in contending with difficulties. All History will convince you of this, and that wisdom and penetration are the fruits of experience, not the Lessons of retirement and leisure.
>
> Great necessities call out great virtues. When a mind is raised, and animated by scenes that engage the Heart, then those qualities which would otherways lay dormant, wake into Life, and form the Character of the Hero and the Statesman. (III,268; January 19, 1780)

This wisdom is sent to a boy of merely thirteen who accompanied his father to Europe at that young age. As Abigail penned these well-intended comments, she must have had her husband John in front of her eyes as her hero and aspiring statesman. Little did she know that their son John Quincy would become that well educated "genius" who rose to the presidency in 1825. All of this is summarized to a degree in a letter from Abigail to her sister Elizabeth Shaw that alludes to the proverb "Example is better than precept":

> The longer I live in the world, and the more I see of mankind, the more deeply I am impressed with the importance and necessity of good principles and virtuous examples being placed before youth, in the most amiable and engaging manner, whilst the mind is uncontaminated, and open to impressions. Yet precept without example is of little avail, for habits of the mind are produced by the exertion of inward practical principles. The "soul's calm sunshine" can result only from the practice of virtue, which is congenial to our natures. (LA,278; March 4, 1786)

Mere words in the form of precepts, maxims or proverbs as well as the best education that people could attain are simply not enough if that wisdom is not followed by responsible and virtuous deeds. Abigail knew well of what she spoke, having been responsible for the education of their four children Abigail (Nabby), John Quincy, Charles, and Thomas Boylston (another daughter, Susanna, died at the age of two), before the boys went off to Harvard. Of course, she kept instructing and educating them with her letters throughout her life.

"Hope Springs Eternal in the Human Breast"— Forever Optimism

As matriarch of the Adams family, Abigail cared deeply for her children, loved and supported her husband, and was forever involved in the extended family, but she also never lost sight of the well being and future of the United States that she in her own way helped to establish. At the time of the war of 1812, she wrote thoughts to her friend Mercy Otis Warren that are of universal application long beyond their inception:

> So long as we are inhabitants of this earth and possess any of our faculties, we cannot be indifferent to the state of our country, our posterity and our friends. [...] We have passed through one revolution and have happily arrived at the goal, but the ambition, injustice and plunder of foreign powers have again involved us in war, the termination of which is not given us to see. [...]
>
> If I give an opinion with respect to the conduct of our native State [of Massachusetts], I cannot do it with approbation. She has had much to complain of as it respected a refusal of naval protection, yet that cannot justify her in paralyzing the arm of government when raised for her defence and that of the nation. A house divided against itself—and upon that foundation do our enemies build their hopes of subduing us. May it prove a sandy one to them. (LA,412–413; December 30, 1812)

There was no need for Abigail to cite the Bible proverb "A house divided against itself cannot stand" (Mark 3:25) in its entirety. Her friend and her contemporaries knew it only too well, and so did Abraham Lincoln when he utilized it as an authoritative *leitmotif* before the Civil War in his arguments for maintaining the Union at all costs.[56] The proverb has been used on the political scene repeatedly since these earlier occurrences, always with the intent of placing national unity above the interests of individual states, certain groups of people, and policies or actions that might tear the nation apart.

As a strong Federalist and social conservative, Abigail had the interest of the entire country in mind when she acted as an adviser to her husband. She explained this conviction through yet another Bible proverb to Mercy Otis Warren, clearly stating that faith in the American government and society will overcome major obstacles in due time:

> I shall [...] turn my attention to my own country, which, though not terrified with the prospect of a profligate prince to govern it, appears to be in an untranquillized state, embarrassed in its finances, distressed in its commerce, and unbalanced in its governments. But I have faith that will remove mountains [Matthew 17:20]; and, as distress and difficulties in private life are frequently spurs to diligence, so have we seen public industry excited in the same manner. (LA,324; May 14, 1787)

It is interesting to note that Abigail appropriates the religious proverb "Faith will move mountains" by relating it not so much to faith in God but to faith in her own abilities. This calls into memory her most beloved proverb "God helps them who help themselves" that also emphasizes the fact that people have to work on their own fate. But there is a third element to the equation of faith in one's own abilities and the resolve to action, and that is hope in the future that appears to be a definite part of the American worldview.[57] As a great admirer of Alexander Pope (1688–1744), Abigail turned to a quotation from his famous *Essay on Man* (1733) to find the proper wording, namely "Hope springs eternal in the human breast."[58] This quotation has long since turned proverb, and by today it is often cited in the truncated form of "Hope springs eternal" without any reference to Pope. In any case, Abigail cites it once as a proverb without any quotation marks or reference to Pope in a letter of June 20, 1784, as a personal explanation for having reached the decision to cross the Atlantic in order to end the long separation from her husband: "I am going to embark very soon upon the mighty waters. Never did I think I could have been persuaded to such an undertaking unaccompanied with Husband son or some near connection, but thus it is. Hope that springs Eternal in the Humane Breast, I pray may in some early day realize to me the promised blessing" (V,350; June 20, 1784; letter to Elizabeth Ellery Dana). In a second employment of this encouraging piece of wisdom, Abigail is hoping to see her sister Mary Cranch again soon, especially since she has been experiencing a rather troublesome period in her life:

> My mind is not in the most cheerful state. Trials of various kinds seem to be reserved for our gray Hairs, for our declining years. Shall I receive

good and not evil? I will not forget the blessings which sweeten Life.
One of those is the prospect I have before me of meeting my dear sister
soon, I hope in health and spirits. A strong immagination is said to be
a refuge from sorrow, and a kindly solace for a feeling Heart. Upon this
principle it was that Pope founded his observation, that "hope springs
eternal in the human breast." (NL,253; May 26, 1800)

Whatever troubled Abigail, be they family matters or political issues,
she always mustered up enough faith, resolve, and hope to carry on as one
of the truly remarkable women of the American Revolution and the first
few decades of the new American nation. The three proverbs "Faith will
remove mountains," "God helps them who help themselves," and "Hope
springs eternal (in the human breast)" encapsulate the life, action, and
worldview of this great matriarch. Faith, resolve, and hope served her well
as she dedicated herself with love and commitment to her husband, family,
and country, making her a proverbial *prima inter pares* in the distinguished
group of founding fathers of the United States. Her vast correspondence
and several biographies about her tell the intriguing and touching story of
this great American woman, whose words and deeds were to a considerable
degree informed by the wisdom of proverbs.

4

"A House Divided Against Itself Cannot Stand"
From Biblical Proverb to Abraham Lincoln and Beyond

Biblical proverbs have permeated vernacular languages throughout the world, and the masterfully translated King James Bible helped to spread ancient wisdom literature in the form of new English proverbs with much vigor and success. One of these proverbs appears in three slightly altered variants in three of the gospels of the New Testament, thereby literally assuring its spread through the English-speaking world. Matthew records Jesus as having stated that "Every kingdom divided against itself is brought to desolation; and every city or house divided against itself shall not stand" (Matthew 12:25), while Mark has Jesus make the same statement in a somewhat simpler way as "And if a kingdom be divided against itself, that kingdom cannot stand. And if a house be divided against itself, that house cannot stand" (Mark 3:24–25). Luke, finally, has the more complex variant "Every kingdom divided against itself is brought to desolation; and a house divided against a house falleth" (Luke 11:17). Since Mark's statement is the closest to the way it was cited by Americans before Lincoln and by him as well, it is stated here in its biblical context (Mark 3:22–27). As can be seen, it is a passage where Jesus talks about the evil powers of the devil, which in the 1850s could be equated with the devilish aspects of slavery:

> 22 And the scribes which came from Jerusalem said, He [Jesus] hath Beelzebub, and by the prince of the devils casteth he out the devils.
>
> 23 And he called them unto him, and said unto them in parables, How can Satan cast out Satan?
>
> 24 And if a kingdom be divided against itself, that kingdom cannot stand.
>
> 25 And if a house be divided against itself, that house cannot stand.
>
> 26 And if Satan rise up against himself, and be divided, he cannot stand, but hath an end.
>
> 27 No man can enter into a strong man's house, and spoil his goods, except he will first bind the strong man; and then he will spoil his house.

Not surprisingly, proverb collections and notably those referring to American usage tend to list both variants or merely the "house" variant, where the more domestic image can refer to the home as well as to the government in general. In these variants it is the house as such that will fall if it is not kept in familial, organizational or governmental order.[1] By the time references of the proverb appear in the early American colonies, the preferred choice is, with very few exceptions, the "house" variant.[2] But still, the fact that this second half of the longer biblical passage is indeed wisdom from the Scriptures is for the most part stated directly or certainly assumed to be recognizable as such by people who knew their Bible. By the turn of the 18th century the standard short form of the biblical proverb turned folk proverb has become "A house divided against itself cannot stand" in the North American colonies. As time progressed, the proverb's religious connotations faded until it became a secularized piece of wisdom to be employed frequently in various and very different contexts.

Pre-Lincoln Use of the Proverb

The earliest American reference to the proverb is contained in a journal from the year 1704 in which Thomas Chalkley describes the worries of his mother after an attack by Indians on a Quaker settlement in New England put the peaceful coexistence of the native population and new settlers into question: "My mother would often say, 'A house divided could not stand;' and she could not tell what to do, although she had most peace in staying, yet she had thoughts of moving."[3] Clearly the use of the proverb in this context refers primarily to social issues, and that is also the case in a fascinating broadsheet from after 1765 entitled "Poetical Thoughts on the Difficulties Our Fore-Fathers Endured in Planting Religious and Civil Liberty in this Western World" that included the following two didactic quatrains:

> So long as we are disagreed,
> The house divided cannot stand,
> So let us take all care with speed,
> To dwell in love with heart and hand.

> That we might share among the rest,
> Those towns that's in America,
> From North to South, from East to West
> Our homage to our God we'll pay.[4]

It is important to note here that while the proverb might also refer to religious division, it is used with equal effectiveness to bemoan basic human, social, and political disunity. It was Thomas Paine, with his remarkable essay on *Common Sense; Addressed to the Inhabitants of America* (1776), who launched the biblical proverb into becoming a commonplace of sorts in political discourse. Right in the first section "On the Origin and Design of Government in General, with Concise Remarks on the English Constitution" he uses the proverb to describe the English form of government as one that could not work in America:

> Some writers have explained the English constitution thus: the king, say they, is one, the people another; the peers are a house in behalf of the king, the commons in behalf of the people; but this hath all the distinctions of a house divided against itself; and though the expressions be pleasantly arranged, yet when examined they appear idle and ambiguous.[5]

Even though Paine does not cite the complete text of the proverb, he is well aware of the fact that his readers will understand the indirect implication that this form of government could not possibly exist in America.

By 1787, a fascinating "Address to all Federalists" by one Curtius appeared in the first volume of *The American Museum*. The author argues vigorously for unity among all factions in the newly proclaimed country, and the final paragraph foreshadows in many ways the words that Abraham Lincoln will utter some seventy years later:

> Let us, then, be of one heart, and one mind. Let us seize the golden opportunity to secure a stable government, and to become a respectable nation. Let us be open, decided, and resolute, in a good cause. A HOUSE DIVIDED AGAINST ITSELF CANNOT STAND. Our national existence depends as much as ever upon our union: and ITS CONSOLIDATION MOST ASSUREDLY INVOLVES OUR PROSPERITY, FELICITY, AND SAFETY.[6]

Politicians of this era found the proverbial metaphor of the "house divided" extremely useful for the purpose of political argumentation and persuasion. Its biblical character endowed it with moral and didactic overtones, and the argument for unified strength was splendidly enhanced by the opposite image of a house or government crumbling.

By the time of the War of 1812, Abigail Adams uses the proverb in its political sense in a letter of December 30, 1812, to Mrs. Mercy Warren. She is clearly worried about the state of the union at this troubled time, and the proverb comes to her mind as a unifying slogan, as it will be employed later by Lincoln and other public figures to the present day:

> We cannot be indifferent to the state of our country, our posterity, and our friends. [...] We have passed through one revolution, and happily arrived at the goal; but the ambition, injustice, and plunder of foreign powers have again involved us in war, the termination of which is not given us to see. [...] Yet I hear from our pulpits, and read from our presses, that it is an unjust, a wicked, a ruinous, and unnecessary war. [...]
>
> A house divided against itself, and upon that foundation do our enemies build their hopes of subduing us. May it prove a sandy one to them![7]

The integration of merely the partially cited proverb is a stylistic masterpiece! Abigail Adams refuses to cite its pessimistic conclusion, since she does not want to agree with the country's enemies that the United States is plagued by disunity. These false conclusions of a crumbling house are then ironically linked with the allusion to the proverbial expression of "to build on sand." The misconceptions of the enemies that the United States might be a house divided are thus, she hopes, built on a sandy foundation, i.e., they are indeed false and will be proven wrong by her victorious country.

By the year 1822, the proverb is for the first time brought up in connection with the issue of slavery, quite indirectly still, but certainly foreshadowing the big slave issues of the middle of the 19th century:

> Ragamuffins vote as well as men of property; and to make the best of it, they are governed by slaves and negroes: for the people to the southward, have votes according to the number of their slaves. We expect to hear shortly of blackamoor senators and governors. [...]: the house that is divided against itself cannot stand [...]: they will soon separate.[8]

This pronouncement is certainly an early hint at a possible separation of the South with its slaves from a Union that is regarded to be anything but perfect.

While in England the dramatist John Thomas Haines could write *A House Divided* (1836) as a farcical comedy in two acts with an obvious allusion to the biblical proverb in its title,[9] the proverb was in much more serious and repeated use by a president of the United States. In fact, Andrew Jackson employed it at least seven times in his published writings, but he clearly used this favorite expression of his on many more occasions. For example, on November 28, 1830, Jackson complains bitterly to Mrs. Andrew J. Donelson about intrigues and dishonesty around him. He starts the following paragraph with a well-known proverb about friendship and concludes it with a direct quotation of the "House divided" proverb:

> I have suffered much and may suffer much more in feeling, but never can I separate from my friend without cause. What a wretch he must be who can. "A friend in need is a friend indeed," and he who can forsake his friend in distress [...] will get into difficulties, from which danger of disgrace may arise. "A House divided cannot stand."[10]

For the most part, the proverb becomes a *leitmotif* of sorts in the letters of Andrew Jackson. He uses it not so much as a political argument for national policy, but rather as a biblical saying to warn against strife among friends and family members. The proverb thus never takes on the crucial meaning that it occupies in Abraham Lincoln's political life, and its use is also not yet connected with the thought of the nation splitting apart over the slavery issue.

Sam Houston, Daniel Webster, and Edmund Quincy

By the 1850s the schism between North and South and the divergence of opinions over slavery are beginning to tear the Union apart. It is at this time that the biblical proverb is starting to play a noticeable role in this struggle, and while it does not completely lose its religious connotations, the proverb clearly becomes a secularized slogan to give moral and political expression to a heart-wrenching struggle. Three powerful and telling uses of the proverb in the early 1850s stand out, and they are part of some of the most significant speeches ever delivered on this issue.

The first reference is to be found in an impassioned speech which Senator Sam Houston from Texas delivered on February 8, 1850, in the Senate. His colleague Senator Henry Clay from Kentucky had placed a resolution before the legislators which became known as the Compromise of 1850. Under this compromise, California was admitted as a free state, i.e., free of slavery, to the United States, while some new territories were allowed to decide for themselves whether they would open up to slavery or not. The debates over this compromise were fierce indeed, and the fear of destroying the Union loomed everywhere. Houston closed his lengthy speech with a strong call for maintaining the Union, not at all that different from Abraham Lincoln's later plea:

I beseech those whose piety will permit them reverentially to petition, that they will pray for the Union, and ask that He who buildeth up and pulleth down nations will, in mercy, preserve and unite us. For a nation divided against itself cannot stand. I wish, if this Union must be dissolved, that its ruins may be the monument of my grave, and the graves of my family. I wish no epitaph to be written to tell that I survived the ruin of this glorious Union.[11]

With great oratorical skill Houston altered the biblical proverb under discussion to "A nation divided against itself cannot stand," a poignant reformulation of the proverb which interestingly enough was never employed by Lincoln. It might, of course, also be possible that Houston had the biblical passage "And if a kingdom be divided against itself, that kingdom cannot stand" (Mark 3:24) in mind when he formulated his statement.

It is a known fact that Abraham Lincoln was a great admirer of Daniel Webster, who as Senator of Massachusetts was known as one of the greatest orators of the time. On May 22, 1851, in Buffalo, with the divisive problem of slavery growing ever more heated, Webster spoke out against slavery and for the Union and its Constitution, drawing on the biblical proverb to warn people of the danger of destroying the nation:

There is but one question in this country now; or, if there be others, they are but secondary, [...] can we preserve the union of these States, by such administration of the powers of the Constitution [...]. If a house be divided against itself, it will fall, and crush every body in it. We must see that we maintain the government which is over us. We must see that we uphold the Constitution, and we must do so without regard to party. [...]

It is obvious to every one, and we all know it, that the origin of the great disturbance which agitates the country is the existence of slavery in some of the States; but we must meet the subject; we must consider it; we must deal with it earnestly, honestly, and justly.[12]

In this significant speech Daniel Webster did, as usual, show concern for the fate of the slaves, but his primary goal was to stress the maintenance of the Union under the Constitution.

That was, of course, quite different from declared abolitionists of this time, something that Lincoln most assuredly was not. In fact, the abolitionist Edmund Quincy published an article entitled "The House Divided Against Itself" in the March 25, 1852, issue of the *National Anti-Slavery Standard,* beginning with an oblique reference to the Bible and with a direct quotation of the proverb:

It was said more than eighteen hundred years ago, that a house divided against itself cannot stand, and the truth of the saying is written on every page of history, antecedent and subsequent. It is not unlikely that the history of our country may furnish fresh and pregnant examples [...]. The great national element of division we need hardly say is Slavery. The point of the wedge was inserted next the cornerstone of our institutions by their founders themselves [...]. By the everlasting laws of moral mechanics it must either be withdrawn or its pressure must grow stronger and stronger and at last make a fissure that will shatter into heaps the proud structure upon the heads of those that put their trust in it.[13]

What Edmund Quincy's thoughts and language as well as those of Sam Houston and Daniel Webster show is that—with due respect to Abraham Lincoln's rhetorical prowess—the beginning of his famous speech is quite in line with other orators and writers of his time.

Abraham Lincoln's Use of Biblical Proverbs

For someone who "adopted at several stages of his career the practice of daily Bible reading,"[14] it became natural to cite quotations or at least paraphrased verses from the Bible with high frequency in oral as well as written statements. Lincoln scholars have not failed to comment on this preoccupation with biblical phrases, claiming that "his familiarity with and use of biblical phraseology was remarkable even in a time when such use was more common than now."[15] There is no doubt that "his greatest speeches reflect both biblical style and biblical teaching."[16]

But scholars dealing with Lincoln's use of biblical language have forgotten to comment on the numerous biblical phrases that long ago turned into folk proverbs and metaphors. These proverbial utterances gave Lincoln the opportunity to speak and write both authoritatively and somewhat colloquially, adding much imagery and color to his arguments of persuasion or otherwise rather factual letters. This preoccupation with biblical phraseology can take on rather overpowering proportions, as in his written reply of May 30, 1864, to a delegation of Baptists:

To read the Bible, as the word of God himself, that "In the sweat of *thy* face shalt thou eat bread [Genesis 3:19]," and to preach there from that, "In the sweat of *other mans* [sic] faces shalt thou eat bread," to my mind can scarcely be reconciled with honest sincerity. When brought to my final reckoning, may I have to answer for robbing no man of his goods [...]. When, a year or two ago, those professedly holy men of the South, met in the semblance of prayer and devotion, and, in the Name of Him who said "As ye would all men should do unto you, do ye even so unto them" [Matthew 7:12] appeal to the christian world to aid them in doing to a whole race of men, as they would have no man do unto themselves, to my thinking they contemned and insulted God and His church, far more than did Satan when he tempted the Saviour with the Kingdoms of the earth. The devil's attempt was no more false, and far less hypocritical. But let me forbear, remembering it is also written "Judge not, lest ye be judged" [Matthew 7:1].[17]

What a paragraph! What a rhetorical masterpiece! Without even mentioning that horrid word "slavery," Lincoln employs three biblical proverbs known to everybody, and certainly to the Baptist ministers, and ridicules countless numbers of slaveholders of the South who have earned their bread through the work of their slaves. He also points out proverbially that they have forgotten the "Golden Rule," and by quoting its proverbial wording, he shows vividly how false their behavior has been. But lest he were to elevate himself to an exaggerated self-righteousness, Lincoln closes his "mini-sermon" with the proverb that warns everybody against sitting in judgment over others and forgetting that all people commit sinful acts. The message is direct, clear, and authoritative, and the three biblical proverbs add a didactic and ethical persuasiveness to this masterful statement.[18]

With plenty of biblical proverbs at his disposal at the time of drafting his acclaimed "House divided" speech for the Republican State Convention of Illinois, one wonders whether Lincoln was aware of the interesting fact that he had actually used the "House divided" proverb at least once before in writing on March 4, 1843, in an "Address to the People of Illinois" which he had put forth jointly with S. T. Logan and A. T. Bledsoe as a campaign circular for the Whig Party. In this early use of the proverb the subject matter is, however, not that of slavery but rather an argument for the adoption of the convention system for nomination of candidates for national office:

> That "union is strength" is a truth that has been known, illustrated and declared, in various ways and forms in all ages of the world. [...]; and he whose wisdom surpasses that of all philosophers, has declared that "a house divided against itself cannot stand." It is to induce our friends to act upon this important, and universally acknowledged truth, that we urge the adoption of the Convention System.[19]

Lincoln is about thirty-four years old at this time and stands at the very beginning of his political career, and yet he already begins to write effective paragraphs based on proverbial argumentation. It is interesting to note that in this case he cites a classical proverb lacking any metaphor whatsoever to start with, but he is quick in adding the biblical proverb as a metaphorical antipode. By also pointing out, albeit in an indirect way, that this proverb carries with it the authority of Jesus, it is made very clear what will happen if political union moves towards disunion. It seems strange, however, that Lincoln never returned to the classical proverb as a positive argument later in his political career. Somehow the apocalyptic "House divided" proverb must have seemed more appropriate to him in light of the troublesome times.

The "House Divided" Speech of June 16, 1858

There really is no particular reason why Lincoln should have remembered his use of this proverb twenty-five years later, especially since its early use was not brought about by its connection to slavery and its danger to the preservation of the Union. However, he did use the biblical proverb in its applicability to the questions of slavery and political union in a significant fragment of a speech that he delivered on May 18, 1858 in Edwardsville, i.e., one month prior to his famed Springfield address. In fact, Roy P. Basler, editor of the *Collected Works of Abraham Lincoln,* argues convincingly that the fragment's key passages became a preliminary draft of the June 16th speech.[20] It is of interest that the proverb is cited in the fragment as a separate and centered heading followed by sentences which are basically the same as the speech delivered one month later in Springfield:

> *A house divided against itself cannot stand.*
> I believe the government cannot endure permanently half slave and half free. [...] I do not expect the Union to be dissolved. I do not expect the house to fall; but I do expect it will cease to be divided. It will become all one thing or all the other. Either the opponents of slavery will arrest the further spread of it, and put it in course of ultimate extinction,; or its advocates will push it forward till it shall become alike lawful in all the States, old as well as new.[21]

Two important matters must be observed regarding this fragment: First, the proverb is not yet integrated effectively as the centerpiece of the paragraph as will be the case in the "House divided" speech, and secondly, this unpublished fragment had, of course, no immediate influence. It is not even known whether Lincoln actually iterated the proverb in Edwardsville on May 18, 1858.

This would help to explain an otherwise baffling statement which Lincoln is to have made in connection with writing his "House divided" speech:

> It is said that when he was preparing his Springfield speech of 1858, he spent hours trying to find language that would express the idea that dominated his entire career—namely, that a republic could not permanently endure half free and half slave, and that finally a Bible passage flashed through his mind and he exclaimed, "I have found it! 'A house divided against itself cannot stand.'" And probably no other Bible passage ever exerted as much influence as this one in the settlement of a great controversy.[22]

If this account could in fact be authenticated,[23] Lincoln might have meant to indicate by it that he found a way to place the proverb into the center part of the introductory section of his speech. After all, as has been stated, he had just used it as a section title in a speech fragment a week earlier, and it is doubtful that he would not have remembered this (even if this fragment were dated late December 1857, as has been suggested recently).[24]

Of the numerous statements of this sort surrounding Lincoln's convention speech, there is at least one that has been sufficiently authenticated to deserve some credence. He made it to his law partner, friend, and confidant William Herndon just an hour or so before he delivered his address in the evening of June 16, 1858. Lincoln had decided to read his prepared speech privately to Herndon, and when Herndon asked him after having heard the first section whether such strong language was politic, Lincoln is supposed to have said:

> That makes no difference. That expression is a truth of all human experience: a house divided against itself cannot stand, and he that runs may read.[25] [...] I want to use some universally known figure, expressed in simple language as universally known, that it may strike home to the minds of men in order to rouse them to the peril of the times. I would rather be defeated with the expression in the speech and it held up and discussed before the people than to be victorious without it.[26]

The problem with this alleged statement is, of course, that William Herndon has referred to it in different phrasings, putting its authenticity into question. Don E. and Virginia Fehrenbacher have done superb detective work to trace virtually every statement that Lincoln is ever to have made but not preserved in his own writing in their massive collection of *Recollected Words of Abraham Lincoln* (1996). These scholars give this quotation an authenticity rating with more than average doubt, and others of a similar type are judged to be probably not authentic. This is particularly true for the claims that Lincoln read the speech to a number of friends in addition to Herndon. Regarding these claims and descriptions of what took place at this prereading of the speech to Herndon and several party leaders, the Fehrenbachers speak of "splendid example[s] of [the] Lincoln myth in the process of elaboration and decoration."[27]

There is, to be sure, no doubt about the fact that Abraham Lincoln's first words during his evening address on June 16, 1858, to the Republican convention in Springfield, Illinois, electrified the audience. People had expected a noncontroversial speech that everybody could listen to without any concerns or turmoil. Instead, Lincoln presented them with a carefully crafted platform that brought the slavery issue and the concern about the Union into the open. His Republican supporters at the convention rightfully felt that this radical statement would cost Lincoln and them the Senatorial election, and it did do exactly that. But Lincoln also accomplished his goal with his bold and not at all rash declaration that "A house divided against itself cannot stand." It lost him the Senate seat, but it helped bring about his debates with Stephen A. Douglas, it put him into the limelight of national politics, and it certainly put this courageous and ethical person on the path to the White House.

The "opening paragraph [of the 'House Divided' speech] has already become one of the most celebrated passages in the political literature of the country," wrote Joseph H. Barret in his early *Life of Abraham Lincoln* in 1865, claiming that "there is moral sublimity in the rugged honesty and directness with which the grand issues in this whole slavery agitation are presented."[28] The ethical nature of the beginning of the speech was no doubt enhanced by the biblical proverb "The house divided against itself cannot stand," which surely was known to most if not all members of the audience. Lincoln did not need to mention that he was quoting Jesus, "whose wisdom surpasses that of all philosophers,"[29] as he had previously done in his campaign circular for the Whig Party on March 4, 1843. It took modern scholars to forget that this famous proverbial utterance had its origin in the Bible. Of course, Lincoln's name is now irrevocably attached to it, especially in the minds of American citizens. Yet to go so far as to state that Lincoln "had coined a quotable but debatable phrase"[30] or that "Lincoln had done the thing which fans a leader's fame without clarifying his position: he had coined a quotable phrase"[31] exceeds historical facts. He had not coined the phrase, but rather brought it into the consciousness of the entire Union. That it was debatable, questionable and even radical for the time in its secularized context of slavery and politics is, of course, true.

But what is it then that Abraham Lincoln said on that eventful evening in Springfield, Illinois? Here is what he said:

> If we could first know *where* we are, and *whither* we are tending, we could then better judge *what* to do, and *how* to do it.
>
> We are now far into the *fifth* year, since a policy was initiated, with the *avowed* object, and *confident* promise, of putting an end to slavery agitation.
>
> Under the operation of that policy, that agitation has not only, *not ceased,* but has *constantly augmented.*
>
> In *my* opinion, it *will* not cease, until a *crisis* shall have been reached, and passed.
>
> "A house divided against itself cannot stand."
>
> I believe this government cannot endure, permanently half *slave* and half *free.*
>
> I do not expect the Union to be *dissolved*—I do not expect the house to *fall*—but I *do* expect it will cease to be divided.
>
> It will become *all* one thing, or *all* the other.
>
> Either the *opponents* of slavery, will arrest the further spread of it, and place it where the public mind shall rest in the belief that it is in course of ultimate extinction; or its *advocates* will push it forward, till it shall become alike lawful in *all* the States, *old* as well as *new*—*North* as well as *South.*[32]

While these few minute paragraphs make up only 5% of the entire speech, they represented "an electrifying challenge to conflict."[33] Carl Sandburg in the first part of his celebrated *Abraham Lincoln* (1926) biography states quite appropriately: "This was so plain that two farmers fixing fences on a rainy morning could talk it over. [...] What interested the country most, as many newspapers published the speech in full, was its opening paragraph. It became known as the 'House Divided' speech. It went far."[34] The second part of the speech (72%) deals with a review of the history of slavery in the United States, stressing especially the tumultuous debate of the 1850's over the question of slavery in new states and territories. Stephen A. Douglas as Chairman of the Senate Committee on Territories had pushed the Kansas-Nebraska Act through Congress in 1854, which stated that the citizens of the new territories would decide whether they wanted to admit slavery or not. This concept of "popular sovereignty" basically brought to an end the famed Missouri Compromise of 1820 that was hammered out by such renowned Senators as Henry Clay and Daniel Webster. This agreement had argued that slavery was prohibited in any part of the original Louisiana Purchase outside the state of

Missouri north of Missouri's southern boundary of latitude 36°30'. Lincoln strongly agreed with this position, feeling that slavery should be contained within its original boundaries where it would eventually be driven to natural extinction. In addition to Douglas's argument of "popular sovereignty," the Supreme Court in 1857 had handed down the Dred Scott decision which established that Congress did not have the constitutional right to bar slavery from new territories. All of this Abraham Lincoln opposed vigorously, going so far as to accuse Stephen A. Douglas and Supreme Court Justice Roger B. Taney, as well as Presidents Franklin Pierce and James Buchanan unfairly of a conspiracy to allow slavery to spread throughout the Union (third part or 23% of the speech).[35]

Much has been written about this seminal speech, and there is certainly not a book on Lincoln which will not have the term "House divided" in its index. The actual discussions range from a couple of pages[36] to entire chapters and separate pamphlets. From the point of view of modern thoughts on racism, the speech did not really go far enough. Lincoln did not go on record as being an abolitionist, and while his introductory statement seemed radical at first, it was in fact rather conservative, in that it argued only for the restriction of slavery in the states where it already existed. It would take the revered Lincoln of today still a number of years and the horrors of the Civil War until he would and could issue the Emancipation Proclamation on January 1, 1863. In a letter of August 22, 1862, to Horace Greeley, Lincoln was still adhering to this policy, as he had made clear so many times ever since his convention speech four years earlier:

> My paramount object in this struggle is to save the Union, and is not either to save or destroy slavery. If I could save the Union without freeing *any* slave I would do it, and if I could save it by freeing *all* the slaves I would do it; and if I could save it by freeing some and leaving others alone I would also do that. What I do about slavery, and the colored race, I do because I believe it helps to save the Union; and what I forbear, I forbear because I do *not* believe it would help to save the Union.[37]

Lincoln has thus been called "essentially a middle-of-the-roader in his attitude toward slavery,"[38] while an extremist abolitionist judged Lincoln in a newspaper article of January 24, 1866, much more harshly: "Lincoln was an emancipationist by compulsion. [...] Lincoln was made a saint and liberator in spite of himself; he was cuffed into the calendar; he was kicked into glory."[39] Perhaps it is best to simply state that "time proved that his straightforwardness was, after all, the best strategy"[40] to get things on the political table. What was definitely clear to Lincoln was that "slavery could not be denationalized; it had either to grow or die."[41] But he certainly had no intention of taking the matter to a civil war. "There will be no war, no violence,"[42] he declared openly during the seventh debate on October 15, 1858.

THE PROVERB AND THE LINCOLN-DOUGLAS DEBATES

Whether Abraham Lincoln intended it so or not, his "House divided" speech became "the keynote for the Lincoln-Douglas debates to follow in the Senate campaign, themselves the most famous examples of political debate in American history."[43] The shrewd and experienced debater Douglas used the short first part of Lincoln's convention speech to brand him a warmongering abolitionist. In fact, the speech in one way or another is cited in twenty of the twenty-one speeches (Lincoln's opening remarks during the fourth debate on September 18, 1858, in Charleston being the one exception), and Douglas carried Lincoln's speech in a little notebook along to the debates and other stump speeches to cite freely from it in order to unveil Lincoln's supposed abolitionist extremism. On the other hand, Lincoln also had with him his "House divided" speech, parts of the Declaration of Independence, segments of Henry Clay's speeches, and various clippings from newspapers pasted into a little leather book for the debates.[44] Douglas twisted Lincoln's views to such a degree that he also argued that they were contrary to the views of the Founding Fathers, i.e., against keeping slavery at least in those states where it had traditionally existed. David Zarefsky has summed up Douglas's plan of attack in the following manner: "Douglas's strategy, then, was to draw on the filiopiety of the age in suggesting that the 'House Divided' speech put Lincoln at odds with the revered Fathers, further proving that the challenger was a dangerous radical who could not be trusted with a seat in the U.S. Senate."[45]

Douglas knew he had Lincoln on the defensive, and right from his opening remarks during the first debate on August 21, 1858, in Ottawa, he branded Lincoln as an abolitionist ready to go to war to end slavery:

> In his speech at Springfield to the convention which nominated him for Senate, he [Lincoln] said:
>> In my opinion it will not cease until a crisis shall have been reached and passed. "A house divided against itself cannot stand." I believe this Government *cannot endure permanently half Slave and Half free.* I do not expect the Union to be dissolved—I do not expect the house to fall—*but I do expect it will cease to be divided.* [...]
>> Why can it not exist divided into free and slave States? Washington, Jefferson, Franklin, Madison, Hamilton, Jay, and the great men of that

day, made this Government divided into free States and slave States, and left each State perfectly free to do as it pleased on the subject of slavery. Why can it not exist on the same principles on which our fathers made it? ("It can.") They knew when they framed the Constitution that in a country as wide and broad as this, with such a variety of climate, production and interest, the people necessarily required different laws and institutions in different localities. [...] One of the reserved rights of the States, was the right to regulate the relations between Master and Servant, on the slavery question. At the time the Constitution was formed, there were thirteen States in the Union, twelve of which were slaveholding States and one a free State. Suppose this doctrine of uniformity preached by Mr. Lincoln, that the States should all be free or all be slave had prevailed and what would have been the result? Of course, the twelve slaveholding States would have overruled the one free State, and slavery would have been fastened by a Constitutional provision on every inch of the American Republic, instead of being left as our fathers wisely left it, to each State to decide for itself.[46]

That is strong and powerful rhetoric and medicine. It is, of course, an argument for popular sovereignty with respect to slavery, something Lincoln vehemently opposed. Douglas presented logical and clear arguments, and the difficulty was that Lincoln had to agree with some of them. This made his position in the response especially difficult. And what is missing from both contestants is, of course, any discussion whatsoever on moral grounds. The whole argument is more one between popular sovereignty versus national policy regarding slavery. These arguments seem like hairsplitting to modern readers, but they were the hot issues of the day and the beginning at least of questioning slavery as such. In his response to Douglas, Lincoln starts with a discussion of his "House divided" proverb, and he even refers to a "moral constitution of men's minds." But there is no moral commitment to the extinction to slavery yet. There is only the hope of final extinction if it remains confined to the present slave States. But here is part of Lincoln's response, starting with a bit of humor at Douglas's expense:

He [Douglas] has read from my speech in Springfield, in which I say that "a house divided against itself cannot stand." Does the Judge say it *can* stand? [Laughter.] I don't know whether he does or not. [...] I would like to know if it is his opinion that a house divided against itself *can stand.* If he does, then there is a question of veracity, not between him and me, but between the Judge and an authority of a somewhat higher character.

[...] When he undertakes to say that because I think this nation, so far as the question of Slavery is concerned, will all become one thing or all the other, I am in favor of bringing about a dead uniformity in the various States, in all their institutions, he argues erroneously. The great variety of the local institutions in the States, springing from differences in the soil, differences in the face of the country, and in the climate, are bonds of the Union. They do not make "a house divided against itself," but they make a house united. If they produce in one section of the country what is called for by the wants of another section, and this other section can supply the wants of the first, they are not matters of discord but bonds of union, true bonds of union. But can this question of slavery be considered as among *these* varieties in the institutions of the country? I leave it to you to say whether, in the history of our government, this institution of slavery has not always failed to be a bond of union, and, on the contrary, been an apple of discord and an element of division in the house. [...] lately, I think, that he [Douglas], and those acting with him, have placed that institution on a new basis, which looks to the *perpetuity and nationalization of slavery.* [Loud cheers.] And while it is placed upon this new basis, I say, and I have said, that I believe we shall not have peace upon the question until the opponents of slavery arrest the further spread of it, and place it where the public mind shall rest in the belief that it is in the course of ultimate extinction [...][47]

Great oratory indeed! But it must have been difficult then, and it is so today, to understand how this "ultimate extinction" of slavery was to come about. Did people think that all black people would die out naturally during the next hundred years? What becomes clear from these two long quotations is that neither Douglas nor Lincoln was yet discussing the real issues, namely the immorality of slavery and the liberation of the slaves. The time for the Emancipation Proclamation had not yet come! After so much discussion of the biblical proverb "A house divided against itself cannot stand," it was appropriate for Douglas not to mention it again in his half-hour rejoinder at the end of the first debate. Even though some of the water is murky between the two candidates, their basic positions on slavery has become clear: Douglas argues for popular sovereignty, and Lincoln claims that slavery is a national problem.

By the time of the sixth debate on October 13, 1858, in Quincy, Douglas is on a roll with ever new twists to this proverb. Lincoln had not used it in his opening speech, but Douglas employed it mercilessly in his hour-and-a-half-long response, this time making sure that people would look at Lincoln and his party as abolitionists. He even goes so far as to paint Lincoln as a possible exterminator of the slaves:

Mr. Lincoln told his Abolition friends that this government could not endure permanently, divided into free and slave States as our fathers made it, and that it must become all free or all slave, otherwise, that the government could not exist. How then does Lincoln propose to save the Union, unless by compelling all the States to become free, so that the house shall not be divided against itself? he intends making them all free; he will preserve the Union in that way, and yet, he is not going to interfere with slavery anywhere it now exists. How is he going to bring it about? [...] He will hem them [the slaves] in until starvation seizes them, and by starving them to death, he will put slavery in the course of ultimate extinction. If he is not going to interfere with slavery in the States, but intends to interfere and prohibit it in the territories, and thus smother slavery out, it naturally follows, that he can extinguish it only by extinguishing the negro race, for his policy would drive them to starvation. This is the humane and Christian remedy that he proposes for the great crime of slavery.[48]

This is a vicious and slanderous and above all false statement, and Douglas knew it! Nevertheless, he made it and thus can stake the claim of having lowered the spirit of the debate to what is today referred to as a mud-slinging campaign. Lincoln responded somewhat indirectly to this nasty outbreak with some humorous relief and then got in a harmless yet effective slam himself:

I wish to return Judge Douglas my profound thanks for his public annunciation here today, to be put on record, that his system of policy in regard to the institution of slavery *contemplates that it shall last forever.* We are getting a little nearer the true issue of this controversy, and I am profoundly grateful for this one sentence. [...] When Judge Douglas undertakes to say that as a matter of choice the fathers of the government made this nation part slave and part free, *he assumes what is historically a falsehood.* More than that; when the fathers of the government cut off the source of slavery by the abolition of the slave trade, and adopted a system of restricting it from the new Territories where it had not existed, I maintain that they placed it where they understood, and all sensible men understood, it was in the course of ultimate extinction; and when Judge Douglas asks me why it cannot continue as our fathers made it, I ask him why he and his friends could not let it remain as our fathers made it?[49]

This time the damage was to Douglas, but do notice how generously and politely, albeit with a bit of irony, Lincoln develops his rhetorical blows.

He takes the high road, and in due time people recognized it, just as he came to realize that all this talk needed real action, namely the eventual Emancipation Proclamation of January 1, 1863.

Lincoln used the proverb three more times in speeches during September of 1859 in the context of referring to his "House divided" speech.[50] On December 7, 1860, he even went so far as to prepare a transcript in pencil of the "House divided" section of his 1858 speech for Edward B. Pease, a hardware dealer from Springfield. Surely this citizen must have asked Lincoln for this favor.[51] As president during the Civil War Lincoln interestingly enough used the proverb but once in his published works. In a letter to Major General Nathaniel P. Banks of November 5, 1863, Lincoln expresses certain worries about what type of state government would be established in Louisiana:

> If a few professedly loyal men shall draw the disloyal about them, and colorably set up a State government, repudiating the emancipation proclamation, and reestablishing slavery, I can not recognize or sustain their work. I should fall powerless in the attempt. This government, in such an attitude, would be a house divided against itself.[52]

The fear of even the slightest chance of reintroducing slavery reminded him of his old biblical proverb which he seemingly had put aside once the Civil War had started. Understandably so, for the proverb "A house divided against itself cannot stand" had proven to be true as far as Lincoln was concerned. The Civil War was proof of the wisdom of this biblical proverb. The house had really fallen, and the future of the Union now depended on the outcome of the war.

Post-Lincoln Use of the Proverb

In the fourth quarter of the nineteenth century, the phrase "The house divided against itself cannot stand" became canonized in quotation dictionaries as belonging to Lincoln in some way or another, while it is cited in proverb dictionaries as a folk proverb without any reference to the Bible or Lincoln. As cultural literacy continues to decline, the proverb will more and more push aside its connection to the Bible and Lincoln. This liberation of the proverb "The house divided against itself cannot stand" from its biblical origin and its significant association with Abraham Lincoln is ever more noticeable today. Introductory formulas specifically referring to the Bible or Lincoln are falling by the wayside, except in such cases where books or articles deal either with religious subjects or Lincoln and the Civil

War. But usually the proverb is cited without any such hints, and it stands on its own feet just like any other folk proverb for which the origin is lost in obscurity. For some people the proverb will always be connected with the Bible and Abraham Lincoln, and to others it will simply be one of those hundreds of anonymous little pieces of wisdom that float around and find their use whenever the shoe fits.

Obviously Lincoln's name was very much attached to the proverb during the Civil War and immediately after his death. Thus it will not be surprising that the young minister Phillips Brooks cited the proverb in his sermon on "The Character, Life, and Death of Abraham Lincoln" which he delivered on April 23, 1865, while Lincoln's body lay in state at Independence Hall in Philadelphia:

> The President came to his power full of the blood, strong in the strength of Freedom. He came there free, and hating slavery. He came there, leaving on record words like these spoken three years before and never contradicted. He had said, "A house divided against itself cannot stand. I believe this Government cannot endure permanently, half slave and half free. I do not expect the Union to be dissolved; I do not expect the house to fall; but I expect it will cease to be divided. It will become all one thing or all the other." When the question came, he knew which thing he meant that it should be. His whole nature settled that question for him.[53]

It is interesting to note that the pastor does not place the proverb into quotation marks as Lincoln had done. Nor does he refer to the Bible at all, something that Lincoln and Douglas both had done on occasion in their use of the proverb during the debates. Phillips Brooks is thus already this early in the development of the biblical proverb after Lincoln making it an expression that was coined by the President.

About a month later, on June 1, 1865, the Reverend Richard Fuller delivered a sermon with the interesting title "A City or House Divided Against Itself." As if to explain the title, he added the biblical proverb "And every city or house divided against itself, shall not stand—Matt. xii:25."[54] Reverend Fuller did well in quoting the proverb from the Gospel of Matthew instead of Mark or Luke in his sermon on the need for positive reconstruction after the Civil War. While Mark and Luke, and thus also Lincoln, use only the house image, Matthew speaks of "every city or house divided against itself," thus alluding to the fact that as the Union is healing from the wounds of the war, individual houses as well as entire cities must be rebuilt. He mentions Lincoln only in passing, whose "blood, shed by the hand of an assassin, fell upon the altar which he was building to generosity, to liberty, to conciliation."[55] Almost becoming the voice of Lincoln, Fuller closes his plea for reconciliation between the South and the North as follows:

> Let all who truly love the Union now bury dissensions in oblivion. Recollect that schemes for the dissolution of that Union have been cherished and may again be cherished in other quarters besides the South. [...] Let us go home resolving to cherish in our own hearts, and to shed around us, in the church, in our families, in the community, the gentle spirit of peace and love.[56]

Interestingly enough, however, there is no reference to Lincoln's use of the "House divided" proverb in this sermon. Did Reverend Fuller simply feel that his audience would make that connection all by itself, or did he think that by stressing the variant from Matthew, he really wanted to make a different point, thus leaving Lincoln's repeated use of the proverb unmentioned?

But around the turn of the century, literary references to the proverb generally ignore both the Bible and Lincoln connection. The following excerpt out of William Cowper Brann's collection of essays entitled *Brann, the Iconoclast* (1898) makes this quite clear, even though it deals with church matters:

> "I have suffered and sacrificed much for this people," he said at length, as though speaking to himself, "and it has borne so little fruit. The world misunderstood me. The church planted by toil and nurtured with my blood has split up into hundreds of warring factions, despite my warning that a house divided against itself cannot stand.[57]

In this quotation, at least, the entire proverb is still cited. But in the following excerpt from Booth Tarkington's *The Conquest of Canaan* (1905) the proverb has been reduced to a mere allusion, giving readers not much of a chance to make any connections with the Bible or Lincoln: "On this, the house divided, one party maintaining that Joe had thus endeavored to evade recognition, the other that the reply was a distinct admission of identity and at the same time a refusal to grant any favors on the score of past acquaintanceship."[58]

When Carl Sandburg used the proverb in a wording quite close to the original in his epic poem *The People, Yes* (1936), he probably had Lincoln's use of it in mind. After all, Sandburg had already written the first part of his celebrated biography *Abraham Lincoln: The Prairie Years* (2 vols., 1926) and was working on the second part with the title *Abraham Lincoln: The War Years* (4 vols., 1939). In his long poem Sandburg deals with a more modern divided house in America, one that is not so much politically motivated as economically:

> Said the scorpion of hate: 'The poor hate the rich. The rich hate the poor. The south hates the north. The west hates the east. The workers hate their bosses. The bosses hate their workers. The country hates the towns. The towns hate the country. We are a house divided against itself. We are millions of hands raised against each other. We are united in but one aim—getting the dollar. And when we get the dollar we employ it to get more dollars.'[59]

In B. English's detective novel *War* (1971) appears a version with the noun "city" that is reminiscent of the proverb as cited in Matthew 12:25. Of special interest is, of course, that the author refers specifically to the fact that he is citing a proverb, and most likely one from folk tradition and not from the Bible or Lincoln: "The city was a divided one, and very often, true to the proverb, it did not stand."[60] This is quite an appropriate statement for a novel dealing with war and its destruction of cities.

Generally speaking, modern authors have no particular interest in connecting the proverb with Lincoln or the Bible for that matter, unless they write about those subjects. The proverb, originally rooted in the New Testament and then attached to Lincoln, has definitely undergone a liberation process. It is evermore becoming a folk proverb free of any particular associations and ready to serve as a strategic communicative device when called upon. And, more often than not, it is simply cited as the "House divided" remnant.

In fact, a computer search for such titles on the Online Computer Library Center (OCLC) database yielded 373 titles in January of 1998. There were some duplications of individual titles, and such nondescript allusions as *(A) House Divided* or *(A) Divided House* appear again and again. At times books with these titles do not have subtitles, and one wonders how prospective readers are to know what divisive issues are possibly dealt with in these publications. It would be absurd to cite almost 400 titles at this point, but representative titles of books covering various subject areas will illustrate the incredible versatility of the titular manipulation of the proverb.

On the purely literary scene, H. B. Marriott Watson published a novel entitled *The House Divided* (1901) taking place in the 18th century, followed by Pearl S. Buck's Chinese novel *A House Divided* (1935). But then followed a third novel of epic proportions by Ben Ames Williams. He gave his work of 1514 pages the short title *House-Divided* (1947), and this time the title does in fact reflect its content by indirectly referring to the sociopolitical strife in the United States before and during the Civil War. But there are also four plays with titles alluding to the proverb without an indication what divisive problem is brought to the stage in them: A. W. Futter, *Divided House* (1950), P. Joynson-Wreford, *A House Divided* (1981), W. Stuart McDowell, *A House Divided,* and Stephen Barber, *A House Divided* (1992). There are more books with this basic title where it is impossible to know from a computer search whether they are novels, plays, or whatever. The only thing that this type of title accomplishes is to suggest that some kind of problem is being dealt with that has brought about a separation of sorts.

The proverbial remnant "A House divided" has become a household term to be used whenever any schism is being discussed. Often it is doubtful whether Lincoln was on the minds of the authors. However, that is doubtless the case in the following titles that employ parts of the proverb and actually also mention Lincoln as well. Here the authors are very well aware of the fact that Lincoln used the proverb and that an allusion to it will immediately call to mind the strife between the North and the South:

- McMaster, John Bach. *Our House Divided: A History of the People of the United States During Lincoln's Administration.* Greenwich, Connecticut: Fawcett Publications, 1961 (the first edition of 1883 did *not* have the proverbial title).
- Forgie, George B. *Patricide in the House Divided: A Psychological Interpretation of Lincoln and His Age.* New York: Norton, 1979.
- Foner, Eric, and Olivia Mahoney. *A House Divided: America in the Age of Lincoln.* Chicago: Chicago Historical Society, 1990.

It is also quite natural that scholars writing about the Civil War will draw on the proverb, associated with Lincoln as it was, to create somewhat catchy titles. Some of them tend to get close to verbatim repetition, and authors of the future would do well to run a computer check on titles to avoid unnecessary repetition. There is always still a possibility to find an innovative subtitle:

- Sewell, Richard H. *A House Divided: Sectionalism and Civil War, 1848–1865.* Baltimore, Maryland: Johns Hopkins University Press, 1988.
- Linden, Glenn M., and Thomas J. Pressly (eds.). *Voices from the House Divided: The United States Civil War as Personal Experience.* New York: McGraw-Hill, 1995.

• Dolan, Edward F. *The American Civil War: A House Divided.* Brookfield, Connecticut: Millbrook Press, 1997.

It is interesting to note from this list that now authors are beginning to cite the informative title first, using the "House divided" statement as an all-encompassing subtitle.

A few final examples of titles deal with social and racial problems in the United States. The metaphorical proverb remnant "A House divided" fits perfectly to illustrate the divisive nature of these issues. One could, of course, ask whether the day will come that authors will be able to change the pessimistic image into one of positive change and hope:

• Lokos, Lionel. *House Divided: The Life and Legacy of Martin Luther King.* New Rochelle, New York: Arlington House, 1968.
• Melady, Thomas Patrick. *House Divided: Poverty, Race, Religion, and the Family of Man.* New York: Sheed & Ward, 1969.
• Newsome, Yvonne D. *A House Divided: Conflict and Cooperation in African American-Jewish Relations.* Diss. Northwestern University, 1991.

Especially studies that deal with racial issues in America will probably have once again used the "House divided" proverb allusion with thoughts of Lincoln and his fight against slavery in mind.

One last reference merits mentioning since it is, in a way, a liberation from the original proverb. On June 25, 1997, a short legal report on a case involving a telephone pole as taxable property appeared on the Internet with the headline "N.H. Supreme Court: A Pole Divided May Stand." The first paragraph helps to understand this absurd title: "A single pole carrying telephone, cable and power lines can be taxable property for one company but not for others, the New Hampshire Supreme Court said in an advisory opinion to legislators."[61] But no matter how far fetched this variation might be, the basic structure of the proverb "A house divided against itself cannot stand" is easily discernible. Whoever dreamt up this innovative rephrasing of an old proverb certainly must have enjoyed the wordplay tremendously. This title is also one more indication of what is still to come.

GERMANY: A HOUSE DIVIDED NO LONGER

It has been argued that, especially in its shortened form of "A House divided," the biblical proverb that became attached to Lincoln's name in the middle of the nineteenth century is barely reminiscent, if at all, of Jesus' wisdom or that of Lincoln. The original proverb is, in fact, not cited very often anymore today. In a world where things are communicated by sound bytes it is only the short cliché without the deeper meaning which gets plucked into verbal communication. But there is one major exception to all of this, and that is the role which the proverb "A house divided against itself cannot stand" was to play during the reunification of Germany.

It must be noted at the beginning of a short account of this intriguing story that this biblical proverb did not become very current in Germany. None of the major German quotation dictionaries include the Bible reference, and with one exception they don't include any well-known quotations from Abraham Lincoln either.[62] Carl Schulze's specialized collection of German biblical proverbs entitled *Die biblischen Sprichwörter der deutschen Sprache* (1860) does list "Ein jeglich Reich, so es mit ihm selbst uneins wird, das wird wüste" (Every kingdom divided against itself is brought to desolation; Matthew 12:25), but it does not add the next verse that contains the "House divided" proverb.[63] Karl Friedrich Wilhelm Wander's massive *Deutsches Sprichwörter-Lexikon* (1867–1880) also includes only this one text from the Bible in a slightly different wording "Wenn ein Reich mit jhm selber vneins wird, so kan es nicht bestehen (Matth. 12,25; also Mark 3:24)" (If a kingdom is divided against itself it cannot stand).[64] What this means is that neither the "kingdom" nor the "house" proverb from the synoptic gospels has become truly proverbial in German. This is quite different from the popularity of these two proverbs in the Anglo-American language, and it shows that there is a considerable difference between the biblical proverbs from one language to another.[65]

A German version of the "House divided" proverb may, however, still gain some currency in Germany, and if that were to become the case, the credit most assuredly should go to Willy Brandt, former mayor of West Berlin (1957–1966) and chancellor of the Federal Republic of Germany (1969–1974). The reason for such a possible spread of this biblical proverb in Germany goes back to the year 1959 when Brandt, then mayor of West Berlin, was invited by the city of Springfield, Illinois, to give a lecture at the sesquicentennial celebration of Abraham Lincoln's birthday on April 12th. It is not known, of course, whether Brandt wrote his address himself, but he certainly was fluent in English, and he was able to address dignitaries and normal citizens alike on that day in perfect English. Whoever prepared this speech knew a considerable amount about the legacy of Abraham Lincoln. Among a number of quotations from Lincoln's famous speeches cited by Brandt was also the "House divided" proverb. In light of the fact that Brandt came from a divided city and country, this was the perfect metaphor for him to speak about at this memorable event:

> Abraham Lincoln spoke of the duty of the whole people to never entrust to any hands but their own the preservation of their liberties, a duty which, after bitter experience, the great majority of the German people also acknowledge.
>
> He spoke of the eternal struggle between democracy and tyranny. We know that this struggle has torn apart the European continent and that it has assumed world-wide dimensions. He quoted the passage from the Bible about the house divided against itself, and expressed his conviction that this government cannot endure permanently half slave and half free.
>
> The truths which Lincoln spoke here in Springfield in June, 1858, are perhaps even more applicable to the present situation of the German people than to the one which he faced: that is, to the arbitrary disruption of their lives, for which, of course, they are not without guilt themselves.[66]

A German version of this speech appeared with the fitting title "Amerikanische und deutsche Einheit" (American and German Unity) in a journal in Germany, indicating explicitly that Brandt's speech dealt with the idea of a "union" just as Lincoln's speech had done almost exactly one hundred years earlier. The center paragraph just cited in English was translated from the following German text:

> Er sprach von dem ewigen Kampf zwischen Demokratie und Tyrannei. Wir wissen, daß diese Auseinandersetzung den europäischen Kontinent zerrissen und daß sie weltweite Formen angenommen hat. Er stützte sich auf das Wort vom geteilten Haus, das keinen Bestand hat, und gab seiner Überzeugung Ausdruck, daß ein Staat nicht auf die Dauer mit einer versklavten und einer freien Hälfte bestehen kann.[67]

Obviously the contextualized use of the proverb in the nontraditional wording of "das Wort vom geteilten Haus, das keinen Bestand hat" (translated as: "the passage from the Bible about the house divided against itself") could not be of any influence in spreading the biblical proverb or Lincoln's quotation of it in the German language. German readers of the speech were not even made aware of the fact that Lincoln was quoting the Bible. Whoever translated this speech must have been solidly steeped in cultural literacy. It seems that this speech was written by a German who had studied American history and politics and who was literally translating this particular passage from the English when creating the German text for Willy Brandt. In that case the word "Wort" could in a way stand for "passage from the Bible." But again, it would have been the rarest German reader who would have made the connection to the Bible.

But be that as it may, Willy Brandt did not forget the proverbial metaphor in his subsequent political career, which saw him rise to the position of chancellor and European politician. As a person dedicated to the idea of unifying Germany, Brandt used the proverb "A house divided against itself cannot stand" as a fitting *leitmotif* that gave figurative expression to the desire for reunification. Just as Lincoln most likely used the biblical proverb frequently in oral communication, Brandt probably did the same in his many political discussions. Fortunately some of these have been recorded, notably an interview which political journalists of the German news magazine *Der Spiegel* conducted on August 28, 1978. In fact, in the following quotation Brandt states explicitly that he quoted Lincoln *frequently* when he argued for German unity abroad. In such discussions Brandt would have been speaking in English most of the time, and he could count on the fact that his audience would know either the biblical proverb or Lincoln's use of it or both:

> Ich habe über viele Jahre hinweg im Ausland um Verständnis gebeten, daß wir auf die Dauer nicht als ein wegen der Nazi-Zeit innerlich gespaltenes Volk leben könnten. Ich habe mich häufig auf einen Satz von Lincoln, der auch nicht von ihm kommt, sondern den er wieder aus der Bibel hat—was ja auch keine Schande ist—, bezogen, daß ein in sich gespaltenes Haus keinen Bestand haben kann.[68]
>
> (For many years I have asked for understanding abroad that we [Germans] cannot live forever as an internally divided people because of the Nazi era. I have often referred to a sentence by Lincoln which does not stem from him but which he in turn got from the Bible—a fact that is nothing to be ashamed of—that a house divided against itself cannot stand.)

Brandt specifically tells the journalists and thus their German readers that the proverb which he is citing from Lincoln does in fact have a biblical origin. This obviously is of considerable importance for the possible dissemination of the proverb/quotation as a loan translation in Germany.

A dozen years later during the tumultuous and truly exciting time of German reunification in 1990, Brandt not surprisingly remembered his previous fascination with this proverb which so aptly fit the German political situation for several decades. In an address on January 31, 1990, in Tutzing with the title "Die Sache ist gelaufen" (The Matter [Reunification] Has Run Its Course), Brandt made the following extremely important statement at the end of his remarks. First of all he declares that he has made the "House divided" proverb the closing *leitmotif* in all of the speeches that he delivered throughout the recently liberated former East Germany. Then he cites the proverb in German together with the English version and its association with Lincoln. He does not mention the Bible though, thus spreading the new German loan proverb primarily as one originating with Lincoln:

> Meine Kundgebungen in der DDR schließe ich nicht von ungefähr mit den schönen Lincoln-Worten, daß ein in sich gespaltenes Haus nicht Bestand hat. "A house divided against itself cannot stand." Das gilt für die gespaltene deutsche Nation; über die aktuellen Aufregungen hinaus auch für die Zukunft der DDR, die wieder zusammenfinden muß und nicht in Haß und Rache untergehen darf.[69]
>
> (I don't close my speeches in the GDR for nothing with the beautiful words by Lincoln that a house divided against itself cannot stand. "A house divided against itself cannot stand." That is true for the German nation; beyond the present-day excitement also for the future of the GDR which must find its way to reunion and which must not vanish in hate and revenge.)

By citing both the German translation and the English original in his speeches, Brandt was not only trying to indicate the linguistic dependence of the German version. He knew very well that many if not most Germans could perfectly well understand the English text quoted from Lincoln. If the proverb has in fact gained some currency in Germany today, it is most likely cited either in German or preferably in English. The incredible influence of the Anglo-American language has, as is well known, brought a flood of English words and phrases into the German language.[70]

If the proverb were ever to become current in the German language, it would be in the wording "Ein in sich gespaltenes Haus hat keinen Bestand." The German biblical versions of "Eine jegliche Stadt oder Haus, so es mit sich selbst uneins wird, kann's nicht bestehen" (Matthew 12:25) and "Wenn ein Haus mit sich selbst uneins wird, kann es nicht bestehen" (Mark 3:25)[71] have not attained proverbial status in hundreds of years and they will not do so considering the diminishing role that religion plays in German society. If this useful and historically rich proverb ever were to become current in German or English in Germany, then the credit would definitely have to go to Willy Brandt who used it frequently as a metaphor to argue for German reunification and subsequently as a warning to keep the newly established union intact. There is no doubt that Brandt admired Lincoln, and Lincoln in turn would have had equal respect for Brandt. Two great minds and politicians who used the same proverb to keep their people together!

The use of the "House divided" proverb in connection with Germany has been picked up in more recent publications, illustrating that it is in fact a fitting metaphor for the German situation. Stephen J. Silvia entitled a scholarly pamphlet on collective bargaining in the reunited Germany by employing the long established formulaic remnant of the proverb: *A House Divided: Employers and the Challenge to Pattern Bargaining in a United Germany* (1995).[72] And during the writing of this chapter an English translation of Hans-Dietrich Genscher's autobiography *Erinnerungen* (Memoirs) appeared. As Germany's longest serving Foreign Minister (1974–1989), Genscher had played an important role in moving Germany step by step towards reunification and also in bringing the Cold War to an end. When the marketing strategists at Broadway Books in New York planned an appropriate title for the American edition of Genscher's memoirs, the following title must have come to them almost naturally: *Rebuilding A House Divided: A Memoir by the Architect of Germany's Reunification* (1998).

From everything that has been said and presented in this chapter, it comes almost as a surprise that the title *Rebuilding A House Divided* has not been used before. It would have been most fitting for the many studies that have treated the period of reconstruction that followed the Civil War. Perhaps Abraham Lincoln used it orally before his tragic death as he began to concentrate on the rebuilding of the Union. The same might be true for Willy Brandt before his death as he struggled to reconstruct Germany after its division had ceased. But there is no need for speculation at the end of this study of the proverb "A house divided against itself cannot stand." There is no doubt that it expresses in a metaphorical fashion and thus by means of the "art of indirection"[73] a fundamental truth about sociopolitical reality and human behavior confronting it. Its message since the Bible and through the age of Abraham Lincoln on to the modern age rings loud and clear for all to hear: "A house divided against itself cannot stand."

5

"Do Unto Others as You Would Have Them Do Unto You"
Frederick Douglass's Proverbial Struggle for Civil Rights

There is no doubt that Frederick Douglass (1818–1895) was the most visible and influential African American of the nineteenth century. Together with Abraham Lincoln, he belongs to a select group of truly outstanding public figures of that age. Son of a slave and an unidentified white man, Douglass escaped from slavery in 1838 after secretly having taught himself how to read and write. Lacking any formal education whatsoever, he nevertheless quickly became a driving force in the antislavery movement, impressing abolitionist audiences with his oratorical eloquence and imposing presence. He subsequently gained considerable fame both in the United States and in Great Britain as a vocal abolitionist, civil rights activist, and publisher of social reform journals. Nothing it seems could stop this vigorous crusader from fighting for a better world where people of both genders and all races could live together in harmony. His autobiography *Narrative of the Life of Frederick Douglass, Written by Himself* (1845; expanded twice in 1855 and 1893) became a classic in his lifetime, and the two sets of five massive volumes of *The Life and Writings of Frederick Douglass* (1950–1975), ed. by Philip S. Foner, and *The Frederick Douglass Papers* (1985–1992), ed. by John Blassingame, bear witness to his rhetorical skills and moral courage.

Frederick Douglass became the collective voice of the three to four million enslaved African Americans, a number that grew to about eight million by the end of his long activist life. He assumed their narrative identity, and when he spoke or wrote, his words were based on the authority of the Bible and the democratic ideals of the United States. He fought his valiant battle against slavery not with the gun but with words before and during the Civil War and until the passing in 1865 of the Thirteenth Amendment outlawing slavery and in 1870 of the Fourteenth Amendment giving African Americans the right to vote. But even after these victories he continued to raise his powerful voice for the causes of women's rights, various minorities, temperance, free public education, and other social causes. He was a social and political agitator in the best sense of that word, always arguing for the strength of morality, equality, and democracy.

His rhetorical prowess is legendary, but scholars have hitherto ignored one major element of that oratorical power, namely his repeated use of biblical and folk proverbs to add authoritative and generational wisdom to his arguments. For example, in the following list of rhetorical devices and techniques employed by Douglass a direct reference to proverbs is sorely missed: "hypothesis, explanation, illustration, personal example, irony, definition, refutation, exposé, testimony from authority, personification, comparison-contrast, narrative, dramatic scenarios, naming names, denunciation, the rhetorical question, *catachresis, accumulation, anaphora, reductio ad absurdum,* antithesis, apostrophe, the pointed term, metaphor, analogy, visual aids [advertisements, wanted posters, books, ankle irons], slogans, invectives, the rhetorical jeremiad, and biblical and classical allusions."[1] Three unpublished theses dealing explicitly with Douglass's language and style also ignore his propensity for citing proverbs. They speak rather generally of his use of "figurative language, illustration, and analogy,"[2] "literal and figurative analogies,"[3] and "figures of comparison and contrast such as analogy, metaphor, and antithesis."[4] Even when on occasion a proverb might be cited to illustrate the metaphorical style of Douglass, both literary and historical scholars seem to miss the obvious fact that the great orator is very consciously integrating proverbs into his oral speech and autobiographical, epistolary, and journalistic writings. William G. Allen, in a lecture on "Orators and Orations" delivered on June 22, 1852 in New York, quite appropriately spoke of "Douglass [who] is not only great in oratory, tongue-wise, but, considering his circumstances in early life, still more marvelous in composition, pen-wise."[5] Surely Allen is not merely speaking of "wise" in the sense of "like" here but is also implying wisdom as well. And clearly he is proverb-wise as well, using proverbial wisdom wherever possible to advance his committed fight for justice and liberty.

In a lecture appropriately titled "The Decision of the Hour," delivered on June 16, 1861, at Rochester, New York, Douglass has perhaps unwittingly put forth his sociolinguistic *modus operandi:*

> Men have their choice in this world. They can be angels, or they can be demons. In the apocalyptic vision, John describes a war in heaven [Rev. 12:7–9]. You have only to strip that vision of its gorgeous Oriental drapery, divest it of its shining and celestial ornaments, clothe it in the simple and familiar language of common sense, and you will have before you the eternal conflict between right and wrong, good and evil, liberty

and slavery, truth and falsehood, the glorious light of love, and the appalling darkness of human selfishness and sin. (3,119; III,437)[6]

At least to a degree, this "simple and familiar language of common sense" is what characterizes proverbs. As "monumenta humana,"[7] as the Finnish proverb scholar Matti Kuusi has defined proverbs somewhat poetically, they contain the collected insights and experiences of people without representing a logical or universal system of philosophical thought. Instead, proverbs very much reflect the dichotomies and contradictions of life, as Douglass has described them in the cited passage.[8] Depending on the context in which they appear, they can take on different functions and meanings, and they may serve good as well as evil designs.[9] Contrary to common belief, proverbs are anything but simple formulaic expressions, and Frederick Douglass's use of them is ample proof of their importance as verbal strategies for social communication.[10]

"If You Give a Nigger an Inch, He Will Take an Ell"

Frederick Douglass is well aware of the ambivalent nature of proverbs whose wisdom can well be a two-edged sword. This becomes quite evident in his depiction of how slaveholders employ evil proverbs to justify the inhuman institution of slavery. A striking example is found in the very first paragraph of Douglass's earliest recorded speech of October 1841 addressing white abolitionists in Lynn, Massachusetts:

> My friends, I have come to tell you something about slavery—what I
> *know* of it, as I have *felt* it. [...] I have suffered under the lash without the
> power of resisting. Yes, my blood has sprung out as the lash embedded
> itself in my flesh. And yet my master [Thomas Auld] has the reputation
> of being a pious man and a good Christian. He was a class leader in the
> Methodist church. I have seen the pious class leader cross and tie the
> hands of one of his young female slaves, and lash her on the bare skin
> and justify the deed by the quotation from the Bible, "he who knoweth
> his master's will and doeth it not, shall be beaten with many stripes."
> Our masters do not hesitate to prove from the Bible that slavery is right,
> and ministers of the Gospel tell us that we were born to be slaves. (I,3)

The vicious proverbial justification of slave beating is a willful misinterpretation of a biblical passage where the "Master" (Luke 12:13), Christ, tells his followers, referred to as servants, that they should prepare themselves and wait for their lord:

But and if that servant say in his heart, My lord delayeth his coming; and shall begin to beat the menservants and maidens ... [t]he Lord of that servant will come in a day when he looketh not for him, and at an hour when he is not aware, and will cut him in sunder, and will appoint him his portion with the unbelievers. And that servant, which knew his lord's will, and prepared not himself, neither did according to his will, shall be beaten with many stripes. (Luke 12:46–47).

The context makes it clear that the slaveholder is in fact the faithless servant who beats his own people and who as a consequence will be beaten for failing to follow the Lord's commands. But that did not matter to the shrewd and mischievous class of slaveholders. They simply twisted part of the biblical parable into a precise utterance. Its frequent verbal use and its actual physical and painful performance rendered it into a slaveholders' proverb that served as a sagacious formula to control the slaves.

Douglass quotes this slavery justification proverb numerous times in his speeches of the 1840s, and he certainly recalled it when writing his widely disseminated *Narrative of the Life of Frederick Douglass, Written by Himself* (1845):

I have said my master found religious sanction for his cruelty. As an example, I will state one of many facts going to prove this charge. I have seen him tie up a lame young woman, and whip her with a heavy cowskin upon her naked shoulders, causing the warm red blood to drip; and, in justification of the bloody deed, he would quote this passage of Scripture—"He that knoweth his master's will, and doeth it not, shall be beaten with many stripes." Master would keep this lacerated young woman tied up in this horrid situation four or five hours at a time. I have known him to tie her up early in the morning, and whip her before breakfast; leave her, go to his store, return at dinner, and whip her again, cutting her in the places already made raw with his cruel lash. (N,53)[11]

This is a slightly more drastic rendering of the terrible scene with its emphasis on the running blood. It is, of course, hard to comprehend how a religious person, as Douglass's master Hugh Auld claimed to be, would think he could justify his inhuman acts by misquoting the Bible. Worse demagogues, notably Adolf Hitler, have done the same with biblical quotations and proverbs trying to justify the killing of millions of people.[12]

Of special interest is also a hitherto unrecorded proverb which expresses the disregard for the life of a slave as well as his murdered body: "It was a common saying, even among little white boys, that it was worth a half-cent to kill a 'nigger,' and a half-cent to bury one" (N,32). In his second autobiography *My Bondage and My Freedom* (1855), Douglass explains this inhuman attitude further and calls it clearly a proverb, thus attesting to its widely held claim: "One of the commonest sayings to which my ears early became accustomed, on Col. Lloyd's plantation and elsewhere in Maryland, was, that it was *'worth but half a cent to kill a nigger, and half a cent to bury him;'* and the facts of my experience go far to justify the practical truth of this strange proverb" (B,204; L,516–517). In a short essay of August 1863 in his journal *Douglass' Monthly,* he returns once again to this telling proverb, recalling its sick validity: "When a boy, on a slave plantation the saying was common: 'Half a cent to kill a Negro and half a cent to bury him.'—The luxury of killing and burying could be enjoyed by the poorest members of Southern society, and no strong temptation was required to induce white men thus to kill and bury the black victims of their lust and cruelty" (3,369).

There were, of course, many slaves who survived such pecuniary killings, but in that case the slaveholders tried to kill the minds of their "chattels." But such mind control did not always work, for naturally intelligent slaves outwitted their masters, as Douglass explains through a fascinating contextualization of a well-known proverb: "Ignorance is a high virtue in a human chattel; and as the master studies to keep the slave ignorant, the slave is cunning enough to make the master think that he succeeds. The slave fully appreciates the saying, 'where ignorance is bliss, 'tis folly to be wise'" (B,172). This formulation represents a fine example of Douglass's use of irony which easily turns the tables on the schemes of the slaveholders.[13]

And, to be sure, he knew from his own experience as a young boy what it means to have one's intellectual growth stunted. In 1826, at the young age of eight, he was sent to Baltimore to live with Hugh and Sophia Auld and serve as a companion to their two-year-old son, Tommy. Things went very well at first, with Sophia Auld beginning to teach him how to read. But this fruitful arrangement was soon to stop for obvious reasons:

> She very kindly commenced to teach me the A, B, C. After I had learned this, she assisted me in learning to spell words of three or four letters. Just at this point of my progress, Mr. Auld found out what was going on, and at once forbade Mrs. Auld to instruct me further, telling her, among other things, that it was unlawful, as well as unsafe, to teach a slave to read. To use his own words, further, he said, "If you give a nigger an inch, he will take an ell. A nigger should know nothing but to obey his

master—to do as he is told to do. Learning would *spoil* the best nigger in the world. Now," he said, "if you teach that nigger (speaking of myself) how to read, there would be no keeping him. It would forever unfit him to be a slave. he would at once become unmanageable, and of no value to his master. As to himself, it could do him no good, but a great deal of harm. It would make him discontented and unhappy." [...] From that moment, I understood the pathway from slavery to freedom. [...] Though conscious of the difficulty of learning without a teacher, I set out with high hope, and a fixed purpose, at whatever cost of trouble, to learn how to read. (N,37; B,217; L,527)

The "harm" of having been introduced to reading was already done, as Douglass states by interpreting Mr. Auld's perversion of the 16th century proverb "Give him an inch and he'll take an ell"[14] to his own advantage: "From this time I was most narrowly watched. If I was in a separate room any considerable length of time, I was sure to be suspected of having a book, and was at once called to give an account of myself. All this, however, was too late. The first step had been taken. Mistress, in teaching me the alphabet had given me the inch, and no precaution could prevent me from taking the ell" (N,40; B,223; L,531).

His autodidactic education could no longer be stopped, and Douglass has narrated the fact that he learned a great deal from studying the Bible and the primers of white boys in the streets of Baltimore. And in 1830, at the mere age of twelve, he put his meager savings to good use and bought himself a used copy of *The Columbian Orator* (1797), a popular collection of speeches and dialogues compiled by Caleb Bingham for the purpose of rhetorical and moralistic instruction.[15] He read and reread passages from this book, putting many a passage into memory to draw upon in later life. Here he encountered speeches by such great orators as Cato, Cicero, George Washington, Benjamin Franklin, and William Pitt, and he was introduced to all aspects of human rights. Of special instructional use was a lengthy introductory essay on "General Directions for Speaking—Extracted from Various Authors" which provided Douglass with the rhetorical skills for his later life as a public speaker.[16] Very much to the point, Booker T. Washington in his biography *Frederick Douglass* (1907) speaks of the fact that these texts "gave to young Douglass a larger idea of liberty than was included in his mere dream of freedom for himself, and in addition they increased his vocabulary of words and phrases."[17] In fact, his deep rooting in the language of the Bible, together with his reading of such linguistically sophisticated excerpts by great minds, created a linguistic prowess in Douglass that seemed alien to early abolitionist audiences who listened to his eloquent speeches. While he was also influenced by the sermonic and at times colloquial style of Black preachers and the rich traditional songs of the slaves,[18] he refrained almost completely from employing the dialect of the plantation and its quarters. In his late pamphlet *Why Is the Negro Lynched?* (1894), Douglass makes the telling statement that "when a black man's language is quoted, in order to belittle and degrade him, his ideas are often put in the most grotesque and unreadable English, while the utterances of Negro scholars and authors are ignored" (4,507). Wanting to illustrate and prove that the intelligence of black people can match that of the white, Douglass very consciously chose to employ standard English and proved himself to be a master at it.[19]

That he used proverbs at all was primarily due to his interest in the Bible as well as the sermonic style of Black preachers, a role that he himself took on during many a Sunday morning in church. Religious rhetoric has long been based on proverbial language, using both biblical and folk proverbs to reach and educate the congregation.[20] The other reason might well be that he found them in that incredibly influential *Columbian Orator* which Douglass read so often that he knew many passages by heart. In a three-page "Extract from the Eulogy on Dr. Franklin, Pronounced by the Abbé Fauchet, in the Name of the Commons of Paris, 1790," he found, for example, the following high praise of proverbial wisdom: "The proverbs of 'Old Henry,' and 'Poor Richard,' are in the hands of both the learned and the ignorant; they contain the most sublime morality, reduced to popular language, and common comprehension; and form the catechism of happiness for all mankind."[21] And in the "Extract from Mr. Pitt's Speech, in Answer to Lord Mansfield, on the Affair of Mr. Wilkes, 1770," Douglass found the passage "My lords, there is one plain maxim, to which I have invariably adhered through life; that in every question in which my liberty or property were concerned, I should consult and be determined by the dictates of common sense. I confess, my lords, that I am apt to distrust the refinements of learning, because I have seen the ablest and most learned men equally liable to deceive themselves, and to mislead others."[22] In a speech on March 26, 1860, at Glasgow, Douglass mentions that "common sense, common justice, and sound rules of interpretation all drive us to the words of the law for the meaning of the law" (III,349), and in an article on "Reconstruction" in the *Atlantic Monthly* of December 1866, Douglass speaks quite similarly of "the plain, common-sense way of doing this work [of reconstruction]" (4,203). And no doubt "Douglass impressed audiences with his sincerity, honesty, integrity, and common sense"[23] during "his war with slavery through language."[24]

"The Crushed Worm May Yet Turn under the Heel of the Oppressor"

When Frederick Douglass turned to proverbs to make his invaluable arguments against slavery, he could indeed count on being understood by his entire audience or readership. His use of folk proverbs in particular added a colloquial and metaphorical flavor to his arguments, and it is this figurative use of language that increased the general appeal of his serious messages. What follows is but a small chronological selection of contextualized proverb examples, in which each proverbial message represents Douglass's typical "common sense" philosophy. He could at times be a bit long-winded in his argumentation, and some of his sentences are loosely constructed. Proverbs help to focus or conclude such invectives:

> Negro pews in the church; Negro boxes in the theatre; Negro cars on the railroad; Negro berths in the steamboat; Negro churches and Negro schools in the community, are all pernicious fruit of a wicked, unnatural, and blasphemous prejudice against our God-given complexion; and as such stand directly in the way of our progress and equality. The axe must be laid at the root of the tree. This whole system of things is false, foul, and infernal, and should receive our most earnest and unceasing reprobation. (5,72; March 10, 1848)
>
> The times create their own watch-words; and the watch-words of one generation may not always be appropriate to another. We would as willingly fight the battle of liberty and equality under the banner of "Free Sons and Free Men," as that of the Declaration of American Independence. "Deeds, not words," is our motto. (5,87–88; Sept. 1, 1848)
>
> The old proverb, "united we stand, divided we fall," has been fully and painfully illustrated by our anti-slavery experience, and it is quite time that we had learned its lesson of wisdom. Moral enterprises, not less than political and physical ones, require union of feeling, union of aim, union of effort. Too long, we think, has this important truth been underestimated. Why should the friends of abolition stand longer divided? Why should they not come together, and do their utmost to establish an abolition organization upon which all may honorably stand and labor together for the extirpation of the common evil of the country? (2,524–525; Oct. 1860)
>
> Happily, however, in standing up in their cause I do, and you do, but stand in defense of the cause of the whole country. The circumstances

of this eventful hour make the cause of the slaves and the cause of the
country identical. They must fall and flourish together. A blow struck
for the freedom of the slave, is equally a blow struck for the safety and
welfare of the country. As Liberty and Union have become identical,
so slavery and treason have become one and inseparable. I shall not
argue this point. It has already been most ably argued. All eyes see it,
all hearts begin to feel it; and all that is needed is the wisdom and the
manhood to perform the solemn duty pointed out by the stern logic of
our situation. It is now or never with us. (III,494; Feb. 5, 1862; 3,215;
Feb. 12, 1862)

"Now or never"—that is indeed a proverbial slogan for the final military
struggle against slavery during the Civil War. But as all of these references
have shown, Douglass expresses his fears and hopes through proverbs, thus
showing the humanity of this fight. Douglass is without doubt the agitator
par excellence, calling things the way he sees them. And when he attacks the
slaveholders of the South in ever new tirades, he is even capable of a proverb
sentence like "Honesty is the best policy even in dealing with slaveholders"
(5,247; II,400; Oct. 14, 1852) to add a bit of biting satire to it all.

Even though he did not condone the idea of planning a militant uprising
of the slaves, he uttered the serious warning that it might just come to this
in an anti-slavery lecture delivered on December 8, 1850, in his hometown,
Rochester. It is a rhetorical masterpiece how he integrates the sixteenth-
century English proverb "Tread on a worm and it will turn" in the middle
of his argument. The metaphor of the "worm" stands, of course, for the
miserable life of the slave, who has been reduced by the slaveholders to the
lowest status of animal life:

> I would warn the American people, and the American government, to be
> wise in their day and generation. I exhort them to remember the history
> of other nations; and I remind them that America cannot always sit "as
> a queen," in peace and repose; that prouder and stronger governments
> than this have been shattered by the bolts of a just God; that the time
> *may* come when those they now despise and hate, may be needed; when
> those whom they now compel by oppression to be enemies, may be
> wanted as friends. What has been, may be again. There is a point beyond
> which human endurance cannot go. The crushed worm may yet turn
> under the heel of the oppressor. I warn them, then, with all solemnity,
> and in the name of retributive justice, *to look to their ways;* for in an
> evil hour, those sable arms that have, for the last two centuries, been
> engaged in cultivating and adorning the fair fields of our country, may

yet become the instruments of terror, desolation, and death, throughout our borders. (2,148–149;II,271)

Anybody who experienced the civil rights marches and the struggles to keep them peaceful under the leadership of Martin Luther King and others will be experiencing a *déjà vu* here. This is a very precarious situation to which Douglass draws attention metaphorically and indirectly, but still clear enough for anybody to understand. And the ever acute Douglass noted well that his warnings and those of others were not necessarily heeded. Seven years later, on May 11, 1857, at New York City, he felt compelled to draw on the "worm" proverb again to paint a very gloomy prophecy, adding the proverbial expression "to fight the devil with fire" at the end for good measure:

The time may come when even the crushed worm may turn under the tyrant's feet. Goaded by cruelty, stung by a burning sense of wrong, in an awful moment of depression and desperation, the bondman and bondwoman at the south may rush to one wild and deadly struggle for freedom. Already slaveholders go to bed with bowie knives, and apprehend death at their dinners. Those who enslave, rob, and torment their cooks, may well expect to find death in their dinnerpots.

The world is full of violence and fraud, and it would be strange if the slave, the constant victim of both fraud and violence, should escape the contagion. He, too, may learn to fight the devil with fire, and for one, I am in no frame of mind to pray that this may be long deferred. (2,412–313; III,169–170)

What a reality check, to use a modern expression to characterize this powerful jeremiad! Douglass very honestly indicates that his pacifist attitude is stretched to the brink and that the philosophy of non-violence might just not be workable much longer. Three years later the Civil War broke out without the occurrence of a mass uprising of the slaves. But little wonder that Frederick Douglass and his sons became staunch supporters of the war effort, helping to recruit black soldiers of the North to fight for the struggle to liberate the "crushed worms" of the South who could finally "turn" and stand up for freedom and human dignity.

Throughout his life's struggles, Douglass never gave up hope that the lot of the slaves and then freed African Americans would improve with time and effort. To argue this point, he often returned to biblical proverbs to strengthen his authoritative argument that slaveholders will in due time be punished for their evil deeds. Now the slaveholders might not simply wind up in captivity themselves, they might also die (at least figuratively) by the proverbial sword for their crimes:

> The slaveholders are sleeping on slumbering volcanoes, if they did but know it; and I want every colored man in the South to remain there and cry in the ears of the oppressors, "Liberty for all or chains for all." I want them to stay there with the understanding that the day may come—I do not say it *will* come, I do not say that I would hasten it, I do not say that I would advocate the result or aim to accomplish or bring it about,—but I say it *may* come; and in so saying, I only base myself upon the doctrine of the Scriptures, and upon human nature, and speaking out through all history. "Those that lead into captivity shall go into captivity" [Rev. 13:10]. "Those that take up the sword shall perish by the sword" [Rev. 13:10, Matt. 26:52]. Those who have trampled upon us for the last two hundred years, who have used their utmost endeavors to crush every noble sentiment in our bosom, and destroy our manly aspirations; those who have given us blood to drink for wages, may expect that their turn will come one day. It was in view of this fact that Thomas Jefferson, looking down through the vista of the future, exclaimed: "I tremble for my country when I reflect that God is just, and that his justice cannot sleep forever." (5,113–114; II,151–152)

It is of interest to note how Douglass in this superb piece of agitation circles quite literally around the idea of direct revenge by the victims on the oppressors. But he does not commit himself to advocate real action. His dual biblical proverb message remains a sincere warning, and by adding Jefferson's warning of a just God to it all, he argues that punishment will surely come in due time, expressed proverbially as "their turn will come one day." This does, in fact, occur once the Civil War is in full swing. Now the deserved punishment of the slaveholders has its justification, and Douglass cites merely the more violent "sword" proverb to seal the fate of the guilty slaveholders:

> Slavery has chosen to submit her claims to the decision of the God of battles. She has deliberately taken the sword and it is meet that she should perish by the sword. Let the oppressor fall by the hand of the oppressed, and the guilty slaveholder, whom the voice of truth and reason could not reach, let him fall by the hand of his slave. It is in accordance with the All-wise orderings of Providence that it should be so. Eternal justice can thunder forth no higher vindication of her majesty nor proclaim a warning more salutary to a world steeped in

cruelty and wickedness, than in such a termination of our system of slavery. Reason, argument, appeal,—all moral influences have been applied in vain. The oppressor has hardened his heart, blinded his mind and deliberately rushed upon merited destruction. Let his blood be upon his own head. (3,376; Aug. 16, 1863)

Now the proverbial *leitmotif* rages military and personal revenge on the perpetrators, and Douglass shows no restraint or mercy as slavery is slowly but surely wiped out. This is not a pacifist speaking but rather a man who has experienced slavery and who knows of the evil deeds of the transgressors. The proverb has no figurative meaning any longer, but it must be acted out so that slavery can be destroyed.

"There Is no Peace for the Wicked"

The whole path towards the Civil War was for Frederick Douglas "a moral revolution" (II,481; May 10, 1854), and by getting involved in it as a great agitator and orator, he became "the moral leader and spiritual prophet of his race."[25] In a speech on August 3, 1857, at Canandaigua, New York, Douglass expressed his moral philosophy in a succinct statement that continues to serve as a motto for any strife for civil rights:

> Let me give you a word of the philosophy of reform. The whole history of the progress of human liberty shows that all concessions yet made to her august claims, have been born of earnest struggle. The conflict has been exciting, agitating, all-absorbing, and for the time being, putting all other tumults to silence. It must do this or it does nothing. If there is no struggle[,] there is no progress. Those who profess to favor freedom and yet depreciate agitation, are men who want crops without plowing up the ground, they want rain without thunder and lightning. They want the ocean without the awful roar of its many waters.
>
> This struggle must be a moral one, or it may be a physical one, and it may be both moral and physical, but it must be a struggle. Power concedes nothing without a demand. It never did and it never will. (III,204)

Several scholars have noted this passage, and Steven Kingston concludes his book on *Frederick Douglass: Abolitionist, Liberator, Statesman* (1941) by quoting its wisdom as the most appropriate composite description of Douglass's life-long crusade for civil rights: "His life is the finest testimony to his own saying: 'If there is no struggle, there is no progress.'"[26] It is good to know that in 1980 this sentence finally found its way into the fifteenth edition of John Bartlett's *Familiar Quotations* as one of Douglass's most significant formulaic statements.[27] It should survive as a quotation, and its concise parallel structure and fundamental wisdom might well turn it into a proverb yet.[28] As Francis J. Grimké mentioned in his "Obituary Sermon" for Frederick Douglass on March 10, 1895, in the Fifteenth Street Presbyterian Church at Washington, D.C., Douglass "possessed a mind of remarkable acuteness and penetration, and of great philosophical grasp. [...] With the skill of a trained dialectician, [he] knew how to marshall all the arguments at his command, in the form of facts and principles. [...] He had a strong, mighty intellect. They called him the Sage of Anacostia; and so he was—all that the term implies—wise, thoughtful, sound of judgment, discriminating, far-seeing."[29]

Frank M. Kirkland has summarized Frederick Douglass's struggle towards enlightened progress with the idea of "moral suasion," which he understands to be "the presupposition that the language of morality directly influences conduct. That is to say, moral suasion requires the belief that it can awaken through rhetoric moral sensibility and, as a consequence, motivate us to do what is good. Moreover, moral suasion is buttressed by Douglass's affirmation of Enlightenment ideas concerning a universal humanism, i.e., a singular human nature, and the sanctity of life, liberty, and happiness."[30] But what Kirkland does not mention is that folk proverbs in general and biblical proverbs[31] in particular are by their very sapient nature expressions of moral suasion.

Even though the conflict of slavery and liberty might not be a religious topic as such, Douglass repeatedly uses two biblical proverbs to argue that these ways of life are absolutely incompatible. In this first example from a speech delivered on February 12, 1846, at Arbroath, Scotland, his proverbial argument becomes the stronger since he is in fact attacking the organized churches for being on the side of the slaveholders:

> I maintain to the last that man-stealing is incompatible with Christianity—that slave-holding and true religion are at war with each other—and that a Free Church should have no fellowship with a slave church;—that as light can have no union with darkness, Christ has no concord with Beelzebub; and as two cannot walk together except they be agreed [Amos 3:3], and no man can serve two masters [Matt. 6:24],—so I maintain that freedom cannot rightfully be blended with slavery. Nay, it cannot, without stabbing liberty to the heart. (5,23; I,159)

Fifteen years later he repeats the first proverb in a short essay on "Shall Slavery Survive the War?" in *Douglass' Monthly* and replaces the second text by a folk proverb: "Slavery and free institutions can never live peacefully

together. They are irreconcilable in the light of the laws of social affinities.—
How can two walk together, except they be agreed. Water and oil will not
mix. Ever more, stir them as you will, the water will go to its place, and the
oil to its. There are elective affinities in the moral chemistry of the universe,
as well as in the physical, and the laws controlling them are unceasingly
operative and irrepealable" (3,143; Sept. 1861). One page later in the same
essay Douglass feels compelled to return to this message, now pulling in the
second Bible proverb after all: "Liberty of conscience, of speech, and of the
press has no real life in a slave State, and can have none for any considerable
length of time. It must either overthrow slavery, or be itself overthrown
by slavery. 'No man can serve two masters.' No society can long uphold
two systems radically different and point blank opposed, like slavery and
freedom" (3,144). But not quite three months later, in a major address of
December 3, 1861, at Boston, Douglass adds a third biblical proverb and an
allusion to a fourth folk proverb to this by now standard argumentation: "The
trouble is fundamental. Two cannot walk together except they be agreed.
No man can serve two masters. A house divided against itself cannot stand
[Matt. 12:35]. It is something to ride two horses going the same way, but
impossible when going opposite ways" (III,465; repeated almost identically
on Jan. 14, 1862, at Philadelphia; see 3,200; III,479). While the proverb
allusion probably is a play on the proverb "When two ride one horse, one
must sit behind" found in William Shakespeare's *Much Ado About Nothing*
(1598),[32] Douglass might well have thought of Abraham Lincoln's famous
"House Divided" speech of June 16, 1858 that secularized the proverb's
message in light of the slavery issue, when he chose this biblical proverb to
argue against the possible co-existence of slavery and freedom.[33]

Frederick Douglass always takes the high road of moral suasion, as can
be seen from yet another powerful Bible proverb which appears for several
decades in his sermonic prophecies that evil doings will surely be punished,
for "There can be no peace, saith the God, unto the wicked" (Isaiah 48:22).
Douglass's words are haunting and threatening, arguing with all his prophetic
might that there is no escape from secular or divine punishment for one's
wickedness.

> While this nation is guilty of the enslavement of three millions of innocent
> men and women, it is as idle to think of having a sound and lasting
> peace, as it is to think there is no God, to take cognizance of the affairs
> of men. There can be no peace to the wicked while slavery continues in
> the land, it will be condemned, and while it is condemned there will be
> agitation; Nature must cease to be nature; Men must become monsters;
> Humanity must be transformed; Christianity must be exterminated; all

ideas of justice, and the laws of eternal goodness must be utterly blotted out from the human soul, ere a system so foul and infernal can escape condemnation, or this guilty Republic can have a sound and enduring Peace. (2,139; II,259; Dec. 1, 1850)

On October 30, 1854, at Chicago, Douglass declares his guilty verdict once again with utmost satirical force: "Our parties have attempted to give peace to slaveholders. They have attempted to do what God has made impossible to be done; and that is to give peace to slaveholders. 'There is no peace to the wicked, saith my God.' In the breast of every slaveholder, God has placed, or stationed an anti-slavery lecturer, whose cry is *guilty,* GUILTY, GUILTY; 'thou art verily guilty concerning thy brother'" (2,323; II,548). What a rhetorical stroke of genius to turn the anti-slavery lecturer into the conscience of the slaveholder!

In March of 1862, in an essay on "The Situation of the War" in his *Douglass' Monthly,* Douglass, quite predictably by now, drew on yet another proverb from the Bible to make the following prophecy: "'Be not deceived, God is not mocked, whatsoever a man soweth that shall he reap' [Gal. 6:7]. This is no dream of prophecy, but a clear reading of the philosophy of social and political forces, illustrated by no remote experience, but by the facts of the present hour" (3,230). A year later, at the height of the Civil War in April 1863, this time in an essay on "Do Not Forget Truth and Justice" in the same magazine,[34] Douglass simply queries "Shall we never learn that whatsoever we, as a nation, shall sow, that we shall certainly reap?" (3,340). On November 20, 1883, he connects the plant imagery of the proverb more directly with general ethical ideas of social politics in a speech at Washington, D.C., once again wanting to explain that all actions will have their results and that the price for wrongdoings will have to be paid:

> I think it will be found that all genuine reform must rest on the assumption that man is a creature of absolute, inflexible law, moral and spiritual, and that his happiness and well-being can only be secured by perfect obedience to such law. All thought of evasion, by faith or penance, or by any means, must be discarded. "Whatever a man soweth, that shall he also reap," and from this there is no appeal. (V,139)

Towards the end of his third autobiography *Life and Times of Frederick Douglass* (1893), he returns once more to the same interpretation of this biblical proverb: "I recognize that the universe is governed by laws which are unchangeable and eternal, that what men sow they will reap, and that there is no way to dodge or circumvent the consequences of any act or deed" (L,914). Only the great moral values can lead to a better life for all people in hopefully more perfect societies, as Douglass has pointed out by means of one more biblical proverb: "Men do not live by bread alone [Deut. 8:3; Matt. 4:4], so with nations. They are not saved by art, but by honesty. Not by the gilded splendors of wealth, but by the hidden treasure of manly virtue. Not by the multitudinous gratification of the flesh, but by the celestial guidance of the spirit" (2,430; III,193–194; Aug. 3, 1857).

"All Men Are Created Equal"

Throughout his long struggle for human progress, Frederick Douglass saw himself by his own definition "as an humble advocate of equal rights—as defender of the principle of human freedom" (2,121; May 30, 1850). And looking back on his life on October 21, 1890, in a speech at Washington, D.C., he openly declared that some gains have been made and that there is hope for the future: "I have seen dark hours in my life, and I have seen the darkness gradually disappearing and the light gradually increasing. One by one I have seen obstacles removed, errors corrected, prejudices softened, proscriptions relinquished, and my people advancing in all the elements that go to make up the sum of general welfare. And I remember that God reigns in eternity, and that whatever delays, whatever disappointments and discouragements may come, truth, justice, liberty, and humanity will ultimately prevail" (V,456). Among these great moral values, liberty seems to be the all-encompassing principle. Proverbially speaking, he chose the folk proverb of decisive and engaged action to argue for his comprehensive scheme of liberty: "Strike while the iron is hot. Let us have no country but a free country, liberty for all and chains for none. Let us have law, one gospel, equal rights for all, and I am sure God's blessing will be upon us and we shall be a prosperous and glorious nation" (IV,31). These encouraging words were spoken on April 12, 1864, at Boston while the Civil War was raging in full force.

Douglass never gave up on his fight for liberty of the slaves, and he chose the famous proverbial words of Patrick Henry from March 23, 1775, as his own revolutionary battle cry in an open letter dated February 8, 1854, in his own *Frederick Douglass' Paper* magazine:

> The inspiration of liberty must be breathed into them [the slaves], till it shall become manifestly unsafe to rob and enslave men. The battle of freedom in America was half won, when the patriotic Henry exclaimed, *Give me Liberty or Give me Death*. Talking of insurrection, yes, my friends, a moral and bloodless one. An insurrection has been raging in this country for more than two hundred years. The whip has been cracking

and the chains clanking amid the shouts of liberty, which have gone up
in mockery before God. The Negro has been shot down like a dog, and
the Indian hunted like a wolf, by our prayer-making and hymn-singing
nation.—Yes, let us have moral insurrection. Let the oppressed and down-
trodden awake, arise, and vindicate their manhood by the presentations
of their just claims to liberty and brotherhood. Let them think and speak
of liberty till their chains shall snap asunder; and their oppressors shall
feel it no longer safe to ensnare and plunder them. (5,313–314)

Douglass wants to be absolutely clear that words must be followed by deeds
if liberty is to be achieved at all. And if freedom is gained, there is always the
danger, of course, that it might be lost again. To warn of such a fate, Douglass
employs yet another famous quotation that has long become a standard proverb
in common parlance. It originated with John Philpot Curran in his "Speech
upon the Right of Election" on July 10, 1790, and not with Thomas Jefferson,
as has been claimed by some. The precise wording was: "The condition upon
which God has given liberty to man is eternal vigilance; which condition if he
break, servitude is at once the consequence of his crime, and the punishment
of his guilt."[35] At Douglass's time as well as today the shorter variants "The
price of liberty is eternal vigilance" or "Eternal vigilance is the price of liberty"
have become the common way of expressing this wisdom. Douglass employed
the proverb the first time on March 17, 1848, in an essay on "The North and
the Presidency" in his *The North Star* journal:

It is in strict accordance with all philosophical, as well as all experimental
knowledge, that those who unite with tyrants to oppress the weak and
helpless, will sooner or later find the groundwork of their own rights and
liberties giving way. "The price of liberty is eternal vigilance." It can only
be maintained by a sacred regard for the rights of all men. (1,296–297)

This is a serious warning especially to all slaveholders. But in a speech
of December 28, 1862, four days before Abraham Lincoln's "Emancipation
Proclamation" on January 1, 1863, Douglass directs the proverb to the
slaves who are about to be freed. While he called his speech at Zion Church
in Rochester, New York, quite appropriately "A Day for Poetry and Song"
in eager anticipation of the day of liberation, he has to do a bit of good old
preaching. And what a prophecy this sermon were to become in due time:

This is no time for the friends of freedom to fold their hands and consider
their work at an end. The price of Liberty is eternal vigilance. Even after
slavery has been legally abolished, and the rebellion [i.e., the Civil War]

substantially suppressed, even when there shall come representatives to Congress from the States now in rebellion, and they shall have repudiated the miserable and disastrous error of disunion, or secession, and the country shall have reached a condition of comparative peace, there will still remain an urgent necessity for the benevolent activity of the men and the women who have from the first opposed slavery from high moral conviction.

Slavery has existed in this country too long and has stamped its character too deeply and indelibly, to be blotted out in a day or a year, or even a generation. The slave will yet remain in some sense a slave, long after the chains are taken from his limbs; and the master will retain much of the pride, the arrogance, imperiousness and conscious superiority and love of power, acquired by his former relation of master. Time, necessity, education, will be required to bring all classes into harmonious and natural relations. (3,311; III,544–545)

The ensuing period of Reconstruction proved Douglass right, and still today, several generations after the emancipation of the slaves, the American society is confronting racial and social injustices.

It should not be surprising, after what has been said about Douglass's effective use of the two proverbs "Give me liberty or give me death" and "The price of liberty is eternal vigilance," that he turned to yet a third famous quotation that quickly turned into a proverb. It was coined and penned by Thomas Jefferson in his "Declaration of Independence" (1776) that begins with the memorable statement: "We hold these truths to be self-evident: that all men are created equal; that they are endowed by their creator with certain inalienable rights; that among these are life, liberty, and the pursuit of happiness." Douglass knew these phrases well, and he cited them repeatedly, especially the proverb that "All men are created equal," in order to argue for equality and liberty:

It is a significant fact, that while meetings for almost any purpose under heaven may be held unmolested in the city of Boston, that in the same city, a meeting cannot be peaceably held for the purpose of preaching the doctrine of the American Declaration of Independence, "that all men are created equal." The pestiferous breath of slavery taints the whole moral atmosphere of the north, and enervates the moral energies of the whole people. (2,146; II,268; Dec. 8, 1850)

You [the American people] declare, before the world, and are understood by the world to declare, that you *"hold these truths to be self evident, that all men are created equal; and are endowed by their Creator with certain inalienable rights; and that, among these are life, liberty, and the pursuit of happiness;"* and yet, you hold securely, in a bondage which, according to your own Thomas Jefferson, *"is worse than ages of that which your fathers rose in rebellion to oppose,"* a seventh part of the inhabitants of your country. (2,200; II,383; July 5, 1852)[36]

The following final example relating to the "Declaration of Independence" and its proverbial wisdom that "All men are created equal" shows a truly impressive trait of Frederick Douglass as a public agitator. He worked on his facts, and yes, albeit without any formal education, he did research to get the true facts out before the public. There was a great deal of detailed knowledge necessary for Douglass to stand in Halifax, England, on January 6, 1860, to deliver these intriguing remarks about the manuscript development of Jefferson's document:

> At first, the reference to slavery was very feeble [in it]. In the first draft of the declaration of American independence, there was a condemnation of slavery, and one of the charges brought against George III, was that he had forced upon the American colonies, by violence and cruelty, the inhuman traffic of selling men and women.[37] It was in consequence of the power of slavery at that time that this passage was struck out from the original document. The declaration which was afterwards published appeared without these words. That declaration declared that this truth was self-evident; that all men were created equal, and had all an equal right to life, liberty, property, and the pursuit of happiness. The word "white," which the modern abettors of slavery would interpolate, did not appear, but the passage said "all men," all kindreds, tongues, and tribes on the face of the earth. (III,301–302)

Amen! Those are words that should not be forgotten today as the civil rights movement continues to fight for equal rights. The emphasis in the proverb "All men are created equal" is on "all," and the word "men" is clearly meant to denote men and women of all races and creeds. It should be no surprise then to learn that "All Rights For All"[38] was chosen for the motto of the *Frederick Douglass' Paper* weekly journal when it began publication in 1851 to spread the message of equality and liberty for all people.

"Be the Architect of Your own Fortune"

Frederick Douglass had the opportunity to observe for thirty years after the Civil War how the fate of the African Americans would play out. And what he saw would have crushed almost any crusader for equality and justice. With the Civil War still raging, Douglass expressed plenty of fears for the future of his race in a talk on "The Mission of the War" on January 13, 1864, in New York City. He begins with an allusion to the proverb "Great oaks from little acorns grow" and then argues against the "universal" truth that "Revolutions never go backward":

> I know that the acorn involves the oak, but I know also that the commonest accident may destroy its potential character and defeat its natural destiny. One wave brings its treasure from the briny deep, but another often sweeps it back to its primal depths. The saying that revolutions never go backward must be taken with limitations. The revolution of 1848 was one of the grandest that ever dazzled a gazing world. It overturned the French throne, sent Louis Philippe into exile, shook every throne in Europe, and inaugurated a glorious Republic. Looking from a distance, the friends of democratic liberty saw in the convulsion the death of kingcraft in Europe and throughout the world. Great was their disappointment. Almost in the twinkling of an eye, the latent forces of despotism rallied. The Republic disappeared. [...] Though the portents are that we shall flourish, it is too much to say that we cannot fail and fall. (3,387; IV,4–5)

The paragraph does not mention slavery in particular or the future of the slaves in general, but it is implied that much caution will be necessary once the war will be over that newly gained rights and privileges will not be lost again.

But it is race, racial prejudice to the point of hate and murder, that occupies the fighting spirit of this champion of civil rights at every turn. The so-called "color line" is growing stronger instead of weaker during this period, while Douglass struggles with all of his verbal might to break it down:

> Can this prejudice against color, as it is called, be accounted for by circumstances outside and independent of race or color? If it can be thus explained, an incubus may be removed from the breasts of both the white and the black people of this country, as well as from that large intermediate population which has sprung up between these alleged irreconcilable extremes. It will help us to see that it is not necessary that the Ethiopian shall change his skin, nor needful that the white man shall change the essential elements of his nature, in order that mutual respect and consideration may exist between the two races. (4,347)

In this passage from his essay on "The Color Line," published in *The North American Review* in June 1881, Douglass alludes to the biblical proverb "Can the Ethiopian change his skin, or the leopard his spots?" (Jer. 13:23) to indicate the impossibility and nonnecessity for whites or blacks to change their color.[39] All that is needed is "mutual respect and consideration," something that holds true today in any racial tensions.

But Douglass returns to the proverb that "A leopard cannot change his spots" in a major address on "The Nation's Problem" on April 16, 1889, at Washington, D.C. This time he makes the interesting point that "pride" in both races might prevent them from having that "mutual respect." He wants equality, not superiority of either race:

> But it may be said that we shall put down race pride in the white people by cultivating race pride among ourselves. The answer to this is that devils are not cast out by Beelzebub [proverbial expression from Matt. 12:24], the prince of devils. The poorest and meanest white man when he has nothing else to command him says: "I am a white man, I am." We can all see the low extremity reached by that sort of race pride, and yet we encourage it when we pride ourselves upon the fact of our color. Let us do away with this supercilious nonsense. If we are proud let it be because we have had some agency in producing that of which to be proud. Do not let us be proud of what we can neither help nor hinder. The Bible put us in the condition in this respect of the leopard, and says that we can no more change our skin than the leopard his spots. If we were unfortunate in being placed among a people with whom our color is a badge of inferiority, there is no need of our making ourselves ridiculous by forever, in words, affecting to be proud of a circumstance due to no virtue in us, and over which we have no control. (V,412)

Note, though, that Douglass is not saying that the black people should not be proud of their achievements as they carve out ever better lives for themselves. The pride should come from making progress, a typical point of view for Frederick Douglass. That is exactly what he had said about six years earlier in a lecture appropriately called "Our Destiny is Largely in Our Own Hands," delivered on April 16, 1883, in the nation's capital: "There is power in numbers, wealth and intelligence, which can never be despised nor defied. All efforts thus far to diminish the Negro's importance as a man and as a member of the American body politic, have failed" (4,359; V,65). The proverb that "There is power in numbers," together with its extension to include money and education, expresses Douglass's dream for the black

race, i.e., to become independent, self-sufficient and respected members of
the American society.

Despite prophetic warnings, Douglass is always hopeful that there
might just be light at the end of the tunnel. Why warn of danger if there
is no chance for avoiding it! During the troubled times of Reconstruction,
Douglass returned to one of his major lectures which he wrote and delivered
for the first time in 1859 and read more than fifty times to audiences across
the United States, Canada, and Great Britain. The address is called "Self-
Made Men," and it contains a number of proverbs that stress the fact that the
American ideal of finding one's own way in life also applies to the black man.
In March, 1893, Douglass repeated the speech at Carlisle, Pennsylvania,
and it is in these comments that he gives his people hope for a better future.
All that seems to be needed is good old solid work, a bit of elbow grease,
and two feet to stand on. Douglass does not use the pragmatic proverb "If at
first you don't succeed, try, try, try again," but it could stand for a summary
of this message. The proverbial expression of "To pull oneself up by one's
bootstraps" might also serve the purpose of describing Douglass's idea of
self-made men, who certainly must be willing to work:

> We may explain success mainly by one word and that word is WORK!
> WORK!! WORK!!! WORK!!!! Not transient and fitful effort, but patient,
> enduring, honest, unremitting and indefatigable work, into which the
> whole heart is put, and which, in both temporal and spiritual affairs, is
> the true miracle worker. Every one may avail himself of this marvelous
> power, if he will. There is no royal road to perfection. [...] The lesson
> taught at this point by human experience is simply this, that the man
> who will get up will be helped up; and the man who will not get up will
> be allowed to stay down. This rule may appear somewhat harsh, but in
> its general application and operation it is wise, just and beneficent. I
> know of no other rule which can be substituted for it without bringing
> social chaos. Personal independence is a virtue and it is the soul out of
> which comes the sturdiest manhood. (V,556–557)

Obviously Douglass knew what he was talking about in all of the
repetitions of this speech, for "in the truest sense of the word, he became a
'self-made' man."[40] Based on solid Protestant work ethics, Douglass developed
a sort of "myth of success,"[41] but it must be remembered his "standard
speech on 'Self-Made Men' accentuated the morality of success rather than
its economics."[42] Be that as it may, "self-reliance was the answer,"[43] even if
the path to success is difficult if not treacherous. This is, of course, what the
proverb "There is no royal road to perfection" is meant to say.

Douglass's reliance on proverbs in this speech based on a pragmatic approach to life does not end there. Wanting to stress that it is high time that black men take their life in their own hands, and that there is great need that they do so, he begins a subsequent paragraph with an appropriate proverb that is then explained as a sound piece of advice:

> Necessity is not only the mother of invention, but the mainspring of exertion. The presence of some urgent, pinching, imperious necessity, will often not only sting a man into marvelous exertion, but into a sense of the possession, within himself, of powers and resources which else had slumbered on through a long life, unknown to himself and never suspected by others. A man never knows the strength of his grip till life and limb depend upon it. Something is likely to be done when something must be done. (V,558)

All of this is true, of course, for the struggling black people. Only hard work and self-reliance will get them into the mainstream of American society, as yet another short paragraph based on two additional proverbs, one of classical and the other of sixteenth-century British origin, makes perfectly clear:

> The primary condition upon which men have and retain power and skill is exertion. Nature has no use for unused power. She abhors a vacuum. She permits no preemption without occupation. Every organ of body and mind has its use and improves by use. "Better to wear out than to rust out," is sound philosophy as well as common sense. (V,559)

But speaking of common sense, Douglass remembers a whole string of other proverbs and proverbial phrases to add to his sermon on success and progress. His audiences, well acquainted with these bits of folk speech and wisdom, must have been delighted with the following paragraph, hopefully taking heed of its serious advice:

> As a people, we have only a decent respect for our seniors. We cannot be beguiled into accepting empty-headed sons for full-headed fathers. As some one has said, we dispense with the smoke when the candle is out. In popular phrases we exhort every man as he comes upon the stage of active life, "Now do your level best!" "Help yourself!" "Put your shoulder to the wheel!" "Make your own record!" "Paddle your own canoe!" "Be the architect of your own fortune!" (V,570)

And then comes yet another final paragraph with two proverbs, asserting that a good time will be coming for the black race because America, where self-made men are possible, is a wonderful exception as far as the rest of the world is concerned:

> We have as a people no past and very little present, but a boundless and glorious future. With us, it is not so much what has been, or what is now, but what is to be in the good time coming. Our mottoes are "Look ahead!" and "Go ahead!," and especially the latter. Our moral atmosphere is full of the inspiration of hope and courage. Every man has his chance. If he cannot be President he can, at least, be prosperous. In this respect, America is not only the exception to the general rule, but the social wonder of the world. (V,571)

Is this not moral suasion at its best? In the true spirit of the tradition of jeremiads, Douglass reminds the black citizens that their past was horrid slavery, that their present is problematic at best, but their future looks bright because at least they have a chance! The struggle to become a self-made man, and a good one at that, exists for each of them, and so the march for civil rights and a good life based on moral principles goes on with hopeful self-assurance. With the future-oriented worldview of Americans as an uplifting concept,[44] the proverb "Hope springs eternal" does indeed hold true.

"Do unto Others as You Would Have Them Do unto You"

Morality and religion were one and the same thing for Frederick Douglass, and it should come as no surprise that the so-called "Golden Rule" of Christianity, in the form of the proverb "Do unto others as you would have them do unto you" (Matt. 7:12), would become the perfect expression of human equality for him. It appears again and again for over fifty years in his speeches and writings, and it must be considered as Douglass's rhetorical and philosophical *leitmotif*. Having made this claim, it is of special interest how Douglass used it for the first time in only his fifth recorded speech on "The Southern Style of Preaching to Slaves" on January 28, 1842, in Boston. He repeated the following excerpt many times, and this satirical masterpiece has come to be known as the "Slaveholder's Sermon" among Douglass scholars. In it Douglass ridicules the hypocritical behavior of preachers who in their preaching would pervert Jesus' word to justify the evil schemes of slavery:

But what a mockery of His [Christ's] religion is preached at the South! I have been called upon to describe the style in which it is set forth. And I find our ministers there learn to do it at the northern colleges. I used to know they went away somewhere I did not know where, and came back ministers; and this is the way they would preach. They [the southern ministers] would take a text—say this:—"Do unto others as you would have others do unto you." And this is the way they would apply it. They would explain it to mean, "slaveholders, do unto *slaveholders* what you would have them do unto you:"—and then looking impudently up to the slaves' gallery, (for they have a place set apart for us, though it is said they have no prejudice, just as is done here in the northern churches;) looking high up to the poor colored drivers and the rest, and spreading his hands gracefully abroad, he says, (mimicking,) "And you too, my friends, have souls of infinite value—souls that will live through endless happiness or misery in eternity. Oh, *labor diligently* to make your calling and election sure. Oh, receive into your souls these words of the holy apostle—'Servants, be obedient unto your masters.' (Shouts of laughter and applause.) Oh, consider the wonderful goodness of God! Look at your hard, horny hands, your strong muscular frames, and see how mercifully he has adapted you to the duties you are to fulfil! (continued laughter and applause) while to your masters, who have slender frames and long delicate fingers, he has given brilliant intellects, that they may do the *thinking*, while you do the *working.*" (Shouts of applause.) It has been said here at the North, that the slaves have the gospel preached to them. But you will see what sort of a gospel it is:—a gospel which, more than chains, or whips, or thumb-screws, gives perpetuity to this horrible system. (I,16–17)[45]

As can be seen from the shouts and applause from the audience, this must have been quite a performance by Douglass with plenty of sarcasm and mimicry: "His voice and the movements of his body drew everyone to him. The physicality—the sexuality—reached round to encircle the audience as he reached out to them and they to him, making complete this ritual of oratory said and heard [and seen!]."[46] Even though this was a memorable show by the young and eager abolitionist, Douglas was nevertheless very serious about his attack on the misappropriation of one of the noblest laws of life.[47]

Being thoroughly entrenched in the abolitionist movement for personal and humanitarian reasons, Douglass gave the noble cause a solid endorsement in his speech on March 30, 1847, at London, now even placing abolitionism on the basic truth of the Golden Rule:

> When the history of the emancipation movement shall have been fairly
> written, it will be found that the abolitionists of the nineteenth century
> were the only men who dared to defend the Bible from the blasphemous
> charge of sanctioning and sanctifying Negro slavery. [...] It will then be seen
> that they were the men who planted themselves on the immutable, eternal,
> and all-comprehensive principle of the sacred New Testament—"All things
> whatsoever ye would that men should do unto you, do ye even so unto
> them"—that, acting on this principle, and feeling that if the fetters were
> on their limbs, the chain upon their own persons, the lash falling quick
> and hard upon their own quivering bodies, they would desire their fellow
> men about them to be faithful to their cause; and, therefore, carrying out
> this principle, they have dared to risk their lives, fortunes, nay, their all, for
> the purpose of rescuing from the tyrannous grasp of the slaveholder these
> 3,000,000 of trampled-down children of men. (1,217; II,32)

Looking at matters a bit more globally, Douglass exclaimed: "I despise
that religion that can carry Bibles to the heathen on the other side of the
globe and withhold them from heathen on this side[48]—which can talk about
human rights yonder and traffic in human flesh here. I love that which
makes its votaries do to others as they would that others should do to them"
(II,100; Sept. 24, 1847).

But Douglass is certain that the slaveholders will pay for their sins in
due time (beginning the following statement with an allusion to the proverb
"There can be no peace for the wicked" discussed above), and even if the law
cannot touch them, they will be haunted by their own guilty conscience:

> Verily there is a God to bring to nought the counsels of wicked men.
> They seek peace for the Slaveholder, but to the Slaveholder there can be
> no peace; his is a bad business; to him, while a Slaveholder, there can be
> neither peace of mind nor peace of conscience. If they could close up all
> Anti-Slavery Conventions, take all our Publications, *Uncle Tom's Cabin*,
> and the portions of the Bible which teach that men should do to others as
> they should wish to be done by, place them in the District of Columbia,
> set a match to them until the flames reached the sky; if they could have
> every abolitionist's tongue cut out, thus to procure their silence, they will
> not have obtained their object, for deep down in the secret corners of the
> Slaveholder's soul, God Almighty has planted an abolition sentinel in his
> monitor, the conscience. (II,465; April 13, 1854)

That is a true fire and brimstone sermon by a skilled orator and preacher.
If only the slaveholders would have heard Douglass, but they didn't attend

the abolition conventions, of course. Nevertheless, if there was any decency left in them, their guilty conscience must have tormented them at night and on their deathbed.

Douglass certainly agreed that after the Civil War ended and slavery had been abolished, the problematic era of Reconstruction brought at least some improvements to the lot of the former slaves. There was even progress being made in the field of human rights, but then, on October 15, 1883, the United States Supreme Court declared the Civil Rights Act of 1875 null and void, a great shock and disappointment to all who were struggling for universal equal rights.[49] Frederick Douglass reacted with his impassioned speech "The Decision Has Humbled the Nation" on October 22, 1883, at Lincoln Hall in Washington, D.C., right under the very eyes of the Supreme Court:

> Social equality does not necessarily follow from civil equality, and yet for the purpose of a hell black and damning prejudice, our papers still insist that the Civil Rights Bill is a Bill to establish social equality.
>
> If it is a Bill for social equality, so is the Declaration of Independence, which declares that all men have equal rights; so is the Sermon on the Mount, so is the Golden Rule, that commands us to do to others as we would that others should do to us; so is the Apostolic teaching, that of one blood God has made all nations to dwell on all the face of the earth; so is the Constitution of the United States, and so are the laws and customs of every civilized country in the world; for no where, outside of the United States is any man denied civil rights on account of his color. (4,403; V,123; L,979–980)

Douglass knew very well and had expressed it many times, that social equality must be earned through hard work, and his idea of the "self-made man" had been making progress towards this goal ever so slowly when the Civil Rights Bill unfortunately was struck down by the highest court in the country. But civil equality is a fundamental right, as he states with plenty of frustration and satire in his voice. In fact, so agitated was he about this setback that he devotes an entire chapter to this debacle in his third autobiography *Life and Times* (1893), where he also reprints this particular passage.[50] This was indeed a major setback, and its effects led eventually to the Civil Rights Movement of the twentieth century under the nonviolent leadership of Martin Luther King. The "Golden Rule" proverb "Do unto others as you would have them do unto you" served Frederick Douglass and his various causes extremely well, and there is no reason why this most humane wisdom should not continue to be the guiding light for civil rights in this country and throughout the world.

"No Man Liveth unto Himself"

In closing, it might be well to return one more time to Frederick Douglass's famous lecture on "Self-Made Men" of March 1893. He begins it with an appropriate quotation from Alexander Pope's *An Essay on Man* (1733–1734): "The saying of the poet that 'The proper study of mankind is man,'[51] and which has been the starting point of so may lectures, essays and speeches, holds its place, like all other great utterance, because it contains a great truth and truth alike for every age and generation of men. It is always new and can never grow old. It is neither dimmed by time nor tarnished by repetition; for man, both in respect of himself and of his species, is now, and evermore will be, the center of unsatisfied human curiosity" (V,546). Over thirty years earlier, in one of the first versions of this often repeated and varied speech entitled "The Trials and Triumphs of Self-Made Men" (1860), Douglass had called on a quotation of William Shakespeare to make a similar philosophical point: "To the great dramatic poet, all the world is a stage,[52] and men but players; but to all mankind, the world is a vast school. From the cradle to the grave, the oldest and the wisest, not less than the youngest and the simplest, are but learners; and those who learn most, seem to have most to learn" (III,291; Jan. 4, 1860). And Frederick Douglass was both a good student and a good teacher of mankind and the world. As an engaged participant on the stage of nineteenth-century America in particular, he heeded the advice of the Bible as well, as he states towards the end of his autobiography *Life and Times* (1893), beginning his reflections with yet another quotation from the Bible which, just like the two worldly quotations just mentioned, has long since become a wise proverb among the people:

> No man liveth unto himself, or ought to live unto himself. My life has conformed to this Bible saying, for, more than most men, I have been the thin edge of the wedge to open for my people a way in many directions and places never before occupied by them. It has been mine, in some degree, to stand as their defense in moral battle against the shafts of detraction, calumny and persecution, and to labor in removing and overcoming those obstacles which, in the shape of erroneous ideas and customs, have blocked the way to their progress. (L,941)

Those are deep philosophical yet simple and humble words. Douglass does not even mention in addition to his constant battle for the black race his fight for women and for civil rights in general. In all of these struggles, he was always the superb communicator. One hears talk today of that or the other national politician being a great communicator, but they don't even come close to touching the rhetorical and persuasive genius of Douglass. This unique man worked untiringly to serve his fellow men, he never lost sight of his goals, and he even had a good sense of humor to deal with it all. During an interview on September 6, 1891, in Baltimore, the seventy-four-year-old Douglass said with much vigor and proverbial wit: "I am unwilling to be an idler, but hope to exert whatever influence I may possess so long as my life lasts. [...] Mr. Douglass then said, laughing heartily: It is true I am now growing old, but I can say like Dr. Jackson said to President Quincy, of Harvard University, when asked when he expected to die, 'I shall die, I suppose, when I am in need of a doctor, when I am about ninety years old and not before then.' But I certainly shall wear, and not rust out" (V,478–479). So he ends with yet another folk proverb that has been in general currency for several centuries. At this particular moment he is using its wisdom for a good measure of humor, but both proverbs of the Bible and folk proverbs also served him extremely well as he made himself understood to people of all races, creeds, and genders through his engaged voice and pen. He believed in the rhetoric of common sense, and proverbs were the perfect verbal tools for his efforts. He never used the proverb "Progress never stands still," but his own formulation of "If there is no struggle, there is no progress" deserves to be entered into the annals of American proverbs. May the struggle for civil rights continue, and may it be based on Frederick Douglass's principles of morality, justice, liberty, humanity, and, last but not least, common sense.

6

"It's Not a President's Business to Catch Flies"
Proverbial Rhetoric in Presidential Inaugural Addresses

After yet another American presidential election in which the political rhetoric of the two principal candidates John Kerry and George W. Bush seemed rather uninspired, trite and devoid of colorful metaphors, it might be of general interest to take a glance at the verbal prowess of previous American presidents. Modern presidents, certainly since Harry S. Truman, are relying ever more on speech writers and advisors who put words into their mouths that lack emotional vigor and instead are replete with statistics and factual information. It is, however, to be hoped that presidents of this large nation will at least continue to labor on their own inaugural addresses as relatively short public speeches that attempt to set the stage for the new presidency.

Obviously every president in his turn has delivered more influential and significant addresses than that at the beginning of his presidential years in office, but choosing the inaugural speeches as the corpus of this investigation makes it possible to investigate the use and function of proverbial language in one precise type of address. Karlyn Kohrs Campbell and Kathleen Hall Jamieson, in their informative book *Deeds Done in Words: Presidential Rhetoric and the Genres of Governance* (1990), have convincingly shown that inaugural addresses are a distinct rhetorical genre: "Presidential inaugurals are epideictic rhetoric because they are delivered on ceremonial occasions, link past and future in present contemplation, affirm or praise the shared principles that will guide the incoming administration, ask the audience to gaze upon traditional values, employ elegant, literary language, and rely on heightening of effect by amplification and reaffirmation of what is already known and believed."[1] Regarding the special language of the "epideictic timelessness"[2] of these addresses, the two authors also observe that "the language of great inaugurals captures complex, resonant ideas in memorable phrases. Americans still recall [...] Lincoln's 'With malice toward none, with charity for all' [...] and John Kennedy's 'Ask not what your country can do for you; ask what you can do for your country' remains memorable. Such phrases illustrate special rhetorical skill in reinvigorating traditional values; in them familiar ideas become fresh and take on new meaning."[3] This is true, of course, but it should be noted that some of these "memorable phrases" have in fact become American proverbs. Furthermore, and perhaps even more importantly, the inaugural speeches do not only use "elegant, literary language" but rather to a noticeable extent proverbial expressions, including biblical and folk proverbs. As the new presidents wish to communicate with *all* the American people, the common language and wisdom of proverbs is perfectly suitable for effective rhetoric at these inaugural rites of passage. No note has hitherto been taken of this significant proverbial aspect of the special rhetoric at presidential inaugurations.

In order to show what role traditional proverbial language has played in inaugural addresses, all fifty-five ceremonial speeches by thirty-eight presidents have been carefully studied. (John Tyler, Millard Fillmore, Andrew Johnson, Chester A. Arthur, and Gerald Ford did not give an inaugural address, since they took over the presidency after a death or assassination.) Rather than citing the references from the inaugural speeches from the published papers of the individual presidents, this chapter makes use of John Gabriel Hunt's edited volume on *The Inaugural Addresses of the Presidents* (1997). It should be noted at the outset that the proverb "It's not a president's business to catch flies"[4] is the only American proverb registered in *A Dictionary of American Proverbs* (1992) that refers to the presidency. It was recorded during the second half of the twentieth century in the state of Illinois, and it was not used by any presidents, as far as is known. Nevertheless, it does express with much imagination and a colorful metaphor that presidents deal with big issues. Had one of the two presidential candidates used this proverb or others during the most recent campaign, they might well have scored some points or gained a few points just because of the expressiveness of this folk wisdom. Instead they talked and argued in platitudes and bureaucratic jargon that lacked any sign of proverbial insight into the seriousness and humor of the people.

From George Washington to John Quincy Adams

A comparison of the words uttered by George Washington in his concise first inaugural address delivered on April 30, 1789, with those spoken during the political campaign of the year 2004 makes it abundantly clear that the political rhetoric in the United States is at a low level. This is not to say that Washington amasses proverbs and proverbial expressions in his speech. Not at all, but he couches his language in proverb allusions, and his audience will most certainly have understood the wisdom expressed in the following words:

> The foundation of our national policy will be laid in the pure and
> immutable principles of private morality, and the preeminence of free
> government [will] be exemplified by all the attributes which can win
> the affections of its citizens and command the respect of the world. [...]
> There is no truth more thoroughly established than that there exists
> in the economy and course of nature an indissoluble union between
> virtue and happiness; between duty and advantage; between the genuine
> maxims of an honest and magnanimous policy and the solid rewards of
> public prosperity and felicity. (6)[5]

The two "maxims" (proverbs) alluded to are most likely "Honesty is the
best policy" and "Happiness is the best reward," two bits of folk wisdom
that the people of the young nation could embrace with conviction and
commitment. Washington's second inaugural address of March 4, 1793,
consists of merely two very short paragraphs in which he expresses his
willingness to take over the heavy burdens of the government once again. It
definitely makes sense that he chose not to include a proverb in this short
text that expresses no particular philosophical or pragmatic message.

John Adams, as the second president of the United States, did not
employ any proverbs in his considerably longer inaugural address on March
4, 1797. However, he starts his remarks with some historical thoughts whose
complexity is rhetorically eased by the inclusion of the proverbial expression
of "the middle course" that was no longer possible at the founding of this
country:

> When it was first perceived, in early times, that no middle course for
> America remained between unlimited submission to a foreign legislature
> and a total independence of its claims, men of reflection were less
> apprehensive of danger from the formidable power of fleets and armies they
> must determine to resist than from those contests and dissensions which
> would certainly arise concerning the forms of government to be instituted
> over the whole and over the parts of this extensive country. (13–14)

As the third president, Thomas Jefferson also stayed away from proverbs
in his two inaugural addresses of March 4, 1801 and 1805. However, in the
introductory paragraph of his first address, Jefferson makes use of one of the
many proverbial metaphors that speaks of the state as a ship or vessel that
needs to be steered by a presidential captain:

> Utterly, indeed should I despair did not the presence of many whom I
> here see remind me that in the other high authorities provided by our

Constitution I shall find resources of wisdom, of virtue, and of zeal
on which to rely under all difficulties. To you, then, gentlemen, who
are charged with the sovereign functions of legislation, and to those
associated with you, I look with encouragement for that guidance and
support which enable us to steer with safety the vessel in which we are all
embarked amidst the conflicting elements of a troubled world. (24)

I can't recall having heard either George W. Bush or John Kerry use
the proverbial phrase of "the ship of state" that needs to be piloted in our
truly troubled world today, even though this fitting metaphor has been in
use since classical antiquity.[6] Other presidents have used it, and in Frederick
Douglass's speeches and essays the proverbial phrase became a *leitmotif*.[7] But
finally, even though Jefferson did not employ proverbs in his two inaugural
addresses, it must not be forgotten that we owe him one of the most
powerful proverbs of them all. After all, his statement in the Declaration
of Independence (1776) that "All men are created equal"[8] has long become
proverbial in the English speaking world.

James Madison, the fourth president of the young nation, faced a vexing
problem with the War of 1812 which had gone badly at the time of his
second inauguration on March 4, 1813. In his comments on this situation
he most certainly has the proverb "One sword (drawn) keeps another in its
scabbard" in mind:

To render the justice of the war on our part the more conspicuous, the
reluctance to commence it was followed by the earliest and strongest
manifestations of a disposition to arrest its progress. The sword was scarcely
out of the scabbard before the enemy was apprised of the reasonable
terms on which it would be resheathed. Still more precise advances were
repeated, and have been received in a spirit forbidding every reliance not
placed on the military resources of the nation. These resources are amply
sufficient to bring the war to an honorable issue. (46)

One is reminded here of the war of words during the Cold War period
in the second half of the twentieth century, one that was also fought with
proverbial rhetoric expressed in words, caricatures, and cartoons.[9]

The fifth president, James Monroe, delivered two rather lengthy
inaugural addresses on March 4, 1817, and March 5, 1821. However, he
does not exhibit any particular inclination towards proverbial language.
Merely during some general introductory comments in his first speech
does he have recourse to a proverbial phrase. He is, of course, quite right in

stating that new presidents have an obligation of "shedding much light" on what their upcoming administration will do:

> In commencing the duties of the chief executive office it has been the practice of the distinguished men who have gone before me to explain the principles which would govern them in their respective administrations. In following their venerated example my attention is naturally drawn to the great causes which have contributed in a principal degree to produce the present happy condition of the United States. They will best explain the nature of our duties and shed much light on the policy which ought to be pursued in the future. (50)

In fact, Monroe provides future presidents with a definition and purpose of these inaugural addresses.

John Quincy Adams, sixth president and until George W. Bush the only son of a former president, made use of the proverbial phrase "to enjoy the fruits of one's labor" in his inaugural speech of March 4, 1825: "We now receive it [the government] as a precious inheritance from those to whom we are indebted for its establishment, doubly bound by the examples which they have left us and by the blessings which we have enjoyed as the fruits of their labors to transmit the same unimpaired to the succeeding generation" (76). Of course, enjoying the benefits of the hard labor of previous generations also means the obligation of handing the precious country on in good shape, a motif that is often used today in political parlance when politicians speak of making this country a better place to be for the children. Adams concludes his speech by calling on God to help him with his daunting task as the new president, a rhetorical topos that has been part of these speeches throughout history. By citing the biblical proverb "Except the Lord keep the city, the watchman waketh but in vain" (Psalms 127:1), he humbly places his presidency under the ultimate guidance of the Almighty:

> To the guidance of the legislative councils, to the assistance of the executive and subordinate departments, to the friendly cooperation of the respective state governments, to the candid and liberal support of the people so far as it may be deserved by honest industry and zeal, I shall look for whatever success may attend my public service; and knowing that 'except the Lord keep the city the watchman waketh but in vain,' with fervent supplications for His favor, to His overruling providence I commit with humble but fearless confidence my own fate and the future destinies of my country. (83)

FROM ANDREW JACKSON TO JAMES BUCHANAN

As the seventh president of the United States, Andrew Jackson presented somewhat of a shopping list of his governmental priorities in his first inaugural address on March 4, 1829. He is not particularly proverbial in his speech, but he does at least make use of the proverbial phrase "to be the exception to the rule" in his comments: "With regard to a proper selection of the subjects of impost with a view to revenue, it would seem to me that the spirit of equity, caution, and compromise in which the Constitution was formed requires that the great interests of agriculture, commerce, and manufactures should be equally favored, and that perhaps the only exception to this rule should consist in the peculiar encouragement of any products of either of them that may be found essential to our national independence" (88–89). He then continues singling out such matters as education and the military, and one is reminded of similar statements by more modern presidents.

Martin Van Buren, in his four years as the eighth president, did not prove to be a very popular or successful occupant of the White House due to an economic depression and the vexing problem of slavery. He was well aware, in his inaugural address of March 4, 1837, that he was to tread in the proverbial footsteps of his predecessors:

> The practice of all my predecessors imposes on me an obligation I cheerfully fulfill—to accompany the first and solemn act of my public trust with an avowal of the principles that will guide me in performing it and an expression of my feelings on assuming a charge so responsible and vast. In imitating their example I tread in the footsteps of illustrious men, whose superiors it is our happiness to believe are not found on the executive calendar of any country. (97)

Unfortunately he slipped only too quickly out of the footsteps of the early presidential giants and can hardly be considered an illustrious president.

Even though William Henry Harrison, the ninth president, gave the longest inaugural address (23 pages) on March 4, 1841, he shows no predilection for proverbial rhetoric.[10] He merely employs the adjective "proverbial" to describe the impressive commercial vigor of the American citizens: "The resources of the country are abundant, the enterprise and activity of our people proverbial, and we may well hope that wise legislation and prudent administration by the respective governments, each acting within its own sphere, will restore former prosperity" (128–129). It is almost surprising that Harrison does not add such proverbs as "Business before pleasure" or "Business is business" which were already current at that time.[11] Of course, President Harrison had no chance to prove himself as the man who brought the country back to economic prosperity. He died of pneumonia after only one month in office. Vice President John Tyler took over the reigns as the tenth president without an inaugural address[12] and was so unsuccessful in his job that he did not decide to seek the presidency in 1844. In fact, the next three presidents also lasted only one term each, as the issues over slavery and the maintenance of the federal union became ever more prevalent. Neither James Polk nor Zachary Taylor employed proverbial language in their inaugural addresses, and Vice President Millard Fillmore, who became the thirteenth president after the death of President Taylor, did not deliver a speech when he was sworn in on July 10, 1850.

Franklin Pierce as the fourteenth president addressed international concerns in his inaugural address on March 4, 1853, assuring his listeners in this country and abroad that he would, proverbially speaking, leave no blot upon the hitherto peaceful record of the United States:

> We have nothing in our history or position to invite aggression; we have everything to beckon us to the cultivation of relations of peace and amity with all nations. Purposes, therefore, at once just and pacific will be significantly marked in the conduct of our foreign affairs. I intend that my administration shall leave no blot upon our fair record, and trust that I may safely give the assurance that no act within the legitimate scope of my constitutional control will be tolerated on the part of any portion of our citizens which cannot challenge a ready justification before the tribunal of the civilized world. (166)

But with the inauguration of James Buchanan as the fifteenth president on March 4, 1857, the nation had gained a leader who sided with slavery interests. Buchanan made it perfectly clear in his inaugural address that he was a strong believer in popular sovereignty, i.e., the right of individual states to decide for themselves whether to tolerate slavery within their boundaries. And to appease strong slavery interests, he made shrewd use of the proverb "Time is a great corrective," which also brings to mind such variants as "Time assuages everything" or "Time changes everything." But here is what he actually said, clearly using the proverb as a dangerous manipulative tool:

> The whole territorial question being thus settled upon the principle of popular sovereignty—a principle as ancient as free government itself— everything of a practical nature has been decided. No other question remains for adjustment, because all agree that under the Constitution

slavery in the states is beyond the reach of any human power except that of the respective states themselves wherein it exists. May we not, then, hope that the long agitation on this subject is approaching its end [...]. Most happy will it be for the country when the public mind shall be diverted from this question to others of more pressing and practical importance. [...] It [the agitation] has alienated and estranged the people of the sister states from each other, and has even seriously endangered the very existence of the Union. Nor has the danger yet entirely ceased. Under our system there is a remedy for all mere political evils in the sound sense and sober judgment of the people. Time is a great corrective. Political subjects which but a few years ago excited and exasperated the public mind have passed away and are now forgotten. [..] Let every Union-loving man, therefore, exert his best influence to suppress this agitation, which since the recent legislation of Congress is without any legitimate object. (177–178)

This is indeed effective proverbial rhetoric, with the proverb serving as the ultimate appeaser in this case. Little wonder that Buchanan strongly supported the ill-conceived Dred Scott decision of the Supreme Court during the very first year of his presidency. It unfortunately opened the floodgates of slavery into territories hitherto not open to slavery.

From Abraham Lincoln to William McKinley

Fortunately the great sixteenth American president, Abraham Lincoln, elevated the principles of the Union above those of the states in regard to slavery. It took a Civil War to wipe out this inhuman institution, during which time Lincoln used powerful rhetoric in which proverbs take on a strong argumentative and persuasive role.[13] His first inaugural address of March 4, 1861, is not especially memorable, but it certainly establishes a firm agenda to combat slavery throughout the country while trying to maintain the Union. Lincoln did not succeed with avoiding the Civil War, but by the time he uttered his second inaugural speech exactly four years later on March 4, 1865, one of the greatest American presidents ever spoke words of wisdom that are still remembered today. He did see the end of this gruesome war before he himself was assassinated, but in this speech a few weeks earlier he rose to oratorical heights that have not been surpassed by any subsequent president.

But what made his short remarks at the second inauguration so very special? Obviously Lincoln was expected to say something about slavery, and he did exactly that. However, he also cites two proverbs from the Bible to underscore his major point that slavery is indeed wrong while at the same time warning his listeners to be careful in their judgments of others. In all of his condemnations of slavery Lincoln is ready and willing to find a way to bring North and South back together and to save the Union, especially as the Civil War is drawing to an end. For him, all Americans deserve to be treated alike:

> One-eighth of the whole population [of the United States] were colored slaves, not distributed generally over the Union, but localized in the southern part of it. These slaves constituted a peculiar and powerful interest. All knew that this interest was somehow the cause of the war. To strengthen, perpetuate, and extend this interest was the object for which the insurgents would rend the Union even by war, while the government claimed no right to do more than to restrict the territorial enlargement of it. Neither part expected for the war the magnitude or the duration which it has already attained. Neither anticipated that the cause of the conflict might cease with or even before the conflict itself should cease. Each looked for an easier triumph, and a result less fundamental and astounding. Both read the same Bible and pray to the same God, and each invokes His aid against the other. It may seem strange that any men should dare to ask a just God's assistance in wringing their bread from the sweat of other men's faces, but let us judge not, that we be not judged. The prayers of both could not be answered. That of neither has been answered fully. The Almighty has His own purposes. [...] Fondly do we hope, fervently do we pray, that this mighty scourge of war may speedily pass away. Yet, if God wills that it continue until all the wealth piled by the bondsman's 250 years of unrequited toil shall be sunk, and until every drop of blood drawn with the lash shall be paid by another drawn with the sword, as was said three thousand years ago, so still it must be said "the judgments of the Lord are true and righteous altogether." (200–201)

While he changes the proverb "In the sweat of thy face shalt thou eat bread" (Genesis 3:19) to ridicule the exploitive and inhuman treatment of the slaves by slaveholders, he cites the cautionary proverb "Judge not, lest ye be judged" (Matthew 7:1) with but a small change. And yet, his use of the personal pronoun "we" gives this comment a sense of humility by the leader of those who are about to win the Civil War. To the double proverbial wisdom Lincoln adds yet another Bible quotation, albeit without any claim to proverbiality. Nevertheless, the biblical claim that "The judgments of the Lord are true and righteous altogether" (Psalms 19:9) place the entire conflict and its resolution squarely into God's hands.

But as if these three well-known Bible references do not already have enough rhetorical and moral persuasiveness, Lincoln adds his by now famous concluding paragraph to it to signal that he as president will deal humanely with the perpetrators once the Civil War is over:

> With malice toward none, with charity for all, with firmness in the right as God gives us to see the right, let us thrive on to finish the work we are in, to bind up the nation's wounds, to care for him who shall have borne the battle and for his widow and his orphan, to do all which may achieve and cherish a just and lasting peace among ourselves and with all nations. (201)

The subsequent era of Reconstruction would certainly have proceeded on a more humane footing if President Lincoln could have lived out his second term. The phrase "With malice toward none, with charity for all" is not a proverb, but it most certainly is proverbially known and has long entered standard dictionaries of quotations as one of the greatest statements ever made by an American president.[14]

Vice President Andrew Johnson served out Lincoln's remaining term (actually almost all four years of it). Then the Republicans chose the victorious General Ulysses S. Grant as their presidential candidate in 1868. His skill as a field commander did not make him Lincoln's equal in oratorical ability. In his second inaugural address, Grant as the eighteenth president merely uses the rather plain proverbial expression "In God's own good time" to bring his point across that the country will surely move towards an ever greater nation:

> In future, while I hold my present office, the subject of acquisition of territory must have the support of the people before I will recommend any proposition looking to such acquisition. I say here, however, that I do not share in the apprehension held by many as to the danger of governments becoming weakened and destroyed by reason of their extension of territory. Commerce, education, and rapid transit of thought and matter by telegraph and steam have changed all this. Rather do I believe that our Great Maker is preparing the world, in His own good time, to become one nation, speaking one language, and when armies and navies will be no longer required. (213)

If Grant could survey the United States at the beginning of the twenty-first century, he might well have to cite the proverb "God's mills grind slowly" to describe the present state of affairs.

Rutherford B. Hayes, James A. Garfield, Chester A. Arthur, Grover Cleveland, Benjamin Harrison, and again Grover Cleveland as the nineteenth to twenty-fourth presidents, did not bother with proverbial language in their inaugural addresses. But that changes with the remarks which William McKinley, the twenty-fifth president, gave at his two inaugurations. He begins his first address on March 4, 1897, with the topos of humility in the face of his daunting task and argues proverbially that he intends to walk in the footsteps of God: "Our faith teaches that there is no safer reliance than upon the God of our fathers, who has so singularly favored the American people in every national trial, and who will not forsake us so long as we obey His commandments and walk humbly in His footsteps" (277). But he departs rather quickly from these rather standard references to the Almighty by turning to the "almighty dollar,"[15] as the phrase goes:

> Our financial system needs some revision; our money is all good now, but its value must not further be threatened. [...] Most of our financial laws are the outgrowth of experience and trial, and should not be amended without investigation and demonstration of the wisdom of the proposed changes. We must be both "sure we are right" and "make haste slowly." If, therefore, Congress, in its wisdom, shall deem it expedient to create a commission to take under early consideration the revision of our coinage, banking and currency laws, and give them that exhaustive, careful and dispassionate examination that their importance demands, I shall cordially concur in such action. (278)

Thus spoke a fiscal conservative at the end of the nineteenth century, and the two proverbs "Be sure you're right, then go ahead" and "Make haste slowly" suited him extremely well in his argument for monetary stability.

Two pages later, still talking about financial matters, President McKinley turns to the early nineteenth-century proverb "Pay as you go" as a sapiential rule for how the government should conduct its business: "The best way for the government to maintain its credit is to pay as it goes—not by resorting to loans, but by keeping out of debt—through an adequate income secured by a system of taxation, external or internal, or both" (280). When he turns to diplomatic issues, he comes up with the statement that "Our diplomacy should seek nothing more and accept nothing less than is due us" (285). There is a sententious if not proverbial ring to this concise formulation (perhaps based on the old proverb "Give everyone his due"), but the utterance has not found its way into any books of memorable phrases thus far. It might be seen, however, as a sign that presidents do attempt to come up with memorable phrases in their inaugural addresses.

As can be seen from the speech at his second inauguration on March 4, 1901, William McKinley has an inclination towards proverbial rhetoric. Looking into the future of his powerful and thriving country, he makes use of three proverbs in but one powerful paragraph:

> Distrust of the capacity, integrity, and high purposes of the American people will not be an inspiring theme for future political contests. Dark pictures and gloomy forebodings are worse than useless. These only becloud, they do not help to point the way of safety and honor. "Hope maketh not ashamed." The prophets of evil were not the builders of the Republic, nor in its crises since have they saved or served it. The faith of the fathers was a mighty force in its creation, and the faith of their descendants has wrought its progress and furnished its defenders. They are obstructionists who despair, and who would destroy confidence in the ability of our people to solve wisely and for civilization the mighty problems resting upon them. The American people, entrenched in freedom at home, take their love for it with them wherever they go, and they reject as mistaken and unworthy the doctrine that we lose our own liberties by securing the enduring foundations of liberty to others. Our institutions will not deteriorate by extension, and our sense of justice will not abate under tropic suns in distant seas. As heretofore, so hereafter will the nation demonstrate its fitness to administer any new estate which events devolve upon it, and in the fear of God will "take occasion by the hand and make the bounds of freedom wider yet." If there are those among us who would make our way more difficult, we must not be disheartened, but the more earnestly dedicate ourselves to the task upon which we have rightly entered. The path of progress is seldom smooth. New things are often found hard to do. Our fathers found them so. We find them so. They are inconvenient. They cost us something. But are we not made better for the effort and sacrifice, and are not those we serve lifted up and blessed? (291–292)

The biblical proverb "Hope maketh not ashamed" (Romans 5:5) is well suited to argue for a positive outlook on the future of the Union, one that befits the future-oriented worldview of the American people.[16] President McKinley's optimistic claims are strengthened by the use of the classical proverb "Take occasion by the hand (forelock)" and the fittingly altered version of Shakespeare's quotation long turned proverb "The path of true love never runs smooth" from the play *Midsummer Night's Dream*. This is indeed a magisterial employment of biblical, literary, and folk proverbs, and his enthusiastic audience no doubt reacted with pride to this string of proverbial statements.

The end of McKinley's second inaugural address is also of interest, and not only because he does not complete his remarks with the more or less traditional humility topos of placing the ultimate fate of the country into the hands of God. Instead, he discusses expansionist policies regarding the Philippines which the United States as a new world power had taken into its possession during the Spanish-American War. To add a bit of patriotic fervor to his statement, he draws on the proverbial triad of "life, liberty and the pursuit of happiness" of Thomas Jefferson's Declaration of Independence: "The greater part of the inhabitants [of the Philippines] recognize American sovereignty and welcome it as a guarantee of order and security for life, property, liberty, freedom of conscience, and the pursuit of happiness" (295). This certainly is an interesting use of this slogan of independence as the United States is occupying a foreign country.

FROM THEODORE ROOSEVELT TO HERBERT HOOVER

The "Rough Rider" Theodore Roosevelt, who had become the twenty-sixth president after McKinley's assassination in September of 1901, delivered his inaugural address for his own four-year-term in office on March 5, 1905. One might have expected to find some solid proverbial rhetoric in the speech by this vital and dynamic politician. But in his short comments of not even three pages he did no more than allude to the proverb "Deeds, not words," a piece of wisdom that is certainly in accord with his own activity level:

> Much has been given us, and much will rightfully be expected from us.
> We have duties to others and duties to ourselves; and we can shirk neither.
> We have become a great nation, forced by the fact of its greatness into
> relations with other nations of the earth, and we must behave as beseems
> a people with such responsibilities. Toward all other nations, large and
> small, our attitude must be one of cordial and sincere friendship. We
> must show not only in our words, but in our deeds, that we are earnestly
> desirous of securing their goodwill by acting toward them in a spirit of
> just and generous recognition of all their rights. (300)

These are rather humble words by the energetic veteran and hero of the Spanish American War, whose down-to-earth forthrightness made him a very popular president indeed.

With Theodore Roosevelt's help, William Howard Taft became the twenty-seventh president, presenting his rather long inaugural address (fifteen pages) on March 9, 1909. Like his predecessor, Taft is not particularly colloquial in his remarks. In fact, he merely uses a proverbial expression to make the point that care must be taken in race relations, that good intentions for increased governmental appointments of Blacks may "do more harm than good." This does not seem to be a particularly engaged statement for civil rights. But here are his own words:

> The Negroes are now Americans. [...] We are charged with the sacred duty of making their path as smooth and easy as we can. Any recognition of their distinguished men, any appointment to office from among their number, is properly taken as an encouragement and an appreciation of their progress, and this just policy should be pursued when suitable occasion offers. But it may well admit of doubt whether, in the case of any race, an appointment of one of their number to a local office in a community in which the race feeling is so widespread and acute as to interfere with the ease and facility with which the local government business can be done by the appointee is of sufficient benefit by way of encouragements to the race to outweigh the recurrence and increase of race feeling which such an appointment is likely to engender. Therefore the executive, in recognizing the Negro race by appointments, must exercise a careful discretion not thereby to do it more harm than good. On the other hand, we must be careful not to encourage the mere pretense of race feeling manufactured in the interest of individual political ambition. (318)

This is a rather convoluted paragraph with too many *if's* and *but's* instead of straight language for integration of the government, even though Taft continues by stating, "Personally, I have not the slightest race prejudice or feeling" (318). Taft is much more forthright a page later when he discusses the need for "laws for the application of safety devices to save the lives and limbs of employees of interstate railroads" (319). In fact, he repeats his alliterative binary formula by proclaiming, "I shall be glad, whenever any additional reasonable safety device can be invented to reduce the loss of life and limb among railway employees, to urge Congress to require its adoption by interstate railways" (319). But where is the call for laws protecting the civil rights of the Blacks and other minorities?

With Woodrow Wilson as the two-term twenty-eighth president, the White House had as its occupant an intellectual who had previously been president of Princeton University. As one might expect, Wilson struck a rather philosophical note in his first inaugural address on March 4, 1913. While he too begins his speech with mentioning the great past of this country, he cautions that "the evil has come with the good" (324). And then follow two paragraphs that amass such proverbial expressions as "To see the bad with the good," "To have fair play," "To have second thoughts," "To have the scales fall of one's eyes," and "To make up one's mind." He clearly wants to confront the citizens with what we would call today a "reality check," and he adds quite a bite to his jeremiad by satirically reducing the prevailing American philosophy of life to the proverb "Every man for himself." The fact that he cites two variations of the proverb that indicate the all-pervasiveness of this worldview from one generation to another makes his statement especially powerful:

> At last a vision has been vouchsafed us of our life as a whole. We see the bad with the good, the debased and decadent with the sound and vital. With this vision we approach new affairs. Our duty is to cleanse, to reconsider, to restore, to correct the evil without impairing the good, to purify and humanize every process of our common life without weakening or sentimentalizing it. There has been something crude and heartless and unfeeling in our haste to succeed and be great. Our thought has been "Let every man look out for himself, let every generation look out for itself," while we reared giant machinery which made it impossible that any but those who stood at the levers of control should have a chance to look out for themselves. We had not forgotten our morals. We remembered well enough that we had set up a policy which was meant to serve the humblest as well as the most powerful, with an eye single to the standards of justice and fair play, and remembered it with pride. But we were very heedless and in a hurry to be great.
>
> We have come now to the sober second thought. The scales of heedlessness have fallen from our eyes. We have made up our minds to square every process of our national life again with the standards we so proudly set up at the beginning and have always carried at our hearts. Our work is a work of restoration. (325)

This is quite a proverbial wake-up call for the nation. The last paragraph with its appropriate integration of the proverbial phrase "To hang in the balance" concludes this humanely inspired speech. This is not a boisterous president who speaks only of the greatness of the United States. Instead, one senses the sincerity and humility of Abraham Lincoln in these remarks, a man who did not have the intellectual schooling of Wilson but who certainly equalled him in moral wisdom. As Woodrow Wilson put it: "This is not a day of triumph; it is a day of dedication. Here muster, not the forces of party, but the forces of humanity. Men's hearts wait upon us; men's lives hang in the balance; men's hopes call upon us to say what we will do. Who shall live up to the great trust? Who dares fail to try? I summon all honest men, all patriotic, all forward-looking men, to my side. God helping me, I will not fail them, if they will but counsel and sustain me!" (327–328).

Little did Woodrow Wilson know that the next year World War I would break out in Europe! In fact, one month after his second inaugural address on March 5, 1917, the United States declared war on Germany. This speech lacks proverbial passages save one in the first paragraph. Here Wilson looks back at the accomplishments of his first term in office, and it is with considerable pride that he speaks proverbially of having put the governmental house back in order:

> The four years which have elapsed since last I stood in this place have been crowded with counsel and action of the most vital interest and consequence. Perhaps no equal period in our history has been so fruitful of important reforms in our economic and industrial life or so full of significant changes in the spirit and purpose of our political action. We have sought very thoroughly to set our house in order, correct the grosser errors and abuses of our industrial life, liberate and quicken the processes of our national genius and energy, and lift our politics to a broader view of the people's essential interests. (329–330)

With the horrors of World War I fading, Warren G. Harding, the twenty-ninth president, had campaigned on the promise of returning the country once and for all to "normalcy." Arguing for a more vigorous trade policy in time of peace, he paraphrased the biblical proverb "Give and you shall receive (Give, and it shall be given unto you)" (Luke 6:38) to add traditional wisdom to his economic message: "We must understand that ties of trade bind nations in closest intimacy, and none may receive except as he gives. We have not strengthened ours in accordance with our resources or our genius, notably on our continent, where a galaxy of republics reflects the glory of new-world democracy, but in the new order of finance and trade we mean to promote enlarged activities and seek expanded confidence" (340). Still speaking of economic matters, Harding argues proverbially that there must be plenty of "give and take" in getting matters back on track:

> The business world reflects the disturbances of war's reaction. [...] The normal balances have been impaired, the channels of distribution have been clogged, the relations of labor and management have been strained. We must seek the readjustment with care and courage. Our people must

give and take. Prices must reflect the receding fever of war activities. Perhaps we shall never know the old levels of wages again, because war invariably readjusts compensations, and the necessaries of life will show their inseparable relationship, but we must strive for normalcy to reach stability. (343)

Echoing his immediate predecessor, Woodrow Wilson, Harding also calls for putting the proverbial house in order: "We contemplate the immediate task of putting our public household in order. We need a rigid and yet sane economy, combined with fiscal justice, and it must be attended by individual prudence and thrift, which are so essential to this trying hour and reassuring for the future" (342). And also in keeping with Wilson's moral stance, Harding places the goal of his administration on the proverb "Do unto others as you would have them do unto you" (Matthew 7:12), the Golden Rule: "Service is the supreme commitment of life. I would rejoice to acclaim the era of the Golden Rule and crown it with the autocracy of service. I pledge an administration wherein all the agencies of government are called to serve, and ever promote an understanding of government purely as an expression of the popular will" (346). Those are truly noble words, and the Golden Rule in one of its proverbial variants ought to be the guiding principle of all governments and their people.[17] It is surprising that later presidents (except for mere allusions to it by Calvin Coolidge and Richard Nixon) have not picked up on this fundamental law of human ethical behavior in their inaugural addresses.

On March 4, 1925, Calvin Coolidge from the rural state of Vermont became the thirtieth president of the United States. Like other presidents before him, he begins his inaugural address with a short historical glance at the greatness of the American nation:

Because of what America is and what America has done, a firmer courage, a higher hope, inspires the heart of all humanity. These results have not occurred by mere chance. They have been secured by a constant and enlightened effort marked by many sacrifices and extending over many generations. We cannot continue these brilliant successes in the future, unless we continue to learn from the past. [...] We must realize that human nature is about the most constant thing in the universe and that the essentials of human relationship do not change. We must frequently take our bearings from these fixed stars of our political firmament if we expect to hold a true course. If we examine carefully what we have done, we can determine the more accurately what we can do. (350)

The seafaring proverbial expression "to hold a true course" is a perfect fit for the thoughts of a person who is taking over the helm of the ship of State. As to the sententious remark on what has been done and what can be done, it might well be structured on a truly famous speech by Abraham Lincoln. He had started his well-known "House Divided" speech of June 16, 1858, with the statement "If we could first know *where* we are, and *whither* we are tending, we could then better judge *what* to do, and *how* to do it."[18] It was in this speech that Lincoln employed the biblical proverb "A house divided against itself cannot stand" (Mark 3:25) to describe how slavery was threatening the survival of the Union.[19]

Even though the American language owes the proverb "The business of America is business"[20] to Calvin Coolidge, this taciturn president actually attempted to stay away from fixed phrases. Right at his inauguration he stated that "If we wish to continue to be distinctively American, we must continue to make that term comprehensive enough to embrace legitimate desires of a civilized and enlightened people determined in all their relations to pursue a conscientious and religious life. We cannot permit ourselves to be narrowed and dwarfed by slogans and phrases. It is not the adjective, but the substantive, which is of real importance. It is not the name of the action, but the result of the action, which is the chief concern" (351). But later in his speech he clearly builds on the two biblical proverbs "Judge not, lest ye be judged" and "Do unto others as you would have them do unto you" and adds the folk proverb of "God helps those who help themselves" for good measure:

> Our program is never to oppress, but always to assist. But while we do justice to others, we must require that justice be done to us. With us a treaty of peace means peace, and a treaty of amity means amity. We have made great contributions to the settlement of contentious differences in both Europe and Asia. But there is a very definite point beyond which we cannot go. We can only help those who help themselves. Mindful of these limitations, the one great duty that stands out requires us to use our enormous powers to trim the balance of the world. (354–354)

These comments are thoroughly based on proverbial slogans, and the change of the proverb "God helps those who help themselves" to the collective "We [Americans] can only help those who help themselves" is a clear indication of the president's willingness to flex the powerful muscles of the country in world affairs. The altered proverb might also imply the unseemly but not uncommon attitude that Americans (collectively) *are* God—or at least God's surrogate decision makers in world affairs.

Towards the end of his speech on various principles for which America stands, the new president draws a very positive picture for the future of the country:

> The encouraging feature of our country is not that it has reached its destination, but that it has overwhelmingly expressed its determination to proceed in the right direction. It is true that we could, with profit, be less sectional and more national in our thought. It would be well if we could replace much that is only false and ignorant prejudice with a true and enlightened pride of race. But the last election showed that appeals to class and nationality had little effect. We were all found loyal to a common citizenship. The fundamental precept of liberty is toleration. We cannot permit any inquisition either within or without the law or apply any religious test to the holding of office. The mind of America must be forever free. (359–360)

The claim that "The fundamental precept of liberty is toleration" is clearly of a linguistic structure and conciseness that gives it the ring of a sententious remark or slogan. It has not gained proverbiality, but it is surprising that it has not entered the many dictionaries of quotations.[21] Be that as it may, Coolidge and his natural terseness of language appears to have a natural inclination to formulaic statements, and he seems to have failed in his attempt to avoid them!

The thirty-first president, however, was more successful in not reducing American ideals to readymade phrases. Herbert Hoover in his inaugural speech of March 4, 1929, basically repeated what Calvin Coolidge had said earlier: "These ideals and aspirations [of America] are the touchstones upon which the day-to-day administration and legislative acts of government must be tested. More than this, the government must, so far as lies within its proper power, give leadership to the realization of these ideals and to the fruition of these aspirations. No one can adequately reduce these things of the spirit to phrases or to a catalogue of definitions" (373). Consequently, his first speech as president is void of quotable phrases and proverbs. But there is, perhaps, one exception to this claim. It appears that he might allude to the proverb "There is no royal road to learning (success)" in the following comment:

> There is no short road to the realization of these aspirations. Ours is a progressive people, but with a determination that progress must be based upon the foundation of experience. Ill-considered remedies for our faults bring only penalties after them. But if we hold the faith of men in our

mighty past who created these ideals, we shall leave them heightened and strengthened for our children. (373)

Whether President Coolidge in his time in office was more proverbial than President Hoover in his turn can, of course, only be ascertained by investigating all of their speeches and writings.

From Franklin Delano Roosevelt to Dwight D. Eisenhower

Never again will there be a president of the United States who will have the opportunity of delivering four inaugural addresses! But Franklin Delano Roosevelt as the thirty-second president did exactly that, and he did so with much pervasive rhetorical power. The beginning paragraph of his speech at the first inauguration on March 4, 1933, is a telling example of his oratorical abilities that were to dominate American politics during the next twelve years, while Winston Churchill soared to rhetorical heights in Great Britain and Adolf Hitler manipulated the German language to bring about World War II and the Holocaust. All three political leaders made ample use of proverbial language to convince their respective people of their plans and intentions.[22] Roosevelt himself began his first inaugural speech with a statement that included the three proverbial texts "To speak the truth, the whole truth, and nothing but the truth," "The only thing we have to fear is fear itself," and "To be a dark hour":

> I am certain that my fellow Americans expect that on my induction into
> the presidency I will address them with a candor and a decision which the
> present situation of our nation impels. This is preeminently the time to
> speak the truth, the whole truth, frankly and boldly. Nor need we shrink
> from honestly facing conditions in our country today. This great nation
> will endure as it has endured, will revive and will prosper. So, first of all,
> let me assert my firm belief that the only thing we have to fear is fear
> itself—nameless, unreasoning, unjustified terror which paralyzes needed
> efforts to convert retreat into advance. In every dark hour of our national
> life a leadership of frankness and vigor has met with that understanding
> and support of the people themselves which is essential to victory. I am
> convinced that you will again give that support to leadership in these
> critical days. (377–378)

As Roosevelt promised the country a New Deal after the devastating depression, he chose his words well when he proclaimed with much optimism that "The only thing we have to fear is fear itself." This statement has long found its way into quotation dictionaries and even into the *Dictionary of American Proverbs* (1992).[23] However, the editors of these collections of quotations and proverbs are quick to point out that Roosevelt based his sententious remark on a number of possible sources:

> Whenever conscience commands anything, there is only one thing to fear, and that is fear (St. Theresa of Avila, c. 1575)
>
> The thing I fear most is fear (Michel Eyquem de Montaigne, 1580)
>
> Nothing is terrible except fear itself (Francis Bacon, 1623)
>
> The only thing I am afraid of is fear (Arthur Wellesley, Duke of Wellington, 1831)
>
> Nothing is so much to be feared as fear (Henry David Thoreau, 1851)[24]

Perhaps Roosevelt alone or with the help of speech writers coined this variant of the formulaic theme of fearing fear, but it might also have been formulated in knowledge of some of these earlier statements. In any case, in its unique wording it has correctly become associated with Franklin D. Roosevelt,[25] and in the mind of most Americans he did in fact invent it.

With a sense of optimism and courage and the willingness to be innovative in governmental programs, Roosevelt called the nation into revitalized action. Little wonder that he cites the proverbial expression "To put the house in order" at this occasion, as Woodrow Wilson and Warren G. Harding had done before him. But Roosevelt now adds the proverb "First things first" in order to stress that certain priorities have to be set in getting the country back on its feet:

> Through this program [the New Deal] of action we address ourselves to putting our own national house in order and making income balance outgo. Our international trade relations, though vastly important, are in point of time and necessity secondary to the establishment of a sound national economy. I favor as a practical policy the putting of first things first. I shall spare no effort to restore world trade by international economic readjustment, but the emergency at home cannot wait on that accomplishment. (380)

Four years later, on January 20 (new date for inaugural addresses), 1937, Roosevelt begins the speech at his second inauguration with the justified claim that the government had succeeded in adhering to the proverb "First things first" in its recovery program:

> When four years ago we met to inaugurate a president, the Republic, single-minded in anxiety, stood in spirit here. We dedicated ourselves to the fulfillment of a vision—to speed the time when there would be for all the people that security and peace essential to the pursuit of happiness. We of the Republic pledged ourselves to drive from the temple of our ancient faith those who had profaned it; to end by action, tireless and unafraid, the stagnation and despair of that day. We did those first things first. (383)

Later on in the same speech, Roosevelt speaks with considerable pride of the changes that have come about, because the New Deal was not just a proverbial patchwork job but a program that, proverbially speaking, will meet with even more success in the long run:

> Our progress out of the depression is obvious. But that is not all that you and I mean by the new order of things. Our pledge was not merely to do a patchwork job with secondhand materials. By using the new materials of social justice we have undertaken to erect on the old foundations a more enduring structure for the better use of future generations. [...] Out of the collapse of prosperity whose builders boasted their practicality has come the conviction that in the long run economic morality pays. (385)

By the time of his third inauguration on January 20, 1941, Roosevelt was already addressing the question whether the United States would have to enter into World War II. Not surprisingly, his short speech on that occasion deals with the idea that "Democracy is not dying" (390). He praises the traditional values of America, especially the importance of maintaining freedom: "Sometimes we fail to hear or heed these voices of freedom because to us the privilege of our freedom is such an old, old story" (292–393). The proverbial expression "To be an old story" serves him well in this case to warn against the feeling that freedom is something old that does not need constant vigilance. Many a puristic stylist might look at this traditional phrase as a cliché of no communicative value,[26] but that would miss Roosevelt's important message.

At the height of World War II, the country elected Roosevelt to a fourth term, but due to the tense situation, Roosevelt's inaugural speech on January 20, 1945, comprised barely a page and a half. And yet, at this somber moment, President Roosevelt cites two proverbial expressions and a proverb to remind people of the necessity to find peace in the world by being a player on the world scene. Isolationism is clearly not a choice for a world power like the United States:

> Today, in this year of war, 1945, we have learned lessons—at a fearful cost—and we shall profit from them. We have learned that we cannot live alone, at peace; that our own well-being is dependent on the well-being of other nations far away. We have learned that we must live as men, not as ostriches, nor as dogs in the manger. We have learned the simple truth, as Emerson said, that "the only way to have a friend is to be one." We can gain no lasting peace if we approach it with suspicion and mistrust or with fear. We can gain it only if we proceed with the understanding, the confidence, and the courage which flow from conviction. (396)

The metaphors of the proverbial expressions "To be an ostrich" and "To be a dog in the manger" serve Roosevelt well to express the two ideas that America cannot afford to be blind to the events in the world and that it cannot retreat selfishly on its own territory, leaving the rest of the world to its own devices. Instead, the United States needs to be a friend to all other free nations, as Roosevelt explains it by quoting a line from Ralph Waldo Emerson's essay on *Friendship* (1841), a line that had long since become a proverb.[27]

Harry S. Truman as the thirty-third president of the United States continued Roosevelt's policies, but he himself deserves the credit for the Marshall Plan, the North Atlantic Treaty Organization, and the start of the United Nations. Although his inaugural speech of January 20, 1949, does not show it, Truman delighted in using proverbs and proverbial expressions in his speeches, news conferences and many books.[28] In fact, he was proud of his plain speaking. He also knew his American history extremely well and wrote essays on former American presidents. It is not surprising then that he includes Thomas Jefferson's sentence-turned-proverb "All men are created equal" in his inaugural speech:

> The American people stand firm in the faith which has inspired this nation from the beginning. We believe that all men have a right to equal justice under law and equal opportunity to share in the common good. We believe that all men have the right to freedom of thought and expression. We believe that all men are created equal because they are created in the image of God. From this faith we will not be moved. The American people desire, and are determined to work for, a world in which all nations and all

peoples are free to govern themselves as they see fit and to achieve a decent
and satisfying life. Above all else, our people desire, and are determined
to work for, peace on earth—a just and lasting peace—based on genuine
agreement freely arrived at by equals. (402–403)

With characteristic optimism he puts the country back on a course
towards prosperity. He does this deliberately, basing his step-by-step
policy on the proverb "Slowly but surely" when it comes to national and
international concerns: "If we are to be successful in carrying out these
policies, it is clear that we must have continued prosperity in this country
and we must keep ourselves strong. Slowly but surely we are weaving a world
fabric of international security and growing prosperity. We are aided by all
who wish to live in freedom from fear" (408).

The thirty-fourth president, Dwight D. Eisenhower fades in rhetorical
abilities in comparison to Harry Truman. In his first inaugural speech of
January 20, 1953, he speaks of "our faith in the deathless dignity of man,
governed by eternal moral and natural laws. This faith defines our full view
of life. It establishes, beyond debate, those gifts of the Creator that are man's
inalienable rights, and that make all men equal in His sight" (413). Just
like Truman before him, Eisenhower clearly alludes to Jefferson's proverb
"All men are created equal" in this passage. Later in the speech Eisenhower
outlines several guiding principles for world peace. In one of the paragraphs
it is the old general speaking: "Realizing that common sense and common
decency alike dictate the futility of appeasement, we shall never try to placate
an aggressor by the false and wicked bargain of trading honor for security.
Americans, indeed all free men, remember that in the final choice a soldier's
pack is not so heavy a burden as a prisoner's chains" (416). The last sentence
has a proverbial ring to it, but it has hitherto not been registered in proverb
or quotation dictionaries.

Eisenhower's second inaugural speech of January 21, 1957, takes place
in an atmosphere of Cold War politics and propaganda. The President
speaks rather generally of these international concerns and couches his call
for peace in the three proverbial expressions "The winds of change," "To
turn the back on someone," and "To pay the price." These metaphors give
his speech some emotional fervor, but there is not the youthful vigor that
was to characterize the inaugural speech of his successor, John F. Kennedy.
But here are Eisenhower's words:

> Thus across all the globe there harshly blow the winds of change. And,
> we—though fortunate be our lot—know that we can never turn our
> back to them. We look upon this shaken earth, and we declare our firm

and fixed purpose—the building of a peace with justice in a world where moral law prevails. The building of such a peace is a bold and solemn purpose. To proclaim it is easy. To serve it will be hard. And to attain it, we must be aware of its full meaning—and ready to pay its full price. We know clearly what we seek, and why. We seek peace, knowing that peace is the climate of freedom. And now, as in no other age, we seek it because we have been warned, by the power of modern weapons, that peace may be the only climate possible for human life itself. (421)

From John F. Kennedy to Jimmy Carter

When the youthful and vigorous John F. Kennedy was sworn in on January 20, 1961,[29] as the thirty-fifth president, he might well be referring to this paragraph by Eisenhower in the first part of his memorable inaugural address: "Let every nation know, whether it wishes us well or ill, that we shall pay any price, bear any burden, meet any hardship, support any friend, oppose any foe, in order to assure the survival and the success of liberty" (428). Kennedy, like Eisenhower, is ready to pay any price, proverbially speaking, to guarantee liberty in this country.

This is a definite pledge by Kennedy, and he adds a few others to this fundamental claim. Three of these pledges integrate, if somewhat indirectly, a basic proverb, thus giving each short paragraph an additional expressive effectiveness. In the first of these pledges, Kennedy must have had the following limerick in mind: "There was a young lady of Niger / Who smiled as she rode on a tiger; / They returned from the ride / With the lady inside, / And the smile on the face of the tiger,"[30] but he might also have alluded to the proverb "He who rides the tiger can never dismount":

> To those new states whom we welcome to the ranks of the free, we pledge our words that one form of colonial control shall not have passed away merely to be replaced by a far greater iron tyranny. We shall not always expect to find them supporting our view. But we shall always hope to find them strongly supporting their own freedom—and to remember that, in the past, those who foolishly sought power by riding the back of the tiger ended up inside. (428)

The second pledge seems to center on the proverb "God helps those who help themselves," once again replacing "God" by the "We" (Americans):

> To those people in the huts and villages across the globe struggling to break the bonds of mass misery, we pledge our best efforts to help

them help themselves, for whatever period is required—not because
the Communists may be doing it, not because we seek their votes, but
because it is right. If a free society cannot help the many who are poor, it
cannot save the few who are rich. (429)

Finally, the third pledge calls to memory the short proverb "Deeds, not
words." Of course, Kennedy might well have used the proverb "Actions
speak louder than words" in this case:

> To our sister republics south of the border, we offer a special pledge—to
> convert our good words into good deeds, in a new Alliance for Progress,
> to assist free men and free governments in casting off the chains of
> poverty.

But there are, to be sure, two memorable and quotable statements in this
refreshing inaugural speech. Clearly Kennedy and his sophisticated speech
writers (primarily Theodore C. Sorenson) formulated them by adopting the
parallel structure of so many proverbs.[31] Speaking of the danger of the Cold
War with its arms race, Kennedy calls upon both sides to remember "that
civility is not a sign of weakness, and sincerity is always subject to proof. *Let
us never negotiate out of fear. But let us never fear to negotiate*" (430). The last
sentence has found its way into John Bartlett's *Familiar Quotations*,[32] but it
would probably go too far to assign a proverbial character to it.

This leads us to the antithetical phrase "Ask not what your country can
do for you; ask what you can do for your country"[33] towards the end of the
speech:

> In the long history of the world, only a few generations have been
> granted the role of defending freedom in its hour of maximum danger.
> I do not shrink from this responsibility—I welcome it. I do not believe
> that any of us would exchange places with any other people or any other
> generation. The energy, the faith, the devotion which we bring to this
> endeavor will light our country and all who serve it—and the glow from
> that fire can truly light the world. *And so, my fellow Americans, ask not
> what your country can do for you; ask what you can do for your country. My
> fellow citizens of the world: Ask not what America will do for you, but what
> together we can do for the freedom of man.* (431)

As one would expect, the proverb-like utterance "Ask not what your
country can do for you; ask what you can do for your country" has made it

into Bartlett's *Familiar Quotations* as well. In fact, this reliable resource cites the following statement from an address delivered on May 30, 1884, by Oliver Wendell Holmes as a possible source: "For, stripped of the temporary associations which gave rise to it, it is now the moment when by common consent we pause to become conscious of our national life and to rejoice in it, to recall what our country has done for each of us, and to ask ourselves what we can do for our country in return."[34] It is hard to imagine that Kennedy's famous civic slogan was not taken from this speech by Oliver Wendell Holmes. But be that as it may, it has now in the precise wording by John F. Kennedy become a sententious remark and is well along to become an American proverb as well.

Lyndon Baines Johnson served out Kennedy's term as the thirty-sixth president and after having been elected president in his own right presented his inaugural address on January 20, 1965. He continued Kennedy's social agenda, but he also became ever more entangled in the civil war in Vietnam. But at his inauguration, he declared sententiously that "For every generation, there is a destiny" (436)[35] and then spoke proverbially of this country where one can be one's own man (person):

> Our destiny in the midst of change will rest on the unchanged character of our people, and on our faith. They came here—the exile and the stranger, brave but frightened—to find a place where a man could be his own man. They made a covenant with this land. Conceived in justice, written in liberty, bound in union, it was meant one day to inspire the hopes of all mankind; and it binds us still. If we keep its terms, we shall flourish. (436)

Choosing the proverbial phrases "To work shoulder to shoulder" and "To reopen old wounds," Johnson continued to call for serious commitment to social progress:

> No longer need capitalist and worker, farmer and clerk, city and countryside, struggle to divide our bounty. By working shoulder to shoulder, together we can increase the bounty of all. We have discovered that every child who learns, every man who finds work, every sick body that is made whole—like a candle added to an altar—brightens the hope of all the faithful. So let us reject any among us who seek to reopen old wounds and to rekindle old hatreds. They stand in the way of a seeking nation. Let us now join the reason to faith and action to experience, to transform our unity of interest into a unity of purpose. (438)

President Johnson wanted to build a great nation of social fairness, but the war in Vietnam discouraged him to the point that he did not seek reelection.

When Richard Milhous Nixon as the thirty-seventh president gave his first inaugural address on January 20, 1969, he picked up on this general theme of greatness. He had informed himself well on what earlier presidents said at their inaugurations. In fact, he studied all of their speeches in preparation of his own address.[36] So Nixon begins with an allusion to the proverb "Nothing is more simple than greatness" and also warns proverbially against promising more than one can deliver:

> Greatness comes in simple trappings. The simple things are the ones most needed today if we are to surmount what divides us, and cement what unites us. To lower our voices would be a simple thing. In these difficult years [referring indirectly to the Vietnam controversy], America has suffered from a fever of words; from inflated rhetoric that promises more than it can deliver; from angry rhetoric that fans discontents into hatreds; from bombastic rhetoric that postures instead of persuading. We cannot learn from one another until we stop shouting at one another—until we speak quietly enough so that our words can be heard as well as our voices. (445–446)

One might recall here what Leo Tolstoy wrote in his epic novel *War and Peace* (1865–1869): that "There is no greatness where there is not simplicity, goodness, and truth,"[37] but most likely Nixon's statement is based on Ralph Waldo Emerson's observation that "Nothing is more simple than greatness; indeed, to be simple is to be great" in his essay on *Literary Ethics* (1840).[38]

In an exceedingly negative analysis of this speech as "Rhetoric That Postures," Robert L. Scott claims that "The noise of the speech was not that of blustering, impotent fury but that of verbal posturing in the face of well-recognized perils. Into the strained fissures from which hell itself threatens to boil forth, the President plunked clichés made all the more hollow by the tincture of old, oratorical bombast."[39] The few examples that Scott cites, and he quotes particularly the paragraph that follows below, do not seem banal and clichéd as Scott argues, especially in light of the fact that all inaugural speeches follow more or less a set of expected rhetorical steps. As Karlyn Kohrs Campbell and Kathleen Hall Jamieson have shown so convincingly, "In order to be invested, presidents must demonstrate their qualifications for office by venerating the past and showing that the traditions of the institution [of the Presidency] continue unbroken in them. They must affirm that they will transmit the institution intact to their successors. Consequently, the language of conservation, preservation, maintenance, and renewal pervades these speeches."[40]

It is then not surprising, but rather to be expected, that Nixon returns once again to Jefferson's proverbial declaration that "All men are created equal" in his admittedly not very eloquent speech:

> As we measure what can be done, we shall promise only what we know we can produce, but as we chart our goals we shall be lifted by our dreams. No man can be fully free while his neighbor is not. To go forward at all is to go forward together. This means black and white together, as one nation, not two. The laws have caught up with our conscience. What remains is to give life to what is in the law: to ensure at last that as all are born equal in dignity before God, all are born equal in dignity before man. As we learn to go forward together at home, let us seek to go forward together with all mankind. Let us take as our goal: where peace is unknown, make it welcome; where peace is fragile, make it strong; where peace is temporary, make it permanent. (447)

In his second inaugural speech of January 20, 1973, Richard Nixon in his role as a Republican president emphasizes the need for less government, especially a smaller emphasis on the power of Washington as the all-too-powerful center of the United States. It certainly was a rhetorical stroke of genius to argue against the pervasive paternalism of the central government by altering the appropriate proverb "Father knows best" to a satirically interpreted "Washington knows best" in this paragraph:

> Abroad and at home, the key to new responsibilities lies in the placing and the division of responsibility. We have lived too long with the consequences of attempting to gather all power and responsibility in Washington. Abroad and at home, the time has come to turn away from the condescending policies of paternalism—of "Washington knows best." A person can be expected to act responsibly only if he has responsibility. This is human nature. So let us encourage individuals at home and nations abroad to do more for themselves, to decide more for themselves. Let us locate responsibility in more places. Let us measure what we will do for others by what they will do for themselves. That is why today I offer no promise of a purely governmental solution for every problem. (454)

It is interesting to note that Nixon's sententious request "Let us measure what we will do for others by what they will do for themselves" appears to be structurally modelled on Kennedy's "Ask not what your country can do for you; ask what you can do for your country." But obviously he is also basing this sentence on the Golden Rule "Do unto others as you would have them do unto you" from the Bible and the proverb "God helps those who help themselves."

Towards the end he refers much more directly to Kennedy's "inaugural proverb," and perhaps it was not mere political expedience that made Nixon do this. It must not be forgotten that Kennedy had defeated Nixon very narrowly in the national election of 1960. Especially regarding international politics, Nixon might well have had considerable respect for Kennedy's vigorous policies of dealing with the Soviet Union. In any case, here is what Nixon, indirectly quoting Kennedy, said:

> Let us remember that America was built not by government, but by people—not by welfare, but by work—not by shirking responsibility, but by seeking responsibility. In our own lives, let each of us ask—not just what will government do for me, but what can I do for myself? In the challenges we face together, let each of us ask—not just how can government help, but how can I help? Your national government has a great and vital role to play. And I pledge to you that where this government should act, we will act boldly and we will lead boldly. But just as important is the role that each and every one of us must play, as an individual and as a member of his own community. (455)

Nixon's rephrasing of Kennedy's by now proverbial remark does, of course, emphasize the individual rather than society in general as Kennedy had intended his message.

After Nixon's disgraceful behavior and resignation from the presidency, Gerald Ford took over the helm of the country as the thirty-eighth president in August of 1974. He lost the 1976 election to Jimmy Carter, who delivered his inaugural address as the thirty-ninth president on January 20, 1977. It is surprising that as a deeply religious, honest, and unpretentious man he did not include any proverbial wisdom in his speech. He merely speaks of the proverbial place in the sun that all people of the world deserve to achieve:

> The world itself is now dominated by a new spirit. Peoples more numerous and more politically aware are craving and now demanding their place in the sun—not just for the benefit of their physical condition, but for basic human rights. The passion for freedom is on the rise. Tapping this new spirit, there can be no nobler nor more ambitious task for America to undertake on this day of a new beginning than to help shape a just and peaceful world that is truly humane. (465)

The phrase of "A place in the sun" was used originally by the German Chancellor Bernard von Bülow in a *Reichstag* speech of December 6, 1897, when he described and justified Germany's colonial ambitions thus: "In a word, we desire to throw no one into the shade, but we also demand our own place in the sun [Platz an der Sonne]."[41] Typical for the ethical Carter, he reinterpreted the political phrase to argue for social and racial fairness.

From Ronald Reagan to George W. Bush

With Ronald Reagan as the fortieth president, the nation had found a so-called "great communicator"[42] to guide it through an increased military buildup and the implementation of supply-side economics in the form of spending cuts and tax cuts.[43] Reagan has been criticized and satirized for his inclination towards sound-byte rhetoric, but his two inaugural addresses do not necessarily bear witness to this phenomenon. His infamous one-liners were usually during supposedly spontaneous remarks, while he and his speech writers obviously labored on his comments made at his two inaugurations. Nevertheless, in a paragraph in his first inaugural speech, January 20, 1981, Reagan, as the first of forty presidents, finally cites the well-known proverbial definition of the American form of government which Abraham Lincoln had immortalized in his famous Gettysburg Address of November 19, 1863: "We here highly resolve [that] these dead shall not have died in vain; that this nation [under God] shall have a new birth of freedom—and that [this] government of the people, by the people, [and] for the people, shall not perish from the earth."[44] To emphasize that the American people must work together, Reagan added the two proverbial expressions "To bear the burden" and "To pay the price" (used previously by Dwight D. Eisenhower) to his message:

> In this present [economic] crisis, government is not the solution to our problem. From time to time, we have been tempted to believe that society has become too complex to be managed by self-rule, that government by an elite group is superior to government for, by, and of the people.[45] But if no one among us is capable of governing himself, then who among us has the capacity to govern someone else? All of us together, in and out of government, must bear the burden. The solutions we seek must be equitable, with no one group singled out to pay a higher price. (473)

In fact, Reagan picks up the proverbial expression "To have fair play" that Woodrow Wilson had used in his first inaugural address. Reagan argues that "All must share in the productive work of this 'new beginning' and all must share in the bounty of a revived economy. With the idealism and fair play which are the core of our system and our strength, we can have a strong and prosperous America at peace with itself and the world" (473–474). And then, turning to his theme that less government is best, Reagan employs the proverbial phrase "To pay the price" for a second time to point out that life in a free country is full of responsibilities: "Freedom and the dignity of the individual have been more available and assured here [in America] than in any other place on earth. The price for this freedom at times has been high, but we have never been unwilling to pay that price" (474). And there is even a third time that Reagan relies on this traditional phrase by adding the classical proverbial expression "To stand on the shoulders of giants" to it in a moving tribute to the truly great American presidents:

> This is the first time in history that this [inaugural] ceremony has been held on this west front of the Capitol. Standing here, one faces a magnificent vista, opening up on this city's special beauty and history. At the end of this open mall are those shrines to the giants, on whose shoulders we stand. Directly in front of me, the monument to a monumental man: George Washington, Father of Our Country. A man of humility who came to greatness reluctantly. He led America out of revolutionary victory into infant nationhood. Off to one side, the stately memorial to Thomas Jefferson. The Declaration of Independence flames with his eloquence. And then beyond the Reflecting Pool the dignified columns of the Lincoln Memorial. Whoever would understand in his heart the meaning of America will find it in the life of Abraham Lincoln. Beyond those monuments to heroism is the Potomac River, and on the far shore the sloping hills of Arlington National Cemetery with its row on row of simple white markers bearing crosses or stars of David. They add up to only a tiny fraction of the price that has been paid for our freedom. (477)

Reagan did not repeat his favorite maxim of having to pay the price in his second inaugural address of January 21, 1985. Perhaps he had become aware of the fact that his "reaganomics" was too high a price to be paid by the less privileged people of the United States. In any case, he now used the somewhat similar proverbial expression "To have mountains to climb" to spur people on to greater and better things: "We are creating a nation once again vibrant, robust, and alive. But there are many mountains yet to climb. We will not rest until every American enjoys the fullness of freedom, dignity, and opportunity as our birthright" (481). Reagan remained the eternal optimist, arguing that "we, the present-day Americans, are not given to looking backward. In this blessed land, there is always a better tomorrow" (480). The actual proverb simply states that "There is always a tomorrow,"[46] but as the addition of the word "better" indicates, President Reagan could always see the proverbial silver lining on the political clouds.

The inaugural address of George H. W. Bush as the forty-first president is perhaps not particularly memorable, but he will most certainly be remembered for having created the proverbial phrase "Read my lips!" during his acceptance speech on August 18, 1988, at the Republican National Convention in New Orleans: "The Congress will push me to raise taxes, and I'll say no, and they'll push, and I'll say no, and they'll push again. And all I can say to them is read my lips: No New Taxes."[47] But his inaugural address of January 20, 1989, is replete with proverbial expressions as no other inauguration speech has been. In the following paragraph, for example, he amasses five of them, citing the phrase "A new breeze is blowing" twice at the beginning:

> I come before you and assume the presidency at a moment rich with promise. We live in a peaceful, prosperous time, but we can make it better. For a new breeze is blowing, and a world refreshed by freedom seems reborn; for in man's heart, if not in fact, the day of the dictator is over. The totalitarian era is passing, its old ideas blown away like leaves from an ancient, lifeless tree. A new breeze is blowing, and a nation refreshed by freedom stands ready to push on. There is new ground to be broken, and new action to be taken. There are times when the future seems thick as a fog; you sit and wait, hoping the mists will lift and reveal the right path. But this is a time when the future seems a door you can walk right through into a room called tomorrow. (490–491)

Like other presidents before him, Bush has absolute trust in the American form of government: "We don't have to talk late into the night about which form of government is better. We don't have to wrest justice from the kings. We only have to summon it from within ourselves. We must act on what we know. I take as my guide the hope of a saint: In crucial things, unity; in important things, diversity; in all things, generosity" (491). It would indeed have been considerate if President Bush had told us what saint he had in mind. Most likely he thought of Saint Augustine, to whom the Latin motto "In necessariis unitas, in dubiis libertas, in omnibus caritas" has occasionally been ascribed. The earliest printed reference found thus far dates, however, only from Rupertus Meldenius's treatise on *Praenesis votiva pro pace ecclesiae* (1626).[48] In any case, the English translation would be "In necessary things, unity; in doubtful things, liberty; in all things, charity." Bush and his speech writers varied the sententious motto somewhat, but for the most part it expresses the spirit of the original.

In his National Convention acceptance speech mentioned above, Bush also spoke of the diverse American population as a "thousand points of light in a broad and peaceful sky." Even though the light metaphor was most likely taken from Thomas Wolfe's novel *The Web and the Rock* (1939),[49] the phrase is now associated with George Bush who repeated it in his inaugural address: "I have spoken of a thousand points of light, of all the community organizations that are spread like stars throughout the nation, doing good. We will work hand in hand, encouraging, sometimes leading, sometimes being led, rewarding" (493). In his forward-looking message, Bush claims proverbially that "We can't turn back the clocks, [...] and we don't wish to turn back time" (494). And he even changes the pecuniary proverb "Money begets money" into an expression of faith and goodwill: "There are today Americans who are held against their will in foreign lands, and Americans who are unaccounted for. Assistance can be shown here, and will be long remembered. Goodwill begets goodwill. Good faith can be a spiral that endlessly moves on" (494).

But speaking of money and the need of bringing the deficit down, Bush uttered the following fascinating proverbial words: "We have more will than wallet; but will is what we need. We will make the hard choices, looking at what we have and perhaps allocating differently, making our decisions based on honest need and prudent safety. And then we will do the wisest thing of all: we will turn to the only resource we have that in times of need always grows—the goodness and the courage of the American people" (492). The phrase "To have more will than wallet" with its striking alliteration is nowhere to be found in dictionaries of formulaic language. However, Bush probably based it on the phraseological structure of "To have more X than Y," as for example in "To have more luck than brains (sense)," "To have more cry than wool," etc. In addition, it seems that the President also had the old proverb "Where there is a will, there is a way" in mind.

The six pages of Bush's inaugural speech are certainly a solid testimony that proverbial language is part of this ceremonial performance by newly elected presidents. In this particular case, there is even a proverbial *leitmotif* in that George Bush returns two more times to the proverbial expression "A new breeze is blowing." Regarding the Vietnam war, Bush said: "That war cleaves us still. But, friends, that war began in earnest a quarter of a century ago; and surely the statute of limitations has been reached. This is a fact: the final lesson of Vietnam is that no great nation can long afford to be sundered by a memory. A new breeze is blowing, and the old bipartisanship must be made new again" (493). And then, in the final crescendo of his speech, Bush cites the "breeze" phrase one more time and connects it with an allusion to his earlier sententious motto of unity, diversity, and generosity, certainly an example of a carefully structured oration:

> Some see leadership as a high drama, and the sound of trumpets calling, and sometimes it is that. But I see history as a book with many pages, and each day we fill a page with acts of hopefulness and meaning. The new breeze blows, a page turns, the story unfolds. And so today a chapter begins, a small and stately story of unity, diversity, and generosity— shared, and written, together. (495)

Yet the masterful craftsman of proverbial rhetoric lost his bid for a second term in the White House to a newcomer on the national scene. An economic recession and the unkept promise of "No new taxes" swept George Bush out of office, and in came Bill Clinton for two terms as the forty-second president.

Clinton began his first inaugural address on January 20, 1993, by quoting the famous proverbial triad from the Declaration of Independence, as William McKinley had done at his second inauguration in 1901. Spring had just sprung in Washington, D.C., and this led Clinton to his idea of reinventing America while holding on to its basic principles:

> A spring reborn in the world's oldest democracy, that brings forth the vision and courage to reinvent America. When our Founders boldly declared America's independence to the world and our purposes to the Almighty, they knew America, to endure, would have to change. Not change for change's sake, but change to preserve America's ideals—life, liberty, the pursuit of happiness. Though we march to the music of our time, our mission is timeless. Each generation of Americans must define what it means to be an American. (500)

Clinton follows up his proverbial call "to march to the music of our time" with the metaphorically appropriate proverbial request: "My fellow Americans, you, too, must play your part in our renewal" (503). His merely four-page address ended with a quotation of the Bible: "As we stand at the edge of the twenty-first century, let us begin anew with energy and hope, with faith and discipline, and let us work until our work is done. The Scripture says, 'And let us not be weary in well-doing, for in due season, we shall reap, if we faint not' [Galatians 6:9]" (504). Certainly this little known Bible passage called into memory the biblical proverb "As you sow, so shall you reap" (Galatians 6:7).[50] Clinton did well not to cite this threatening proverb decreeing punishment.

Instead his Bible passage promises rewards to the patiently faithful and hopeful along the lines of the proverb "Good things come to those who wait."

Bill Clinton began his second inaugural address on January 20, 1997, with the old standby proverbial quotation from the Declaration of Independence: "The promise of America was born in the eighteenth century out of the bold conviction that we are all created equal. It was extended and preserved in the nineteenth century, when our nation spread across the continent, saved the Union, and abolished the scourge of slavery. Then, in turmoil and triumph, that promise exploded onto the world stage to make this the American century. What a century [i.e., the twentieth century] it has been! America became the world's mightiest industrial power, saved the world from tyranny in two world wars and a long cold war, and time and again reached across the globe to millions who longed for the blessings of liberty" (506).

After this short history lesson, Clinton moved on to a glance into the challenges of the twenty-first century, declaring that "the future is up to us" (507). This latter statement might well be a shortened version of the longer proverb "The future belongs to those who prepare for it." The only other proverbial utterance in this nondescript speech comes at its end, where Clinton talks about his upcoming problems of having to deal with both houses of Congress being in Republican hands:

> The American people returned to office a president of one party and a Congress of another. Surely they did not do this to advance the politics of petty bickering and extreme partisanship they plainly deplore. No, they call all of us instead to be repairers of the breach and to move on with America's mission. America demands and deserves big things from us, and nothing big ever came from being small. Let us remember the timeless wisdom of Cardinal [Joseph] Bernardin [of Chicago, 1928–1996] when facing the end of his own life. He said, "It is wrong to waste the precious gift of time on acrimony and division." We must not waste the precious gift of this time, for all of us are on that same journey of our lives. And our journey too will come to an end, but the journey of our America must go on. (511)

On the one hand Clinton succeeds splendidly in coining a statement that has the ring of a folk proverb to it. He even integrates the idiomatic meaning of the phrase "to be small" in the sense of being uncooperative into his memorable phrase "Nothing big ever came from being small." But then, as if he perhaps thought this successful pun too trite to conclude his important speech, he adds the awkward and not (if at all) known quotation of Cardinal Bernardin to it, destroying his successful slogan by an awkward and artificial statement. One would have preferred to hear Clinton's own words, and if he wanted yet another quotable sentence about "the precious gift of time," he could have found many of them among folk proverbs. For a start, the three American proverbs "Time wasted getting even could be saved by getting ahead," "Time wasted is time lost," and "Time wasted is never regained"[51] come to mind as suitable possibilities.

This brings us to the much anticipated fifty-fourth inaugural address delivered on January 20, 2001, by George W. Bush as the forty-third president of the United States. Speculation in the media was rampant about what Bush would say and whether he could indeed rise to the rhetorical challenge. As Roderick Hart, Professor of Communication and Government at the University of Texas, had put it quite negatively: "You take a person with no love of language or sense of timing, comparatively devoid of vision, he's a rhetorical disaster area."[52] And yet, immediately after his inaugural address television commentators had considerable praise for this inexperienced public speaker. The day after newspapers followed suit, as can be seen from the analysis by Frank Bruni and David E. Sanger in *The New York Times:* "Mr Bush turned to a loftiness of oratory that he had often avoided in the past, when he would regularly prune his speechwriters' language to fit his folksy, unpretentious image of himself. His remarks today were sprinkled with elegant locutions, artful syntax and alliterative phrases. He spoke to many audiences."[53] This was a speech calling for unity of a country divided, not only because of the bitterly contested election. As Bush had said on December 13, 2001, after the Supreme Court of the United States had in fact made him the new president: "Our nation must rise above a house divided."[54] The allusion to the Bible proverb "A house divided against itself cannot stand," echoing Abraham Lincoln's use of it in his struggle to keep the Union together, was well chosen for this momentous occasion. It had been my conjecture that Bush would incorporate this fitting piece of traditional wisdom in its entirety into this inaugural speech, but he and his speechwriter Michael Gersen decided against it.

Possibly this speech will be counted among the more memorable inaugural addresses. As veteran reporter Bob Schiefer of the CBS network remarked to anchorman Dan Rather immediately following the address, this speech will probably be referred to as the "Four C's Speech." With much eloquent humility George W. Bush had stated that "Today we affirm a new commitment to live out our nation's promise through civility, courage, compassion and character."[55] Of course, there were other "c"-words, such as "commitment," "common good," "citizen," and "community." The most memorable utterance might well be: "I ask you to be citizens. Citizens, not spectators. Citizens, not subjects. Responsible citizens, building communities of service and a nation of character." If then this speech were to go down as the "C-Speech," it will not be because of its mediocre oratorical character but rather because of its message of civic responsibility.

While speaking of civility,[56] courage, compassion, and character, Bush might well have chosen the proverb "Where there is a will, there is a way" to add some traditional authority to his pledge to these ideals. He comes close to doing so by choosing the structure of this proverb to add a considerable proverbial ring to his commitment to compassion: "Where there is suffering, there is duty. Americans in need are not strangers, they are citizens; not problems, but priorities; and all of us are diminished when any are hopeless." A bit later, speaking of basic fairness and human decency, he underscores his pledge to compassion by a significant quotation: "Sometimes in life we are called to do great things. But as a saint of our times has said, every day we are called to do small things with great love. The most important tasks of a democracy are done by everyone."[57] While many listeners might not have been aware that Bush was quoting Mother Teresa, his message of humility certainly touched their hearts.

After his indirect reference to this modern saint, George W. Bush concludes his address quite appropriately with a Bible quotation long turned proverb that once again alludes metaphorically to his theme of humility for the citizens of this great nation:

> After the Declaration of Independence was signed, Virginia statesman John Page wrote to Thomas Jefferson: "We know the race is not to the swift, nor the battle to the strong. Do you not think an angel rides in the whirlwind and directs this storm?" Much time has passed since Jefferson arrived at his inauguration. The years and changes accumulate. But the themes of this day he would know: our nation's grand story of courage, and its simple dream of dignity. [...]
>
> Never tiring, never yielding, never finishing, we renew that purpose today: to make our country more just and generous, to affirm the dignity of our lives and every life.
>
> This work continues. This story goes on. And an angel rides the whirlwind and directs this storm.
>
> God bless you all, and God bless America.

Perhaps Bush is also alluding to the cautionary biblical proverb "They that sow the wind shall reap the whirlwind" (Hosea 8:7) in these final comments. With the two proverbial metaphors he makes the best possible use of folk wisdom, namely that of indirection.[58] On the one hand he sends an indirect message to the world that America will continue to be a strong defender of human rights, freedom and democracy. But on the other hand he also warns the American citizens not to give in to pride and superiority, for "The race is not to the swift, nor the battle to the strong" (Ecclesiastes 9:11), at least not always. But there is hope and a willingness by the new president that an angel or God will guide him and all Americans in a life dedicated to compassion, dignity, humility and civility in the service of all citizens.

Forty years ago, after the energizing and spirited inaugural address of John F. Kennedy, the editors of *The New Yorker* began their laudatory comments with the observation that "As rhetoric has become an increasingly dispensable member of the liberal arts, people have abandoned the idea, held so firmly by the ancient Greeks and Romans, that eloquence is indispensable to politics. Perhaps President Kennedy's achievements in both spheres will revive a taste for good oratory—a taste that has been alternately frustrated by inarticulateness and dulled by bombast." Stressing Kennedy's adherence to Aristotle's and Cicero's insistence on logical, emotional, and ethical persuasion in the ideal oration, they expressed the hope that Kennedy had "reestablished the tradition of political eloquence."[59] After George W. Bush's first inaugural address there was hope for more eloquent rhetoric once again, an amazing achievement for the new president whose rhetorical skills had been ridiculed. Unfortunately Bush's years as president have not been marked by verbal eloquence, and his second inaugural address, delivered on January 20, 2005, contained no particularly memorable phrase or proverbial statement.

But be that as it may, all presidents have tried to give memorable inaugural addresses. Thus far, the speeches by Abraham Lincoln, Franklin Delano Roosevelt, and John F. Kennedy stand out by far. Not surprisingly, their speeches also contain some of the most often quoted eloquent phrases which have found their way into dictionaries of quotations and proverbs. Presidents address a very heterogeneous audience, and they must find a common denominator in their rhetoric that will be grasped and appreciated by the largest possible number of people, both here in the United States and throughout the world. In an enlightening article on "Maxims, 'Practical Wisdom,' and the Language of Action: Beyond Grand Theory" (1996) in the renowned journal *Political Theory*, the political scientist Ray Nichols argued convincingly that political rhetoric must be characterized by "'practical wisdom,' 'practical knowledge,' 'practical reason,' [and] 'practical judgment.'"[60] The common sense of such practical wisdom expressed in quotable phrases or proverbs definitely adds to the communicative and emotional quality of presidential rhetoric. Inaugural addresses especially are meant to be timely and timeless, and a memorable phrase or a traditional proverb represents a preformulated and commonly known bit of wisdom that underscores the value system and mentality of the people. All of this must be understood with an obvious caveat, of course. As with everything in life the proverbs "Everything in moderation" and "Nothing in excess" also hold true for the use of proverbs in inaugural addresses. But now and then a solid statement of timeless folk wisdom in the form of a proverb will clearly do no harm, as some of the very best inaugural addresses by American presidents make abundantly clear. An occasional proverb at the right moment will not hinder the call for eloquence in political rhetoric.

7

"We Are All in the Same Boat Now"
Proverbial Discourse in the Churchill-Roosevelt Correspondence

Recounting his second visit to Washington in mid-June of 1942 in his celebrated six-volume personal history of *The Second World War* (1948–1954), Prime Minister Winston S. Churchill relates how at a meeting President Franklin Delano Roosevelt and General George C. Marshall agreed spontaneously to let the British armed forces have an urgently needed supply of Sherman tanks and guns. Still overwhelmed years later by this generous and philanthropic action, Churchill cites the proverb "A friend in need is a friend indeed"[1] to underline this clear proof of the close friendship that existed between the United States and Great Britain during the war years. But this piece of traditional wisdom could on a more comprehensive level also serve as a proverbial *leitmotif* to characterize the remarkable friendship that tied these two remarkable world leaders together in their fight against the common enemy in Europe and Asia.

They expressed their friendship for each other during telephone calls and at several high-level meetings, but these oral exchanges were of course not recorded. But there is their extensive correspondence that bears witness to the fact that the two leaders had a special relationship during almost six years between 1939 and 1945. Hardly a day went by when not at least one telegram, memorandum or letter was exchanged, with 1161 and 788 messages sent by Churchill and Roosevelt respectively. Warren F. Kimball has edited this invaluable historical record in three massive volumes of *Churchill & Roosevelt: The Complete Correspondence* (1984) that bring to light the communicative and rhetorical prowess of both men. Since the messages were private and secretive, shared only with very close family members and advisors, they reflect a "candid, friendly, informal atmosphere that both men worked to create and preserve" (I,3).[2] And when certain exchanges were prepared by advisors (primarily in the case of Roosevelt[3]), casual remarks concerning private matters would be added at the end, giving the letters or at least part of them an air of refreshing informality and at times colloquial spontaneity.

Much has been said and written about this friendship, and the numerous comprehensive biographies are replete with factual accounts and at times apocryphal stories.[4] But there are also several book-length studies that deal with their special relationship,[5] with Keith Alldritt's *The Greatest of Friends: Franklin D. Roosevelt and Winston Churchill* (1995) and Jon Meacham's *Franklin and Winston: An Intimate Portrait of an Epic Friendship* (2003)[6] describing and analyzing their friendship without over-romanticizing their "love" for each other. After all, it was Churchill who depended on Roosevelt and the American forces and who had to submit to Roosevelt's idiosyncracies more often than Roosevelt had to put up with Churchill's robust nature. As the war went on and Roosevelt realized that the world would be divided between the United States and the Soviet Union, Churchill was repeatedly made to feel like the third man out among Roosevelt, Stalin, and himself representing the waning British Empire. One is reminded of the proverb "Two is company but three's a crowd," which does not, however, appear in the correspondence.

THE PROVERBIAL PROWESS OF TWO WORLD LEADERS

Churchill and Roosevelt did their best to keep on friendly terms, and whenever there were "lover's quarrels" in their increasingly problematic relationship, both took care to make amends as they fought their common enemies. Great orators and stylists that they were, they always found the right tone and words to heal the wounds inflicted by the game of power politics. In the long run, their friendship survived and their common goal of defeating the Axis powers was achieved. Roosevelt clearly also had his friend Winston Churchill in mind when, at the height of the Second World War, he included the following remarks in his fourth inaugural speech on January 20, 1945: "We have learned that we cannot live alone, at peace; that our own well-being is dependent on the well-being of other nations far away. We have learned that we must live as men, not as ostriches, nor as dogs in the manger. We have learned the simple truth, as Emerson said, that 'the only way to have a friend is to be one.'"[7] The metaphors of the proverbial expressions "to be an ostrich" and "to be a dog in the manger" added much expressiveness to Roosevelt's argument that the United States cannot be blind to world events and that it also cannot retreat into isolationism. Instead, America needs to act as a friend to all free nations, as expressed with the quotation from Ralph Waldo Emerson's essay on *Friendship* (1841) that has long since become a proverb.[8]

Turning from their valiant deeds as politicians to their rhetorical ability, both Churchill and Roosevelt have uttered concise statements that have become part of the sententious if not proverbial repertoire of the Anglo-American language. Two famous examples readily come to mind: Roosevelt, on March 4, 1933, began his first inaugural address with the claim that "the only thing we have to fear is fear itself,"[9] thus rallying the American people to accept his New Deal that would get them out of the devastating depression. And on May 13, 1940, Churchill electrified members of the House of Commons and the entire British nation with his statement "I have nothing to offer but blood, toil, tears and sweat,"[10] getting the British people behind his vigorous struggle against Nazi Germany. Especially regarding Churchill, much has been made of his capacity as a "phrase forger"[11] and his interest in employing the English language as an effective rhetorical weapon.[12] In fact, his predisposition to proverbial rhetoric, something that Adolf Hitler matched with his manipulative use of proverbial language on the other side,[13] has been studied in considerable detail.[14] Roosevelt's careful attention to his oratorical skills at public speeches, press conferences, and especially during his famous "fireside chats" has also been scrutinized,[15] but his quite similar inclination towards the use of proverbs and proverbial expressions has hitherto gone completely unnoticed. There is merely a very short study that refers to Churchill's and Roosevelt's "use of clichés,"[16] but there are no textual examples (!) and proverbial matters are not even mentioned.

To make things worse, scholars have paid very little attention to the style of the letters by these two linguistic giants. Letters as a textual corpus have not received enough attention by language-oriented investigators, and it is amazing that the scrupulous editor of the Churchill and Roosevelt correspondence does not say one word about the rhetorical nature of these important letters in his otherwise highly informative introduction (I, 3–20). And yet, both men were such keen observers and practitioners of language, with Churchill receiving the Nobel prize for literature in 1953, clearly also a recognition of his linguistic abilities. Despite their superb university educations and privileged family backgrounds, the two political leaders were well aware of the fact that they needed to find language with which to relate their ideas clearly and somewhat plainly to the common people. This deep interest in communicating with the masses of their two democracies caused them to craft and deliver speeches (albeit in the case of Roosevelt with the help of highly capable speechwriters) that could reach the general population.

Proverbial expressions and proverbs were most certainly part of this common linguistic ground, and this proverbial language also carried over into their secretive war correspondence. While many letters contain factual paragraphs relating to pragmatic matters of conducting the war, there is always room for personal comments to underscore emotional states, ranging from frustrations and disappointments to expressions of thankfulness and friendship. It is in such tense or joyful passages that the colloquial language of proverbs and proverbial expressions enters, giving their letters a deeply emotional and heart-warming touch. And the two friends are an even match proverbially, with Churchill using 238 proverbial statements in his 1161 letters, messages, and telegrams (an average of one phrase per 4.88 letters), and Roosevelt employing 206 such phrases in his 788 epistolary texts (one phrase per 4.86 letters). This might not be a very high frequency of proverbial utterances, but it must be remembered that some messages are merely a line or two long, while the longer documents are often procedural or planning documents that were composed in matter-of-fact wording. But be that as it may, a close analysis of the proverbial language of this unparalleled correspondence by two superb politicians, admirable human beings, and special friends will show that these colorful metaphors and pieces of folk wisdom added much to their communicative process in highly troubled times.

"Two Hearts that Beat as One"—Personal Touches

It was Roosevelt who on September 11, 1939, shortly after the beginning of World War II, contacted Churchill, thus setting the stage for several years of support and friendship between them as they built a powerful and necessary alliance against the Nazi menace:

> It is because you and I occupied similar positions in the World War that I want you to know how glad I am that you are back again in the Admiralty. Your problems are, I realize, complicated by new factors but the essential is not very different. What I want you and the Prime Minister [Chamberlain] to know is that I shall at all times welcome it if you will keep me in touch personally with anything you want me to know about. You can always send sealed letters through your pouch or my pouch. (I,24)

The fact that both men had been in their respective navies helped to bond them as comrades in their struggles, and they quite obviously delighted in using nautical phrases in their letters as time went on. For now, they are content in proverbially "staying in touch," but also wishing to meet personally, as Roosevelt states on February 1, 1940: "I wish much that I could talk things over with you in person—but I am grateful to you for keeping me in touch, as you do" (I,34). Much, of course, was already at stake for Churchill in his lone fight against Nazi Germany, while the United States still pursued a somewhat isolationist course. Much hoping to draw

America into the war as an ally, Churchill used indirect proverbial language (i.e., "fair play" and "to be at stake") on November 6, 1940, to hint that the newly reelected President needs to look closely at the responsibilities of his country regarding the threatened free world: "I feel that you will not mind my saying that I prayed for your success and that I am truly thankful for it. This does not mean that I seek or wish anything more than the full fair and free play of your mind upon the world issues now at stake in which our two nations have to discharge their respective duties. We are now entering upon a somber phase of what must evidently be a protracted and broadening war, and I look forward to being able to interchange any thoughts with you in all that confidence and goodwill which has grown up between us since I went to the Admiralty at the outbreak" (I,81; repeated on November 8, 1944 [III,383]). This is proverbial pleading by indirection, and Roosevelt, while staying out of the war, helped as much as he could, encouraging his troubled friend on May 1, 1941, by simply stating proverbially: "Keep up the good work" (I,180).

With the United States having entered the war, Churchill wrote a two-line birthday message to his distant friend on January 30, 1942, which shows how political and familial matters add up to a strong personal relationship: "Many happy returns of the day, and may your next birthday see us a long lap forward on our road. Please give my kindest regards to Mrs. Roosevelt" (I,335). Roosevelt responded one day later with a most touching declaration of their friendship: "Thank you ever so much for your wire. It is fun to be in the same decade with you" (I,337).[17] About six weeks later, on March 18, 1942, Roosevelt chose the proverbial expression "to take a leaf out of someone's book" to remind his friend in a very personal manner to take good care of himself:

> I know you will keep up your optimism and your grand driving force, but I know you will not mind if I tell you that you ought to take a leaf out of my notebook. Once a month I go to Hyde Park for four days, crawl into a hole and pull the hole [*sic*] in after me. I am called on the telephone only if something of really great importance occurs. I wish you would try it, and I wish you would lay a few bricks or paint another picture. (I,422)

And when his wife Eleanor went on a good-will visit to Great Britain in October 1942, Franklin sent a short letter along with her that began with "I confide my Missus to take care of you and Mrs. Churchill. I know our better halves will hit it off beautifully" (October 19, 1942; I,633). In addition to this twofold use of proverbial phrases, Roosevelt ends his short note with yet another proverbial metaphor, indicating that he and Churchill were facing similar concerns with the media: "My trip to the west coast was well worth while and the people are all right—not the newspaper owners. You have that same headache" (I,633).

Such short notes referring to their similar situations as President or Prime Minister are often couched in proverbial language, giving them a personal and emotional touch. This is certainly the case in a short personal and secret message that Churchill wrote on July 31, 1943, regarding the Anglo-American policy in the Italian campaign: "I have not had time to consult my colleagues but I have no doubt whatever that our joint draft as amended expresses in perfect harmony the minds of our 2 governments on the broad policy to be pursued [in the case of Italy's surrender]. It seems to be a case of 'Two hearts that beat as one'" (II,367). But there is also humor, as for example in the thank-you note that Churchill included with a portrait of himself for Roosevelt on May 1, 1944: "My dear Franklin, You kindly sent me recently a portrait of yourself which I like very much and have hung in my bedroom. Here is a tit for your tat. I hope you will accept it, flattering though it be to me, and like it as much as I do yours. Yours ever, Winston S. C." (III,120). Churchill also used a bit of proverbial humor in a letter of May 28, 1944, trying to convince his friend to agree to a major strategic meeting: "Doctor Churchill informs you that a sea voyage in one of your great new battleships would do you no end of good" (III,149). Roosevelt clearly enjoyed this type of light-hearted communication to counterbalance the seriousness of the war situation, as seen from his response on the following day: "I should like very much to accept Dr. Churchill's advice to make a sea voyage in your direction and I hope to do so at a later date" (III,151).

And Churchill was persistent in his insistence on a meeting, including also their ally Joseph Stalin (called by them Uncle Joe). In his letter of July 16, 1944, he goes so far as to tell Roosevelt that proverbially speaking, he is completely in his hands, i.e., utterly dependent on Roosevelt's good will: "When are we going to meet and where? That we must meet soon is certain. It would be better that U. J. came too. I am entirely in your hands. I would brave the reporters at Washington or the mosquitos of Alaska!" (III,249). The meeting of the "big three" took place eventually at Yalta between February 4 and 11, 1945,[18] and it was here where Roosevelt openly snubbed Churchill while trying to build a relationship with Stalin who, admittedly, would become a more important partner in world politics after the war than Churchill's declining British Empire. But Churchill, obviously hurt, could forgive (but not forget), addressing his letter of March 17, 1945 quite formerly with "Prime Minister to President Roosevelt." And yet, at the end he signs the letter with his first name Winston, with his epistle stating once again that their friendship has been and will continue to be, proverbially expressed, a rock on which the free world could be helped back on its feet:

> I hope that the numerous telegrams I have to send you on so many of our difficult and intertwined affairs are not becoming a bore to you. Our friendship is the rock on which I build for the future of the world so long as I am one of the builders. [...] I remember the part our personal relations have played in the advance of the world cause now nearing its first military goal. [...] Peace with Germany and Japan on our terms will not bring much rest to you and me (if I am still responsible). When the war of the giants is over, the wars of the pygmies will begin. There will be a torn, ragged and hungry world to help to its feet: and what will Uncle Joe or his successor say to the way we should both like to do it?" (III,574)

Always forward looking, Churchill made amends with his old friend before Roosevelt died on April 12, 1945, leaving Churchill to carry on the fight for democracy as the "iron curtain" fell in Europe and the Cold War commenced.[19]

"The Sooner the Better"—Proverbial Plans

The friendship between Churchill and Roosevelt was in part based on the necessity of working together towards the same goal. The President certainly had it right when on December 25, 1942, he sent this short message to London: "The Roosevelts send the Churchills warm personal Christmas greetings. The old teamwork is grand" (II,88). And for this proverbially grand team of work horses to succeed, it was necessary "to take (keep) the same line" and "to be in step" with each other. These not particularly metaphorical phrases act as *leitmotifs* throughout the letters, giving the two men a colloquial way of reminding each other how important a joint approach to war strategies was: "It is important that we should take the same line although we need not necessarily adopt exactly the same wording" (Churchill, October 14, 1944; III,356); "I have today sent the following to Stalin. You will see that we are in step" (Roosevelt, December 30, 1944; III,482); "I am delighted with our being in such perfect step" (Churchill, April 1, 1945; III,602); and "Please tell me how you think the matter should be handled so that we may keep in line together" (Churchill, April 11, 1945; III,624).

The expressions "to be at stake" and "high stakes" are also repeatedly employed to tell each other in plain language how important various missions are: "Don't you think perhaps it would be beneficial to us both if this leak [to the press] could be run down and so avoid another one in the future when there is more at stake" (Roosevelt, October 4, 1943; II,491); and "The stakes are very high on both sides and the suspense is long-drawn. I feel sure we shall win" (Churchill, March 4, 1944; III,18). For Churchill, who so very much relied on American help, the repeated use of the proverbial expression "to bridge the gap" took on a special sense of urgency as he asked or begged for support: "Immediate needs are: first of all, the loan of forty or fifty of your older destroyers to bridge the gap between what we have now and the large new construction we put in hand at the beginning of the war" (Churchill, May 15, 1940; I,37). And the understanding of the immediacy of assistance and action on both sides of the Atlantic is also well expressed in the non-metaphorical proverb "The sooner, the better" that adds a bit of persuasive power to their statements: "It seems to me in the light of your recent cable the sooner this mission [to discuss Russian supply requirements] gets to Moscow the better" (Roosevelt, September 8, 1941; I,240); "Grand [Churchill's plan to visit the United States]. The quicker the better including the receiver's wife" (Roosevelt, June 10, 1942; I,508); and when it was suggested later that another meeting could take place at Casablanca, Churchill responded immediately and forcefully: "Yes, certainly; the sooner the better. I am greatly relieved. It is the only thing to do" (Churchill, December 21, 1942; II,86). And Roosevelt also relied on this rather blasé proverb in the following year when Churchill agreed to come to Washington: "I am really delighted you are coming. I agree most heartily that we have some important business to settle at once; the sooner the better" (Roosevelt, May 2, 1943; II,206).

The somewhat more metaphorical expression "to be at (break) a deadlock," conjuring up the image of locking brakes on a cart, is quite naturally called upon by the Prime Minister and President to refer to an impasse in negotiations or to an apparently unsolvable problem. Considering the incredible challenges both men faced in executing various plans and actions, this overused English phrase takes on a pressing significance that is anything but a cliché: "I have been much concerned at the delay in reaching an agreement in respect to the naval and air bases [in Great Britain]. Indeed, the negotiations appear to be deadlocked on a number of points of considerable importance" (Roosevelt, February 25, 1941; I,138); "It seems to me that the situation [on the Russian front] is changing so rapidly that we should do well to let a week or so pass before ourselves taking steps to break the deadlock [over letting Anglo-American planes operate behind Russian lines]" (Churchill, December 3, 1942; II,59); and "We must not let this great Italian battle degenerate into a deadlock" (Churchill, October 26, 1943; II,563). Churchill had even been reluctant to send representatives to hold discussions with the Russians: "I deprecate sending our military representatives to Moscow. It will only lead to a deadlock and queer the pitch" (Churchill, December 3, 1942; II,55). Roosevelt might well have had some difficulty understanding the primarily British proverbial expression "to queer the pitch" in the meaning of jeopardizing one's chances beforehand. The "pitch" signifies a place of performance and an interruption could "queer" or spoil the entire matter.[20] In any case, it is of interest to note how Churchill very shrewdly strengthens his "deadlock" metaphor with this somewhat exotic Briticism. It must have struck his friend Franklin somewhat "queer" or odd, while enjoying Winston's proverbial *tour de force*, no doubt!

But as expected, there are also numerous instances where both Churchill and Roosevelt employ much more colorful proverbial expressions and proverbial comparisons. Of particular interest is, for example, Churchill's reversal of the phrase "to make mountains out of molehills" in his message of March 10, 1941, to his American friend: "I have been working steadily about the [American lease of] bases [in England] on turning the mountains back into molehills, but even so, the molehills remain to be disposed of. I hope to send you a cable on Monday leaving very little that is not cleared away. Please lend a hand with the shovel if you can" (I,145). Of course, Roosevelt was more than willing to help wherever he could, stating that "we may still pull some of the chestnuts out of the fire" (May 14, 1941; I,187), the perfect metaphor for performing difficult tasks for an ally. Referring to his commitment to increased production of planes, Roosevelt writes "we will let no grass grow under our feet" (October 19, 1942; I,633), thus underscoring his promise with a colorful image. The headache of finding the best relationship between the production of merchant ships and military escort vessels is also circumscribed proverbially, with the phrase of "having your cake and eating it too" indicating that Roosevelt was aware of the fact that he was expecting too much: "I presume that we shall never satisfy ourselves as to the relative need of merchant ships versus escort vessels. In this case I believe we should try to have our cake and eat it too" (November 20, 1942; II,44). In other words, he was pushing the problem aside, something that he unfortunately also did regarding the vexing Polish problem. Churchill recognized early on that Stalin had his eye on taking control over Poland, but Roosevelt argued with two well-placed proverbial expressions against making an issue out of the matter: "I still think the future government [of Poland] and matters like boundaries can be put on ice until we know more about it. This, in line with my general thought that we ought not to cross bridges till we come to them" (March 16, 1944; III,48). Clearly the President is employing the proverbial phrases here as a convenient ready-made rationalization process of his non-action at the time. Regarding France and its future after D Day and the end of the war, Roosevelt also chose a colorful metaphor to tell Churchill that in the long run France would be his problem: "I am absolutely unwilling to police France and possibly Italy and the Balkans as well. After all, France is your baby and will take a lot of nursing in order to bring it to the point of walking alone. It would be very difficult for me to keep in France my military force or management for any length of time" (February 7, 1944; II,709).

Churchill, the masterful stylist, was perfectly able to match Roosevelt's steady use of proverbial phrases that give his messages a certain conversational tone. More than Roosevelt, he also integrates expressive proverbial comparisons into his explanatory comments, as for example: "Meanwhile all operations for ROUNDUP [code name of a plan for a major invasion of western Europe from England in 1943] should proceed at full blast, thus holding the maximum enemy forces opposite England. All this seems to me as clear as noonday" (July 14, 1942; I,529); "Have just returned from watching the assault [i.e., invasion of southern France] from considerable distance. Everything seems to be working like clockwork here and there have been few casualties so far" (August 16, 1944; III,278); and "It is as plain as a pike staff that his [Vyacheslav Molotov's] tactics are to drag the business [of dealing with Poland] out" (March 27, 1945; III,587). Referring to various other problems, Churchill had also written proverbially to his friend Franklin: "I hope however that you will chase these clouds away" (August 25, 1943; II,436), and referring to the egocentric Charles de Gaulle having become a bit more reasonable, he quite befittingly speaks of the general's former desire to run "a one-man show" of French interests: "I am satisfied that he [de Gaulle] is being increasingly caged and tamed by the Committee [of National Liberation] and that there is no longer any danger of a one-man show" (January 30, 1944; II,693). And very appropriately, Churchill relied on the expression "to be a gamble" regarding the timing of the D Day invasion, stressing the incredible risk factor involved: "I go every weekend to see the armies preparing here and I have visited some of your finest divisions. Even more striking are all the extraordinary structures and mass of craft already prepared. The weather is a great gamble but otherwise I am full of hope" (May 25, 1944; III,143). And the proverbial gamble worked with the massive invasion on the Normandy beaches marking the true beginning of the end of the Third Reich.

"The Pilot Who Weathered the Storm"—Naval Idioms

Both former naval administrators had no problems whatsoever understanding each other's use of maritime expressions. A number of scholars have commented on their predilection towards military metaphors in general and nautical images in particular, adding up to a pervasive war imagery in all modes of oral and written communication.[21] But in the case of studies on Roosevelt, it is as if their authors have never heard of proverbs or proverbial expressions. These genre designations are nowhere to be found, and with very rare exceptions only metaphors are cited as examples without even mentioning the rich proverbial language of both naval persons. They were very cognizant of their earlier employment in their respective navies, with Churchill often referring to himself as "Former Naval Person" in his letters and Roosevelt commenting once: "As Naval people you and I fully understand the vital strength of the fleet [...] and command of the seas means in the long run the saving of democracy and the recovery of those suffering temporary reverses" (June 14, 1940; I,48). In the proverbial "long run" they did, of course, exactly that as captains of their respective "ships of state."[22] Addressing an envelope on January 20, 1941, to "A Certain Naval Person," Roosevelt sent this short note with a quotation from Henry Wadsworth Longfellow's poem "Building of the Ship" to his treasured comrade:

> I think this verse applies to you as it does to us:
> "Sail on, Oh Ship of State!
> Sail on, Oh Union strong and great.
> Humanity with all its fears
> With all the hope of future years
> Is hanging breathless on thy fate." (I,131)

About four weeks later Roosevelt employed the proverbial expression "to stem the tide" to tell the former naval person Churchill that the British war efforts in Greece have made a real difference. By choosing a maritime expression, he was certain to let his friend know how much his efforts in this struggle were appreciated: "I think the feeling in America is that the efforts which your country made to stem the tide in Greece was a worthy effort and the delaying action which you fought there must have greatly weakened the Axis" (May 10, 1941; I,184). And about a week later Churchill made use of the proverbial phrase "to swim against the stream" to reflect on the loss of ships in the Atlantic and the difficulty in building new ones: "Where have we got to then? Just making time and swimming level with the bank against the stream" (May 19, 1941; I,190).

Roosevelt also relied on the proverbial expression of "to be at the helm" to draw Churchill's attention to the risk of crossing the Atlantic by ship: "My one reservation is the great personal risk to you—believe this should be given most careful consideration for the Empire needs you at the helm and we need you there too" (December 10, 1941; I,286). Knowing that Roosevelt would understand his metaphor, Churchill thought it best to couch his thoughts on the final date for the Normandy invasion into naval phraseology as well: "You will see that all plans are related to the X date [the mid-May 1944 schedule of the landing] and if as I think increasingly probable the Y date [June 1944] prevails there is a lot of rope to veer and haul on" (January 8, 1944; II,657). And Roosevelt, instead of writing that the health of his major advisor Harry Hopkins was getting better, turns to the naval phrase "to be on deck" as a fitting metaphor: "Harry is improving slowly following a severe attack of influenza. This however was complicated by a recurrence of his old digestive disturbance. I hope that he will be on deck again in a month's time, but it is a slow job" (January 20, 1944; II,689). And when Roosevelt, as once promised to Churchill, could not be in England for the upcoming June invasion in 1944, he chose the proverbial phrase "to miss the boat" to express his disappointment: "I do not believe I can get away for over a month. Of course, I am greatly disappointed that I could not be in England just at this moment, but perhaps having missed the boat it will be best not to make the trip until the events of the near future are more clear" (May 20, 1944; III,139). Among those future events was also Roosevelt's fourth campaign for the presidency, and it was Churchill who paid his friend in arms a touching compliment after his reelection, drawing very appropriately on the maritime phrase of "to weather the storm" to tell Roosevelt how glad he is that he will continue to be the "pilot" of the American ship of state: "I always said that a great people could be trusted to stand by the pilot who weathered the storm. It is an indescribable relief to me that our comradeship will continue and will help to bring the world out of misery" (November 8, 1944; III,383).

There are many additional phraseological references in the letters that reflect bellicose times, as for example: "We are determined to fight to the last inch and ounce for Egypt" (Churchill, May 3, 1941; I,182); "We hope soon to turn the bombing heat on to Italy" (Churchill, November 13, 1942; I,670); "We must close our ranks on every front for the prosecution of the war" (Roosevelt, April 30, 1943; II,204); "We have under development a project [flying B-29 bombers out of India and China against Japan] whereby we can strike a heavy blow at our enemy in the Pacific early next year with our new heavy bombers" (Roosevelt, November 10, 1943; II,594); and "It may well be that the French losses will grow heavier on and after D Day, but in the heat of battle, when British and United States troops will probably be losing at a much higher rate, a new proportion [regarding these losses] establishes itself in men's minds" (Churchill, May 7, 1944; III,123).

Yet clearly the most important proverbial exchange between Churchill and Roosevelt took place on December 7, 1941, the very day the Japanese had attacked the American naval base at Pearl Harbor. Roosevelt called Churchill to tell him of the event and to inform him that he would ask Congress for a declaration of war against Japan on the next day, with Churchill pledging to do the same. Five years later Churchill recalled the short conversation as follows:

> In two or three minutes Mr. Roosevelt came through. "Mr President, what's this about Japan?" "It's quite true," he replied. "They have attacked us at Pearl Harbor. We are all in the same boat now ...." I got on again and said, "This certainly simplifies things. God be with you," or words of that effect. (I,281)

This recollection of the use of the classical proverbial expression "to be in the same boat" is substantiated by a short exchange between the President and the Prime Minister on the two subsequent days. Having delivered his "war message" to Congress on December 8, 1941,[23] referring at the beginning to the attack as "a date which will live in infamy," Roosevelt wrote this short telegram to Churchill:

> The Senate passed the all-out declaration of war eighty-two to nothing, and the House has passed it three hundred eighty-eight to one. Today all of us are in the same boat with you and the people of the Empire and it is a ship which will not and cannot be sunk. (I,283)

And Churchill telegraphed back on December 9, using the proverbial phrase once again to express their common fate and struggle in a most fitting naval metaphor:

> I am grateful for your telegram of December 8. Now that we are as you say "in the same boat" would it not be wise for us to have another conference. We could review the whole war plan in the light of reality and new facts, as well as the problems of production and distribution. I feel all these matters, some of which are causing me concern, can best be

settled on the highest executive level. It would also be a very great pleasure to me to meet you again, and the sooner the better. (I,282–284)

It is questionable whether Roosevelt or Churchill were aware of the fact that their "boat" metaphor is an English translation of the classical Latin proverbial expression "in eadem es navi" that has been traced back to a letter by Cicero from 53 B.C.[24] But they most assuredly were in the same boat now, and their large and powerful vessel with its massive war machinery moved forward "full blast" (Churchill, September 6, 1942; I,592) towards final victory. The proverbial expression "to be in the same boat," uttered at one of the deciding moments in world history, served Roosevelt and Churchill well as the penultimate metaphor for their joint struggle, and as such is convincing proof that proverbial language does indeed run the whole gamut from banal cliché to sublime wisdom.

"We Are on Our Way Shoulder to Shoulder"—Somatic Phrases

Somatic expressions are prevalent in the discourse of both Churchill and Roosevelt, with the latter being particularly conscious of body metaphors due to his own physical disability.[25] They use proverbial expressions to add emotional intensity to their messages, clearly showing that this colloquial language enables them to let their feelings show during extremely stressful times. These phrases also gave the leaders the opportunity to communicate complicated matters in vivid and easily recognizable imagery. It must, of course, be said that Roosevelt and Churchill were fortunate in that they were both native English speakers. These metaphors certainly created ample problems for translators, especially during the meetings with Stalin.[26]

A good example of Churchill's use of somatic phrases appears in his letter of May 17, 1941, where he reports to Roosevelt that Rudolf Hess, Deputy Führer and a major Nazi leader, had landed by parachute in Scotland wanting to negotiate a separate British-German settlement: "But condition was attached that Hitler would not negotiate with [the] present Government in England. This is the old invitation to us to desert all our friends in order to save temporarily the greater part of our skin" (I,188). A few additional proverbial references from Churchill's letters and telegrams include the following: "I do not like these days of personal stress and I have found it difficult to keep my eye on the ball" (February 20, 1942; I,364); "Anything like a serious difference between you and me would break my heart and surely deeply injure both our countries at the height of this terrible struggle" (April 12, 1942; I,449); "I appeal to all patriotic men on both sides of the Atlantic Ocean to stamp their feet on mischief makers and sowers of tares, wherever they may be found, and let the great machines roll into battle under the best possible conditions for our success" (February 11, 1943; II,145); "At this time four years ago our nation and empire stood alone against an overwhelming and implacable enemy, with our backs to the wall" (June 2, 1944; III,158); and "Why can you and I not keep this [matters in Greece] in our own hands considering how we see eye to eye about so much of it?" (June 11, 1944; III,180). This last statement shows how Churchill is quite willing to couple two somatic phrases to add a certain metaphorical persuasiveness to his argument.

Roosevelt proceeds on similar grounds, always ready to include a body metaphor to indicate a human element to his statements, as for example in this plain and simple sentence of June 17, 1941, to his British friend: "I have the distinct feeling in my bones that things are looking up with you and with us" (I,210). A few additional examples show the always encouraging and optimistic Roosevelt, as he tries to help Churchill along, who also was not lacking in positive willpower to carry on the fight: "I hope you will be of good heart in these trying weeks because I am very sure that you have the great confidence of the masses of the British people" (February 18, 1942; I,362); "What Harry [Hopkins] and [General] Geo. Marshall will tell you all about has my heart and *mind* in it" (April 3, 1942; I,441); "Molotov's visit is, I think, a real success because we have got on a personal footing of candor and as good friendship as can be acquired through an interpreter" (May 31, 1942; I,503); "I cannot help feeling that the past week represented a turning point in the whole war and that now we are on our way shoulder to shoulder" (July 27, 1942; I,544; see also June 17, 1943; II,255); "Please let me know when you send [the] message to Stalin and I will immediately send him a similar message, but I am certain both our messages should be so phrased as to leave a good taste in his mouth" (October 5, 1942; I,617); "Best of luck in getting rid of our mutual headache [i.e., Charles de Gaulle's involvement in North Africa]" (June 4, 1943; II,230); "I still keep my fingers crossed. I hope Uncle Joe will agree with us [concerning de Gaulle]" (June 24, 1943; II,277); and "Over here new political situations crop up every day but so far, by constant attention, I am keeping my head above water" (June 2, 1944; III,161).

The letters and telegrams abound with such somatic phrases, often appearing at the end of the message, thereby supplying the previously discussed military or political issues with a bit of humanity. As such, these body metaphors are not "eye wash" (Churchill, August 14, 1942; I,563) or nonsense, but rather significant signals of two great allies, who "must stand shoulder to shoulder, identically and simultaneously through this miserable mess" (Roosevelt, June 17, 1943; II,255).

"Giving the Cat Another Canary to Swallow"— Animal Metaphors

Animal expressions are not as frequent in the Churchill and Roosevelt correspondence as are somatic phrases. But when they do appear, they take on a significant communicative function (including the dehumanization of the enemy), quite often with a bit of irony or humor. Churchill obviously enjoyed writing the following paragraph to Roosevelt on September 14, 1942, clearly having a bit of fun in playfully varying the proverbial phrase "to kill two birds with one stone" to sum up his argument:

> Unless we can offer Stalin something definite for say December, we shall not get the full facilities we need for preparing airfields etc thereabouts. Moreover if we are able to make a firm offer, albeit contingent on favorable events in Egypt, it would be possible at the same time to ask for some favors for the Poles. Stalin has given us sixty thousand Poles with thirty thousand dependents out of which two and a half Divisions are being made, but no provision has been made for recruitment of further Poles, Officers and men, to keep these forces going. Of these there are great numbers in various sorry plights throughout Russia. I thought we might help two birds with one piece of sugar. (I,594)

What an ingenious summation of a rather convoluted argument, driving the major point home with a colorful image in which the traditional "stone" has been replaced by a saccharine substitute of manipulative diplomacy.

Roosevelt also delighted in this type of linguistic play, as for example in the following statements based on animal phrases: "You will readily see that I do not trust the Chicago *Tribune* further than you can throw a bull by the tail but I do think we need a paper of our own for the soldiers in England" (October 6, 1942; I,620); "I went to Hyde Park for five days; got full of health in glorious zero weather—came back here [to Washington] last week and have been feeling like a fighting cock ever since" (March 17, 1943; II,156); "The newspapers here [...] had a field day over General Marshall's duties. The drums were beaten rather loudly by the rest of the press for a few days but it is pretty much of a dead cow now" (October 4, 1943; II,489); "I prefer to leave things [unconditional-surrender declaration concerning Germany] as they are for the time being and we really do not know enough about opinions in Germany itself to go on any fishing expedition there at this time" (January 6, 1944; II,652); and there is also this delightful innovation of the Bible proverb "A leopard cannot change his spots" (Jeremiah 13:23): "It seems clear that prima donnas [here Charles de Gaulle] do not change

their spots" (June 12, 1944; III,181), a turn of phrase that must have met
with hundred percent approval by Winston Churchill.

Charles de Gaulle proved to be a constant headache for both Roosevelt
and Churchill, especially as he sought to solidify Gaullist control in Africa
by pressing for the replacement of Pierre Boisson as Governor General of
West Africa. When General Henri Giraud left de Gaulle behind in Algiers
on a trip to Washington, Churchill rightfully wrote a deeply concerned
telegram to the President on June 25, 1943:

> I am somewhat concerned at Giraud leaving Algiers at this juncture on
> a visit to you. If both [Giraud and de Gaulle] were invited it would be
> all right, but I think it dangerous to leave the field open to De Gaulle,
> especially while the position of Boisson is so uncertain. While the mouse
> is away the cat will play two groups undecipherable. (II,279)

Warren Kimball as editor added the following comment to this short
message: "The final phrase, 'two groups undecipherable,' appears in both the
British and American source documents and would seem to be equivalent of a
phrase made popular in transcripts of the Nixon White House tapes—expletive
deleted!" (II,279). It might well be that Churchill had closed his missive with
something like "God dammit!," but of even greater interest is his most fitting
"anti-proverb"[27] "While the mouse is away the cat will play," the precise inversion
of the traditional proverb "While the cat's away the mice will play" to explain
that the catty de Gaulle would cause even more trouble while being left to his
own devices. This is clearly one of the best examples of proverbial indirection
in this fascinating correspondence replete with proverbial language.

Churchill enjoyed using proverbial metaphors to describe or relate to
certain situations or persons, as for example in "Don't you think the time
has very nearly come when we might let P.Q. [codeword for the joint Anglo-
American appeal to the Italian people] out of the bag? Otherwise we might
lose the psychological effect" (July 13, 1943; II,322); "You will I am sure
share my relief that Leros [an island off the west coast of Turkey] has so far
managed to hold out. 'The dogs under the table eat of the childrens [sic]
crumbs'" (October 23, 1943; II,557); and the somewhat humorous but at
the same time frustrated beginning of yet another letter of February 1, 1944:
"The following has just arrived from U.J. and as I do not know whether you
have a separate copy I repeat it to you with the following comment 'What
can you expect from a bear but a growl?'" (II,694).

But there is one final play with the proverbial comparison "to look like
a (the) cat ate (swallowed) a (the) canary" of 19th-century American origin
with the meaning of being well satisfied with oneself.[28] To understand this

metaphorical game played by the President and Prime Minister, it must be kept in mind that "cat" for them meant the press, while the "canary" stood for a German submarine. Roosevelt began the verbal game with his letter of July 15, 1943, in which he opposed making a special announcement of recent sinkings of German U-boats, lest Americans would get the unfortunate impression that victory was in sight:

> The wave of optimism that has followed recent successes and our latest release on the anti-submarine situation is definitely slowing down production. We cannot afford to further inflate this costly public disregard of the realities of the situation, and therefore I doubt the wisdom at this time of giving the cat another canary to swallow. (II,327)

The linguistically adept Churchill caught on quickly to the metaphor, responding the next day with a two-line telegram that must have tickled Roosevelt: "My cat likes canaries and her appetite grows with eating. However, news is now outdated as we have altogether 18 canaries this month" (II,328). Four days later, on July 20, 1943, Roosevelt kept up the game, but this time "canary" stands for the two islands taken by the allied forces, who are referred to somewhat jokingly as "pussycats." The additional use of the proverbial phrase "to fall into someone's lap" helps to underscore the obvious delight over this easy success: "By-the-way, Martinique and Guadaloupe became ripe and fell into our laps without loss of life or any slowing up of the main war effort—another canary for us pussycats" (II,338). When Churchill writes again on July 25, 1943, the indirect reference to submarines and the media is back again: "Up to date in July, we have caught 26 canaries, which is good for 25 days. There should be quite a good meal for our cats when the time comes" (II,345). And about a week later, on July 31, 1943, he once again has a bit of fun with this proverbial game: "The July canaries to date number 35 making a total of 85 in the 91 days since May 1. Good hunting. Instead of making any announcement as agreed on August 10 let us settle together on the 12th what food our cats are to have" (II,368). Thus ends a proverbial play that at first sight appears to trivialize the dreadful submarine warfare in the Atlantic. But that was by no means the intent by Roosevelt or Churchill, who played the game merely as a bit of humorous relief in a time of terrible stress and loss of thousands of lives on both sides of the raging war.

"All War Is a Struggle for Position"—Proverbial Wisdom

Neither Churchill nor Roosevelt used many proverbs or quotations in their relatively short letters and telegrams. It was one thing to add some metaphorical spice to these messages in the form of proverbial phrases and proverbial comparisons, but folk wisdom or sententious remarks might have added too much of a didactic or authoritative tone to the sensitive correspondence. The Prime Minister and the President in their own way did enough explaining and at times teaching in their letters, and clearly they did not want to add fuel to the fire with ready-made bits of wisdom. And yet, in one of his longer letters to Roosevelt of November 12, 1940, Churchill included the following explanatory paragraph ending with one of Napoleon's famous maxims that clearly has a proverbial ring to it in military circles:

> From this brief summary it must be apparent to you how terribly narrow is the margin upon which we are operating today. Our prospects of victory depend upon our holding all the main theatres we do today, the Atlantic, the Mediterranean including Gibraltar and Suez, the passage from the North to the South Atlantic around the Cape of Good Hope, while you hold the Pacific, till the beginning of 1942, when your great increment of armament comes in. If we give up any of these positions, or the enemy break through, then, the positions from which he can attack become immensely extended, the blockade is impaired, and totalitarian power begins to crowd in on ourselves, on South America, and on you. Never was there a clearer case of Napoleon's maxim: "All war is a struggle for position." (I,91)

And outlining Adolf Hitler's *modus operandi* in his war of aggression, Churchill makes use of the classical proverb "One thing at a time" to describe how the dictator is proceeding step by step: "Hitler has shown himself inclined to avoid the Kaiser's mistake. He does not wish to be drawn into a war with the United States until he has gravely undermined the power of Great Britain. His maxim is 'one at a time'" (December 7, 1940; I,106). Here the proverb served Churchill very well to pinpoint Hitler's method of conquest.

Roosevelt employed proverbs and quotations in a similar vein. In his letter of November 19, 1942, he reports to Churchill how he had used a fascinating non-English proverb during a recent press conference to explain to reporters why he was dealing both with the Vichy French Admiral Jean Darlan and National Liberation General Charles de Gaulle in North Africa, clearly a contradiction but seemingly a necessary evil: "I told the press yesterday in confidence an old orthodox church proverb used in the Balkans that appears applicable to our present Darlan-de Gaulle problem. 'My children, it is permitted you in time of grave danger to walk with the devil

until you have crossed the bridge'" (II,22). This certainly was an apt use of
a proverb to explain a complex strategic maneuver. But there are, of course,
also very straightforward and less serious examples of proverbs in the letters.
Thus, when Roosevelt was dealing with the possible location of a meeting
with Churchill somewhere in North Africa, he writes his friend somewhat
humorously: "I asked General Smith, who left here four or five days ago,
to check up confidentially on some possible tourist oasis as far from any
city or large population as possible. One of the dictionaries says 'an oasis is
never wholly dry.' Good old dictionary!'" (December 14, 1942; II,74), and
when the matter of Roosevelt not receiving a couple of Churchill's telegrams
gets resolved, the Prime Minister writes: "Naturally I was puzzled at not
receiving an answer, so rang up Harry [Hopkins]. All's well that ends well"
(July 13, 1942; I,527).

But there are a few more significant occurrences of proverbs in the
letters, where the folk wisdom helps to clarify a major strategic point, as for
example in the case of what to do with Mussolini and his fascist partners after
their fall from power. Roosevelt once again made use of a proverb to make
his point to Churchill: "It is my opinion that an effort to seize the 'head
devil' in the early future would prejudice our primary objective which is to
get Italy out of the war. We can endeavor to secure the person of the 'head
devil' and his assistants in due time, and then to determine their individual
degrees of guilt for which 'the punishment should fit the crime'" (July 30,
1943; II,362). In other words, Roosevelt is making a promise here that the
fascist leaders will be held accountable in front of a tribunal. And Churchill
also turned to a well-known proverb to argue for the announcement of what
generals will be entrusted with the major D Day invasion: "I am hoping this
can be settled soon. To give OVERLORD the best chance the commanders
should be at it now. The eye of the master maketh the horse fat" (October
22, 1943; II,551). This is powerful metaphorical medicine for President
Roosevelt finally to announce that General Eisenhower would be the
supreme commander for the invasion.

The Normandy beaches but also the future of France were always on
Churchill's and Roosevelt's minds. Especially Churchill worried about a
possible civil war in that country, arguing to Roosevelt that "to carry civil war
into France is to lose the future of that unfortunate country and prevent the
earliest expression of the will of the people as a whole, in fact, we should be
lending ourselves to a process of adding to the burdens and sacrifices of our
troops and of infringing our fundamental principle, 'All governments derive
their just powers from the consent of the governed'" (December 23, 1943;
II,630). Churchill did well to quote this famous phrase from the American
Declaration of Independence (1776), knowing only too well that this would

strike a sympathetic chord in Roosevelt. Churchill was also concerned that the United States might break diplomatic relations with the military government in Argentina, thus interrupting the steady flow of supplies from that country to Great Britain. Again he employs a common folk proverb to plead his case: "Our Chiefs of Staff consider that an immediate cessation of Argentine supplies will rupture military operations on the scale planned for this year. I cannot cut the British ration lower than it is now. We really must look before we leap. We can always save up and pay them back when our hands are clear. I must enter my solemn warning of the gravity of the situation which will follow an interruption of Argentine supplies" (January 23, 1944; II,678). It is important to note how Churchill personalizes the proverb "Look before you leap" by changing it to "We must look before we leap," clearly arguing from the point of view of the Anglo-American alliance and the friendship between Roosevelt and himself.

Finally, there is also Winston Churchill's statement of December 10, 1944: "My guiding principle is 'No peace without victory'" (III,451), a maxim that most certainly expressed Franklin Roosevelt's philosophy as well, as the two world leaders and friends joined forces to defend the democracies against fascist and dictatorial powers. It has not been registered in any of the books of quotations, but President Woodrow Wilson did use a similar formulation during his address to the Senate of the United States on January 22, 1917: "It must be a peace without victory. [...] Only a peace between equals can last."[29] Of course, at the end of World War I, the idealistic Wilson did not get his way of such a peace on equal footing, a failure that in the long run helped to bring about World War II. At the end of this second European catastrophe, both Churchill and Roosevelt understandably felt that idealism once again had to give way to the reality of unconditional surrender and final victory. The crimes against humanity by the Axis powers had been too severe, and the principle of "No peace without victory" had to prevail. Unfortunately, as both Churchill and Harry S. Truman[30] as Roosevelt's successor recognized only too quickly, the victors would very soon slither into a new type of war that became the menace for the next fifty years, the so-called Cold War.

"Lovers' Quarrels Are the Renewal of Love"—
Lasting Friendship

The friendship between the two world leaders became ever more strained during the last year before Roosevelt's death. When they met with Stalin in February of 1945 at Yalta, "it was the true twilight of Roosevelt and Churchill's friendship,"[31] with Roosevelt pushing Churchill aside rather unfairly in favor of building a relationship with Stalin in preparation of dealing with the Soviet Union as a super power after the war. Roosevelt and Churchill also strongly disagreed over Churchill's insistence of an all-out thrust toward Berlin by General Eisenhower so that Berlin could be taken by Anglo-American forces. But the Americans were content with letting the Russian troops march into Berlin first, a situation that later resulted in the division of Germany, the dropping of the iron curtain across Europe, and the beginning of the Cold War. But even though Churchill lost his important plea with Roosevelt and Eisenhower, he chose to accept this unfortunate defeat gracefully in a letter of April 5, 1945, to his friend Roosevelt. Quoting a classical Latin proverb dating back to Terence[32] that is well-known in its English translation of "Lovers' quarrels are the renewal of love," Churchill signalled his continued willingness to maintain his friendship with Roosevelt that had weathered various storms throughout the war:

> My personal relations with General Eisenhower are of the most friendly character. I regard the matter [of the delayed advance by the Allies towards Berlin] as closed and to prove my sincerity I will use one of my very few Latin quotations, "Amantium irae amoris integratio est." (III,612)

Of course, Churchill was perfectly capable of quoting Latin proverbs and sententious remarks,[33] but the fact that he did it in this letter adds a bit of irony to his statement, since it sent Roosevelt's staff scrambling to find a translation. Churchill had, so to speak, a small moment of intellectual one-upmanship, but he nevertheless meant what he said! When the deep friendship between him and Roosevelt came to an abrupt end six days later on April 12, 1945, Churchill must definitely have been glad that he had written this message of loving friendship just before the death of the President.

But it is also one last proverbial exchange between the weary warriors bound together by common goals and, despite their differences towards the very end, by their love and friendship for each other. Their correspondence shows that proverbs and proverbial expressions played a considerable role in their almost daily exchange of messages, and these ready-made phrases of folk speech did much to bring about a mutual international understanding of war strategies and world affairs.[34] It certainly behooves social scientists, linguists, phraseologists and paremiologists to pay much closer attention to the language of political leaders, as they make critical decisions about war and peace throughout the world.[35] While many proverbial statements not mentioned here are of no particular relevance as clichés, those contextualized references discussed take on very important communicative functions, be they emotional, manipulative, explanatory, didactic, or argumentative in nature. In the case of the unique wartime correspondence between Winston S. Churchill and Franklin Delano Roosevelt, this special proverbial language gave both great men the opportunity to build a relationship based on trust and friendship that made it possible for them and the Anglo-American alliance to be and travel "in the same boat" together.

8

"Good Fences Make Good Neighbors"
The Sociopolitical Significance of an Ambiguous Proverb

Contrary to popular opinion, those seemingly plain and simple truths called proverbs are anything but straightforward bits of traditional wisdom. A glance into any proverb collection quickly reveals their contradictory nature, as can be seen from such well-known proverb pairs as "Absence makes the heart grow fonder" and "Out of sight, out of mind." Proverbs are not universal truths, and their insights are not based on a logical philosophical system. Instead, they contain the general observations and experiences of humankind, including life's multifaceted contradictions. But matters are even more complex, since the actual meaning of a particular proverb depends on its function in a given context.[1] In fact, Kenneth Burke was absolutely correct when he stated that metaphorical "proverbs are strategies for dealing with situations. In so far as situations are typical and recurrent in a given social structure, people develop names for them and strategies for handling them. Another name for strategies might be attitudes."[2] By naming social situations, proverbs express generalizations, influence or manipulate people, comment on behavioral patterns, satirize societal ills, strengthen accepted beliefs or, in short, make positive or negative comments regarding practical social conduct.[3] Above all, proverbs are used to disambiguate complex situations and events, but since proverbs as analogies are themselves ambiguous, i.e., open to multiple interpretations, they can prove to be of a vexing and paradoxical analogic ambiguity.[4]

This is certainly true for the appearance of the well-known proverb "Good fences make good neighbors" in such different contextual environments as literary works, legal briefs, mass media, advertisements, and, of course, oral communication on a personal or sociopolitical level. Simply stated, the inherent ambiguity of the proverb lies in the fact that its metaphor contains both the phenomenon of fencing in someone or something while at the same time fencing the person or thing out. This being the case, it is only natural to ask such questions as: When and why do good fences make good neighbors? When and why should we build a fence or wall in the first place? and When and why should we tear such a structure down? In other words, the proverb contains within itself the "irresolvable tension between boundary and hospitality,"[5] between demarcation and common space, between individuality and collectivity, and between many other conflicting attitudes that separate people from each other, be it as neighbors in a village or city or as nations on the international scene. Much is obviously at stake when it comes to erecting a fence or a wall, no matter whether the structure is meant for protection or separation from the other, to wit the Great Wall of China, the Berlin Wall, the walls that separate Americans from Mexicans or Israelis from Palestinians, and one individual neighbor from another. What for heavens sake is the folk wisdom of the proverb "Good fences make good neighbors"? After all, should it not be the goal of humankind to tear down fences and walls everywhere? How can anybody justify the erection or maintenance of barriers between people and neighbors?

In order to answer these legitimate questions, a wealth of materials concerning the history, use, and meaning of the proverb needs to be investigated.[6] The attempt has been made to give as complete a picture of this fascinating proverb as possible, but many additional texts cannot be cited here due to space restrictions. One thing is for certain, however: the study of but one proverb like "Good fences make good neighbors" is an intriguing exercise in culture, folklore, history, language, mentality, psychology, and worldview, indicating clearly that there is no such thing as a simple proverb.

International Proverbs about Fences

People everywhere and at all times have seen the pros and cons of a fence marking property lines and keeping people from infringing on each other's space. Some of them are actually quite similar to the basic idea of the proverb "Good fences make good neighbors," which advocates some distance between neighbors: "There must be a fence between good neighbors" (Norwegian), "Between neighbors' gardens a fence is good" (German), "Build a fence even between intimate friends" (Japanese),"Love your neighbor, but do not throw down the dividing wall" (Indian [Hindi]), and "Love your neighbor, but put up a fence" (Russian). There is even the German proverb "A fence between makes love more keen" that shows how a barrier can, in fact, increase the love between two people who long for each other.[7] If only social and political walls could always bring about love between the parties separated by the fence! Be that as it may, folk wisdom states again and again that some distance between neighbors might be a good idea for the sake of privacy, as can be seen in the basic wisdom expressed in the late medieval Latin proverb

"Bonum est erigere dumos cum vicinis" (It is good to erect hedges with the neighbors).[8]

Two English Antecedents to the Proverb

There are two English proverbs that express the principal idea of "Good fences make good neighbors," albeit in different images and structures. Thus George Herbert printed in his collection of *Outlandish Proverbs* (1640) the text "Love your neighbor, yet pull not downe your hedge."[9] In April of 1754 Benjamin Franklin included the proverb in the wording of "Love thy Neighbor; yet don't pull down your Hedge" in his *Poor Richard's Almanack,*[10] indicating that the proverb had made the jump to North America. An almanac of the year 1811 repeated the proverb with a clear explanation: "Love thy neighbor; yet pull not down thy hedge. That is to say, be courteous, friendly, and neighborly, but never lay yourself open to exposure to anyone."[11] Some fifty years earlier, the British playwright Arthur Murphy had warned in his play *The Citizen* (1763): "You have taught me to be cautious in this wide world—Love your neighbor, but don't pull down your hedge."[12] And there is also this telling allusion to the "hedge" proverb in Margaret Oliphant's Scottish novel *Neighbors on the Green* (1889):

> They [some neighbors] were so friendly, that it was once proposed to cut it [a hedge] down, and give me and my flowers more air; but we both reflected that we were mortal; circumstances might change with both of us; I might die, and some one else come to the cottage whose inspection might not be desirable; or the Admiral might die, and his girls marry, and strangers come. In short, the end of it was that the hedge remained; but instead of being a thick holly wall, like the rest of my inclosure, it was a picturesque hedge of hawthorn, which was very sweet, in spring and a perfect mass of convolvulus in autumn; and it had gaps in it and openings.[13]

The "gaps and openings" in the hedge add a particular charm to this allusion, and also in the larger political world such monstrous walls as the Berlin Wall for example had a hole in them from time to time to leap into freedom. Speaking of Germany, the variant "Liebe deinen Nachbar, reiss aber den Zaun nicht ein" (Love your neighbor, but do not pull down the fence) is still in current use.[14]

In 1946, Richard Hofstadter made the following remark in a review of *A Benjamin Franklin Reader* (1946), alluding to Robert Frost's use of the proverb in his celebrated poem "Mending Wall" (1914): "'Love your neighbor; yet don't pull down your hedge.' (Almost two centuries later a New England poet echoes, 'Good fences make good neighbors.')."[15] The "hedge" proverb continues to be registered in various British and American proverb collections,[16] and it was collected in oral use in the United States between 1945 and 1985.[17] Nevertheless, it is hardly in common use any longer in the States, and Hofstadter is correct in assuming that the "fence" proverb has replaced it.

The second related English proverb is "A hedge between keeps friendship green," an early variant of which has been registered in John Mapletoft's *Select Proverbs* (1707) as a Spanish proverb with an English translation: "Por conservar amistad pared en medio. A Wall between both best preserves Friendship."[18] It might be of interest here that Ralph Waldo Emerson included this translated proverb from Spain in a journal entry of May 12, 1832: "A wall between both, best preserves friendship."[19] This proverb also was brought to America by immigrants from the British Isles.[20] While this text is still heard from time to time in oral communication in the English-speaking world, it is basically on its way to extinction due to the widespread currency of the "fence" proverb. The implication is once again that some distance is needed between neighbors or friends if their positive relationship is to last. Hedges, however, are not particularly common in the United States, where fences are used to separate one piece of property from another (in earlier times, of course, also stone walls as in Great Britain). The newer proverb "Good fences make good neighbors" is thus a metaphor more befitting the reality of the American landscape.

Proverbs of the Structure "Good X Make(s) Good Y"

While the two "hedge" proverbs express similar ideas to the "fence" proverb, they certainly don't have the same linguistic structure upon which "Good fences make good neighbors" might have been constructed. Such proverbs do exist, however, in the English language, for example "Good ware makes quick markets,"[21] "Good cause makes a stout heart and a strong arm," "Good harvests make men prodigal, bad ones provident," "Good words make amends for misdeeds,"[22] and "Good horses make short miles."[23] However, these texts contain only the first part of the pattern, namely "Good X make(s) ..." But here are a number of proverbs that are based on the entire structure of "Good X make(s) good Y": "Good beginning maketh [makes a] good ending,"[24] "A good husband makes a good wife," "A good Jack makes a good Jill," "Good masters make good servants," and "A good wife makes a good husband."[25] Any of these texts might well have provided the structure and pattern for the "fence" proverb.

There is one more proverb that must be mentioned as a possible influence, namely the common European proverb "A good lawyer, an evil neighbor" that has been traced back to Randle Cotgrave's *A Dictionarie of the French and English Tongue* (1611).[26] The early American minister and writer Cotton Mather stated in 1710 that "There has been an old Complaint, That a Good Lawyer seldom is a good Neighbor," and Benjamin Franklin cited it in June of 1737 in *Poor Richard's Almanack* as "A good Lawyer, a bad Neighbor."[27] The meaning of this proverb is that lawyers make bad neighbors because they might just use their legal knowledge to their personal advantage against a trusting neighbor. The slightly expanded variant "A good lawyer makes a bad neighbor"[28] is of additional interest due to the fact that the "fence" proverb has occupied lawyers to a large degree as they litigate issues that involve barriers of various types.

The Irish Variant "Good Mearings Make Good Neighbors"

As I reviewed Fionnuala Williams' collection of *Irish Proverbs: Traditional Wit and Wisdom* (2000), I discovered the Irish proverb "Good mearings make good neighbors" in the volume.[29] At that time I queried: "And how about 'Good mearings make good neighbors', where 'a mearing' is a boundary between land owned by different people? Might this be the precursor of what is thought to be an American proverb, namely 'Good fences make good neighbors'? First recorded in the United States in 1846, might Irish people have brought this with them to America?" In the meantime my friend Fionnuala Williams has spent many hours looking for Irish texts of this proverb, and she has found a number of them in the famous *Schools' Manuscript Collection* of folklore with its valuable holdings of Irish proverbs. The "mearing" proverb is still known and used in Ireland today, even though the "fence" proverb is clearly gaining ground with the strong influence of English over Gaelic.

Fionnuala Williams also provided me with the Gaelic variant "Cha raibh cómhursana agat ariamh chomh mhaith le teoranntaibh—You never had neighbors as good as boundary fences. [attached explanation:] Because they prevent so many quarrels and law-suits" out of Énrí Ó Muirgheasa's (Henry Morris) collection of Ulster proverbs *Seanfhocail Uladh* (1907).[30] A similar text was included in Patrick S. Dinneen's *An Irish-English Dictionary:* "Ní raibh cómharsa agat riamh níos feárr 'ná teoirinnte—boundaries are ever one's best neighbors" (1927).[31] But more important, the Gaelic proverb "Fál maith a dhéanus comharsana maithe—Good mearings make good neighbors," as registered by Williams, was originally published in the second volume of Tomás S. Ó Máille's collection of Connacht proverbs *Sean-fhocla*

Chonnacht (1952)[32] with the indication of an earlier publication date of 1936 added to it. This is all of great speculative interest, since it might be possible that the Irish proverb "Good mearings make good neighbors" might have been current in Ireland already in the first half of the nineteenth century. If that was indeed the case, then Irish immigrants could have brought it to America with them. The Gaelic might then have been translated into English, substituting for the unknown word of "mearing" the generally known noun "fence." As this new variant became known, it took a hold in Ireland and Great Britain after the second World War with the ever increasing influence of the American version of the English language.

Whether or not the Gaelic proverb travelled to the United States, where it might have become the proverb "Good fences make good neighbors" by a slight change in translation, must unfortunately remain conjecture at this point. What is needed are references and dates of the Irish text that predate 1936 and go back to before 1846, the year of the first recorded text of the proverb "Good fences make good neighbors" in the United States.[33] There is, of course, also the definite possibility that there is no Irish connection at all. There is such a thing as polygenesis in proverbs (the independent invention of similar texts in different places continues), not surprisingly, perhaps, due to their shortness and formulaic structures.

THE HISTORY OF THE PROVERB BEFORE 1914

Whether of Irish or American origin, the "fence" proverb appears to have had a slow start indeed. If the proverb did not travel from Ireland to the States in the form of "Good mearings make good neighbors," and if therefore polygenesis is at play, then the origin of the American proverb might well be found in a passage of a letter which the Reverend Ezekiel Rogers of a settlement at Rowley, Massachusetts, wrote to Governor John Winthrop on June 30, 1640: "Touching the buisinesse of the Bounds, which we haue now in agitation; I haue thought, that a good fence helpeth to keepe peace betweene neighbors; but let vs take heede that we make not a high stone wall, to keepe vs from meeting."[34] Certainly this text connects fences and neighbors, but it is still a far cry from the "fence" proverb under discussion. In fact, the next reference that comes close in commenting on fences and neighbors and that might have a bit of proverbial ring to it appeared in a farmer's almanac over one hundred sixty years later, in 1804: "Look to your fences; and if your neighbor neglects to repair and keep in order his half, do it yourself; you will get your pay."[35] More to the proverbial point is the following statement in Hugh Henry Brackenridge's book on *Modern Chivalry* (1815), which satirizes various aspects of social and political life in America. Reflecting on Thomas Jefferson as President, he states: "I was always with him in his apprehensions of John Bull; and I deplored his errors only because he left himself in a situation to invite the horns of that maddest of all mad cattle. Good fences restrain fencebreaking beasts, and preserve good neighborhoods."[36] This formulation from 1815 contains the twofold use of the adjective "good" and approaches to a considerable degree the wording of the "fence" proverb. The passage also already mirrors the political interpretation of the proverb that has become quite prevalent in the modern mass media.

A fascinating variant, stressing the negative results of not keeping up one's fences, appeared fifteen years later in *The Vermont Anti-Masonic Almanac for the Year of Our Lord 1831:* "Poor fences make lean cattle and ill-natured neighbors."[37] This text is cited as a piece of farm wisdom, and there is no reason to doubt its proverbiality, even though a few more references would be welcome. It basically is the other side of the coin of the "fence" proverb, especially if one were to simply state "Poor fences make poor neighbors."

It took another fifteen years until the proverb "Good fences make good neighbors" finally appeared in print in that precise wording for the first time in *Dwights American Magazine, and Family Newspaper* of December 5, 1846, with a second reference shortly afterwards in the *Defiance [Ohio] Democrat* newspaper of May 27, 1847.[38] The third early reference was located in *Blum's Farmer's and Planter's Almanac* for 1850, repeated in the same almanac for the year 1861. The folklorist Addison Barker, who found the almanac references one hundred years after their initial publication, published his discovery in a barely half-a-page note in the *Journal of American Folklore* with the commentary that "It is possible that an early editor found 'Good fences make good neighbors' in a New England almanac or farm journal. Or he may have gleaned the proverb from oral currency."[39] Some years ago, in a chapter on the flavor of regional Vermont proverbs for which I had chosen the tongue-in-cheek title "Good Proverbs Make Good Vermonters," I stated as an aside that "I would give a lot to locate the proverb 'Good fences make good neighbors' in a Vermont publication prior to 1850 [now it should be 1846]."[40] Unfortunately I have still not succeeded in doing so, and the honor of the first printed references of the proverb thus far goes to *Dwights American Magazine* from New York, the *Defiance [Ohio] Democrat* newspaper and to Winston-Salem, North Carolina, where *Blum's Farmer's and Planter's Almanac* has been published in large editions since 1828 (more than 200,000 copies in the 1950s). To be sure, there is an illustration of two farmers working on each side of a fence in the *Western Agricultural Almanac* from Rochester, New York, for the month of April 1822.[41] But alas, the proverb was not printed under it as an explanatory comment. This was done only in a reprint of the picture in an article on "Early Almanacs of Rochester"[42] over one hundred years later. No doubt the proverb was in oral circulation during the first half of the nineteenth century, and perhaps it reached New York, Ohio, and the American South from Vermont or another New England state. But be that as it may, for the present study the dates of the first appearances of the proverb in print are the years 1846, 1847, and 1850!

If the proverb was in fact in oral use in the first half of the nineteenth century, the historian James Veech appears not to have known it when he wrote his book on the *Mason and Dixon's Line: A History. Including an Outline of the Boundary Controversy Between Pennsylvania and Virginia* in the year 1857. As the title indicates, this book deals with a major historical boundary, and the precise wording of the "fence" proverb, if in fact it had reached considerable currency, would have been most appropriate. Instead, Veech seems to fumble for a piece of wisdom to end the following paragraph, succeeding only partially in making a somewhat formulaic statement:

> Very many of the marks and monuments upon the line have been removed, or have crumbled down; and its vista is so much grown up as to be hardly distinguishable from the adjacent forests. It should be retraced and remarked. Except in part of Greene county, all the original surveys of lands upon the line were made after it was authoritatively fixed. Hence no inconvenience or trouble has yet arisen from its partial obliteration. But one of the best securities for peace between neighbors is to keep up good division fences.[43]

And yet, as the *Transactions of the State Agricultural Society of Michigan; with Reports of County Agricultural Societies for the Year 1859* show, the proverb had made its way West (perhaps with Vermont farmers moving on for better fields?) to Michigan: "Good fences make good neighbors, and enable the farmer when he retires to bed at night, to awake in the morning conscious that his crops are secure, and that the labor of weeks are [*sic*] not destroyed in an hour by his neighbor's or his own stock."[44] This statement is a precise explanation of the basic meaning of this proverb, describing the need of good fences on farm land, where the maintenance of the fence or wall depends on responsible reciprocity among neighbors.

By April 3, 1885, the proverb found its way into the *Home Advocate,* a newspaper published in Union Parish, Louisiana,[45] and on June 16, 1901, finally, the proverb had its debut in an article on "Impressions of the New South" by James C. Bayles in the ultimate American newspaper, *The New*

York Times: "I also observe that the fence has reached a stage of development in its evolution from the elongated brush pile in which it combines utility with so much of beauty as inheres in right lines. If it be true that good fences make good neighbors, the people of this part of the South must dwell together in great amity."[46] The introductory formula "if it be true" can be understood as a marker indicating the common currency of the "fence" proverb at the end of the nineteenth century.

The Proverb in Dictionaries of Quotations and Proverbs

The numerous dictionaries available to the phrasal sleuth are not of much help in providing early references except for registering that most people today think of the American poet Robert Frost when they hear or use the "fence" proverb. This goes so far that many English speakers, not only in the United States, think that the proverb was coined by Frost. Nigel Rees has observed the matter well in one of his quotation dictionaries: "Good fences make good neighbors. This proverbial thought is best known because of the poem 'Mending Wall' in Frost's *North of Boston* (1914), which includes the lines: "My apple trees will never get across / And eat the cones under his pines, I tell him. / He only says, Good fences make good neighbors."[47] The proverb actually appears twice in this very popular poem, and there can be no doubt that it helped to spread the proverbial wisdom throughout the United States and beyond, either with Frost's name attached to it or standing by itself as a piece of traditional wisdom. As far as quotation dictionaries are concerned, their authors usually cite precisely these three lines of the poem with appropriate credits to Robert Frost, starting as early as 1922, a mere eight years after the original publication of the poem.[48]

Matters are a bit more uncertain in those quotation dictionaries where only the one line with the proverb "Good fences makes good neighbors" is cited together with the name of Robert Frost. Readers might in this case jump to the conclusion that Frost originated the proverb.[49] Elizabeth Knowles has solved this predicament very well in her *The Oxford Dictionary of Phrase, Saying, and Quotation* (1997) by registering the three lines of the poem with the name of Robert Frost in one place and the "fence" proverb by itself as an anonymous bit of folk wisdom in another.[50] Tad Tuleja also succeeds splendidly in the entry in his *Book of Popular Americana* (1994), even though he does not register the three lines of the poem but rather the first line and the adage, i.e., the proverb: "Mending Wall (1914) A poem by Robert Frost recounting the mutual repair of a wall by the poet [more correctly: the speaker] and a neighbor. It is remembered chiefly for its opening line, 'Something there is that doesn't love a wall,' and the neighbor's paradoxical adage 'Good fences make good neighbors.'"[51] This statement also refers once again to the fact that people associate the proverb with Frost's famous poem. The same is true for the entry in *The Dictionary of Cultural Literacy* (1988), whose authors cite the proverb with explanations, clearly stating that Frost is quoting a folk proverb in his poem: *"Good fences make good neighbors.* Good neighbors respect one another's property. Good farmers, for example, maintain their fences in order to keep their livestock from wandering onto neighboring farms. This PROVERB appears in the poem 'Mending Wall,' by Robert Frost."[52]

Before turning to paremiographical dictionaries, it is at least of some interest that Archer Taylor in his celebrated book on *The Proverb* (1931) does not refer to Robert Frost at all. He clearly considers "Good fences make good neighbors" to be a *bona fide* proverb, albeit of a more recent vintage then classical and medieval proverbs based on the structural pattern "Where there is X, there is Y": "We may perhaps see the difference between this type and the modern traditional proverb in the contrast between Ubi bona custodia, ibi bona pax ('Where there is good guarding, there peace is kept') and Good fences make good neighbors."[53] Another folklorist, Harold W. Thompson, was of the same opinion as Taylor in considering the "fence" proverb to be well established in the 1930s. He collected it in the state of New York and interprets its wisdom to be of the type "found in various proverbs of *ironical* and even *Cynical observation,* of which Robert Frost has selected one for a famous poem: 'Good fences make good neighbors.'"[54] And yet, if the proverb was so well established by the mid-20th century, how is it possible that Henry W. Woods failed to include it in his otherwise very useful collection of *American Sayings* (1945)? It also does not appear in David Kin's *Dictionary of American Proverbs* (1955), even though the folklorist W. Edson Richmond had cited it in a small collection of proverbs from Indiana as a perfect example for a "folk proverb."[55] And to add insult to injury, how could the proverb possibly have escaped the editors of the second edition of *The Oxford English Dictionary* (1989), especially since John A. Simpson as one of the two major editors had included it in his valuable *The Concise Oxford Dictionary of Proverbs* (1982)?[56] But such are the pitfalls of lexicography in general and paremiography in particular. It takes time for "new" words and phrases to be picked up, and some expressions never make it into dictionaries and collections.

But not to despair or even worry—the proverb has been registered in many regional and national collections of proverbs in the second half of the twentieth century, a clear indication that it reached wide currency by then.[57] And yet, it is utterly surprising that the extensive Folklore Archives at the University of California at Berkeley do not contain a single reference to the proverb.[58] But there are also those discoveries that bring special joy to the proverb scholar. This happened to me when I discovered the following entry in a collection of "Vermont Proverbs and Proverbial Sayings" which my former colleague Muriel J. Hughes had gathered by means of field research some four decades ago: "No fences—no neighbors. Cf. Robert Frost, *Mending Wall,* 'Good fences make good neighbors.'"[59] This cynical variant claims that fences are needed among neighbors and that congenial life without fences is not possible (on a literal level the proverb could be interpreted as stating the obvious fact that where there are no fences there are also no people to be found, i.e., there are no settlements). The "fence" proverb, on the other hand, states the same idea in a positive and amicable fashion. The proverbs are two sides of the same coin, but only the "fence" proverb has gained vast currency and has been registered in numerous dictionaries of quotations and proverbs.

ROBERT FROST'S POEM "MENDING WALL"

There is no doubt that the appearance of Robert Frost's celebrated poem "Mending Wall" in the year 1914 was of ultimate significance for the general acceptance of the hitherto rather sporadically employed proverb "Good fences make good neighbors." But the poem with its twice repeated "fence" proverb also did not become generally known immediately. It really became only a literary and cultural icon in 1949, when Frost's volume of *Complete Poems* became a household word at least in the United States. As will be shown later, the proverb, and about a third of the time with reference to Frost's use of it in "Mending Wall," became a proverbial "hit" as of the middle of the twentieth century. It owes this tremendous gain in currency to the fascination with Frost's paradoxical poem that helped to zero in on the strikingly ambivalent interpretation possibility of its folk wisdom. Here then is the text of the poem with the twice repeated phrase that "Something there is that doesn't love a wall" and its juxtaposition to the equally repeated proverb "Good fences make good neighbors":

> *Mending Wall*
> Something there is that doesn't love a wall,
> That sends the frozen-ground-swell under it,
> And spills the upper boulders in the sun;
> And makes gaps even two can pass abreast.
> The work of hunters is another thing:
> I have come after them and made repair
> Where they have left not one stone on a stone,

But they would have the rabbit out of hiding,
To please the yelping dogs. The gaps I mean,
No one has seen them made or heard them made,
But at spring mending-time we find them there.
I let my neighbor know beyond the hill;
And on a day we meet to walk the line
And set the wall between us once again.
We keep the wall between us as we go.
To each the boulders that have fallen to each.
And some are loaves and some so nearly balls
We have to use a spell to make them balance:
'Stay where you are until our backs are turned!'
We wear our fingers rough with handling them.
Oh, just another kind of outdoor game,
One on a side. It comes to little more:
There where it is we do not need the wall:
He is all pine and I am apple orchard.
My apple trees will never get across
And eat the cones under his pines, I tell him
He only says. 'Good fences make good neighbors.'
Spring is the mischief in me, and I wonder
If I could put a notion in his head:
'*Why* do they make good neighbors? Isn't it
Where there are cows? But here there are no cows.
Before I built a wall I'd ask to know
What I was walling in or walling out,
And to whom I was like to give offense.
Something there is that doesn't love a wall,
That wants it down.' I could say 'Elves' to him,
But it's not the elves exactly, and I'd rather
He said it for himself. I see him there
Bringing a stone grasped firmly by the top
In each hand, like an old-stone savage armed.
He moves in darkness as it seems to me,
Not of woods only and the shade of trees.
He will not go behind his father's saying,
And he likes having thought of it so well
He says again, 'Good fences make good neighbors.'[60]

Clearly this is a dramatic dialogue containing much irony. Numerous
scholars have attempted to interpret this poem from many points of view,

including aesthetic, folkloristic, literary, and psychological aspects. At least twenty articles have been published on the poem itself, and it is also discussed on several pages in most books on Frost's poetry.[61] The complex meaning of the ambiguous poem can be summarized as follows: it is a poem about boundaries, barriers, (in)determinacy, conventions, tradition, innovation, (dis)agreements, individuality, community, property, behavior, communication, knowledge, and folk wisdom, to be sure. By now it is generally agreed that the speaker of the poem is not Robert Frost, who as the poet intended nothing more or less than to display the confrontation of two neighbors over the maintenance of a wall that, to make things even more difficult, is not really needed any longer for any pragmatic reasons. Commenting on this poem in a letter of November 1, 1927, Frost states that he consciously employed his "innate mischievousness" in setting up the argumentative dialogue in order "to trip the reader head foremost into the boundless."[62] And a great job he did, for readers to this day struggle with the exact meaning of the poem.

It is a shame that so many interpreters of the poem do not identify the "father's saying" as a true proverb, but instead speak of an aphorism,[63] a cliché,[64] a phrase,[65] or a slogan.[66] Speaking for those scholars who recognized the repeated utterance of the neighbor for what it is, the literary folklorist George Monteiro claimed correctly that "when we fail to recognize that the neighbor replies to the poet's [better: speaker's] prodding with a proverb, we miss a good deal of Frost's point."[67] He then proceeds convincingly to explain why this is the case:

> What finally carries through in Frost's poem is the idea that the stock reply—unexamined wisdom from the past—seals off the possibility of further thought and communication. When thought has frozen into folk expression, language itself becomes another wall which cannot know what it would wall in or what it would wall out, but which blindly carries out a new, and perhaps unintended, function. Meeting once a year and insulated from anything beyond simple interaction by their well-defined duties and limits, these 'good' neighbors turn out to be almost incommunicative.[68]

In this interpretation, the proverb would quite literally express the fact that fences create social walls that prevent any type of communication. But are things quite so simple with the meaning of the proverb in the poem and by itself? After all, it is not the "old-stone savage" who initiates the rebuilding of the seemingly senseless wall but rather the intellectually inclined speaker. In other words, perhaps the old-fashioned neighbor really is not such a stubborn blockhead after all. Taking this viewpoint, Fritz Oehlschlaeger suggests the following interpretation:

> The old man's repetition of the saying represents his wise recognition that fences must continually be remade. The saying is itself a fence, for it divides the men while providing a point of contact (and it is only possible to have a point of contact where there is division). As a fence, the saying must be periodically rebuilt against the somethings that 'don't love a wall': most prominently here, the speaker's egotism. After the neighbor's first 'Good fences make good neighbors,' the speaker has intensified his campaign against the wall, and, by extension, against the neighbor's individuality. By the end of the poem it is simply time to hold the speaker in check again, but to do it without giving 'offense.' Thus the neighbor once again goes behind his father's saying.[69]

The old neighbor does in fact understand the meaning of the proverb quite differently from the speaker. He sees the need of the fence to get along with his neighbor, i.e., it is a positive and not a negative barrier or wall. What makes the proverb so difficult to understand in both of its occurrences and different interpretations by the two neighbors is that by its very nature it is a verbal form of indirection. The very fact that the message of the proverb is expressed indirectly through a metaphor makes its dual interpretation possible. Whether the proverb "Good fences makes good neighbors" is looked at positively (valid) or negatively (invalid) very much depends on what side of the fence one is on, whether and what one intends to fence in or fence out, and whether any fence is desirable or necessary in any given situation. Perhaps Robert Frost had nothing else in mind when he wrote this poem but to show that proverbs are verbal devices of mischievous indirection, reflecting by their ambiguous nature the perplexities of life itself. Simply put, Frost is saying that the wisdom of the proverb "Good fences make good neighbors" is in the eye of the beholder. The argument of the neighbors over the (in)validity of the proverb continues to the present day and will not cease to take place. As some scholars have pointed out, the proverb "Good fences make good neighbors" with its possible interpretations also implies the obverse claim that "Good neighbors make good fences."[70] As people deal with forms of appropriate separation (personal space, property, territories, etc.), they do well to stress the need for social interaction and communication across the fence. The "fence" proverb, as it appears in "Mending Wall" (with the emphasis perhaps on mending!) and in oral and written communication, is a perfect metaphor for what keeps people apart or together. It is, in fact, a folkloristic sign for the divergencies and convergencies of life and forces the careful reader into a "deautomatization of cultural conventions of thought and perception."[71]

THE PROVERB IN LITERARY WORKS

It is perhaps not surprising that literary authors have reacted to the ambiguous message of Frost's proverb poem, accusing the poet of "sitting on the fence" when it comes to a clear-cut interpretation of this bit of folk wisdom. In fact, Robert Francis wrote a short prose piece appropriately entitled "Frost as Mugwump" (1980), arguing that Frost "was in favor of walls and he was scornful of walls. In 'Mending Wall' the speaker kids his neighbor for insisting on repairing an unnecessary wall; but the speaker keeps right on doing his share of repairing nevertheless. That was not the only fence that Frost was on both sides of."[72] This is, of course, missing Frost's point of wanting to show the dualistic meaning of the proverb.

The poets who pick up the "fence" proverb after Frost tend to ignore the ambiguous nature of the folk wisdom. Here, for example, is Raymond Souster's four-line poem "The New Fence" (1955) that argues that a fence between good neighbors is simply not necessary:

> *("Good fences make good neighbors"—Robert Frost)*
> Take my next-door neighbor and I,
> waiting eight years to put one up,
> and now that we've actually done it
> wondering why we bothered in the first place.[73]

The Vermont poet Walter Hard, on the other hand, has a typically independent Yankee farmer react quite differently to the proverb in his lengthy poem "Fence and Offense" (1960):

> It is likely that Alvin Paine
> Had never heard of Robert Frost's neighbor,
> The one he walked the line with in spring
> Mending the wall winter's freezing and thawing
> Had made openings in where none were intended.
> Certainly if Alvin had ever heard his convictions,
> That "Good fences make good neighbors,"
> He never showed he took any stock in it.
> Either that or else he had no real desire
> To be a good neighbor if it required
> That he keep his fences mended.
> [...][74]

The poem goes on and shows how the farmer gets into trouble with the new neighbor and the law; they do not want to put up with his meandering cows. This leads to estrangement and anything but neighborliness, showing that the anti-proverb "Bad fences make bad neighbors" has plenty of truth to it. A bit of cooperation would surely have gone a long way, but that would have undermined the farmer's traditional sense of independence. The neighbor slams a lawsuit on him, once again not taking recourse in neighborly communication. Thus the lack of a proper fence leads to offense on both sides.

But here is yet another twist on the proverb and Robert Frost's poem. While the "fence" proverb helps us to preserve our cherished personal independence and freedom, we must be careful not to twist it into the shortsighted and chauvinistic anti-proverb of "Bad neighbors make good fences"—a thought-provoking variation that concludes Richard Eberhart's poem "Spite Fence" (1980):

> After years of bickerings
>
> Family one
> Put up a spite fence
> Against family two.
>
> Cheek for cheek
> They couldn't stand it.
> The Maine village
>
> Looked so peaceful.
> We drove through yearly,
> We didn't know.
>
> Now if you drive through
> You see the split wood,
> Thin and shrill.
>
> But who's who?
> Who made it,
> One side or the other?
>
> Bad neighbors make good fences.[75]

The "Maine village" that Eberhart speaks of could, of course, just as well be located in Frost's Vermont. But then this might also be a place anywhere in the world, where disagreeing neighbors put up a fence to cut off communication. There are plenty of examples which take the wisdom of the proverb variant "Bad neighbors make good fences" far beyond the quiet village scene to the loud arena of international politics, as for example at the border between Israeli and Palestinian territories.

Regarding its appearance in prose literature, it is of interest to note that the proverb basically enters the scene after 1949, the year that Frost's *Collected Poems* appeared and took America by storm. In contrast with the poets, the prose authors cite the proverb as an independent piece of folk wisdom without any direct or indirect reference to Frost's use of it. In his autobiographical account *A Year of Space* (1953), Eric Linklater simply employs the proverb to indicate that demarcations between properties are necessary: "The care and improvement of one's property, moreover, are traditionally a duty, not only to oneself, but to the community. Good fences make good neighbors, and the general well-being, the aggregate comeliness, of any part of the country are dependent on the respect that each man has for his own."[76] But things are a bit more complicated when Alfred Duggan has King Guthrum (9th century) utter the following words in his historical novel *The King of Athelney* (1961): "I have taken no land from the West Saxons, but in the north we have a saying: 'good fences make good neighbors.' We must fix a sure boundary, to avoid quarrels."[77] As has been shown, the proverb did not exist at that medieval time, and it is thus an anachronism. The pitfalls of proverb use are indeed wide and deep, and they ought not to be used as automatically and thoughtlessly as is often the case in oral and written discourse.

John O'Hara, in his novel *The Lockwood Concern* (1965), has one of his characters go well beyond just erecting a wall. Here a person literally throws the unwanted neighbors off their land, yet another situation which has also happened on the large scale of politics: "The only thing to do was get rid of them, lock, stock and barrel. Good fences make good neighbors, they say. But I did more than build a good fence. I transplanted the neighbors to Lebanon County. I'm very fond of the Dietrichs, now that they're forty miles away."[78] Things are not so drastic in Dudley Lunt's *Taylors Gut in the Delaware State* (1968), where several people, "in line with the old saw that good fences make good neighbors [...] arrived at a complicated compromise agreement [about the Mason-Dixon Line]."[79] In other words, the "fence" proverb can indeed be of considerable help in keeping neighbors from cutting off meaningful communication. A bit of distance and space between two parties can go a long way, especially in the case of bad neighbors.

Of course, the proverb has been taught by parents to their children as a cautionary bit of wisdom to keep one's guard up, to keep a barrier between that is just enough to protect one's privacy: *"Good fences make good neighbors, his mother had told him"*;[80] and "Good fences make mighty good neighbors, you hear me child?"[81] And there is also the variant "Strong fences make good neighbors,"[82] arguing more directly perhaps for the need of fences between people. The proverb appears to be accepted as a non-controversial statement, completely ignoring Frost's deliberation on its validity. But that is the function of proverbs in most contexts: they bring closure to a matter by putting an end to any question whatsoever. In other words, fences of some type are needed if people are to get along, as one meaning of the proverb "Good fences make good neighbors" claims so rigidly and convincingly. Any kind of critical analysis or questioning of its wisdom is missing in these literary references, a fact that seems quite surprising after Frost's intriguing ambivalent interpretation of the proverb.

Fences as Practical and Aesthetic Structures

Anybody who wants to sell fences or who wants to build one for practical or aesthetic reasons will quite naturally interpret the proverb in a most positive light. Advertisers in particular use the proverb as a bit of wisdom to convince customers what a great idea it would be to construct a fence. Here are a few texts from the mass media that show the frequent use of the proverb as an expression of common sense. In a total of 48 located texts, Robert Frost is mentioned only 16 times (one third), indicting that it is the folk wisdom that is being stressed in these positive messages:

Fences Remain in Fashion

The old saying, "good fences make good neighbors," could be rewritten to read, "good fences help make good gardens." There are few structural additions to the home that will bring as much lasting beauty and serve so many purposes as a well-designed and well-constructed garden fence.[83]

Good Fences Make Good Neighbors

Fence Sale!
Custom Fence & Railing Inc.
397A Jericho Tpke., Mineola, N.Y. 11501[84]

In Stone Walls, Peace and Unassuming Beauty

Well, there are still some bovines restrained by stone walls, especially in eastern Connecticut. We view such pastoral scenes and a feeling of peace and contentment pervades the soul. Why, we ask? We enjoy a sense of territorial assuredness. This is seen in our suburban yards of neatly defined boundaries. 'Good fences make good neighbors," we believe, and there is security in a wall.[85]

Fancy Fencing Meets Its Residential Match

Good fences make good neighbors, wrote the American poet Robert Frost in 1914. Seventy-five years later, good fences also make good business. "The use of wooden or wooden type fences seems to be on the increase," noted Terry Dempsey, executive vice president of the International Fence Industry Association [...]. "Consumers today seem more interested in esthetics than strictly enclosures.[86]

Good Fences Make Good Neighbors

Call to see our Fencing and Garden Structures.
Eglantine Timber.[87]

Good Fences to Keep Things in or Keep Them out

Good fences make good neighbors. Good fence information makes building a fence less daunting. If there's a fence in your future, visit a fence specialist or home improvement center, to survey styles and prices.[88]

In Defense of the Fence

"Something there is that doesn't love a wall," Robert Frost opines in his famous poem. Twice he notes with disapproval a wall-building neighbor who says, "Good fences make good neighbors." Forgive me for contradicting the bard of New England, but he is wrong. The neighbor is right. Good fences do make good neighbors—with the proviso that the fence is properly designed and placed.[89]

Many more examples could be cited to document this positive interpretation of the "fence" proverb, either with or without reference to Robert Frost. Little wonder that photographer Josephine von Miklos introduced her splendidly illustrated book *Good Fences Make Good Neighbors* (1972) with the appropriate proverbial lines from Robert Frost's poem and the following acute comments:

> "Fence," according to Mr. Webster, is an abbreviation of "defence" thus indicating an unquiet state of affairs between property owners who may not trust one another to trespass over their side of the line which had been established by custom and law. Thus the tradition of the Great

Wall of China, the walls around Vienna to prevent the Turks from entering the inner city, the battlements and ramparts of medieval castles and towns, has not really changed. When the first Europeans came to this country they simply took up the old habits and ideas to protect themselves against dangers lurking everywhere. Fences and walls meant at least some safety. Also, from the beginning, the word "property" must have had a meaning. In time it attained status, and a beautifully carved fence or even just carefully selected and laid rocks became the symbol of a man and his standing in the world.[90]

Looking at these pictures and reading the texts just mentioned, one is indeed inclined to alter the first line of Robert Frost's poem to "Something there is that does love a wall!" But these are surely "simplistic" views of the "fence" proverb, ignoring its ambivalence in exchange of pragmatic aesthetics.

HOUSING FEUDS OVER FENCES

If matters were only that simple even in everyday neighborly coexistence! Fences can in fact become a bone of contention very quickly, as one newspaper account after another signifies (of 46 references, 16 mention Robert Frost, once again about a third). When this is the case, the positive meaning of the "fence" proverb or Robert Frost's asserted positive interpretation of it are debunked at the beginning of a more detailed account of the neighborly dispute. The journalists seemingly delight in showing that the proverb "Good fences make good neighbors" is not always true—that is not much of an insight, but it serves the reporters well in setting the tone for their articles about such recurring feuds:

Fence Foments Two-Family Feud
If good fences make good neighbors, what's a bad fence make? It makes a feud. In northwest Citrus County a disputed fence has made for an all-out battle between two families, the Sweeneys and the Callaways.[91]

Golf Course Fence Called an "Eyesore"
Good fences are supposed to make good neighbors—but the 1,000-foot-long chain link fence erected by the Columbia Association along its golf course construction project has some neighbors crying foul.[92]

De-fence-ive Residents
"Good fences make good neighbors," the renowned poet Robert Frost wrote, but these days, residents along 75th St. in Middle Village might

strongly disagree. They were good neighbors with the owners of an Amaco gas station at the corner of Eliot Ave. and 74th St., they say, until the new owner put up an 8-foot-high chain-link fence along one edge of the property two months ago.[93]

Dispute About New Fence Turns Ugly

Good fences make good neighbors. Unless only one neighbor wants the fence. What started out as a quarrel about a fence has escalated into a border conflict that has prompted the city to consider stricter fence laws.[94]

Neighbors Can Always Find a Reason to Complain

It was Robert Frost, I believe, who once said that good fences make good neighbors. Nowadays, you need the Berlin Wall. Folks still plan neighborhood gatherings. But everyone sends their attorney.[95]

The allusion to legal matters in this last reference is only the tip of the litigious iceberg, as will be explained later. Of course, this neighborly breakdown is not just observed in the United States, as Patricia Crowe shows in her Stanford University dissertation on *Good Fences Make Good Neighbors: Social Networks at Three Levels of Urbanization in Tirol, Austria* (1978). In a more recent fascinating study concerning social, behavioural, and ethical issues with the title "Good Fences and Good Neighbors: John Locke's Positive Doctrine of Toleration" (1999), Anthony Wilhelm shows convincingly that the seventeenth-century English philosopher John Locke had it right when he argued for a civil society, "for the limitations on human understanding in the world require the duty of toleration and good neighborliness to overcome the insidious effects of self-love in human affairs."[96] It is exactly this positive attitude towards the right and duty to toleration that is needed in the modern world. For this a commitment to the social virtues is necessary, "since fences that secure rights are necessary but not sufficient to foster the neighborliness that invigorates a good community."[97] In other words, people will most likely never be able to live without some fences, but they should at least build them together and in agreement on both sides! Matters are not quite as clear cut and universally applicable, as shown in this neighborhood report from Los Angeles:

Neighbors Tear Down Their Fences to Build Extended Family

Robert Frost wrote "good fences make good neighbors," but some neighbors in this agricultural university town beg to differ. They took out their saws and crowbars the other day and, board by board, tore down the 60 or so feet of fence they saw as not only separating their four homes but also blocking out fellowship, fun and neighborly assistance.[98]

This action worked for these neighbors, and that is wonderful, but as another journalist commented on a large scale three months later, "from the Great Wall of China to the Berlin Wall to the hedgerows of England, people have always felt the need to build barriers whether for political or military reasons, as boundary markers or backdrops, as noise or weather guards or, increasingly today, as privacy protection"[99]. Thank God the Berlin Wall came down shortly after this comment, but new walls and fences are erected every day for many reasons, by far not all of them negative. The key issue is that if fences are wanted or needed, the construction should be a united effort for the good of all people on both sides. There should also be mending of the fence by both parties with plenty opportunities for communication and bridge-building.

METAPHORICAL FENCES

As with all metaphorical proverbs, the "fence" proverb too does not always refer merely literally to fences or by extension to walls. A good example is the scholarly title "Good Fences Make Good Neighbors: The Importance of Maintaining the Boundary Between Factual and Fictional Narrative" (1984) that William Siebenschuh chose for a literary article.[100] Many readers will have thought of Robert Frost, but neither his name nor the poem appear on the pages. Merely the thought of a division between factual and fictional writing brought to mind the proverb as a fitting metaphor for this distinction. For the proverb to be a sign for something quite different is, of course, one of its basic functions as it is employed in the communicative role of folkloristic indirection. Not quite a third (14 of 46) of such texts found in the mass media mention Robert Frost, again indicating that the poet's use of the proverb is losing its importance. The declining cultural literacy is probably part of this process, but journalists might also wish to stress the anonymous folk wisdom of the proverb. Not every context, after all, lends itself to yet another reference to Frost, nor is it necessary with this well-known proverb:

Platonic Pleasantries—Loving Thy Neighbor
Good fences may or may not make good neighbors, but shared walls, particularly when the people living on different sides park their electronic equipment against them, do not. Miss Manners would therefore like to spell out some special rules of neighborliness, based on city living.[101]

When the Neighbors Aren't Friendly

A character in a Robert Frost poem thought good fences make good neighbors. Nowadays, with people living close together, maybe sound-proofing would help too. And for those still unable to stay away from each other's throats, there are an increasing number of mediation programs,[102] which may be the best solution of all.[103]

These Floors Can Handle Noise

Good fences make good neighbors, some say, but silent floors can also help cement a good relationship. And slathering light-weight cement across a wooden sub floor goes a long way in creating that quiet floor.[104]

My Walls Came Tumbling Down—Tales from the Boardroom

Good fences make good neighbors, said Robert Frost but with an attitude like that I doubt he could have become a management consultant. The first recommendation in any report they produce is to tear down all artificial barriers [between] inter- and intra-staff and management. Successful corporations—unlike good neighbors—do not need fences.[105]

Keep Your Hedge to Yourself

Writing about his New England farm, poet Robert Frost observed, "Good fences make good neighbors." Over in Britain, it seems, this saying has taken on a new life. Three thousand people have written the government complaining of overgrown hedges in their neighbors' yards. And nothing short of legislation is being considered to address the issue. "We recognize that overgrown garden hedges have caused distress to thousands of people," said Environment Minister Michael Meacher, "and we take these problems very seriously."[106]

County Mediator Program Offers Help Resolving Feuds

An old adage states that good fences make good neighbors. So do good mediators.[107]

The two final examples indicate that at least in some cases legal mediators might just have to be the ones who can solve confrontational problems that cannot be handled by a normal fence any longer. Unfortunately, the next step is litigation, and the law has indeed occupied itself with the "fence" proverb, both practically and theoretically.

THE PROVERB AND THE LAW

Some of the references cited thus far have already alluded to legal implications of the proverb. In older times, villages and municipalities had in fact professional "fence viewers" to oversee the maintenance of commonly held fences by neighbors. As explained in an article on "Viewers of Fences" (1942) by Vermonter John Gould, "'Good fences make good neighbors,' goes an old New England saying. So firmly convinced of this were the early settlers that they chose fence viewers to make sure that good neighborliness did not suffer from neglect. [...] The fence viewer was an arbiter of disputes, [...] simply a court of original jurisdiction to establish each man's obligation toward maintaining a joint fence. Their function was to settle a dispute before it got to the lawing stage. And that's a pretty good purpose in any man's part of the country."[108] Indeed, much effort, time, and money could be saved if such arbiters were at work in other types of arbitration. Regarding religious education in public schools, for example, matters had to go all the way to the United States Supreme Court, until Justice Felix Frankfurter could finally write in his opinion of March 8, 1948: "We renew our conviction that 'we have staked the very existence of our country on the faith that complete separation between state and religion is best for the state and best for religion.' If nowhere else, in the relation between Church and State, 'good fences make good neighbors.'"[109] This is, of course, a marvelous use of the proverb as a metaphorical and thus indirect device to prove a legal point.

Many scholarly articles have been written on legal arguments that have made positive or negative use of the "fence" proverb to untangle boundary reports, to wit David Glenwick's "'Good Fences Make Bad Neighbors—A Community-Oriented Course in Psychology and Criminal Justice" (1978), Hubert Rottleuthner's "Borders Without Flaw: Do Good Fences Make Good Neighbors?" (1994), and Philip Weinberg's "Congress, the Courts, and Solid Waste Transport: Good Fences Don't Always Make good Neighbors" (1995).[110] F. A. Hayek, in his classic study on *Law, Legislation and Liberty* (1973), has perhaps summarized the legal importance of the "fence" proverb the best:

> The understanding that "good fences make good neighbors," that is, that men can use their own knowledge in the pursuit of their own ends without colliding with each other only if clear boundaries can be drawn between their respective domains of free action, is the basis on which all known civilization has grown. Property, in the wide sense in which it is

used to include not only material things, but (as John Locke defined it) the "life, liberty and estates" of every individual, is the only solution men have yet discovered to the problem of reconciling individual freedom with the absence of conflict. Law, liberty, and property are an inseparable trinity. There can be no law in the sense of universal rules of conduct which does not determine boundaries of the domains of freedom by laying down rules that enable each to ascertain where he is free to act.[111]

More than twenty years later, Hayek's University of Chicago Law School colleague, Richard Epstein, echoed these thoughts in his published lecture on *Transaction Costs and Property Rights: Or Do Good Fences Make Good Neighbors?* (1996) with a more direct reference to Frost's "Mending Wall" poem:

> Robert Frost's poem, "Mending Wall," achieved its greatness precisely because its long dialogue showed a deep ambiguity about fences, and perhaps about the boundaries that these were designed to protect. [...] I think that the message that Robert Frost has offered us is a good one: good fences are not necessarily the right way to create good neighbors, nor even to demarcate the boundary lines that exist between neighbors. But by the same token, we should not want to say that bad fences make good neighbors, or indicate that boundaries are themselves unimportant to the way individuals structure their relationships with each other.[112]

The ambivalence about fences and the proverb can be seen again and again in the treatment they receive in the mass media in reports on legal issues (13 of 34 texts, or slightly less than a third, mention Frost's poem). The lawsuits mentioned usually deal with property issues, of course, and the journalists' reference to the proverb makes very clear indeed how important boundary questions are in our litigious society with its demands of private property:

Talking Trees

Good fences are supposed to make good neighbors. But the adage doesn't seem to extend to the trees hanging over those fences. For years the courts have been cluttered with cases disputing the rights, liabilities and responsibilities of homeowners with the trees that are close to a property line. [...] Lawyers agree that certain basic legal tenets will apply in any state. For example, the ownership is normally determined by the trunk. If it is clearly inside a property line then the tree belongs to the owner of that property regardless of how heavily its limbs hang over the neighbor's land.[113]

Rebuilding Fences Can Strain Good-Neighbor Policy

If good fences make good neighbors, then what is to be said of all the fences that turned into rubble with the January earthquake? That's a question that many neighbors are asking themselves as they deal with the task of rebuilding the many fences that were destroyed or damaged and are still in need of repair. Who pays the bill is the focus of contentiousness by many not-so-neighborly neighbors.[114]

New Umpires Put on the Boundary

Robert Frost wrote "good fences make good neighbors." To take it one step further, good laws make good fences, and so ensure good neighbors. Apart from noise, boundary disputes must be the single biggest cause of disputes between people who live next to each other.[115]

My Strife Next Door

Robert Frost was right: good fences make good neighbors. The trouble starts when the very fences are the cause of the upset neighbors, to the point where m'learned friends start to rub their hands at the prospect of another lucrative day before m'lud. Civil dissent keeps a barrister in silk, so to say.[116]

Resolved: Where Maine Begins and N.H. Ends

If it is true that sometimes good fences make good neighbors, then the US Supreme Court has just helped bring an extra measure of civility to New England by settling a long-standing border dispute between New Hampshire and Maine.[117]

At the end of this section on legal issues, let me cite a somewhat longer legal case that took place in Frost's and my state of Vermont in the year 1989. It shows the ambivalent interpretations of the poem which, in turn, lead lawyers and scholars to draw their own conclusions. But by taking sides, they do in fact miss Frost's point, namely that there are two sides to every argument—fence I mean. Things are never just black and white as well-structured, orderly, and legalistic minds would like to have it. In the following text, already in the headline, various misinterpretations of the poem "Mending Wall" occur. For the record once again: Robert Frost saw both arguments for the fence or wall, and mischievous as he was as an intellectual, he chose neither, knowing darn well that the world cannot live without proper boundaries:

Vermont Fence Ruling Sustains Poet

The Vermont Supreme Court, following a poetic precedent by Robert Frost, says good neighbors need not help keep up good fences. The five justices on Tuesday found unconstitutional a 1790 law making a livestock owner and neighbors equally responsible for maintaining the fences between their properties. The ruling came 75 years after Frost published "Mending Wall." In the poem, Frost questions the springtime ritual of helping his neighbor fix the stone wall between their properties, but the old farmer responds, "Good fences make good neighbors." In Tuesday's case, Ernest and Louise Choquette of Newport objected when their neighbors, Robert and Rose Perrault, refused to help pay for a fence to keep the Choquettes' cows off the Perraults' land. The Choquettes sued the Perraults for $316, the amount the town fence viewer ruled that the Perraults owed under state law. Two lower courts ruled in the Choquettes' favor, but the Supreme Court said the Perraults do not have to pay. The high court's ruling turned on the question of whether the public good outweighed the state constitution's ban on giving special consideration to special groups, in this case, landowners with livestock. The court found it made sense in the 18th, 19th and early 20th centuries to say that the public good outweighed the no-special-interests clause. "The land was predominantly open and farmed, and rural landowners were also livestock owners," Justice Ernest W. Gibson 3d wrote. Without the fence law, livestock owners would be solely responsible for keeping their animals from damaging their neighbors' property and solely responsible for the fence, the court said. But Justice Gibson wrote: "As a result of changing land-use patterns, the law more and more often applies to landowners without livestock. In such situations the fence law is burdensome, arbitrary and confiscatory, and therefore cannot pass constitutional muster."

Many have misread Frost's view, saying he approved shared responsibility for fence-mending, said Margaret Edwards, an English professor at the University of Vermont. But she pointed to lines in which Frost says he sees his neighbor carrying stones:

In each hand, like an old-stone savage armed.

He moves in darkness as it seems to me ...

Ms. Edwards said, "The old farmer is really being put down, though it's done so gracefully it almost doesn't seem that way at first glance."

Robert Bent, the lawyer whose argument prevailed at the high court, said a lower court judge had cited the "good fences make good neighbors" line in the Superior Court decision that the high court overturned. Mr. Bent said the Superior Court judge, Alden Bryan, "sort of missed the point that Frost was making, that his neighbor was holding onto hidebound tradition." He added that the legal argument paralleled the poetic: that the Vermont fence law was a narrow tradition best discarded. The Choquettes' lawyer, Robert Davis, said he was disappointed but could understand the court's logic. He pointed to Justice Gibson's comments about shifting land-use patterns, and to a line from another poet named Robert [i.e., Bob Dylan]: "The times, they are a changin'."[118]

Let me stick out my proverbial neck here for a moment: I would give a lot if this case had come up only now, with all the new interpretations of Frost's poem becoming part of the legal case. My distinguished colleague and friend Prof. Margaret Edwards and a number of the lawyers and judges would have to come to the conclusion that matters are not altogether as clear cut as they thought. First of all, as already discussed above, Robert Frost is not the speaker of the poem. Then it is the speaker who initiates the annual mending of the wall, obviously somewhat believing in the purpose of maintaining it despite the fact that no livestock is on the land any longer. The old neighbor, on the other hand, is the one who realizes that some boundary in the form of a fence or wall is necessary if he wants to keep a distance between himself and his intellectualizing neighbor. In the end, they both realize that somewhat of a fence is a necessity after all, that's why both of them are in fact fixing it. So I would say that the reasoning of the professor, lawyers, and judges of this case is not quite right in their use of Frost's poem, but I too understand that the law regarding the joint pecuniary expenses of maintaining the fence needed to be changed. Too bad it had to get to a law suit, though, for one would think or at least hope that neighborly friendship would try a bit harder to resolve matters. Sometimes it might just still be useful to listen to an old-fashioned fence viewer who might, on a second try, work out a compromise that could be satisfactory and save many legal fees and avoid ill feelings between neighbors.

INTERNATIONAL POLITICS AND THE PROVERB

What is the case in local and legal politics also is played out on the international scene, of course. And Robert Frost and his poem are part of it all, as can be seen from a 1941 newspaper report on Frost receiving an honorary "Doctor of Letters" degree from Princeton University: "Robert Frost, recognized by English-speaking peoples everywhere as the most distinguished poet of the generation which brought new life to poetry in America: [...], lover of New England, he finds sermons in stones, and, proclaiming that good fences make good neighbors, proves that no barriers can hem in the pioneering American spirit in its never-ending hunt for the free, the beautiful and the good in nature and in the daily lives of people."[119] This is indeed well put during the time of World War II, for while there were clearly fences between the warring sides, the spirit of humanity had to cross them for a more peaceful world.

In the second half of the twentieth century the "fence" proverb has repeatedly been employed to comment on US and Canadian relations, two countries who are the best of friends and who maintain this friendship through thousands of miles of a common border. Naturally, there have been periods of friction, but generally the fence has worked well. Joseph Barber's book title *Good Fences Make Good Neighbors. Why the United States Provokes Canadians* (1958) tells some of this story, for even though the two countries are as close in many sociopolitical aspects as any, they both want to retain their separate identities.[120] That is what makes the fence between them such a good one indeed, and it behooves the United States to pay attention to this fact. The mass media reflects this state of affairs in numerous reports making use of the metaphorical "fence" proverb:

Canada Is Missing Opportunities with Mexico

Good fences make good neighbors. So goes the famous aphorism regarding Canada—U.S. relations. The Mulroney government has made this point a central feature of Canadian foreign policy and with good reason—over three quarters of Canadian trade is with our U.S. neighbor [...]. But while Canadians are focussing on the neighbor next door, the U.S., what about the neighbor across the street, Mexico? We share the same geographical block, North America; we share the same large neighbor, but what do Canada and Mexico know of each other?[121]

"Good Fences" Keeping Us Canadian

Much of the history of Canada can be seen as the establishment, maintenance, and adjustment of our border, in the largest sense, with the United States. The border is not eroding and the public on both sides may be of a mind to strengthen "good fences, good neighbors." That same task remains key in public policy as we begin the new century and it remains central to foreign policy especially. Canada is an activist middle power resolutely committed to working with others in the pursuit of humanitarian goals and international cooperation.[122]

Security with Liberty

Since good fences make good neighbors, we've been justifiably worried about the border with our friend and neighbor to the north. Because of our special relationship with Canada, the "fence" between us was almost nonexistent before Sept. 11 [2001]. Unfortunately, Canada's lax refugee and immigration controls become our problem. They allowed numerous suspected terrorists to arrive in Canada and disappear—sometimes into the United States. Canada's cooperation is essential and welcome.[123]

Clearly the "9/11" (2001) terrorist attacks on the United States have brought to light the need for secure borders, once again indicating that the "fence" proverb is an essential rule for international relations. As a British journalist had put it some years earlier: "'Good fences make good neighbors' wrote Robert Frost, the New England poet, and this wisdom is as applicable to the affairs of nations as to neighborhoods. Yet it is being ignored by the West's wishful thinking leaders as they seek to fashion a post-cold war world in which all ground is common, all differences can be compromised and all truths are relative"[124]

Of course, there are also serious concerns at the US and Mexican border, primarily dealing with illegal immigrants and drug traffic. Clark Reynolds discussed these problems in his study *Do Good Fences Make Good Neighbors? Recent and Prospective U.S.—Mexican Relations* (1973) more than three decades ago.[125] The mass media is also filled with numerous articles on the strained relations, signaling that a new iron curtain seems to be falling between the two countries:

Good Fences Do not Necessarily Make Good Neighbors

As American and Mexican legislators tear down the boundaries impeding free trade between the two countries, U.S. military forces and the Border Patrol are trying to stop the high-volume trade in drugs and undocumented labor that already passes between them.[126]

Border Watch—Fence Mending

Good fences make good neighbors. That well-known line doesn't always apply to the border between the United States and Mexico: like the border between any two countries, our fence has some intentional holes. After all, a good deal of the traffic in both directions is entirely legal, welcome and economically beneficial to both sides. But there's truth in the observation that if Mexico City and Washington don't get their border law-enforcement act together, much misery and unhappiness is likely to lie ahead.[127]

Neighbor's Changing Face
The man [Vicente Fox] who would be president of Mexico by the end of
the year met yesterday with the man [Bill Clinton] who by then will only
have weeks left as president of the United States and they talked about
whether you really need good fences to be good neighbors.[128]

Judging by this situation and other international borders, it appears that
fences of some type, hopefully humane barriers, are unfortunately needed
for many reasons. Little wonder that the proverb has been used to report
on US—Russian relations,[129] Burma's isolation,[130] Russia's involvement in
Afghanistan,[131] the Bosnian refugee problem,[132] the maintenance of Asian
national borders,[133] the conflicts in the Balkan states,[134] and many others.
Once again the "fence" proverb is cited either with or without mentioning
Robert Frost's poem (interestingly enough again 16 of 48 texts or one third
mention Frost) in its use on the international scene. All these references
basically state that for the most part fences are needed between international
neighbors, both between those actually fighting with each other and those
trying to get along. The well-known columnist William Safire has put it quite
well by referring to Frost's "deeper sense of fence mending." Better than most
literary scholars, he also speaks of how "the poet explains the comradeship
and sense of mutual respect between two men who recognize each other's
limitations." And then he observes that "fences have an important place in
politics. *Fence mending*—talking to local politicians, contributors, workers,
and newsmen—is considered good and necessary, but *sitting on the fence* is
often considered cowardly and *fence straddling* is opportunistic."[135] Safire
adds three proverbial expressions to the proverb itself, but his main point is
obviously that the necessary fences should be erected out of mutual respect
for each other as a reasonable border and demarcation between friend or foe.

This leads to one last but major employment of the "fence" proverb
on the international scene, to wit its use as a most fitting metaphor in the
Israeli—Palestinian conflict in the Near East. As the journalist Aviva Cantor
put it: "'Good fences make good neighbors,' wrote Robert Frost. If his words
apply to any neighbors, it is to Israelis and Palestinians. The two nations are
like a couple mired in distrust, fear, and hatred. But each lives in a dream
world, because neither is going to get all the property, nor will either succeed
in driving the other out. It is time, then, to separate. [...] Here's where the
fence idea comes in—not steel, mines, and barbed wire, but a living fence
established at an international conference under the umbrella of the United
Nations—which has the structure and the experience of maintaining
peacekeeping operations—and guaranteed by the world body."[136] Five years
later, the Israeli journalist Yosef Goell echoed these sentiments by once again

using the proverb, albeit as a quotation from Frost: "'Good fences make good neighbors.' (Robert Frost) Nations should separate as much as possible from each other. That is how friction can be reduced."[137] By the beginning of 1995, Israeli politicians started to think of a real fence that would separate the Israelis from the Palestinians:

Israel Ponders $230-million West Bank Security Fence

Good fences make good neighbors. That concept—a $230-million fence to separate Israel from the 1.2 million Palestinians in the West Bank—is at the heart of a plan being prepared at Prime Minister Yitzhak Rabin's behest.[138]

Barak Mulls Border Fence Plan

Prime Minister Ehud Barak held a meeting yesterday with several of his ministers to discuss the ways and means of setting up a border fence between Israel and the future Palestinian entity. The prime minister has long advocated the creation of such a barrier, quoting often from the Robert Frost poem about how "good fences make good neighbors," and using grand hand motions to illustrate his belief that the best future for his land involves "us here—and them there."[139]

Good Fences Make Good Negotiators

Once, the goal of American diplomacy in the Middle East was to help Israel and Palestinians live together. Now, the best aim is to help them live apart. As quickly as possible. [...] For the near future, maybe the best possibility is a proposal by former Prime Minister Ehud Barak. Under this plan, Israel would evacuate three-quarters of the West Bank, abandoning some settlements and annexing others, and build a fence the length of the border. [...] It would separate Palestinians from the Israeli military and checkpoints, and Israelis from Palestinian suicide bombers. [...] In some cases, good fences make good neighbors or at least non-bleeding ones.[140]

Separation is perhaps truly the most effective way at the moment to keep Israelis and Palestinians from violent confrontation. From the point of view of Frost's poem and its interpretation of the "fence" proverb, there is, however, one problem with the design of the fence in the Middle East that is being constructed by only the Israelis to protect themselves against the terrorism of suicide bombers. Unfortunately the Palestinian authorities are not necessarily playing their part in avoiding the crossing of terrorists into Israeli territory by fencing in these extremists. In the poem both men work on the fence together to create a border between them, to give them breathing space and to allow them to live their lives in peace and privacy. In any case, alluding to the planned fence between Israelis and the Palestinians, the journalist Matt Rees wrote:

Good Fences for Bad Neighbors

Fencing off Terrorists. Desperate to protect itself from Palestinian bombers, Israel begins to build a controversial and costly wall around the West Bank. The planned barrier consists of multiple obstacles for would-be infiltrators and is similar to a network that runs along Israel's border with Jordan. Building it will cost $1.6 million per mile. The government so far has approved construction along 75 miles, and the Defense Ministry hopes to fence off the entire West Bank.[141]

As the headline of this report indicates, a fence might indeed be the only solution at the moment to keep the Israeli and Palestinian neighbors apart or from killing each other. Referring to the new fence and the "fence" proverb, the *London Times* asked two months later on August 17, 2002: "Can you ever a build a bridge by putting up a fence?"[142] The answer ought to be yes, but the necessary bridge building between Israelis and Palestinians would be much enhanced if both sides and not just one were equally committed to building the fence in the first place. Such "good" fences for "bad" neighbors could indeed prove the proverb "Good fences make good neighbors" correct in the case of the Israeli-Palestinian conflict. And yes, communication across the fence could just build a bridge to a better time when the fence could come down again. A fascinating article with the title "Do Good Fences Make Good Neighbors?: Israel and Lebanon after the Withdrawal" (2000) by Laura Eisenberg concludes with a paragraph that can easily be transposed to the Israeli-Palestinian situation: "The Good fence may be locked, but there is a chance that a good fence can make Israel and Lebanon [the Palestinians], if not good friends, then at least neighbors who no longer trespass one another's property or harbor the other's enemies, both with deadly results. Even as good people on both sides must strive to break down the psychological walls of hostility between Israelis and Lebanese [Palestinians], the material fence separating them must remain, for the indefinite future, high and strong."[143] For now, let's maintain the fence on both sides together and build communicative bridges across the fence.

THE NEED OF FENCES

Speaking of the less violent problems of the electronic world of the Internet, an editorial on "Internet Fences" had something very basic to say about the "fence" proverb: "One of Robert Frost's most famous poems, 'Mending Wall' contains the line, 'Good fences make good neighbors,' which means that even good neighbors want it understood that this land is mine and that land is yours. Put another way, good neighbors talk over the fence, but it is important that the fence be there."[144] It is simply not as easy as some modern fence viewers would have it, realizing that their profession is a dying art, of course: "'Good fences make good neighbors,' Robert Frost once wrote. New England fence viewers disagree. They say that the best fence is no fence at all."[145] Another such simplistic statement claimed: "Good fences make good neighbors, they say. But you know what makes really great neighbors? No fences."[146] But the reporter was writing a story about a beautiful flower garden that connected neighbors, a well chosen exception to prove the general rule that fences are usually needed so that people and nations can get along.

This last reference by the journalist Benjamin Forgey on the exhibition "Between Fences" at the National Building Museum in Washington, D.C. is a befitting summary for this investigation of the "fence" proverb. As he reports on the history of fences in the United States, he makes the all too common error of claiming that Robert Frost coined the proverb. Nevertheless, he is aware of its ambiguity in the poem and as a proverb by itself:

The Great Walls of America

"Good fences make good neighbors." Even the poet who coined this most American of proverbs was ambivalent about it. Robert Frost, in "Mending Wall," put the line in his neighbor's mouth, and then proceeded to compare the poor man to "an old-stone savage" moving around in darkness, "not of woods only and shade of trees." This ambivalence is doubtless why the saying became so popular—you can see both sides and both seem equally true. Or maybe not quite that. It depends on who is laying the fence, and where and why. Sometimes it simply depends on which side of the fence you're on.[147]

But we know, of course, that there are always two sides to each fence, to that barrier that both separates and connects, if effective communication and serious commitment to common goals like peace, for example, are present. When people work together on not totally dispensable fences, they might just build bridges across them and learn to tolerate each other in a congenial, humane way. Fences are a necessary evil in human relationships, and it is better to mend them together than to infringe on each other's territory or privacy. Even though "Something there is that doesn't love a wall," there is ample truth in the proverb that "Good fences make good neighbors."

Notes

1. Different Strokes for Different Folks

An earlier version of this chapter was delivered as a lecture on March 5, 2004, at the international symposium on paremiology in memory of Kazys Grigas at Vilnius, Lithuania.

1. See the bibliographies by Otto Moll, *Sprichwörterbibliographie* (Frankfurt am Main: Vittorio Klostermann, 1958); and Wolfgang Mieder, *International Proverb Scholarship. An Annotated Bibliography*, 4 vols. (New York: Garland Publishing, 1982, 1990 and 1993; New York: Peter Lang, 2001).

2. See Kenneth Burke, "Literature [i.e., Proverbs] as Equipment for Living," in K. Burke, *The Philosophy of Literary Form. Studies in Symbolic Action* (Baton Rouge, Louisiana: Louisiana State University Press, 1941), pp. 253–262; Peter Seitel, "Proverbs: A Social Use of Metaphor," *Genre*, 2 (1969), 122–139; also in Wolfgang Mieder and Alan Dundes (eds.), *The Wisdom of Many: Essays on the Proverb* (New York: Garland Publishing, 1981), pp. 122–139; James Obelkevich, "Proverbs and Social History," in Peter Burke and Roy Porter (eds.), *The Social History of Language* (Cambridge: Cambridge University Press, 1987), pp. 43–72; also in Wolfgang Mieder (ed.), *Wise Words: Essays on the Proverb* (New York: Garland Publishing, 1994), pp. 211–252; and Zuzana Profantová, "Proverbial Tradition as Cultural-Historical and Social Phenomenon," in Peter Ďurčo (ed.), *Europhras '97. Phraseology and Paremiology* (Bratislava: Akadémia PZ, 1998), pp. 302–307.

3. See the numerous essays in Wolfgang Mieder (ed.), *Cognition, Comprehension, and Communication. A Decade of North American Proverb Studies (1990–2000)* (Baltmannsweiler: Schneider Verlag Hohengehren, 2003).

4. Wolfgang Mieder, *Proverbs Are Never Out of Season. Popular Wisdom in the Modern Age* (New York: Oxford University Press, 1993).

5. See Wolfgang Mieder, "Prolegomena to Prospective Paremiography," *Proverbium*, 7 (1990), 133–144; Kazys Grigas, "Problems of the Type in the Comparative Study of Proverbs," *Journal of the Baltic Institute of Folklore*, 1 (1996), 106–127; and K. Grigas, "Einige Probleme der modernen Parömiographie und Parömiologie," *Acta Ethnographia Hungarica*, 45 (2000), 365–369.

6. Kazys Grigas, *Lietuvių patarlės. Lyginamasis tyrinėjimas* (Vilnius, Lithuania: Vaga, 1976), p. 294.

7. Grigas, *Lietuvių patarlės*, p. 295.

8. See Kazys Grigas, "The Motif of the Mote in Someone's Eye and the Comparative Study of a Proverb," *Arv: Nordic Yearbook of Folklore*, 51 (1995), 155–159; and K. Grigas, "Das Sprichwort 'Man soll den Tag nicht vor dem Abend loben' in der Geschichte der europäischen Kulturen," *Proverbium*, 15 (1998), 105–136.

9. For a discussion see Wolfgang Mieder, "The History and Future of Common Proverbs in Europe," in Ilona Nagy and Kincső Verebélyi (eds.), *Folklore in 2000. Voces amicorum Guilhelmo Voigt sexagenario* (Budapest: Universitas Scientiarum de Rolando Eötvös nominata, 2000), pp. 300–314; and Vilmos Voigt, "Lithuanian Proverbs and Their Place in European Paremiology," *Tautosakos Darbai / Folklore Studies* (Vilnius), 15 (22) (2001), 11–16.

10. For this proverb see Wolfgang Mieder, *Tradition and Innovation in Folk Literature* (Hanover, New Hampshire: University Press of New England, 1987), pp. 178–228; and W. Mieder, *"Die großen Fische fressen die kleinen." Ein Sprichwort über die menschliche Natur in Literatur, Medien und Karikaturen* (Wien: Edition Praesens, 2003).

11. For such loan translations see Archer Taylor, *The Proverb* (Cambridge, Massachusetts: Harvard University Press, 1931; rpt. ed. by Wolfgang Mieder. Bern: Peter Lang, 1985), pp. 43–65; and Lutz Röhrich and Wolfgang Mieder, *Sprichwort* (Stuttgart: Metzler, 1977), pp. 37–40.

12. For these two proverbs see Wolfgang Mieder, *Proverbs Are Never Out of Season*, pp. 193–224; and W. Mieder, *Strategies of Wisdom. Anglo-American and German Proverb Studies* (Baltmannsweiler, Germany: Schneider Verlag Hohengehren, 2000), pp. 109–144.

13. See Francis de Caro and William K. McNeil, *American Proverb Literature. A Bibliography* (Bloomington, Indiana: Folklore Forum, Indiana University, 1971); and Wolfgang Mieder, *American Proverbs. A Study of Texts and Contexts* (Bern: Peter Lang, 1989), pp. 47–70.

14. Regarding this apparent dearth of proverbs among Native Americans see Gary Gossen, "Chamula Tzotzil [Mayan Indians from southern Mexico] Proverbs: 'Neither Fish nor Fowl'," in Munro S. Edmonson (ed.), *Meaning in Mayan Languages: Ethnolinguistic Studies* (The Hague: Mouton, 1973), pp. 205–233; also in Wolfgang Mieder (ed.), *Wise Words: Essays on the Proverb*, pp. 351–392; and W. Mieder, *American Proverbs. A Study of Texts and Contexts*, pp. 99–110.

15. For a more detailed discussion and examples see Jack L. Daniel, "Towards an Ethnography of Afroamerican Proverbial Usage," *Black Lines*, 2 (1973), 3–12; and Wolfgang Mieder, *American Proverbs. A Study of Texts and Contexts*, pp. 111–128.

16. Selwyn Gurney Champion, *Racial Proverbs. A Selection of the World's Proverbs Arranged Linguistically* (London: George Routledge, 1938), pp. 613–614.

17. Richard Jente, "The American Proverb," *American Speech,* 7 (1931–1932), 342–348; see also Wolfgang Mieder, *American Proverbs. A Study of Texts and Contexts,* pp. 29–45.

18. The various proverbial texts are listed in Wolfgang Mieder, "'Behold the Proverbs of a People': A Florilegium of Proverbs in Carl Sandburg's Poem *Good Morning, America,*" *Southern Folklore Quarterly,* 35 (1971), 160–168; and W. Mieder, "Proverbs in Carl Sandburg's Poem *The People, Yes,*" *Southern Folklore Quarterly,* 37 (1973), 15–36.

19. For proverbs as expressions of worldview or mentality see Alan Dundes, "Folk Ideas as Units of Worldview," in Américo Paredes and Richard Bauman (eds.), *Toward New Perspectives in Folklore* (Austin, Texas: University of Texas Press, 1972), pp. 93–103; Kimberly J. Lau, "'It's about Time': The Ten Proverbs Most Frequently Used in Newspapers and Their Relation to American Values," *Proverbium,* 13 (1996), 135–159; also in Wolfgang Mieder, *Cognition, Comprehension, and Communication,* pp. 231–254; Stan Nussbaum, *The ABC of American Culture. First Steps toward Understanding the American People through Their Common Sayings and Proverbs* (Colorado Springs, Colorado: Global Mapping International, 1998); and Pekka Hakamies, "Proverbs and Mentality," in Anna-Leena Siikala (ed.), *Myth and Mentality. Studies in Folklore and Popular Thought* (Helsinki: Finnish Literature Society, 2002), pp. 222–230.

20. Carl Sandburg, *The Complete Poems of Carl Sandburg* (New York: Harcourt, Brace, Jovanovich, 1970), pp. 328–330 (section eleven).

21. For a complete list see George B. Bryan and Wolfgang Mieder, "The Proverbial Carl Sandburg (1878–1967). An Index of Folk Speech in His American Poetry," *Proverbium,* 20 (2003), 15–49.

22. Wolfgang Mieder, *Yankee Wisdom. New England Proverbs* (Shelburne, Vermont: The New England Press, 1989).

23. Wolfgang Mieder, *Talk Less and Say More. Vermont Proverbs* (Shelburne, Vermont: The New England Press, 1986).

24. See Stuart A. Gallacher, "Franklin's *Way to Wealth:* A Florilegium of Proverbs and Wise Sayings," *Journal of English and Germanic Philology,* 48 (1949), 229–251; and Wolfgang Mieder, *American Proverbs. A Study of Texts and Contexts,* pp. 129–142.

25. For an intriguing explanation of this positive attitude see Alan Dundes, "Thinking Ahead: A Folkloristic Reflection of the Future Orientation in American Worldview," *Anthropological Quarterly,* 42 (1969), 53–72.

26. For Emerson's keen interest in proverbs see Ralph Charles La Rosa, *Emerson's Proverbial Rhetoric: 1818–1838* (Diss. University of Wisconsin, 1969); and Wolfgang Mieder, *American Proverbs. A Study of Texts and Contexts,* pp. 143–169.

27. See Peter Grzybek, "Foundations of Semiotic Proverb Study," *Proverbium,* 4 (1987), 39–85; also in Wolfgang Mieder (ed.), *Wise Words. Essays on the Proverb,* pp. 31–71; and Anna Tóthné Litovkina, "A Few Aspects of a Semiotic Approach to Proverbs, with Special Reference to Two Important American Publications [W. Mieder, *American Proverbs. A Study of Texts and Contexts* (1989) and W. Mieder et al., *A Dictionary of American Proverbs* (1992)]," *Semiotica,* 108 (1996), 307–380.

28. The lecture was delivered on December 10, 1835, and is included in Stephen E. Whicher, Robert E. Spiller, and Wallace E. Williams (eds.), *The Early Lectures of Ralph Waldo Emerson* (Cambridge, Massachusetts: Harvard University Press, 1964), vol. 1, p. 290.

29. Cited from Alfred R. Ferguson and Joseph Slater (eds.), *The Collected Works of Ralph Waldo Emerson* (Cambridge, Massachusetts: Harvard University Press, 1971), vol. 1, pp. 21–22.

30. For this important "new" proverb see Wolfgang Mieder, *American Proverbs. A Study of Texts and Contexts,* pp. 317–332; and Alyce McKenzie, "'Different Strokes for Different Folks': America's Quintessential Postmodern Proverb," *Theology Today,* 53 (1996), 201–212; also in W. Mieder, *Cognition, Comprehension, and Communication,* pp. 311–324.

31. See Lauren Dundes, Michael B. Streiff, and Alan Dundes, "'When You Hear Hoofbeats, Think Horses, Not Zebras': A Folk Medical Diagnostic Proverb," *Proverbium,* 16 (1999), 95–103; also in Wolfgang Mieder (ed.), *Cognition, Comprehension, and Communication,* pp. 99–107.

32. See my essay in Wolfgang Mieder (ed.), *Wise Words. Essays on the Proverb,* 515–542.

33. For many examples see Wolfgang Mieder and Anna Tóthné Litovkina, *Twisted Wisdom. Modern Anti–Proverbs* (Burlington, Vermont: The University of Vermont, 1999).

34. Charles Clay Doyle, "On 'New' Proverbs and the Conservativeness of Proverb Collections," *Proverbium,* 13 (1996), 69–84; also in W. Mieder (ed.), *Cognition, Comprehension, and Communication,* pp. 85–98; see also Nigel Rees, *Sayings of the Century* (London: George Allen & Unwin, 1984).

35. See Geoffrey M. White, "Proverbs and Cultural Models. An American Psychology of Problem Solving," in Dorothy Holland and Naomi Quinn (eds.), *Cultural Models in Language and Thought* (Cambridge: Cambridge University Press, 1987), pp. 152–172.

36. For an impressive survey of this phenomenon see Broder Carstensen and Ulrich Busse, *Anglizismen-Wörterbuch. Der Einfluß des Englischen auf den deutschen Wortschatz nach 1945.* 3 vols. (Berlin: Walter de Gruyter, 1993–1996).

37. For a study of this disturbing proverb see Wolfgang Mieder, *The Politics of Proverbs. From Traditional Wisdom to Proverbial Steretypes* (Madison, Wisconsin: University of Wisconsin Press, 1997), pp. 138–159.

38. For these German variants see Wolfgang Mieder, *Sprichwörtliches und Geflügeltes. Sprachstudien von Martin Luther bis Karl Marx* (Bochum: Norbert Brockmeyer, 1995), pp. 165–174.

39. The proverb's history from the 16th century to the present is treated in Wolfgang Mieder, *"Morgenstunde hat Gold im Munde": Studien und Belege zum populärsten deutschsprachigen Sprichwort* (Wien: Edition Praesens, 1997).

40. See Wolfgang Mieder, "Der frühe Vogel und die goldene Morgenstunde: Zu einer deutschen Sprichwortentlehnung aus dem Angloamerikanischen," in Irma Hyvärinen, Petri Kallio, and Jarmo Korhonen (eds.), *Etymologie, Entlehnungen und Entwicklungen. Festschrift für Jorma Koivulehto* (Helsinki: Société Néophilologique, 2004), pp. 193–206.

41. See Wolfgang Mieder, *Sprichwort, Redensart, Zitat. Tradierte Formelsprache in der Moderne* (Bern: Peter Lang, 1985), pp. 151–154 (with Geeoge B. Bryan).

42. See my treatment of the German and English history of this proverb in Wolfgang Mieder, *Sprichwort—Wahrwort!? Studien zur Geschichte, Bedeutung und Funktion deutscher Sprichwörter* (Frankfurt am Main: Peter Lang, 1992), pp. 191–201; and W. Mieder, *Proverbs Are Never Out of Season*, pp. 135–151.

43. See Wolfgang Mieder, "'Ein Apfel pro Tag hält den Arzt fern': Zu einigen amerikanischen Lehnsprichwörtern im Deutschen," *Revista de Filologia Alemana*, 12 (2004), 143–157.

44. See Wolfgang Mieder, "'Good Fences Make Good Neighbours': History and Significance of an Ambiguous Proverb," *Folklore* (London), 114 (2003), 155–179. The German loan translation is treated in W. Mieder, "'Ein Apfel pro Tag hält den Arzt fern'," pp. 153–155.

45. See my article on this proverb in Wolfgang Mieder (ed.), *Wise Words: Essays on the Proverb*, pp. 515–542. The German loan translation is discussed in W. Mieder, "'Ein Apfel pro Tag hält den Arzt fern'," pp. 155–157.

46. See Wolfgang Mieder, "'Man soll nicht alle Eier in einen Korb legen': Zur deutschsprachigen Entlehnung eines angloamerikanischen Sprichwortes," *Nauchnyi vestnik. Seriia: Sovremennye lingvisticheskie i metodiko-didacticheskie issledovaniia*, no volume given, no. 1 (2004), 21–31.

2. Government of the People, by the People, for the People

This chapter was first published in *Proverbium*, 20 (2003), 259–308.

1. Samuel A. Green, *President Lincoln's Speech at Gettysburg, November 19, 1863* (Boston: Massachusetts Historical Society, 1901), p. 1 (the entire pamphlet comprises a mere three pages).

2. Dewitt Miller, "Abraham Lincoln: Wycliffe Bible," *Notes and Queries*, 10th series, 9 (1908), 10. The claim was made by Ward Hill Lamon, *The*

Recollections of Abraham Lincoln (Chicago: McClurg, 1895), p. 176: "In the preface of the old Wickliffe Bible, published A.D. 1324, is the following declaration: 'This Bible is for the government of the people, by the people, and for the people,' which is identical with that employed by Mr. Lincoln in his Gettysburg speech." I have checked the entire preface of the Wycliffe Bible, and the statement is nowhere to be found.

3. See Robert J. Paterson, "Government for the People, of the People, by the People," *Notes and Queries,* 12th series, 1 (1916), p. 127; and Harry B. Poland, "Government for the People, of the People, by the People," *Notes and Queries,* 12th series, 1 (1916), 197; David Salmon, "Government for the People, of the People, by the People," *Notes and Queries,* 12th series, 1 (1916), 197; G. L. Apperson, "Government for the People, of the People, by the People," *Notes and Queries,* 12th series, 1 (1916), p. 197; and Albert Matthews, "Government for the People, of the People, by the People," *Notes and Queries,* 12th series, 2 (1916), 14–15.

4. Kate Louise Roberts, *Hoyt's New Cyclopedia of Practical Quotations,* completely revised and greatly enlarged (New York: Funk & Wagnalls, 1922), pp. 332–335.

5. Burton Stevenson, *The Home Book of Proverbs, Maxims, and Famous Phrases* (New York: Macmillan, 1948), p. 549.

6. See David Kin, *Dictionary of American Maxims* (New York: Philosophical Library, 1955), p. 214 (Webster), p. 215 (Parker), p. 203 (Webster and Lincoln); Tom Burnam, *The Dictionary of Misinformation* (New York: Thomas Y. Crowell, 1975), p. 98 (Parker and Lincoln); William Safire, *Political Dictionary,* 3rd ed. (New York: Random House, 1978), pp. 319–320 (Parker and Lincoln); John Bartlett, *Familiar Quotations,* 16th ed. by Justin Kaplan (Boston: Little, Brown and Company, 1992), p. 450 (Lincoln), p. 461 (Parker); and Nigel Rees, *Cassell Companion to Quotations* (London: Cassell, 1997), pp. 355–356 (Lincoln, Webster, Parker).

7. See Gabor S. Boritt (ed.), *Of the People, by the People, for the People, and Other Quotations by Abraham Lincoln* (New York: Columbia University Press, 1996), p. XIV (Wycliffe), p. 100 (Lincoln); and Antony Jay, *The Oxford Dictionary of Political Quotations* (Oxford: Oxford University Press, 1996), p. 226 (Lincoln), p. 285 (Parker), p. 395 (Wycliffe).

8. Gregory Titelman, *Dictionary of Popular Proverbs and Sayings* (New York: Random House, 1996), p. 124.

9. E. D. Hirsch, Joseph F. Kett, and James Trefil, *The Dictionary of Cultural Literacy* (Boston: Houghton, Mifflin and Company, 1988), p. 244.

10. I would like to thank my former student, colleague and friend Jake Barickman and my work-study student Erin Regan for their help with finding references from various electronic databases. Their expertise and untiring efforts have been of greatest importance in the compilation of the many references of this chapter.

11. Thomas Cooper, *Some Information Respecting America* (London: J. Johnson, 1794), pp. 52–53 (the entire letter on pp. 48–84).

12. The declaration titled "To the President of the United States" (without date) is published in the *Proceedings of the American Antiquarian Society, at the Annual Meeting Held in Worcester, October 21, 1893* (Worcester, Massachusetts: Charles Hamilton, 1894), pp. 323–325.

13. President John Adams' response titled "To My Fellow Citizens of the County of Westmoreland in the State of Virginia" is also included in the *Proceedings of the American Antiquarian Society, at the Annual Meeting Held in Worcester, October 21, 1893* (Worcester, Massachusetts: Charles Hamilton, 1894), pp. 326–327. There is also a letter of October 26, 1894, by Samuel A. Green to George F. Hoar, that refers to Daniel Webster's and Theodore Parker's use of variants of this phrase (see p. 327).

14. Cited from "McCulloch v. Maryland. Opinion. U.S. Supreme Court, 6 March 1819," in *The Papers of John Marshall*, ed. by Charles F. Hobson (Chapel Hill, North Carolina: University of North Carolina Press, 1995), vol. 8, pp. 254–280 (here p. 262).

15. Benjamin Disraeli, *Vivian Grey* (London: Alexander Moring, 1904), vol. 2, p. 127 (book 6, chapter 7).

16. Earl John Russell, "Ministerial Plan of Parliamentary Reform. Tuesday, March 1, 1831," in *Selections from Speeches of Earl Russell 1817 to 1841 and from Despatches 1859 to 1865* (London: Longmans, Green, and Co., 1870), pp. 301–336 (here pp. 335–336)

17. Alphonse de Lamartine, *Histoire des Girondins* (Paris: Plon, 1984), vol. 2, p. 445 (book 45, section 13).

18. Alphonse de Lamartine, *History of the Girondists,* translated by H. T. Ryde (London: Henry G. Bohn, 1864), vol. 3, p. 104 (book 45, section 13).

19. Daniel Webster, "Second Speech on Foot's Resolution," in *The Works of Daniel Webster* (Boston: Little, Brown and Company, 1853), vol. 3, pp. 271–342 (here p. 321, 333, and 334).

20. Cited from Anne C. Lynch (ed.), *The Rhode-Island Book: Selections in Prose and Verse, from the Writings of Rhode-Island Citizens* (Providence, Rhode Island: H. Fuller, 1841), p. 160.

21. Theodore Parker, "Speech at a Meeting of the Citizens of Boston, in Faneuil Hall, March 25, 1850, to Consider the Speech of Mr. Webster," in Theodore Parker, *Speeches, Addresses, and Occasional Sermons* (Boston: Ticknor and Fields, 1861), vol. 3, pp. 1–37 (here p. 2).

22. Theodore Parker, "Slave Power in America," in Theodore Parker, *Speeches, Address, and Occasional Sermons* (Boston: Ticknor and Fields, 1861), vol. 3, pp. 38–86 (here pp. 41–42).

23. For numerous references by Lincoln see Wolfgang Mieder, *The Proverbial Abraham Lincoln. An Index to Proverbs in the Works of Abraham Lincoln* (New York: Peter Lang, 2000), pp. 135–137 ("Life, liberty and the pursuit of happiness"), and pp. 146–150 ("All men are created equal").

24. *The Collected Works of Abraham Lincoln*, ed. by Roy Basler (New Brunswick, New Jersey: Rutgers University Press, 1953, vol. 7, p. 23. For short discussions of this formulation see Herbert Joseph Edwards and John Erskine Hankins, *Lincoln the Writer: The Development of His Literary Style* (Orono, Maine: University of Maine, 1962), pp. 103–104; Byron D. Murray, "Lincoln Speaks," *Contemporary Review*, 208 (1966), 260–261 (the entire article on pp. 250–261); Lois J. Einhorn, *Abraham Lincoln the Orator: Penetrating the Lincoln Legend* (Westport, Connecticut: Greenwood Press, 1992), pp. 103–104; and Garry Wills, *Lincoln at Gettysburg: The Words that Remade America* (New York: Touchstone, 1992), pp. 107, 129, 145–146.

25. Theodore Parker, "The State of the Nation. Considered in a Sermon for Thanksgiving Day.—Preached at the Melodeon, November 28, 1850," in Theodore Parker, *Speeches, Addresses, and Occasional Sermons* (Boston: Ticknor and Fields, 1861), vol. 3, pp. 180–229 (here pp. 195–196).

26. Theodore Parker, "Some Thoughts on the Progress of America, and the Influence of Her Diverse Institutions. An Address Prepared for the Anti-Slavery Convention in Boston, May 31, 1854," in Theodore Parker, *Additional Speeches, Addresses, and Occasional Sermons* (Boston: Ticknor and Fields, 1861), vol. 2, pp. 1–70 (here p. 25).

27. Theodore Parker, *The Relation of Slavery to a Republican Form of Government. A Speech Delivered at the New England Anti-Slavery Convention, Wednesday Morning, May 26, 1858* (Boston: William L Kent, 1858), pp. 4–5 (21 pages in all).

28. Theodore Parker, "The Effect of Slavery on the American People," in *The Collected Works of Theodore Parker*, ed. by Frances Power Cobbe (London: Trübner, 1863–1871), vol. 8, pp. 132–157 (here p. 138).

29. William H. Herndon and Jesse W. Weik, *Abraham Lincoln. The True Story of a Great Life* (New York: D. Appleton, 1892), vol. 2, p. 65. See also John White Chadwick, *Theodore Parker. Preacher and Reformer* (Boston: Houghton, Mifflin and Company, 1900), p. 323.

30. Theodore Parker, "Transcendentalism," in Robert E. Collins, *Theodore Parker: American Transcendentalist. A Critical Essay and a Collection of His Writings* (Metuchen, New Jersey: The Scarecrow Press, 1973), pp. 49–74 (here pp. 66–67). It was published as *Transcendentalism. A Lecture. Never before printed* (Boston: Free Religious Association, 1876). See also Garry Wills, *Lincoln at Gettysburg. The Words that Remade America* (New York: Touchstone, 1992), pp. 107–108.

31. W. Alfred Jones, "Titles," in W. A. Jones, *Characters and Criticisms* (New York: I. Y. Westervelt, 1857), pp. 230–239 (here p. 239).

32. Abraham Lincoln, "Message to Congress in Special Session," in *The Collected Works of Abraham Lincoln,* ed. by Roy P. Basler (New Brunswick, New Jersey: Rutgers University Press, 1953), vol. 4, pp. 421–441 (here p. 426).

33. Cited from an article on "Ohio Legislature" in the *Ohio State Journal* (February 7, 1852), no pp.

34. Steven Béla Várdy, "Louis Kossuth's Words in Abraham Lincoln's Gettysburg Address," *Eurasian Studies Yearbook,* 71 (1999), 27–32 (here pp. 31–32).

35. See Earl W. Wiley, "Lincoln the Speaker 1816–1830," in Lionel Crocker (ed.), *An Analysis of Lincoln and Douglas as Public Speakers and Debaters* (Springfield, Illinois: Charles C. Thomas, 1968), p. 19 (the entire essay on pp. 5–21).

36. Waldo W. Braden, "'A Remorseless Analyzer': Lincoln's Speech Preparation," in Waldo W. Braden, *Lincoln: Public Speaker* (Baton Rouge, Louisiana: Louisiana State University Press, 1988), p. 51 (the entire chapter on pp. 48–66).

37. Byron D. Murray, "Lincoln Speaks," *Contemporary Review,* 208 (1966), 261 (the entire article on pp. 250–261).

38. See the short note by Thoburn V. Barker, "Lincoln: Rhetorical Copycat?" *Today's Speech,* 15 (1967), 30. The entire note (on pp. 29–30) deals with Lincoln's allusions to Pericles' famous "Funeral Oration" in his own Gettysburg Address. For a superb analysis of Lincoln's immortal speech see Garry Wills, *Lincoln at Gettysburg: The Words that Remade America* (New York: Touchstone, 1992). Regarding the copying of proverbs by another great American public figure see Wolfgang Mieder, "'Early to Bed and Early to Rise': From Proverb to Benjamin Franklin and Back," in Wolfgang Mieder, *Proverbs Are Never Out of Season: Popular Wisdom in the Modern Age* (New York: Oxford University Press, 1993), pp. 98–134.

39. *The Collected Works of Abraham Lincoln,* ed. by Roy P. Basler (New Brunswick, New Jersey: Rutgers University Press, 1953), vol. 7, pp. 18–23 (with variants). The full "final text" is also included in Garry Wills, *Lincoln at Gettysburg. The Words that Remade America* (New York: Touchstone, 1992), p. 263. See also Wolfgang Mieder, *The Proverbial Abraham Lincoln,* pp. 35–37 and 160.

40. Cited from "Second Speech on Foot's Resolution" in *The Works of Daniel Webster,* 7th ed. (Boston: Little, Brown and Company, 1853), vol. 3, pp. 271–342 (here p. 321). See also the insightful analysis by Richard N. Current, "Lincoln and Daniel Webster," *Journal of the Illinois State Historical Society,* 47 (1955), 307–321 (esp. p. 321).

41. The speech is entitled "Slave Power in America" and is cited from Theodore Parker, *Speeches, Addresses, and Occasional Sermons* (Boston: Ticknor and Fields, 1856), vol. 3, pp. 38–86 (here p. 41). See also Herbert Joseph Edwards

and John Erskine Hankins, *Lincoln the Writer: The Development of His Literary Style* (Orono, Maine: University of Maine, 1962), pp. 103–104; Byron D. Murray, "Lincoln Speaks," *Contemporary Review*, 208 (1966), 250–261 (here pp. 260–261); Lois J. Einhorn, *Abraham Lincoln the Orator: Penetrating the Lincoln Legend* (Westport, Connecticut: Greenwood Press, 1992), pp. 103–104; and Garry Wills, *Lincoln at Gettysburg: The Words That Remade America* (New York: Touchstone, 1992), pp. 129, 145–146, and 172–174.

42. Thoburn V. Barker, "Lincoln: Rhetorical Copycat?" *Today's Speech*, 15 (February 1967), 30 (the entire short note linking Lincoln's address with an oration by Pericles from 431 B.C. on pp. 29–30).

43. Cited from *The Frederick Douglass Papers*, ed. by John Blassingame (New Haven, Connecticut: Yale University Press, 1985–1992), vol. 2, p. 223.

44. *The Frederick Douglass Papers*, vol. 3, p. 140.

45. *The Frederick Douglass Papers*, vol. 3, p. 176.

46. *The Frederick Douglass Papers*, vol. 3, p. 361.

47. Cited from *The Life and Writings of Frederick Douglass*, ed. by Philip S. Foner (New York: International Publishers, 1950–1975), vol. 4, pp. 271–272.

48. *The Life and Writings of Frederick Douglass*, vol. 3, p. 291. For these comments on Douglass see also Wolfgang Mieder, *"No Struggle, No Progress": Frederick Douglass and His Proverbial Rhetoric for Civil Rights* (New York: Peter Lang, 2001), pp. 86–95 and 386–389.

49. *The Frederick Douglass Papers*, vol. 4, p. 158.

50. *The Life and Writings of Frederick Douglass*, vol. 2, p. 15.

51. *The Frederick Douglass Papers*, vol. 5, p. 169.

52. *The Frederick Douglass Papers*, vol. 5, p. 48.

53. *The Frederick Douglass Papers*, vol. 5, p. 110. This paragraph is also mentioned by George A. Hinshaw, *A Rhetorical Analysis of the Speeches of Frederick Douglass* (Diss. University of Nebraska, 1972), p. 350.

54. *The Frederick Douglass Papers*, vol. 5, p. 218.

55. *The Frederick Douglass Papers*, vol. 5, p. 369.

56. *The Frederick Douglass Papers*, vol. 5, p. 262.

57. *The Frederick Douglass Papers*, vol. 5, p. 594.

58. Cited from a volume that includes all three versions of the biography: Frederick Douglass, *Autobiographies: Narrative of the Life of Frederick Douglass* [1845], *My Bondage and My Freedom* [1855], *Life and Times of Frederick Douglass* [1893] (New York: Library of America, 1994), p. 960.

59. John Cordner, *The American Conflict: An Address, Spoken Before the New England Society of Montreal on 22 December, 1864* (Montreal: John Lovell, 1865), p. 30.

60. W. E. Hathaway, "A Sketch of Russian History," *The Ladies' Repository*, 9, issue 6 (June 1872), 401–409 (here pp. 408–409).

61. Lyman H. Atwater, "Taxation of Churches, Colleges, and Charitable Institutions," *The Princeton Review*, 3, issue 10 (October 1874), pp. 340–349 (here p. 341).

62. *Proceedings of the Republican National Convention, Held at Cincinnati, Ohio, June 14, 15, and 16, 1876*, reported by M. A. Clancy (Concord, New Hampshire: Republic Press Association, 1876), p. 55.

63. Philip Schaff, "Progress of Christianity in the United States," *The Princeton Review*, 2 (1879), pp. 209–252 (here p. 213).

64. Robert G. Ingersoll, "The Grant Banquet. Chicago, November 13, 1879," in *The Works of Robert G. Ingersoll*, ed. by Emmett F. Fields (New York: C. P. Farrell, 1902), pp. 81–84 (here p. 81).

65. James Russell Lowell, *Democracy and Other Addresses* (Boston: Houghton, Mifflin and Company, 1887), p. 20.

66. Robert G. Ingersoll, "God in the Constitution," in *The Works of Robert G. Ingersoll*, ed. by Emmett F. Fields (New York: C. P. Farrell, 1902), pp. 121–134 (here p. 134).

67. Anonymous, "Against Russian Treaty," *The New York Times* (June 6, 1894), p. 8.

68. Cited from *The Works of Charles Dickens. Letters and Speeches* (New York: Hearst's International Library, 1893), vol. 2, pp. 559–562 (here p. 562). For Dickens' frequent use of proverbial language see George B. Bryan and Wolfgang Mieder, *The Proverbial Charles Dickens. An Index to Proverbs in the Works of Charles Dickens* (New York: Peter Lang, 1997).

69. Cited from *The Complete Works of Oscar Wilde* (New York: William H. Wise, 1927), vol. 10, pp. 1–65 (here p. 22).

70. Robert G. Ingersoll, "Eight to Seven Address," in *The Works of Robert G. Ingersoll*, ed. by Emmett F. Fields (New York: C. P. Farrell, 1902), vol. 9, pp. 227–263 (here p. 256).

71. *The Elizabeth Cady Stanton—Susan B. Anthony Reader. Correspondence, Writings, Speeches*, ed. by Ellen Carol DuBois (Boston: Northeastern University Press, 1992), pp. 208–215 (here pp. 212–213).

72. Archbishop Ireland, "The Country's Path of Duty," *The New York Times* (February 13, 1903), p. 1.

73. Theodore Roosevelt, "A Proclamation," *The New York Times* (November 1, 1903), p. 11.

74. Ambrose Bierce, *The Unabridged Devil's Dictionary*, ed. by David E. Schultz and S. T. Joshi (Athens, Georgia: University of Georgia Press, 2002), pp. 174–175.

75. Anonymous, "England's Reply: A Neutral Suggestion of Points Germany Should Agree to," *The New York Times* (December 24, 1916), p. X8.

76. I came across this information in a half-page entry on "Government of the people, by the people and for the people" in Henry F. Woods, *American Sayings. Famous Phrases, Slogans, and Aphorisms* (New York: Duell, Sloan and Pearce, 1945; rpt. New York: Perma Giants, 1950), p. 41: "The House of Representatives on April 3, 1918 [actually April 6], adopted *The American Creed* formulated by William Tyler Page, which begins, 'I believe in the United States of America as a Government of the people, by the people, for the people.'"

77. Cited from *Congressional Record, Containing the Proceedings and Debates of the Second Session of the Sixty-Fifth Congress of the United States of America* (Washington, D.C.: Government Printing Office, 1918), vol. 56, p. 4745 (Congressional Record—House).

78. See "The American's Creed" in *Congressional Record, Appendix and Index to Parts 1–11 of The Proceedings and Debates of the Second Session of the Sixty-Fifth Congress of the United States of America* (Washington, D.C.: Government Printing Office, 1918), vol. 56, part 12, pp. 286–289.

79. *Ibid.,* p. 287 (left column).

80. *Ibid.,* p. 287 (right column).

81. *Ibid.,* p. 288 (left column).

82. *Ibid.,* p. 289 (left column).

83. Anonymous, "Topics of the Times," *The New York Times* (December 4, 1936), p. 24.

84. Carl Sandburg, *The People, Yes* (New York: Harcourt, Brace and Company, 1936), p. 134 (section 57, pp. 134–139, of the poem is a tribute to Lincoln). See also Wolfgang Mieder, "Proverbs in Carl Sandburg's Poem *The People, Yes,*" *Southern Folklore Quarterly,* 37 (1973), 15–36.

85. Michael Arlen, *The Flying Dutchman* (New York: Doubleday, Doran & Company, 1939). p. 187 (chapter 8).

86. Cited from "Wheeler Condemns Both Old Parties," in *The New York Times* (September 2, 1924), p. 3.

87. A "Public Notice" by John Clinton McGee; cited from *The New York Times* (September 2, 1928), p. 19.

88. Anonymous, "Democracy is Freedom," *The New York Times* (August 13, 1939), p. E8.

89. M. Fellows, "The American Way Viewed as Heritage to Be Guarded," in *The New York Times* (September 1, 1940), p. E7 (letter to the editor).

90. Anonymous, "Topics of the Times," *The New York Times* (February 13, 1943), p. 10.

91. The various texts by George Washington, James Madison, Ralph Waldo Emerson, William Tyler Page, Stephen Vincent Benét, Henry Cabot Lodge, Albert

Einstein, and others are assembled under the headline "'I Am an American': A Creed and a Code," in *The New York Times* (May 21, 1944), p. SM16.

92. *Winston S. Churchill: His Complete Speeches 1897–1963,* ed. Robert Rhodes James (New York: Chelsea House Publishers, 1974), vol. 4, pp. 4206–4211 (here p. 4208). See also Wolfgang Mieder and George B. Bryan, *The Proverbial Winston S. Churchill. An Index to Proverbs in the Works of Sir Winston Churchill* (Westport, Connecticut: Greenwood Press, 1995), p. 331.

93. *The Collected Essays of Sir Winston Churchill,* ed. Michael Wolff (London: Library of Imperial History, 1976), vol. 2, pp. 218–221 (here p. 218 and 220).

94. *The Collected Essays of Sir Winston Churchill,* vol. 1, pp. 360–364 (here p. 361).

95. *Winston S. Churchill: His Complete Speeches 1897–1963,* vol. 6, pp. 6536–6541 (here pp. 6536–6537).

96. *Winston S. Churchill: His Complete Speeches 1897–1963,* vol. 7, pp. 7083–7103 (here p. 7084).

97. *Winston S. Churchill: His Complete Speeches 1897–1963,* vol. 7, pp. 7209–7219 (here p. 7214).

98. *Congressional Record,* vol. 87, part 11 (1941), pp. A1527–A1528 (here p. A1528). See also Wolfgang Mieder and George B. Bryan, *The Proverbial Harry S. Truman. An Index to Proverbs in the Works of Harry S. Truman* (New York: Peter Lang, 1997), pp. 137–138.

99. *Off the Record: The Private Papers of Harry S. Truman,* ed. by Robert H. Ferrell (New York: Harper & Row, 1980), pp. 100–102 (here p. 102).

100. For Truman's ability to use strong language see Eldorous L. Dayton, *Give 'em Hell Harry. An Informal Biography of the Terrible Tempered Mr. T.* (New York: The Devin-Adair Company, 1956); and Mark Goodman (ed.), *Give 'em Hell, Harry* (New York: Award Books, 1974)

101. *Public Papers of the Presidents of the United States: Harry S. Truman.* January 1 to December 31, 1948 (Washington, D.C.: U.S. Government Printing Office, 1964), pp. 526–527 (here p. 527).

102. *Ibid.,* pp. 571–572 (here p. 571).

103. *Ibid.,* pp. 707–708 (here p. 708).

104. *Ibid.,* pp. 753–755 (here pp. 753–754).

105. *Ibid.,* pp. 901–903 (here p. 903).

106. *Public Papers of the Presidents of the United States: Harry S. Truman.* January 1 to December 31, 1849 (Washington, D.C.: U.S. Government Printing Office, 1964), pp. 139–140 (here p. 140).

107. *Public Papers of the Presidents of the United States: Harry S. Truman.* January 1 to December 31, 1950 (Washington, D.C.: U.S. Government Printing Office, 1965), pp. 496–497 (here p. 497).

108. *Public Papers of the Presidents of the United States: Harry S. Truman.* January 1 to December 31, 1951 (Washington, D.C.: U.S. Government Printing Office, 1965), pp. 199–200 (here p. 200).

109. Ronald Reagan, "Remarks on East-West Relations at the Brandenburg Gate in West Berlin, June 12, 1987," *Public Papers of the Presidents of the United States: Ronald Reagan.* 1 January to 3 July 1987 (Washington, D.C.: U.S. Government Printing Office, 1989), pp. 634–638 (here p. 635. See also Wolfgang Mieder, "'Raising the Iron Curtain': Proverbs and Political Cartoons of the Cold War," in W. Mieder, *The Politics of Proverbs: From Traditional Wisdom to Proverbial Stereotypes* (Madison, Wisconsin: University of Wisconsin Press, 1997), pp. 99–137 (here pp. 100–101).

110. *Ibid.,* pp. 370–374 (here p. 371).

111. See Margaret Truman (ed.), *Where the Buck Stops. The Personal and Private Writings of Harry S. Truman* (New York: Warner Books, 1989).

112. *Off the Record. The Private Papers of Harry S. Truman,* pp. 333–336 (here p. 333).

113. *Strictly Personal and Confidential: The Letters Harry Truman Never Mailed,* ed. by Monte M. Poen (Boston: Little, Brown and Company, 1982), pp. 133–134 (here p. 133).

114. David E. Lilienthal, "Our Faith Is Mightier Than Our Atom Bomb," *The New York Times* (March 6, 1949), p. SM11.

115. E. L. Woodward, "A Spade Is a Spade Is a Maybe: Words Loom Large in the World Struggle: Their Meanings Can Be Dangerously Elusive," *The New York Times* (March 16, 1952), pp. 13, 54, 56, 58 (here p. 56). Regarding the proverbial expression "to call a spade a spade," see Wolfgang Mieder, *"Call A Spade a Spade": From Classical Phrase to Racial Slur. A Case Study* (New York: Peter Lang, 2002).

116. President Dwight D. Eisenhower's talk on "Congressional Bills for Labor Reform," in *The New York Times* (August 7, 1959), p. 8.

117. Cited under "Ideas and Men" in *The New York Times* (June 26, 1960), p. E9.

118. Anonymous, "A Day for Plain Speaking," *The New York Times* (September 25, 1961), p. 32.

119. See "Lincoln's Gettysburg Address: Today Is Its 100th Anniversary," *The New York Times* (November 19, 1963), p. 35.

120. Cited from Homer Bigart, "Mrs. Kennedy Spends Rainy Day in Seclusion," *The New York Times* (November 30, 1963), p. 13.

121. Bel Kaufman, *Up the Down Staircase* (Englewood Cliffs, New Jersey: Prentice-Hall, 1964), p. 139.

122. Senator Adlai E. Stevenson's speech (no title given) is cited from *The New York Times* (October 3, 1972), p. 2.

123. Theodore M. Hesburgh, "The Hucksters," *The New York Times* (May 23, 1973), p. 47.

124. Cited from the "Transcript of President Ford's Final Message to Congress on State of the Union," *The New York Times* (January 13, 1977), p. 26.

125. Laurin Hall Healy, "Eight Weapons Against the No-Vote Party," *Christian Science Monitor* (November 3, 1980), p. 23.

126. Don Hewitt from CBS's "60 Minutes"; cited from Max Frankel, "Last Gasp for Fair Air. What Still Remains of TV Regulation Could End the Political Money Chase," *The New York Times* (April 4, 1999), p. SM19.

127. *The New York Times* (May 3, 1981), p. R11.

128. *The New York Times* (February 23, 1983), p. C23.

129. Walter F. Mondale, "3 Things That We Must Do Together," *The New York Times* (February 22, 1984), p. A18.

130. Cited from the "Transcript of Mondale Address Accepting Party Nomination," *The New York Times* (July 20, 1984), p. A2.

131. Charlotte Saikowski, "Two Hundred Years of the Constitution—Can America Govern Itself?" *Christian Science Monitor* (February 13, 1987), p. 20.

132. See Alan Dundes, "Thinking Ahead: A Folkloristic Reflection of the Future Orientation in American Worldview," *Anthropological Quarterly,* 42 (1969), 53–72.

133. Phil-Heiner Randermann, "Reichstag Tells Story of Failed Democracy," *The New York Times* (June 26, 1995), p. A14.

134. William Matthews, *After All. Last Poems* (Boston: Houghton Mifflin, 1998), p. 45.

135. Kathryn L. van Heyningen, "Our Steely Determination," *St. Petersburg Times* (September 16, 2001), p. 6D.

136. Tim Cuprisin, "'Dead Body' Phrase May Mark Bush's Political Life," *Milwaukee Journal Sentinel* (January 8, 2002), p. 6B.

3. God Helps Them Who Help Themselves

1. See Charles W. Meister, *The Founding Fathers* (Jefferson, North Carolina: McFarland, 1987); Joseph J. Ellis, *Founding Brothers. The Revolutionary Generation* (New York: A. Knopf, 2001); and Andrew S. Trees, *The Founding Fathers and the Politics of Character* (Princeton, New Jersey: Princeton University Press, 2004).

2. See the concise but informative portrayal by Linda Myer, "Abigail Adams," *Maryland Committee for the Humanities,* 78 (2001), 9–12.

3. Frank Shuffelton, "In Different Voices: Gender in the American Republic of Letters," *Early American Literature,* 25 (1990), 290 (the entire article on pp. 289–304). See also Howard Anderson and Irvin Ehrenpreis, "The Familiar

Letter in the Eighteenth Century: Some Generalizations," in H. Anderson, Philip B. Daghlian, and I. Ehrenpreis (eds.), *The Familiar Letter in the Eighteenth Century* (Lawrence, Kansas: University of Kansas Press, 1966), pp. 269–282.

4. See Phyllis Lee Levin, *Abigail Adams. A Biography* (New York: St. Martin's Press, 1987), p. 310.

5. Quotations from the letters are taken from the following publications with the precise references listed in parentheses. Their inconsistent and frequently erroneous orthography has been maintained throughout:

   A. *Adams Family Correspondence (1761–1785),* ed. by L. H. Butterfield, 6 vols. (Cambridge, Massachusetts: Harvard University Press, 1963–1993). The volume numbers are cited in Roman numerals followed by the page numbers.

   B. *New Letters of Abigail Adams 1788–1801,* ed. by Stewart Mitchell (Boston: Houghton Mifflin Company, 1947). This volume is identified by NL followed by the page numbers.

   C. *Letters of Mrs. Adams, Wife of John Adams,* ed. by Charles Francis Adams, 4th ed. (Boston: Wilkins, Carter, and Company, 1848). Passages from this volume are identified by LA followed by page numbers.

6. This statement was used as a motto (p. vii) and in part as the title of an invaluable study by Edith B. Gelles, *First Thoughts. Life and Letters of Abigail Adams* (New York: Twayne Publishers, 1998). For the linguistic problems of the largely self-taught Abigail see Lynne Withey, *Dearest Friend. A Life of Abigail Adams* (New York: The Free Press, 1981; New York: Touchstone, 2002), p. xiii.

7. Ralph Ketcham, "The Puritan Ethic in the Revolutionary Era: Abigail Adams and Thomas Jefferson," in Carol V. R. George (ed.), *"Remember the Ladies": New Perspectives on Women in American History. Essays in Honor of Nelson Manfred Blake* (Syracuse, New York: Syracuse University Press, 1975), p. 49 and p. 65 (the entire article on pp. 49–65).

8. This is a reference to the somewhat flirtatious correspondence between Abigail Adams and James Lovell; see Edith B. Gelles, "A Virtuous Affair," in E. B. Gelles, *Portia. The World of Abigail Adams* (Bloomington, Indiana: Indiana University Press, 1992), pp. 57–71.

9. See Edith B. Gelles, "The Abigail Industry," *The William and Mary Quarterly,* 45 (1988), 656–683.

10. Edith B. Gelles, *Portia. The World of Abigail Adams* (Bloomington, Indiana: Indiana University Press, 1992), p. 3.

11. Elaine Forman Crane, "Political Dialogue and the Spring of Abigail's Discontent," *The William and Mary Quarterly,* 56 (1999), 769 (the entire article on pp. 745–774). Crane also refers to the more unlikely source for the Portia pen-name in William Shakespeare's *The Merchant of Venice.*

12. See also the appropriately entitled chapter on "'Cast in the Same Mould'" in Rosemary Keller, *Patriotism and the Female Sex. Abigail Adams and the American Revolution* (Brooklyn, New York: Carlson, 1994), pp. 1–20.

13. See Bartlett Jere Whiting, *Early American Proverbs and Proverbial Phrases* (Cambridge, Massachusetts: Harvard University Press, 1977), p. 438; and Wolfgang Mieder, Stewart A. Kingsbury, and Kelsie B. Harder, *A Dictionary of American Proverbs* (New York: Oxford University Press, 1992), p. 595.

14. Oliver Goldsmith might have taken this phrase from Edward Young's didactic and reflective poem *Night Thoughts on Life, Death, and Immortality* (1742–1745): "Man wants but little; nor that little, long." See Burton Stevenson, *The Home Book of Proverbs, Maxims, and Famous Phrases* (New York: Macmillan, 1948), p. 2444 (no. 8); and Wolfgang Mieder et al., *A Dictionary of American Proverbs,* p. 401.

15. See the many multilingual references in Gyula Paczolay, *European Proverbs in 55 Languages with Equivalents in Arabic, Persian, Sanskrit, Chinese and Japanese* (Veszprém: Veszprémi Nyomda, 1997), pp. 150–154.

16. See Morris Palmer Tilley, *A Dictionary of the Proverbs in England in the Sixteenth and Seventeenth Centuries* (Ann Arbor: University of Michigan Press, 1950), p. 263; and Robert W. Dent, *Shakespeare's Proverbial Language. An Index* (Berkeley, California: University of California Press, 1981), p. 122.

17. See Frances M. Barbour, *A Concordance to the Sayings in Franklin's "Poor Richard"* (Detroit, Michigan: Gale Research Company, 1974), p. 82.

18. Cited from Jared Sparks, *The Works of Benjamin Franklin* (Philadelphia, Pennsylvania: Childs & Peterson, 1840), vol. 2, p. 94; with italics in original. See also Stuart A. Gallacher, "Franklin's *Way to Wealth:* A Florilegium of Proverbs and Wise Sayings," *Journal of English and Germanic Philology,* 48 (1949), 229–251; and Wolfgang Mieder, "Benjamin Franklin's 'The Way to Wealth'," in W. Mieder, *Proverbs. A Handbook* (Westport, Connecticut: Greenwood Press, 2004), pp. 216–224.

19. See Burton Stevenson, *The Home Book of Proverbs,* pp. 980–981 (no. 15); and F. P. Wilson, *The Oxford Dictionary of English Proverbs* (Oxford: Oxford University Press, 1970), pp. 312–313.

20. See Wolfgang Mieder, "'A Man of Fashion Never Has Recourse to Proverbs': Lord Chesterfield's Tilting at Proverbial Windmills," in W. Mieder, *Strategies of Wisdom. Anglo-American and German Proverb Studies* (Baltmannsweiler, Germany: Schneider Verlag Hohengehren, 2000), pp. 55–56 (the entire chapter on pp. 37–68).

21. Edith B. Gelles, "Abigail Adams: Domesticity and the American Revolution," *New England Quarterly,* 52 (1979), 516 (the entire article on pp. 500–521). See also Charles W. Akers, *Abigail Adams. An American Woman,* 2nd ed. (New York: Longman, 2000), pp. 84–85.

22. Richard Jente, "The Untilled Field of Proverbs," in George R. Coffman (ed.), *Studies in Language and Literature* (Chapel Hill, North Carolina: University of North Carolina Press, 1945), p. 116 (the entire article on pp. 112–119).

23. James Obelkevich, "Proverbs and Social History," in Peter Burke and Roy Porter (eds.), *The Social History of Language* (Cambridge: Cambridge University Press, 1987), p. 57 (the entire article on pp. 43–72; also in Wolfgang Mieder (ed.), *Wise Words. Essays on the Proverb* (New York: Garland Publishing, 1994), pp. 229–230 (the entire article on pp. 211–252).

24. For numerous studies see Wolfgang Mieder and George B. Bryan, *Proverbs in World Literature. A Bibliography* (New York: Peter Lang, 1996).

25. Bartlett Jere Whiting, *Early American Proverbs*, p. xviii.

26. See Wolfgang Mieder, "Narrative History as Proverbial Narrative: David McCullough's Best-Selling *John Adams* [2001] Biography," *Proverbium: Yearbook of International Proverb Scholarship*, 19 (2002), 279–322.

27. Kathleen Ann Lawrence, "'Splendid Misery': The Influential Letters of Abigail Adams," in K. A. Lawrence, *The Domestic Idiom. The Rhetorical Appeals of Four Influential Women in Nineteenth-Century America* (Diss. Indiana University, 1989), p. 58 (the entire chapter on pp. 21–85). Lawrence mentions but three examples, namely "God helps them who help themselves" (p. 56), "God helps them that help themselves" (p. 57), and "Revenge is sweet" (p. 58). See also Lawrence's statement that "throughout her letters Adams referred to literature, poetry, historical, classical, biblical, and political sources. Often her 'topoi' or places were found in stories, anecdotes, fables, folklore, parables, and proverbs" (p. 27).

28. Lynne Withey, *Dearest Friend. A Life of Abigail Adams* (New York: The Free Press, 1981), p. 58.

29. This letter is included in the microfilm edition of the voluminous *Adams Papers* of the Massachusetts Historical Society. Cited from Lynne Withey, *Dearest Friend. A Life of Abigail Adams* (New York: The Free Press, 1981), pp. 136–137.

30. See Burton Stevenson, *The Home Book of Proverbs*, p. 1488 (no. 10).

31. Natalie S. Bober, *Abigail Adams. Witness to a Revolution* (New York: Atheneum, 1994), p. 60.

32. See also the following letters to John: June 3, 1776 (II,4); April 17, 1777 (II,213); June 23, 1777 (II,269); July 10, 1777 (II,278–279); July 15, 1778 (III,60); February 13, 1779 (III,167); July 24, 1780 (III,382); June 17, 1782 (IV,326); November 13, 1782 (V,35); April 28, 1783 (V,144); and February 11, 1784 (V,302–303. The emotive if not sensual passages are usually at the beginning or the end of the letters.

33. Lynne Withey, *Dearest Friend. A Life of Abigail Adams* (New York: The Free Press, 1981), p. 134.

34. Cited from Charles Francis Adams (ed.), *The Works of John Adams* (Boston: Little, Brown and Company, 1854), vol. 9, p. 513. See also Edith B. Gelles, "Abigail Adams: Domesticity and the American Revolution," *New England Quarterly,* 52 (1979), 514 (the entire article on pp. 500–521).

35. Edith B. Gelles, "Abigail Adams: Domesticity and the American Revolution," *New England Quarterly,* 52 (1979), 500 (the entire article on pp. 500–521).

36. Kathleen Ann Lawrence, "'Splendid Misery': The Influential Letters of Abigail Adams," in K. A. Lawrence, *The Domestic Idiom. The Rhetorical Appeals of Four Influential Women in Nineteenth-Century America* (Diss. Indiana University, 1989), p. 30 (the entire chapter on pp. 21–85).

37. Edith B. Gelles, *Portia. The World of Abigail Adams* (Bloomington, Indiana: Indiana University Press, 1992), p. 119 (see also pp. 123–125).

38. Cited from David McCullough, *John Adams* (New York: Simon & Schuster, 2001), p. 553.

39. For a discussion of the proverb "Do unto others as you would have them do unto you," see J. O. Hertzler, "On Golden Rules," *The International Journal of Ethics,* 44 (1933–1934), 418–436; and John Marks Templeton, *Worldwide Laws of Life. 200 Eternal Spiritual Principles* (Philadelphia, Pennsylvania: Templeton Foundation Press, 1997,pp. 8–12.

40. See Wolfgang Mieder, "'Do Unto Others as You Would Have Them Do Unto You': The Golden Rule as the Ultimate Wisdom for Equality," in W. Mieder, *"No Struggle, No Progress." Frederick Douglass and His Proverbial Rhetoric for Civil Rights* (New York: Peter Lang, 2001), pp. 95–102 and pp. 184–192.

41. Abigail also referred to these remarks in a letter of April 27, 1776, to her friend Mercy Otis Warren (see I,397).

42. Charles W. Akers, *Abigail Adams. An American Woman,* 2nd ed. (New York: Longman, 2000), p. 48.

43. Cited from Burton Stevenson, *The Home Book of Proverbs,* p. 2404 (no. 10).

44. See Elaine Forman Crane, "Political Dialogue and the Spring of Abigail's Discontent," *The William and Mary Quarterly,* 56 (1999), 763 (the entire article on pp. 745–774).

45. John Bartlett, *Familiar Quotations,* ed. Emily Morison Beck, 15th ed. (Boston: Little, Brown and Company, 1980), p. 392.

46. "Remember the Ladies" is used as chapter headings by Edith B. Gelles, *First Thoughts. Life and Letters of Abigail Adams* (New York: Twayne Publishers, 1998), pp. 14–30; and Charles W. Akers, *Abigail Adams. An American Woman,* 2nd ed. (New York: Longman, 2000), pp. 35–52.

47. See Selwyn Gurney Champion, *The Eleven Religions and Their Proverbial Lore* (New York: E. P. Dutton, 1945); Albert Kirby Griffin, *Religious Proverbs. Over 1600 Adages from 18 Faiths Worldwide* (Jefferson, North Carolina:

McFarland, 1991); and more specific Wolfgang Mieder, *Not by Bread Alone. Proverbs of the Bible* (Shelburne, Vermont: New England Press, 1990).

48. Lynne Withey, *Dearest Friend. A Life of Abigail Adams* (New York: The Free Press, 1981), p. 7.

49. This Bible proverb also appears in a letter of May 12, 1785, to Elizabeth Cranch (see VI,143).

50. See Wolfgang Mieder and George B. Bryan, *The Proverbial Winston S. Churchill. An Index to Proverbs in the Works of Sir Winston Churchill* (Westport, Connecticut: Greenwood Press, 1995), pp. 29–32 and p. 196. See also W. Mieder, "'Make Hell While the Sun Shines': Proverbial Rhetoric in Winston Churchill's The Second World War," in W. Mieder, *The Politics of Proverbs. From Traditional Wisdom to Proverbial Stereotypes* (Madison, Wisconsin: University of Wisconsin Press, 1997), pp. 447–49 (the entire chapter on pp. 39–66).

51. *Adams Papers,* cited from Lynne Withey, *Dearest Friend. A Life of Abigail Adams* (New York: The Free Press, 1981), p. 239.

52. Abigail alludes to this Bible proverb again in another letter to her sister Mary Cranch: "The people who can see and judge for themselves are disposed to do right, but the Ethiopean cannot Change his skin" (NL,159; April 21, 1798)

53. See the many passages in R. B. Bernstein (ed.), *The Wisdom of John and Abigail Adams* (New York: MetroBooks, 2002), pp. 42–63; with Abigail's use of the "fish"-proverb on pp. 45–46.

54. Matti Kuusi, *Parömiologische Betrachtungen* (Helsinki: Suomalainen Tiedeakatemia, 1957), p. 52.

55. See Wolfgang Mieder, "History and Interpretation of a Proverb about Human Nature: 'Big Fish Eat Little Fish'," in W. Mieder, *Tradition and Innovation in Folk Literature* (Hanover, New Hampshire: University Press of New England, 1987), pp. 178–228 and pp. 259–268 (notes). Abigail's use of the proverb is treated on p. 212 of this chapter.

56. See Wolfgang Mieder, *"A House Divided": From Biblical Proverb to Lincoln and Beyond* (Burlington, Vermont: University of Vermont, 1998). See also W, Mieder, *The Proverbial Abraham Lincoln. An Index to Proverbs in the Works of Abraham Lincoln* (New York: Peter Lang, 2000), pp. 10–18.

57. For this see Alan Dundes, "Thinking Ahead: A Folkloristic Reflection of the Future Orientation in American Worldview," *Anthropological Quarterly,* 42, no. 2 (1969), 53–72.

58. See Burton Stevenson, *The Home Book of Proverbs,* p. 1168 (no. 2); and Wolfgang Mieder et al., *A Dictionary of American Proverbs,* p. 309. The quotation/proverb appears in Epistle 1, line 95 of *An Essay on Man.* Stevenson states that this was "the birth of a phrase which promptly became proverbial."

4. A House Divided Against Itself Cannot Stand

This chapter was first published in Warren S. Brown (ed.), *Understanding Wisdom* (Philadelphia, Pennsylvania: Templeton Foundation Press, 2000), pp. 57–102.

1. Only "house" variants are listed in Vincent Stuckey Lean, *Collectanea: Proverbs, Folk Lore, and Superstitions* (Bristol: J. W Arrowsmith, 1903; rpt. Detroit: Gale Research Company, 1969), vol. 3, p. 391; Burton Stevenson, *The Home Book of Proverbs, Maxims, and Famous Phrases* (New York: Macmillan, 1948), p. 1191 (no. 4); Frances M. Barbour, *Proverbs and Proverbial Phrases of Illinois* (Carbondale, Illinois: Southern Illinois University Press, 1965), p. 95; John Simpson, *The Concise Dictionary of Proverbs*, 2nd ed. (Oxford: Oxford University Press, 1992), p. 132. Wolfgang Mieder, Stewart A. Kingsbury, and Kelsie B. Harder in *A Dictionary of American Proverbs* (New York: Oxford University Press, 1992), p. 315 and p. 349, list both the "house" and "kingdom" variants.

2. One of those exceptions, albeit recorded much later, is the variant "A kingdom divided against itself cannot stand" that appears in Emma Louise Snapp's regional collection of "Proverbial Lore in Nebraska," *University of Nebraska Studies in Language, Literature, and Criticism*, 13 (1933), 60 (the entire collection on pp. 51–112).

3. Cited from "A Journal of the Life, Labours, Travels, etc. of Thomas Chalkley" included in *A Collection of the Works of Thomas Chalkley* (Philadelphia: James & Johnson, 1790), p. 43. I owe this as well as the subsequent references including those from Andrew Jackson to the invaluable yet very short citations in Bartlett Jere Whiting, *Early American Proverbs and Proverbial Phrases* (Cambridge, Massachusetts: Harvard University Press, 1977), p. 226.

4. The entire broadsheet with 72 stanzas is included in Olga Elizabeth Winslow, *American Broadside Verse* (New Haven, Connecticut: Yale University Press, 1930), p. 185 (part 2, stanzas 7–8).

5. Thomas Paine, *Political Writings*, ed. Bruce Kuklick (Cambridge: Cambridge University Press, 1989), pp. 6–7. I owe this reference to my graduate student Olga Trokhimenko, who found it through a computer search of the University of Virginia Electronic Library (Modern English Collection) database. Scholars are certain that Lincoln read Thomas Paine, and thus must have known this reference to the proverb. See Roy P. Basler, "Lincoln's Development as a Writer," in Roy P. Basler (ed.), *Abraham Lincoln: His Speeches and Writings* (Cleveland, Ohio: The World Publishing Company, 1946), p. 6 (the entire essay on pp. 1–49).

6. Curtius, "Address to All Federalists," *The American Museum, or, Repository of Ancient and Modern Fugitive Pieces*, 1 (1787), 384 (the entire essay on pp. 381–384).

7. Cited from "Correspondence Between John Adams and Mercy Warren," *Collections of the Massachusetts Historical Society,* 44 (1878), 502 (the entire letter on pp. 501–502).

8. P. Stansbury, *A Pedestrian Tour of Two Thousand Three Hundred Miles, in North America* (New York: J. D. Myers & W. Smith, 1822), p. 153.

9. See Johan Thomas Haines, *A House Divided. A Farcical Comedy in Two Acts* (London: J. Dicks, 1836). A later edition was entitled *Uncle Oliver, or, A House Divided. A Farce in Two Acts* (London: James Pattie, 1839).

10. *Correspondence of Andrew Jackson,* vol. 4, p. 208 (the entire letter on pp. 207–209).

11. Part of the lengthy "Speech of Mr. Houston of Texas, in the Senate of the United States, Friday, February 8, 1850," *Appendix to the Congressional Globe for the First Session, Thirty-First Congress: Containing Speeches and Important State Papers,* (Washington, D.C.: John C. Rives, 1850), vol. 22, part 1, p. 102 (the entire speech on pp. 97–102). I owe this reference as well as the following one from Daniel Webster to a footnote in George B. Forgie, *Patricide in the House Divided: A Psychological Interpretation of Lincoln and His Age* (New York: W. W. Norton & Company, p. 201 (note 2).

12. Daniel Webster, "Reception at Buffalo [May 22, 1851]," *The Writings and Speeches of Daniel Webster* (Boston: Little, Brown, & Company, 1903), vol. 4, pp. 243–244, p. 245, and p. 258 (the entire speech on pp. 242–262).

13. Edmund Quincy, "The House Divided Against Itself," *National Anti-Slavery Standard* (March 25, 1852), p. 174. I owe this valuable reference to Allan Nevins, *Ordeal of the Nation: A House Dividing 1852–1857* (New York: Charles Scribner's Sons, 1947), p. 78. See also Edmund Quincy's much longer treatise entitled *Where Will It End? A View of Slavery in the United States in Its Aggressions and Results* (Providence, Rhode Island: Anthony Knowles, 1863). In this 23-page pamphlet Edmund Quincy (1808–1877) does not cite the proverb again, but he makes the following statement: "The entire history of the United States is but the record of the evidence of this fact [the existence of slavery]. What event in our annals is there that Slavery has not set her brand upon it to mark it as her own? In the very moment of the nation's birth, like the evil fairy of the nursery tale, she was present to curse it with her fatal words" (p. 9).

14. Elton Trueblood, *Abraham Lincoln: Theologian of American Anguish* (New York: Harper & Row, 1973), p. 58. Trueblood includes a revealing chapter on "Lincoln and the Bible" (pp. 48–71) in his informative book. Lincoln also was an avid reader of *The Believer's Daily Treasure; or, Texts of Scripture, Arranged for Every Day in the Year,* 4th ed. (London: The Religious Tract Society, 1852), which was reissued with an introduction by Carl Sandburg and the title *Lincoln's Devotional* (Great Neck, New York: Channel Press, 1957). Many of the Biblical proverbs used by Lincoln are also included in this

book with precise references. It should be noted, however, that the "House divided" proverb does not appear in the collection. I owe this reference to my friend William White.

15. Helen Nicolay, *Personal Traits of Abraham Lincoln* (New York: The Century Co., 1912), p. 364.

16. Herbert Joseph Edwards and John Erskine Hankins, *Lincoln the Writer: The Development of His Literary Style* (Orono, Maine: University of Maine, 1962), p. 98.

17. Roy P. Basler (ed.), *The Collected Works of Abraham Lincoln*, 8 vols. (New Brunswick, New Jersey: Rutgers University Press, 1953), vol. 7, p. 368. This edition also provides an *Index* volume (New Brunswick 1955), a *Supplement 1832–1865* volume (Westport, Connecticut: Greenwood Press, 1974), and a *Second Supplement 1848–1865* volume (New Brunswick, New Jersey: Rutgers University Press, 1990). All citations from Lincoln are from this edition, and they are henceforth indicated by *Collected Works* followed by the volume and page numbers. It should be noted that Lincoln's original spelling has been maintained throughout!

18. For Lincoln's "use of ethical persuasion" (without referring to the employment of proverbs) see Marvin G. Bauer, "Persuasive Methods in the Lincoln-Douglas Debates," *Quarterly Journal of Speech,* 13 (1927), 29–39 (esp. pp. 36–39).

19. *Collected Works,* vol. 1, p. 315 (the entire circular on pp. 309–318).

20. See *Collected Works,* vol. 2, p. 448 (note 1).

21. *Collected Works,* vol. 2, pp. 452–453.

22. William Jennings Bryan, "Lincoln as Orator," in Lionel Crocker, (ed.), *An Analysis of Lincoln and Douglas as Public Speakers and Debaters* (Springfield, Illinois: Charles C. Thomas, 1968), p. 95 (the entire article on pp. 91–95).

23. The fact that the account is not included in Don E. and Virginia Fehrenbacher (eds.), *Recollected Words of Abraham Lincoln* (Stanford, California: Stanford University Press, 1996) can be taken as a solid indication that there is no truth to it.

24. It should be pointed out that the reliable Lincoln scholar Don E. Fehrenbacher has presented an argument that this fragment was most likely already written during the last days of December 1857. This does, however, not change the fact that Lincoln had used the "House divided" proverb in writing shortly before the June 16, 1858, speech. See Don E. Fehrenbacher, "The Origins and Purpose of Lincoln's 'House-Divided' Speech," *Mississippi Valley Historical Review,* 46 (1960), 637–641 (the entire article on pp. 615–646); rpt. in Don E. Fehrenbacher, *Prelude to Greatness: Lincoln in the 1850's* (Stanford, California: Stanford University Press, 1962), 89–94 (the entire chapter

on pp. 70–95). In his recent biography on *Lincoln* (New York: Simon & Schuster, 1995), pp. 206–207 (the entire chapter on pp. 196–229 is entitled "A House Divided"), David Herbert Donald agrees with this earlier date of the fragment.

25. The meaning of the statement "He that runs may read" might cause the modern reader some trouble. It is a Bible quotation that has gained some proverbial status: "And the Lord answered me, and said, Write the vision, and make it plain upon tables, that he may run that readeth it" (Habakkuk 2:2). A couple of meanings are possible for this proverb rarely used today: Referring to Lincoln's "House divided" proverb, it might mean that people who hear (read) it will make haste to escape from the danger of letting the Union be destroyed. It might also simply mean that the "House divided" proverb is so clear that the listener (reader) should be quick in understanding it. See Burton Stevenson, *The Home Book of Proverbs,* p. 1938 (no. 13). It should be noted that Lincoln never used this Biblical proverb in his *Collected Works,* placing immediate doubt on the authenticity at least of this proverb in Herndon's account.

26. This is what William Herndon claimed in a lecture delivered about Lincoln on January 24, 1866, that was published much later with the title "Facts Illustrative of Mr. Lincoln's Patriotism and Statesmanship," *Abraham Lincoln Quarterly,* 3 (1944–1945), 184 (the entire lecture on pp. 179–203. See the same text in Don E. and Virginia Fehrenbacher (eds.), *Recollected Words of Abraham Lincoln,* p. 251. The statement also appears in slightly changed wording in William H. Herndon and Jesse W. Weik, *Abraham Lincoln: The True Story of a Great Life* (New York: D. Appleton and Company, 1892), vol. 2, p. 67. See also the accounts of this popular paragraph in J. G. Holland, *The Life of Abraham Lincoln* (Springfield, Massachusetts: Gurdon Bill, 1866), p. 161; Francis Fisher Browne, *The Every-Day Life of Abraham Lincoln* (New York: G. P. Putnam's Sons, 1886), pp. 178–179; John G. Nicolay and John Hay (eds.), *Complete Works of Abraham Lincoln* (New York: The Tandy-Thomas Company, 1905), vol. 3, pp. 1–2 (note 1); James Morgan, *Abraham Lincoln: The Boy and the Man* (New York: Macmillan Company, 1908), pp. 118–119; and Mildred Freiburg Berry, "Lincoln—The Speaker," *Quarterly Journal of Speech,* 17 (1931), 34–35 (the entire article on pp. 25–49).

27. Don E. and Virginia Fehrenbacher (eds.), *Recollected Words of Abraham Lincoln,* p. 267. Not wishing to spread these myths concerning the speech before and after its delivery any further, I simply refer the reader to several far-fetched accounts presented in this excellent book based on serious scholarly work (see pp. 17–18, 145–146, 250–251, 266–267, 326, 334, 352, 439, 488, 537–538).

28. Joseph H. Barret, *Life of Abraham Lincoln* (New York: Moore, Wilstach & Baldwin, 1865), p. 144.

29. *Collected Works,* vol. 1, p. 315.

30. See J. G. Randall, *Lincoln the President* (New York: Dodd, Mead & Company, 1946), vol. 1, p. 107.

31. Reinhard Henry Luthin, *The Real Abraham Lincoln* (Englewood Cliffs, New Jersey: Prentice-Hall, 1960), p. 193.

32. *Collected Works,* vol. 2, pp. 461–462 (the entire speech on pp. 461–469).

33. See Roy P. Basler, "Lincoln's Development as a Writer," in Roy P. Basler, *Abraham Lincoln: His Speeches and Writings* (Cleveland, Ohio: The World Publishing Company, 1946), p. 24 (the entire essay on pp. 1–49).

34. Carl Sandburg, *Abraham Lincoln: The Prairie Years and The War Years* (New York: Harcourt, Brace and Company, 1954), p. 138 (first published 1926).

35. For a detailed discussion of these three parts of the speech see Don E. Fehrenbacher, "The Origins and Purpose of Lincoln's 'House-Divided' Speech," *Mississippi Valley Historical Review,* 46 (1960), 615–646 (the percentages are given on p. 641); rpt. in Don E. Fehrenbacher, *Prelude to Greatness: Lincoln in the 1850's* (Stanford, California: Stanford University Press, 1962), pp. 70–95 (the percentages on p. 92); Michael C. Leff, *Rhetorical Timing in Lincoln's "House Divided" Speech* (Evanston, Illinois: Northwestern University School of Speech, 1983), pp. 6–9 (the 20-page pamphlet is based on the Van Zelst Lecture in Communication delivered on May 19, 1983 at Northwestern University in Evanston, Illinois); and David Zarefsky, *Lincoln, Douglas and Slavery in the Crucible of Public Debate* (Chicago: University of Chicago Press, 1990), pp. 44–45.

36. For some of these shorter comments see Daniel Kilham Dodge, *Abraham Lincoln: Master of Words* (New York: D. Appleton, 1924), pp. 55–56; J. G. Randall, *Lincoln the President* (New York: Dodd, Mead & Company, 1946), pp. 105–107; David D. Anderson, *Abraham Lincoln* (New York: Twayne Publishers, 1970), pp. 114–121; M. E. Bradford, "Dividing the House: The Gnosticism of Lincoln's Political Rhetoric," *Modern Age,* 23 (1979), 10–24 (esp. pp. 1819); Don E. Fehrenbacher, "The Words of Lincoln," in John L. Thomas (ed.), *Abraham Lincoln and the American Political Tradition* (Amherst, Massachusetts: University of Massachusetts Press, 1986), pp. 31–49 (esp. pp. 41–42); rpt. in Don E. Fehrenbacher, *Lincoln in Text and Context. Collected Essays* (Stanford, California: Stanford University Press, 1987), pp. 270–286 (esp. pp. 279–280); and John Grafton (ed.), *Great Speeches [of] Abraham Lincoln* (New York: Dover Publications, 1991), pp. 24–25.

37. *Collected Works,* vol. 5, p. 388.

38. See Arthur Charles Cole, *Lincoln's "House Divided" Speech: Did It Reflect a Doctrine of Class Struggle?* (Chicago: University of Chicago Press, 1923), p. 6

(the entire pamphlet contains 36 pp. and is the printed version of a lecture delivered before the Chicago Historical Society on March 15, 1923).

39. Arthur Charles Cole, *Lincoln's "House Divided" Speech,* p. 7. Cole cites this reference from the *Columbus (Massachusetts) Crisis* newspaper.

40. See Joseph Fort Newton, *Lincoln and Herndon* (Cedar Rapids, Iowa: The Torsch Press, 1910), p. 174.

41. David D. Anderson, *Abraham Lincoln* (New York: Twayne Publishers, 1970), p. 115.

42. *Collected Works,* vol. 3, p. 316.

43. Mark E. Neely, *The Last Best Hope of [sic] Earth: Abraham Lincoln and the Promise of America* (Cambridge, Massachusetts: Harvard University Press, 1993), p. 50.

44. See Harold Holzer (ed.), *The Lincoln-Douglas Debates* (New York: Harper Collins, 1993), p. 17.

45. David Zarefsky, *Lincoln, Douglas and Slavery in the Crucible of Public Debate* (Chicago: University of Chicago Press, 1990), p. 143 (see also p. 142).

46. *Collected Works,* vol. 3, pp. 7–9.

47. *Collected Works,* vol. 3, pp. 17–18.

48. *Collected Works,* vol. 3, pp. 265–266.

49. *Collected Works,* vol. 7, p. 276.

50. *Collected Works,* vol. 3. p. 407 (September 16, 1859); p. 438 (September 17, 1859); and vol. 3, p. 464 (September 19, 1859).

51. *Collected Works,* vol. 4, p. 147.

52. *Collected Works,* vol. 7, p. 1.

53. Phillips Brooks, "The Character, Life, and Death of Abraham Lincoln," in Waldo W. Braden (ed.), *Building the Myth: Selected Speeches Memorializing Abraham Lincoln* (Urbana, Illinois: University of Illinois Press, 1990), p. 56 (the entire sermon on pp. 49–61 and an introduction by the editor on pp. 47–48).

54. See Richard Fuller, *A City or House Divided Against Itself: A Discourse* (Baltimore: J. F. Weishampel, 1865).

55. Richard Fuller, *A City or House Divided Against Itself,* p. 10 (the entire sermon encompasses 20 printed pages).

56. Richard Fuller, *A City or House Divided Against Itself,* pp. 19–20.

57. William Cowper Brann, *The Complete Works of Brann the Iconoclast* (New York: The Brann Publishers, 1919), vol. 1, p. 73. The original work is entitled *Brann, the Iconoclast: A Collection of the Writings of W. C. Brann,* 2 vols. (Waco, Texas: Knight, 1898). I owe this and the next two references to my student Olga Trokhimenko, who found them on the University of Virginia Electronic Library (Modern English Collection) database.

58. Booth Tarkington, *The Conquest of Canaan* (New York: Harper & Brothers, 1905), p. 101.

59. Carl Sandburg, *The People, Yes* (New York: Harcourt, Brace & World, 1964), p. 71 (end of section 36). See also the significant 57th section on "Lincoln" (pp. 134–139). Here Sandburg cites Lincoln's "government of the people by the people for the people" (p. 134), but he does not quote the "House divided" proverb.

60. Both of these references are cited from Bartlett Jere Whiting, *Modern Proverbs and Proverbial Sayings,* p. 328. They appear on p. 120 and p. 15, respectively, in the novels. Unfortunately I did not succeed in locating these two books, and for this reason no contexts can be cited.

61. This last reference I also owe to my student Olga Trokhimenko.

62. Thirteen quotations from Lincoln in German translation are included in J. H. Kirchberger, *Das Große Krüger Zitaten Buch* (Frankfurt am Main: Wolfgang Krüger Verlag, 1977), pp. 238–239. The "House divided" proverb is not included.

63. See Carl Schulze, *Die biblischen Sprichwörter der deutschen Sprache* (Göttingen: Vandenhoeck und Ruprecht, 1860; rpt. ed. by Wolfgang Mieder. Bern: Peter Lang, 1987), p. 145.

64. See Karl Friedrich Wilhelm Wander, *Deutsches Sprichwörter-Lexikon,* 5 vols. (Leipzig: F. A. Brockhaus, 1867–1880; rpt. Darmstadt: Wissenschaftliche Buchgesellschaft, 1964), vol. 3 (1873), col. 1602 (no. 21).

65. For an interesting comparative study see J. Alan Pfeffer, "Das biblische Zitat im Volksmund der Germanen und Romanen," in Beda Allemann and Erwin Koppen (eds.), *Teilnahme und Spiegelung. Festschrift für Horst Rüdiger* (Berlin: Walter de Gruyter, 1975), pp. 99–111.

66. These paragraphs are quoted from a 12-page double-spaced typed manuscript which Willy Brandt made available to journalists for morning newspapers of Friday, February 13, 1959. It has the title "Address by Willy Brandt, Governing Mayor of Berlin[,] delivered at The Lincoln Sesquicentennial Banquet[,] Springfield, Illinois, February 12, 1959." For an interesting local newspaper report regarding Brandt's speech see "Brandt Tells Of His People's Fight" in the *Illinois State Register* (Springfield, Friday, February 13, 1959), pp. 1–2. In all the secondary literature read for this chapter, I came across only one reference to Brandt's Springfield address: "Illinois's year-long [sesquicentennial] commemoration kicked off with the visit of Willy Brandt, mayor of Berlin, who spoke on Lincoln's birthday;" see Merrill D. Peterson, *Lincoln in American Memory* (New York: Oxford University Press, 1994), p. 366. I would like to thank Nancy Crane and Angus Robertson from the Bailey/Howe Library at the University of Vermont for obtaining a copy of this speech from a "News Kit" housed at the John Hay Library (Special

Collections) of Brown University in Providence, Rhode Island. Nancy Crane also located the newspaper report from the *Illinois State Register* through the help of the town library in Springfield.

67. Willy Brandt, "Amerikanische und deutsche Einheit: Abraham Lincoln zum 150. Geburtstag. Festansprache gehalten am 12. Februar 1959 in Springfield (Illinois), USA," *Außenpolitik,* 10 (1959), 210 (the entire speech on pp. 209–213).

68. Willy Brandt, *Die "Spiegel"-Gespräche,* ed. by Erich Böhme and Klaus Wirtgen (Stutgart: Deutsche Verlags-Anstalt, 1993; rpt. as paperback Reinbek: Rowohlt Verlag, 1995), p. 273. I discovered this and the following references together with my undergraduate student Sonja Eggert; see her Honors Thesis on *"Kleine Schritte sind besser als keine Schritte": Willy Brandts sprichwörtliche Rhetorik* (Burlington, Vermont: The University of Vermont, 1998).

69. Willy Brandt, "Die Sache ist gelaufen," in Willy Brandt, *"... was zusammengehört": Über Deutschland* (Bonn: J. H. W. Dietz, 1993), p. 82 (the entire speech on pp. 74–83).

70. For hundreds of examples with detailed notes and bibliographical references see Broder Carstensen and Ulrich Busse, *Anglizismen-Wörterbuch,* 3 vols. (Berlin: Walter de Gruyter, 1993–1996). As an example of how the American proverb "A picture is worth a thousand words" has entered the German language both as a loan translation and in English see Wolfgang Mieder, "'Ein Bild sagt mehr als tausend Worte': Ursprung und Überlieferung eines amerikanischen Lehnsprichworts," *Proverbium: Yearbook of International Proverb Scholarship,* 6 (1989), 25–37.

71. The passage by the apostle Luke is very different in the German Bible translation, namely "Ein Haus fällt über das andere (11:17)" (One house falls over the other). It also has not reached any proverbial status.

72. Stephen J. Silvia, *A House Divided: Employers and the Challenge to Pattern Bargaining in a United Germany* (Cambridge, Massachusetts: Minda de Gunzburg Center for European Studies, Harvard University, 1995), a 33-page pamphlet.

73. See James Hurt, "All the Living and the Dead: Lincoln's Imagery," *American Literature,* 52 (1980), 352 (the entire article on pp. 351–380). Hurt argues convincingly that "Lincoln's art, then, is an art of indirection, of finding a way of representing a deeply personal vision indirectly through parable—like stories and jokes, and, we might add, images and symbols." Let me simply add that proverbs are clearly part of this "art of indirection," albeit one based on the emotive and expressive power of folk speech.

5. Do Unto Others As You Would Have Them Do Unto You

This chapter was first published in the *Journal of American Folklore,* 114 (2001), 331–357.

1. Ronald K. Burke, *Frederick Douglass: Crusading Orator for Human Rights* (New York: Garland Publishing, 1996), p. 121.
2. Frank W. Hale, *A Critical Analysis of the Speaking of Frederick Douglass* (M.A. Thesis University of Nebraska, 1951), p. 46.
3. George A. Hinshaw, *A Rhetorical Analysis of the Speeches of Frederick Douglass During and After the Civil War* (Diss. University of Nebraska, 1972), p. 260.
4. Lois Belton Kinney, *A Rhetorical Study of the Practice of Frederick Douglass on the Issue of Human Rights, 1840–1860* (Diss. Ohio State University, 1974), p. 254.
5. Cited from Benjamin Quarles (ed.), *Frederick Douglass* (Englewood Cliffs, New Jersey: Prentice-Hall, 1968), p. 101. See also Carolyn Calloway-Thomas, "William G. Allen on 'Orators and Orations'," *Journal of Black Studies,* 18 (1988), 313–336 (the tongue- and pen-wise passage on p. 331).
6. There are two competing editions of Frederick Douglass's speeches and writings: Philip S. Foner (ed.), *The Life and Writings of Frederick Douglass,* 5 vols. (New York: International Publishers, 1950–1975); and John Blassingame (ed.), *The Frederick Douglass Papers,* 5 vols. (New Haven, Connecticut: Yale University Press, 1985–1992). Where a particular source appears in both editions, two references will be cited. The Arabic numeral before the page number refers to Foner's edition, while the Roman numeral preceding the page number relates to Blassingame's edition. This particular quotation is also cited by David W. Blight, "Frederick Douglass and the American Apocalypse," *Civil War History,* 31 (1985), 309–328 (here p. 319); also reprinted in D. W. Blight, *Frederick Douglass' Civil War: Keeping Faith in Jubilee* (Baton Rouge, Louisiana: Louisiana State University Press, 1989), 101–121 (here p. 110).
7. Matti Kuusi, *Parömiologische Betrachtungen* (Helsinki: Suomalainen Tiedeakatemia, 1957), p. 52.
8. For collections of proverbs and proverbial expressions in common use among African Americans in more recent times see Jack L. Daniel, *The Wisdom of Sixth Mount Zion [Baptist Church] from The Members of Sixth Mount Zion and Those Who Begot Them* (Pittsburgh, Pennsylvania: University of Pittsburgh, College of Arts and Sciences, 1979); Alene Leett Barnes-Harden, *African American Verbal Arts: Their Nature and Communicative Interpretation: A Thematic Analysis* (Diss. State University of New York at Buffalo, 1980); Geneva Smitherman, *Talkin and Testifyin: The Language of Black America* (Detroit, Michigan: Wayne State University Press, 1986); and G. Smitherman, *Black Talk: Words and Phrases from the Hood to the Amen Corner* (New York:

Houghton Mifflin, 1994). See also the studies by Jack L. Daniel, "Towards an Ethnography of Afroamerican Proverbial Usage," *Black Lines,* 2 (1973), 3–12; John W. Roberts, "Slave Proverbs: A Perspective," *Callaloo,* 1 (1978), 129–140; and Jack L. Daniel, Geneva Smitherman-Donaldson, and Milford A. Jeremiah, "Makin' a Way outa no Way: The Proverb Tradition in the Black Experience," *Journal of Black Studies,* 17 (1987), 482–508.

9. See Wolfgang Mieder, *Proverbs Are Never Out of Season: Popular Wisdom in the Modern Age* (New York: Oxford University Press, 1993); and W. Mieder, *The Politics of Proverbs: From Traditional Wisdom to Proverbial Stereotypes* (Madison, Wisconsin: University of Wisconsin Press, 1997).

10. See Kenneth Burke, "Literature [i.e., proverbs] as Equipment for Living," in K. Burke, *The Philosophy of Literary Form: Studies in Symbolic Action* (Baton Rouge, Louisiana: Louisiana State University Press, 1941), pp. 253–262; and Peter Seitel, "Proverbs: A Social Use of Metaphor," *Genre,* 2 (1969), 143–161; rpt. in Wolfgang Mieder and Alan Dundes (eds.), *The Wisdom of Many: Essays on the Proverb* (New York: Garland Publishing, 1981; rpt. Madison, Wisconsin: University of Wisconsin Press, 1994), pp. 122–139.

11. Cited from a volume that includes the three versions of the autobiography: Frederick Douglass, *Autobiographies: Narrative of the Life of Frederick Douglass* [1845], *My Bondage and My Freedom* [1855], *Life and Times of Frederick Douglass* [1893] (New York: Library of America, 1994), p. 53. Other references will be cited by the letter N, B, or L plus page numbers. For a discussion of this proverb see Lisa Margaret Zeitz, "Biblical Allusion and Imagery in Frederick Douglass' Narrative," *College Language Association Journal,* 25 (1981), 56–64 (here pp. 57–58); and A. James Wohlpart, "Privatized Sentiment and the Institution of Christianity: Douglass's Ethical Stance in the Narrative," *American Transcendental Quarterly,* 9 (1995), 181–194 (here p. 186).

12. See Wolfgang Mieder, "'As If I Were the Master of the Situation': Proverbial Manipulation in Adolf Hitler's Mein Kampf," in W. Mieder, *The Politics of Proverbs,* pp. 9–38.

13. For a short discussion of this proverb see also Stephen L. Thompson, "The Grammar of Civilization: Douglass and Crummell on Doing Things with Words," in Bill E. Lawson and Frank M. Kirkland (eds.), *Frederick Douglass: A Critical Reader* (Oxford: Blackwell, 1999), pp. 173–203 (here p. 180).

14. See the short comment on this proverb in Stephen L. Thompson, "The Grammar of Civilization," p. 186.

15. See David W. Blight's excellent introduction to the bicentennial edition of Caleb Bingham, *The Columbian Orator Containing a Variety of Original and Selected Pieces together with the Rules, which are Calculated to Improve Youth and Others, in the Ornamental and Useful Art of Eloquence* (New York: New York University Press, 1998), pp. xiii–xxxiii. Of much interest is also

Granville Ganter, "The Active Virtue of *The Columbian Orator,*" *New England Quarterly,* 70 (1997), 463–476.

16. Every biographer of Douglass refers to the influence that *The Columbian Orator* had on his intellectual and rhetorical development; see David W. Blight, *Frederick Douglass' Civil War,* pp. 89–91; William S. McFeely, *Frederick Douglass* (New York: W. W. Norton, 1991), pp. 34–36; and Gregory P. Lampe, *Frederick Douglass: Freedom's Voice, 1818–1845* (East Lansing, Michigan: Michigan State University Press, 1998), pp. 7–13.

17. Booker T. Washington, *Frederick Douglass* (Philadelphia: George W. Jacobs, 1907; rpt. New York: Greenwood Press, 1969), p. 26.

18. For a discussion of songs see Sterlin Stuckey, "'Ironic Tenacity': Frederick Douglass's Seizure of the Dialectic," in Eric J. Sundquist (ed.), *Frederick Douglass: New Literary and Historical Essays* (Cambridge: Cambridge University Press, 1990), 23–46 (here pp. 32–38).

19. For a discussion of Douglass's move from "the simple, concrete speech of the *Narrative* to the Latinate, polysyllabic, inflated rhetoric of the Victorian intelligentsia," see Henry Dan Piper, "The Place of Frederick Douglass's *Narrative of the Life of an American Slave* in the Development of a Native American Prose Style," *Journal of Afro-American Issues,* 5 (1977), 183–191 (here p. 189). Of interest are also Ann Kibbey, "Language in Slavery: Frederick Douglass's *Narrative,*" *Prospects: The Annual of American Cultural Studies,* 8 (1983), 163–182; rpt. in Harold Bloom (ed.), *Frederick Douglass's "Narrative of the Life of Frederick Douglass"* (New York: Chelsea House Publishers, 1988), pp. 131–152; and Edward J. Dupuy, "Linguistic Mastery and the Garden of the Chattel in Frederick Douglass' *Narrative,*" *Mississippi Quarterly,* 44 (1990–1991), 23–33.

20. See Alyce M. McKenzie, *Preaching Proverbs: Wisdom for the Pulpit* (Louisville, Kentucky: Westminster John Knox Press, 1996); and Sw. Anand Prahlad, *African-American Proverbs in Context* (Jackson, Mississippi: University of Mississippi Press, 1996).

21. Caleb Bingham, *The Columbian Orator,* p. 56.

22. Caleb Bingham, *The Columbian Orator,* p. 145.

23. George A. Hinshaw, *A Rhetorical Analysis of the Speeches of Frederick Douglass,* p. 212.

24. John Sekora, "Comprehending Slavery: Language and Personal History in Douglass' *Narrative* of 1845," *College Language Association Journal,* 29 (1985), 157–170 (here p. 165); rpt. in Harold Bloom (ed.), *Frederick Douglass's "Narrative of the Life of Frederick Douglass,"* pp. 153–163 (here p. 159).

25. Kelly Miller, "Frederick Douglass," in K. Miller, *Race Adjustment: Essays on the Negro in America* (New York: Neale Publishing, 1907; rpt. with the new title *Race Adjustment: The Everlasting Stain* (New York: Arno Press, 1968), pp. 211–220 (here p. 220).

26. Steven Kingston, *Frederick Douglass: Abolitionist, Liberator, Statesman* (New York: National Negro Congress, 1941), p. 45. See also Frank W. Hale, "Frederick Douglass: Antislavery Crusader and Lecturer," *Journal of Human Relations,* 14 (1966), 100–111 (here p. 111); and David W. Blight in his introduction to Caleb Bingham, *The Columbian Orator,* p. xxvi.

27. See John Bartlett, *Familiar Quotations,* 15th ed. by Emily Morison Beck (Boston: Little, Brown and Company, 1980), p. 556 (No. 4). It should be noted that Douglass's statement that "Power concedes nothing without a demand. It never did and it never will" has also become well known and is frequently quoted. However, it has not yet been included in Bartlett's collection.

28. For how individual sayings might become general proverbs see Archer Taylor, *The Proverb* (Cambridge, Massachusetts: Harvard University Press, 1931; rpt. ed. by Wolfgang Mieder. Bern: Peter Lang, 1985), pp. 34–43; Shirley L. Arora, "The Perception of Proverbiality," *Proverbium,* 1 (1984), 1–38; rpt. in W. Mieder (ed.), *Wise Words: Essays on the Proverb* (New York: Garland Publishing, 1994), pp. 3–29; and W. Mieder, "Popular Views of the Proverb," *Proverbium,* 2 (1985), 109–143.

29. Cited from Benjamin Quarles (ed.), *Frederick Douglass,* pp. 122–127 (here p. 123).

30. Frank M. Kirkland, "Enslavement, Moral Suasion, and Struggles for Recognition: Frederick Douglass's Answer to the Question—'What is Enlightenment?'," in Bill E. Lawson and F. M. Kirkland (eds.), *Frederick Douglass: A Critical Reader,* pp. 243–310 (here p. 244).

31. A few examples are cited in George A. Hinshaw, *A Rhetorical Analysis of the Speeches of Frederick Douglass,* pp. 347–349. For collections see Selwyn Gurney Champion, *The Eleven Religions and Their Proverbial Lore* (New York: E. P. Dutton, 1945); Burton Stevenson, *The Home Book of Bible Quotations* (New York: Harper & Brothers, 1949); Wolfgang Mieder, *Not By Bread Alone: Proverbs of the Bible* (Shelburne, Vermont: New England Press, 1990); Albert Kirby Griffin, *Religious Proverbs: Over 1600 Adages from 18 Faiths Worldwide* (Jefferson, North Carolina: McFarland, 1991); and John Marks Templeton, *Worldwide Laws of Life: Two Hundred Eternal Spiritual Principles* (Radnor, Pennsylvania: Templeton Foundation Press, 1997).

32. See Wolfgang Mieder, Stewart A. Kingsbury, and Kelsie B. Harder (eds.), *A Dictionary of American Proverbs* (New York: Oxford University Press, 1992), p. 312.

33. See Wolfgang Mieder, *The Proverbial Abraham Lincoln: An Index to Proverbs in the Works of Abraham Lincoln* (New York: Peter Lang, 2000), pp. 10–18.

34. For Douglass as a journalist see Philip S. Foner, *Frederick Douglass. A Biography* (New York: Citadel Press, 1969), pp. 84–100; and Shelley Fisher Fishkin and Carla L. Peterson, "'We Hold These Truths to Be Self-Evident':

The Rhetoric of Frederick Douglass's Journalism," in Eric J. Sundquist (ed.), *Frederick Douglass: New Literary and Historical Essays*, pp. 189–204.

35. Burton Stevenson, *The Home Book of Proverbs, Maxims, and Famous Phrases* (New York: Macmillan, 1948), p. 1388 (no. 3); and John W. Blassingame (ed.), *The Frederick Douglass Papers*, III,544 (note 4).

36. This text is from one of Douglass's most impressive speeches entitled "What to the Slave Is the Fourth of July?" a bitter abolitionist attack delivered in his native Rochester. For detailed analyses of this significant oration see Lois Belton Kinney, *A Rhetorical Study of the Practice of Frederick Douglass on the Issue of Human Rights*, pp. 203–225; James Jasinski, "Rearticulating History in Epideictic Discourse: Frederick Douglass's 'The Meaning of the Fourth of July to the Negro'," in Thomas W. Benson (ed.), *Rhetoric and Political Culture in Nineteenth-Century America* (East Lansing, Michigan: Michigan State University, 1997), pp. 71–89; and John Louis Lucaites, "The Irony of 'Equality' in Black Abolitionist Discourse: The Case of Frederick Douglass's 'What to the Slave Is the Fourth of July?'," in Thomas W. Benson (ed.), *Rhetoric and Political Culture in Nineteenth-Century America*, pp. 47–69.

37. John W. Blassingame, the informed editor of *The Frederick Douglass Papers*, has provided the following explanatory comment here (III,301–302; note 2): Jefferson's earliest "composition draft" of the Declaration of Independence charged the British crown with having "refused us permission to exclude [importation of Negroes] by law." His "original Rough draft" includes a much fuller and more bitter indictment of George III: "[H]e has waged cruel war against human nature itself, violating it's [sic] most sacred rights of life & liberty in the persons of a distant people who never offended him, captivating & carrying them into slavery in another hemisphere, or to incur miserable death in their transportation thither. This piratical warfare, the opprobrium of infidel powers, is the warfare of the CHRISTIAN king of Great Britain, determined to keep open a market where MEN should be bought & sold, he has prostituted his negative for suppressing every legislative attempt to prohibit or to restrain this execrable commerce." Julian P. Boyd et al., eds., *The Papers of Thomas Jefferson* (Princeton, 1950–), I:418,426.

38. See Philip S. Foner, *Frederick Douglass*, p. 88. The motto was proposed by Douglass's friend Gerrit Smith.

39. For discussions of this proverb see Carolyn Prager, "'If I Be Devil': English Renaissance Response to the Proverbial and Ecumenical Ethiopian," *Journal of Medieval and Renaissance Studies*, 17 (1987), 257–279; and Jean Michel Massing, "From Greek Proverb to Soap Advert [*sic*]: Washing the Ethiopian," *Journal of the Warburg and Courtauld Institutes*, 58 (1995), 180–201.

40. Frank W. Hale, "Frederick Douglass: Antislavery Crusader and Lecturer," *Journal of Human Relations*, p. 101.

41. See William L. Andrews, "Introduction," in W. L. Andrews (ed.), *Critical Essays on Frederick Douglass* (Boston: G. K. Hall, 1991), 1–20 (here p. 4).

42. Waldo E. Martin, "Self-Made Man, Self-Conscious Hero," in W. E. Martin, *The Mind of Frederick Douglass* (Chapel Hill, North Carolina: University of North Carolina Press, 1984), pp. 253–278 (here p. 256).

43. Nathan Irvin Huggins, "Self-Reliance," in N. I. Huggins, *Slave and Citizen: The Life of Frederick Douglass* (Boston: Little, Brown and Company, 1980), pp. 44–73 (here p. 71).

44. See Alan Dundes, "Thinking Ahead: A Folkloristic Reflection of the Future Orientation in American Worldview," *Anthropological Quarterly,* 42 (1969), 53–72.

45. This paragraph reoccurs frequently in the Douglass scholarship; see Benjamin Quarles, *Frederick Douglass* (Washington, D.C.: The Associated Publishers, 1948), p. 363; Philip S. Foner (ed.), *The Life and Writings of Frederick Douglass,* vol. 1, p. 50; Frank W. Hale, *A Critical Analysis of the Speaking of Frederick Douglass,* p. 32; Philip S. Foner, *Frederick Douglass: A Biography,* p. 50; and Ronald K. Burke, *Frederick Douglass: Crusading Orator for Human Rights,* pp. 18–19.

46. William S. McFeely, *Frederick Douglass,* p. 100.

47. For a discussion of the proverb "Do unto others as you would have them do unto you," see J. O. Hertzler, "On Golden Rules," *The International Journal of Ethics,* 44 (1933–1934), 418–436; Hans Reiner, "Die 'Goldene Regel': Die Bedeutung einer sittlichen Grundformel der Menschheit," *Zeitschrift für philosophische Forschung,* 3 (1948), 74–105; Claudio Soliva, "Ein Bibelwort [die 'Goldene Regel'] in Geschichte und Recht," *Unser Weg: Werkblatt der Schweizerischen Weggefährtinnen,* no volume given, nos. 6–7 (1964), 51–57; and John Marks Templeton, *Worldwide Laws of Life,* pp. 8–12.

48. This is most likely a reference to the refusal by the American Bible Society to distribute Bibles among those slaves who could read.

49. John W. Blassingame provides the following explanation (note 1): "This law [the Civil Rights Act of 1875], generally regarded as one of the most radical to emerge from the Reconstruction era, instructed the nation that all persons, regardless of race or color, were entitled to full and equal access to public accommodations and facilities, particularly places of lodging, amusement, and transportation" (V, 111).

50. For a short discussion see August Meier, "Frederick Douglass' Vision for America: A Case Study in Nineteenth-Century Negro Protest," in Harold M. Hyman and Leonard W. Levy (eds.), *Freedom and Reform: Essays in Honor of Henry Steele Commager* (New York: Harper & Row, 1967), pp. 127–148 (here pp. 141–142).

51. Alexander Pope, *An Essay on Man* (1733–1734), epistle II, line 2.

52. William Shakespeare, *As You Like It* (1599), act 2, scene 7, lines 139–140.

6. It's Not a President's Business to Catch Flies

This chapter first appeared in *Southern Folklore*, 57 (2000), 188–232.

1. Karlyn Kohrs Campbell and Kathleen Hall Jamieson, *Deeds Done in Words: Presidential Rhetoric and the Genres of Governance* (Chicago: University of Chicago Press, 1990), p. 15. This book includes a chapter on "Inaugural Addresses" (pp. 14–36 and pp. 227–229 [notes]) which was earlier published in more or less identical form by both authors as "Inaugurating the Presidency," *Presidential Studies Quarterly,* 15 (1985), 394–411.

2. See Campbell and Jamieson, *Deeds Done in Words,* p. 36.

3. Campbell and Jamieson, *Deeds Done in Words,* p. 28. See also Burt Solomon: "Inaugural Auguries," *National Journal,* no. 2 (January 13, 2001), pp. 84–90: "Many phrases from past inaugural addresses have made their way into Bartlett's *Familiar Quotations* and have accurately described the spirit of the ensuing Administration" (p. 85). I owe this reference to my colleague Prof. John Burke.

4. See Wolfgang Mieder, Stewart A. Kingsbury, and Kelsie B. Harder (eds.), *A Dictionary of American Proverbs* (New York: Oxford University Press, 1992), p. 482.

5. All page numbers in parentheses refer to John Gabriel Hunt (ed.), *The Inaugural Addresses of the Presidents* (New York: Gramercy Books, 1997). See also the earlier collection of these special speeches by Davis Newton Lott (ed.), *The Inaugural Addresses of the American Presidents from Washington to Kennedy* (New York: Holt, Rinehart and Winston, 1961).

6. See Irene Meichsner, *Die Logik von Gemeinplätzen. Vorgeführt an Steuermannstopos und Schiffsmetapher* (Bonn: Bouvier, 1983).

7. See Wolfgang Mieder, *"No Struggle, No Progress": Frederick Douglass's Proverbial Rhetoric in His Fight for Civil Rights* (New York: Peter Lang, 2001), pp.

8. Mieder et al., *Dictionary of American Proverbs,* p. 398.

9. See Wolfgang Mieder, "'Raising the Iron Curtain': Proverbs and Political Cartoons of the Cold War," in W. Mieder, *The Politics of Proverbs: From Traditional Wisdom to Proverbial Stereotypes* (Madison, Wisconsin: University of Wisconsin Press, 1997), pp. 99–137 and 214–221 (notes).

10. For a statistical analysis of the number of words and sentences in the inaugural speeches of the American presidents see Donald L. Wolfarth, "John F. Kennedy in the Tradition of Inaugural Speeches," *The Quarterly Journal of Speech,* 47 (1961), 124–132. The average length is 2463 words in 84 sentences.

11. See Mieder et al., *Dictionary of American Proverbs,* p. 75.

12. When scholars speak of inaugural addresses, they usually do not include the remarks that the nine Vice Presidents made who took over the position of President because of a death, assassination or resignation. See, however, the chapter on "Special Inaugural Addresses: The Speeches of Ascendant Vice Presidents," in Campbell and Jamieson, *Deeds Done in Words*, pp. 37–51 and 229–232 (notes).

13. See Wolfgang Mieder, *The Proverbial Abraham Lincoln: An Index to Proverbs in the Works of Abraham Lincoln* (New York: Peter Lang, 2000).

14. See for example Burton Stevenson, *The Home Book of Proverbs, Maxims, and Famous Phrases* (New York: Macmillan, 1948), p. 1506 (no. 1); and John Bartlett, *Familiar Quotations*, ed. Justin Kaplan. 16th ed. (Boston: Little, Brown and Company, 1992), p. 450 (no. 11).

15. For the origin of this phrase see Rex Forrest, "[Washington] Irving and 'The Almighty Dollar'," *American Speech*, 15 (1940), 443–444.

16. See Alan Dundes, "Thinking Ahead: A Folkloristic Reflection of the Future Orientation in American Worldview," *Anthropological Quarterly*, 42 (1969), 53–72.

17. For a discussion of the proverb "Do unto others as you would have them do unto you" as a universal law, see J. O. Hertzler, "On Golden Rules," *The International Journal of Ethics*, 44 (1933–1934), 418–436; Hans Reiner, "Die 'Goldene Regel': Die Bedeutung einer sittlichen Grundformel der Menschheit," *Zeitschrift für philosophische Forschung*, 3 (1948), 74–105; Claudio Soliva, "Ein Bibelwort [die 'Goldene Regel'] in Geschichte und Recht," *Unser Weg: Werkblatt der Schweizerischen Weggefährtinnen*, no volume given, nos. 6–7 (1964), 51–57; Brian Burrell, *The Words We Live By: The Creeds, Mottoes, and Pledges that Have Shaped America* (New York: The Free Press, 1997), pp. 13–27; and John Marks Templeton, *Worldwide Laws of Life* (Philadelphia, Pennsylvania: Templeton Foundation Press, 1997), pp. 8–12.

18. Cited from Roy P. Basler (ed.), *The Collected Works of Abraham Lincoln*, 8 vols. (New Brunswick, New Jersey: Rutgers University Press, 1953), vol. 2, p. 461 (the entire speech on pp. 461–469).

19. For a monograph of the secularized use of this proverb see Wolfgang Mieder, *"A House Divided": From Biblical Proverb to Lincoln and Beyond* (Burlington, Vermont: The University of Vermont, 1998).

20. See Mieder et al., *Dictionary of American Proverbs*, p. 76 (without reference to Calvin Coolidge).

21. For presidential quotations in general see the special compilations by Caroline Thomas Harnsberger (ed.), *Treasury of Presidential Quotations* (Chicago: Follett, 1964); Elizabeth Frost (ed.), *The Bully Pulpit: Quotations from America's Presidents* (New York: Facts on File Publications, 1988); Donald L. Miller (ed.), *From George ... to George: 200 Years of Presidential Quotations*

(Washington, D.C.: Braddock Communications, 1989); and Antony Jay (ed.), *The Oxford Dictionary of Political Quotations* (Oxford: Oxford University Press, 1996).

22. See Wolfgang Mieder and George B. Bryan, *The Proverbial Winston S. Churchill: An Index to Proverbs in the Works of Sir Winston Churchill* (Westport, Connecticut: Greenwood Press, 1995); Wolfgang Mieder, "Proverbs in Nazi Germany: The Promulgation of Anti-Semitism and Stereotypes Through Folklore," in W. Mieder, *Proverbs Are Never Out of Season: Popular Wisdom in the Modern Age* (New York: Oxford University Press, 1993), pp. 225–255; and the two chapters on "'As if I Were the Master of the Situation': Proverbial Manipulation in Adolf Hitler's *Mein Kampf*" and "'Make Hell While the Sun Shines': Proverbial Rhetoric in Winston Churchill's *The Second World War*" in W. Mieder, *The Politics of Proverbs: From Traditional Wisdom to Proverbial Stereotypes* (Madison, Wisconsin: University of Wisconsin Press, 1997), pp. 9–38 (notes, pp.193–200) and pp. 39–66 (notes, pp. 200–206).

23. Mieder et al., *Dictionary of American Proverbs*, pp. 203–204, cite an informant stating "Used by Franklin D. Roosevelt in his first inaugural address (1933)."

24. See Stevenson, *Home Book of Proverbs, Maxims, and Famous Phrases*, pp. 783–784 (no. 14); and Bartlett, *Familiar Quotations*, p. 648 (no. 18). For Henry David Thoreau's use of proverbs see J. Russell Reaver, "Thoreau's Ways with Proverbs," *American Transcendental Quarterly*, 1 (1967), 2–7; and Wolfgang Mieder and George B. Bryan, *Proverbs in World Literature: A Bibliography* (New York: Peter Lang, 1996), p. 261.

25. See also the special collection by E. Taylor and Lois F. Parks (eds.), *Memorable Quotations of Franklin D. Roosevelt* (New York: Thomas Y. Crowell, 1965); and Alex Ayres (ed.), *The Wit and Wisdom of Eleanor Roosevelt* (New York: Meridian, 1996).

26. For the positive value of using clichés when appropriate see Edd Miller and Jesse J. Villarreal, "The Use of Clichés by Four Contemporary Speakers [Winston Churchill, Anthony Eden, Franklin Roosevelt, and Henry Wallace]," *Quarterly Journal of Speech*, 31 (1945), 151–155.

27. See Stevenson, *Home Book of Proverbs, Maxims, and Famous Phrases*, p. 896 (no. 3); and Mieder et al., *Dictionary of American Proverbs*, p. 239. For Ralph Waldo Emerson's use of proverbs see Ralph Charles La Rosa, "Necessary Truths: The Poetics of Emerson's Proverbs," in Eric Rothstein (ed.), *George Eliot, De Quincey, and Emerson* (Madison, Wisconsin: University of Wisconsin Press, 1976), pp. 129–192; and Wolfgang Mieder, *American Proverbs: A Study of Texts and Contexts* (Bern: Peter Lang, 1989), pp. 143–169. For further bibliographical references see Mieder and Bryan, *Proverbs in World Literature*, pp. 97–98.

28. See Wolfgang Mieder and George B. Bryan, *The Proverbial Harry S. Truman: An Index to Proverbs in the Works of Harry S. Truman* (New York: Peter Lang, 1997).

29. See the "Analysis of the Style of John F. Kennedy's Inaugural Address" in Edward P. J. Corbett, *Classical Rhetoric for the Modern Student* (New York: Oxford University Press, 1965), pp. 508–518.

30. Cited from Lott (ed.), *The Inaugural Addresses of the American Presidents*, p. 270. Donald L. Wolfarth, "John F. Kennedy in the Tradition of Inaugural Speeches," p. 132, speaks of this proverbial metaphor as a "picturesque admonition," while Edward P. J. Corbett, "Analysis of the Style of John F. Kennedy's Inaugural Address," p. 514, refers to it as a "folksy adage."

31. It is, however, generally believed and accepted that John F. Kennedy wrote his inaugural speech primarily by himself; see Sam Meyer, "The John F. Kennedy Inauguration Speech: Function and Importance of Its 'Address System'," *Rhetoric Society Quarterly,* 12 (1982), 239–250 (here pp. 240–241).

32. Bartlett, *Familiar Quotations,* p. 741 (no. 5). See also the small book by Edward Lewis and Richard Rhodes (eds.), *John F. Kennedy: Words to Remember* (Kansas City, Missouri: Hallmark Cards, 1967).

33. See also Edward P. J. Corbett, "Analysis of the Style of John F. Kennedy's Inaugural Address," p. 512: "And the most memorable line of the speech is cast in the form of an antithesis: '... Ask not what your country can do for you—ask what you can do for your country.' Most of these antitheses of thought are laid out in parallel grammatical structure. The recurring parallelism is appropriate here because although the President is pointing up opposites by his antitheses he wants to suggest that these opposites can be reconciled. Opposites can be reconciled only if they are co-ordinate, and one way to emphasize the co-ordinate value of opposites is to juxtapose them in a parallel grammatical structure." But Corbett fails to see that this parallel (and also proverbial!) structure helped the memorability of this sentence along.

34. Bartlett, *Familiar Quotations,* p. 741 (note 1).

35. For President Johnson's sententious rhetoric see the chapter on "Quotes and LBJ" in Paul F. Boller, *Quotemanship: The Use and Abuse of Quotations for Polemical and Other Purposes* (Dallas, Texas: Southern Methodist University Press, 1967), pp. 406–431.

36. See Barbara Ann Harris, "The Inaugural of Richard Milhous Nixon: A Reply to Robert L. Scott," *Western Speech,* 34 (1970), 233 (the entire article on pp. 231–234).

37. Cited from Bartlett, *Familiar Quotations,* p. 510 (no. 8). For Tolstoy's use of proverbs see Andrew Donskov, "Tolstoy's Use of Proverbs in The Power of Darkness," in Kevin J. McKenna (ed.), *Proverbs in Russian Literature: From*

Catherine the Great to Alexander Solzhenitsyn (Burlington, Vermont: The University of Vermont, 1998), pp. 61–74. Other studies are listed in Mieder and Bryan, *Proverbs in Literature,* p. 262.

38. Cited from Stevenson, *Home Book of Proverbs, Maxims, and Famous Phrases,* p. 2115 (no. 14). See also Mieder et al., *Dictionary of American Proverbs,* p. 267.

39. Robert L. Scott, "Rhetoric That Postures: An Intrinsic Reading of Richard M. Nixon's Inaugural Address," *Western Speech,* 34 (1970), 47 (the entire article on pp. 46–52).

40. Campbell and Jamieson, *Deeds Done in Words,* pp. 21–22.

41. Cited from Nigel Rees, *Phrases & Sayings* (London: Bloomsbury, 1995), p. 382. See also Bartlett, *Familiar Quotations,* p. 557 (no. 3).

42. See Gregg Phifer, "Two Inaugurals [Jefferson and Reagan]: A Second Look," *The Southern Speech Communication Journal,* 48 (1983), 378–385 (here p. 385): "Reagan is often called the Great Communicator. And why not? For the first time in our nation's history we have in the White House a man whose principal source of income prior to the election of 1980 was his mastery of the spoken word, his ability to charm audiences and command large fees for a single talk. A better term, however, would be the Great Persuader or Salesman, since genuine communication requires a two-way flow of ideas."

43. For two collections of his wit and wisdom see Clark Cassell (ed.), *President Reagan's Quotations* (Washington, D.C.: Braddock Publications, 1984); and Bill Adler (ed.), *The Uncommon Wisdom of Ronald Reagan: A Portrait in His Own Words* (Boston: Little, Brown and Company, 1996).

44. Cited from Basler (ed.), *Collected Works of Abraham Lincoln,* vol. 7, pp. 18–23. The words in square brackets indicate different versions of the speech. See also Garry Wills, *Lincoln at Gettysburg: The Words that Remade America* (New York: Touchstone, 1992); and Mieder, *The Proverbial Abraham Lincoln,* pp. 35–37.

45. This proverbial sentence is also cited by Bert E. Bradley, "Jefferson and Reagan: The Rhetoric of Two Inaugurals," *The Southern Speech Communication Journal,* 48 (1983), 119–136 (here p. 125).

46. See Mieder et al., *Dictionary of American Proverbs,* p. 603.

47. Cited from Bartlett, *Familiar Quotations,* p. 753 (no. 12).

48. See Stevenson, *Home Book of Proverbs, Maxims, and Famous Phrases,* p. 321 (no. 4); Bartlett, *Familiar Quotations,* p. 266 (no. 10); and Georg Büchmann, *Geflügelte Worte,* ed. Winfried Hofmann. 40th ed. (Berlin: Ullstein, 1995), pp. 356–357.

49. See Bartlett, *Familiar Quotations,* p. 753 (no. 11).

50. For those 425 texts of the Bible that have become folk proverbs in the English language see Wolfgang Mieder, *Not by Bread Alone: Proverbs of the Bible* (Shelburne, Vermont: New England Press, 1990). See also the much larger collection by Burton Stevenson, *The Home Book of Bible Quotations* (New York: Harper & Brothers, 1949).

51. See Mieder et al., *Dictionary of American Proverbs,* p. 599.

52. Cited from James A. Barnes, "Striking the Right Notes [for the Inauguration Speech]," *National Journal,* no. 2 (January 13, 2001). 110– 122 (here p. 111). I owe this reference to my colleague Prof. John Burke.

53. Frank Bruni and David E. Sanger, "Unity Is a Theme: In Inaugural Speech, He [George W. Bush] Asks Citizens to Seek 'a Common Good'," *The New York Times* (January 21, 2001), p. 1 and p. 14 (the quotation is from this page).

54. Cited from Ron Fournier, "Bush Pledges Reconciliation: Gore Concedes Race; Transition Period Begins," *The Burlington Free Press* (December 14, 1001), p. 1.

55. The entire text of the inaugural address is cited from "President: 'I ask You to Be Citizens'," *The New York Times* (January 21, 2001), pp. 12–13.

56. It might be recalled that John F. Kennedy in his inaugural address had declared that "Civility is not a sign of weakness" regarding his foreign policies during the Cold War. Bush looks at "civility" more from an interpersonal point of view.

57. The modern saint seems to be Mother Teresa, even though I could not find this specific statement in any of my numerous books of quotations. Somehow Melinda Henneberger was able to identify the person behind the quotation; see her article on "In His Address, Bush Lingers on a Promise to Care," *The New York Times* (January 21, 2001), p. 14: "He quoted Mother Teresa, though not by name, saying, 'as a saint of our times has said, every day we are called to do small things with great love'."

58. Both Bible proverbs have long become folk proverbs in the English language; see Mieder at al., *A Dictionary of American Proverbs,* p. 407 and pp. 656–657. For Biblical quotations and proverbs, see Burton Stevenson, *The Home Book of Bible Quotations* (New York: Harper & Brothers, 1949); and Wolfgang Mieder, *Not By Bread Alone: Proverbs of the Bible* (Shelburne, Vermont: New England Press, 1990).

59. Anonymous, "John F. Kennedy's Inaugural Address," *The New Yorker* (February 4, 1961), pp. 23–24. Also reprinted in Edward P. J. Corbett, *Classical Rhetoric for the Modern Student,* pp. 506–508.

60. Ray Nichols, "Maxims, 'Practical Wisdom,' and the Language of Action," *Political Theory,* 24 (1996), 687–705 (here p. 687).

7. We Are All in the Same Boat Now

1. Winston S. Churchill, *The Second World War,* 6 vols. (London: Cassell, 1951), vol. 4, S. 344.

2. All references from Warren F. Kimball's *Roosevelt & Churchill: The Complete Correspondence,* 3 vols. (Princeton, New Jersey: Princeton University Press, 1984) will be identified in parentheses by the volume and page numbers.

3. See Franics L. Loewenheim, Harold D. Langley, and Mamfred Jonas (eds.), *Roosevelt and Churchill. Their Secret Wartime Correspondence* (New York: E. P. Dutton, 1975), p. 4.

4. For detailed accounts see Charles Eade (ed.), *Churchill by His Contemporaries* (London: The Reprint Society, 1953); Frank Freidel, *Franklin D. Roosevelt. A Rendezvous with Destiny* (Boston: Little, Brown and Company, 1990); Robin Edmonds, *The Big Three: Churchill, Roosevelt and Stalin in Peace & War* (New York: Norton, 1991); and Conrad Black, *Franklin Delano Roosevelt. Champion of Freedom* (New York: Public Affairs, 2003).

5. See Joseph P. Lash, *Roosevelt and Churchill, 1939–1941. The Partnership that Saved the West* (New York: Norton, 1976); Keith Sainsbury, *Churchill and Roosevelt at War. The War They Fought and the Peace They Hoped to Make* (New York: New York University Press, 1994); and David Stafford, *Roosevelt and Churchill: Men of Secrets* (Woodstock, New York: Overlook Press, 2000).

6. My work-study student Erin Regan gave me Jon Meacham's book as a sign of appreciation for having been her professor and mentor for almost four years. The reading of this volume resulted in this study. It is with much gratitude and fond memories that I dedicate this chapter to my very special former student.

7. Cited from John Gabriel Hunt (ed.), *The Inaugural Addresses of the Presidents* (New York: Gramercy Books, 1997), p. 396.

8. See Wolfgang Mieder, Stewart A. Kingsbury, and Kelsie B. Harder (eds.), *A Dictionary of American Proverbs* (New York: Oxford University Press, 1992), p. 239.

9. For various analyses of this speech see Halford R. Ryan, *Franklin D. Roosevelt's Rhetorical Presidency* (Westport, Connecticut: Greenwood Press, 1988), pp. 76–78; Davis W. Houck, *FDR and Fear Itself: The First Inaugural Address* (College Station, Texas: Texas A&M University Press, 2002); and H. R. Ryan, "Franklin Delano Roosevelt: Rhetorical Politics and Political Rhetorics," in K. Ritter and M. J. Medhurst (eds.), *Presidential Speechwriting. From the New Deal to the Reagan Revolution and Beyond* (College Station, Texas: Texas A&M University Press, 2003), pp. 21–39 (here pp. 32–34).

10. For a discussion of this famous phrase see Richard H. Crum, "'Blood, Sweat and Tears'," *Classical Journal,* 42 (1947), 299–300; and Wolfgang Mieder,

The Politics of Proverbs. From Traditional Wisdom to Proverbial Sterotypes (Madison, Wisconsin: University of Wisconsin Press, 1997), pp. 53–55.

11. Manfred Weidhorn, "Churchill the Phrase Forger," *Quarterly Journal of Speech,* 58 (1972), 161–174.

12. See above all J. W. Miller, "Winston Churchill, Spokesman for Democracy," *Quarterly Journal of Speech,* 28 (1942), 131–138; Herbert L. Stewart, *Sir Winston Churchill as Writer and Speaker* (London: Sidgwick and Jackson, 1954); W. R. Underhill, "Fulton's Finest Hour [Churchill's 'Iron Curtain' Speech]," *Quarterly Journal of Speech,* 52 (1966), 155–163; Manfred Weidhorn, *Sword and Pen. A Survey of the Writings of Sir Winston Churchill* (Albuquerque, New Mexico: University of New Mexico Press, 1974); Darrell Holley, *Churchill's Literary Allusions. An Index to the Education of a Soldier, Statesman and Litterateur* (Jefferson, North Carolina: McFarland, 1987); M. Weidhorn, *Churchill's Rhetoric and Political Discourse* (Lanham, Maryland: University Press of America, 1987); and Keith Aldritt, *Churchill the Writer: His Life as a Man of Letters* (London: Hutchinson, 1992).

13. For Hitler's ill-conceived use of proverbs see Wolfgang Mieder, *Proverbs Are Never Out of Season. Popular Wisdom in the Modern Age* (New York: Oxford University Press, 1993), pp. 225–255; W. Mieder, *The Politics of Proverbs,* pp. 9–38; and W. Mieder, *Strategies of Wisdom. Anglo-American and German Proverb Studies* (Baltmannsweiler, Germany: Schneider Verlag Hohengehren, 2000), pp. 265–301.

14. See Wolfgang Mieder and George B. Bryan, *The Proverbial Winston S. Churchill. An Index to Proverbs in the Works of Sir Winston Churchill* (Westport, Connecticut: Greenwood Press, 1995); and W. Mieder, *The Politics of Proverbs,* pp. 39–66.

15. See Waldo W. Braden and Earnest Brandenburg, "Roosevelt's Fireside Chats," *Speech Monographs,* 22 (1955), 290–302; Halford R. Ryan, *Franklin D. Roosevelt's Rhetorical Presidency* (Westport Connecticut: Greenwood Press, 1988); Betty H. Winfield, *FDR and the News Media* (Urbana, Illinois: University of Illinois Press, 1990); Suzanne M. Daughton, "Metaphorical Transcendence: Images of the Holy War in Franklin Roosevelt's First Inaugural," *Quarterly Journal of Speech,* 79 (1993), 427–446; H. R. Ryan, "Franklin Delano Roosevelt (1882–1945)," in H. R. Ryan (ed.), *U.S. Presidents as Orators. A Bio-Critical Sourcebook* (Westport, Connecticut: Greenwood Press, 1995), pp. 146–167; Carol Gelderman, *All the Presidents' Words. The Bully Pulpit and the Creation of the Virtual Presidency* (New York: Walker, 1997), pp. 11–35; David M. Ryfe, "Franklin Roosevelt and The Fireside Chats," *Journal of Communication,* 49 (1999), 80–103; Davis W. Houck and Amos Kiewe, *FDR's Body Politics. The Rhetoric of Disability* (College Station, Texas: Texas A&M University Press, 2003), and H. R. Ryan,

"Franklin Delano Roosevelt: Rhetorical Politics and Political Rhetoric," pp. 21–39.

16. Edd Miller and James J. Villarreal, "The Use of Clichés by Four Contemporary Speakers [Winston S. Churchill, Anthony Eden, Franklin D. Roosevelt, and Henry Wallace]," *Quarterly Journal of Speech,* 31 (1945), 151–155.

17. This statement is not particularly well known, but it took on a proverbial ring for me and my deceased friend Prof. George B. Bryan (1939–1996), with whom I co-authored several books on proverbs, among them our volume on *The Proverbial Winston S. Churchill* (1995). Speaking of special friendships, we had stated at the end of our preface to that study: "Working on this book was so joyous that at work sessions we frequently echoed the words of Franklin Roosevelt to Winston Churchill: 'It is fun to be in the same decade with you.'" As I worked on this chapter, my thoughts were often with my dear departed friend.

18. See above all Robin Edmonds, *The Big Three;* and Jon Meacham, *Franklin and Winston: An Intimate Portrait of an Epic Friendship* (New York: Random House, 2003), pp. 313–325.

19. See Fraser J. Harbutt, *The Iron Curtain: Churchill, America, and the Origins of the Cold War* (New York: Oxford University Press, 1986).

20. P. R. Wilkinson, *Thesaurus of Traditional English Metaphors* (London: George Routledge, 1992), p. 470.

21. See Halford R. Ryan, *Franklin D. Roosevelt's Rhetorical Presidency,* pp. 81–84 and 167; S. M. Daughton, "Metaphorical Transcendence," p. 430; and Wolfgang Mieder and George B. Bryan, *The Proverbial Winston S. Churchill,* pp. 32–34.

22. For this common political motif see Irene Meichsner, *Die Logik von Gemeinplätzen. Vorgeführt an Steuermannstopos und Schiffsmetapher* (Bonn: Bouvier, 1983); and Kevin J. McKenna, "A Nation Adrift: The Russian 'Ship of State' in *Pravda* Political Cartoons During the Decade of the 1990's," *Proverbium,* 20 (2003), 237–258.

23. See Hermann G. Stelzner, "'War Message [by President Roosevelt]', December 8, 1941: An Approach to Language," *Speech Monographs,* 33 (1966), 419–437.

24. For a survey of the history of this proverbial expression see Wolfgang Mieder, *Deutsche Redensarten, Sprichwörter und Zitate. Studien zu ihrer Herkunft, Überlieferung und Verwendung* (Wien: Edition Praesens, 1995), pp. 140–159.

25. Davis W. Houck and Amos Kiewe, *FDR's Body Politics,* p. 115.

26. See Julia Nikoláeva, "Vicisitudes ideológicas de la paremiología soviética," *Paremia,* 8 (1999), 359–364.

27. For a discussion of "anti-proverbs" see Wolfgang Mieder, *Proverbs. A Handbook* (Westport, Connecticut: Greenwood Press, 2004), pp. 150–153.

28. The proverbial comparison is recorded in Bartlett Jere Whiting, *Modern Proverbs and Proverbial Sayings* (Cambridge, Massachusetts: Harvard University Press, 1989), p. 101; and P. R. Wilkinson, *Thesaurus of Traditional English Metaphors,* p. 294.

29. John Bartlett, *Familiar Quotations,* ed. by Justin Kaplan. 16th ed. (Boston: Little, Brown and Company, 1992), p. 572.

30. For Harry S. Truman's frequent use of proverbial language see Wolfgang Mieder and George B. Bryan, *The Proverbial Harry S. Truman. An Index to Proverbs in the Works of Harry S. Truman* (New York: Petr Lang, 1997).

31. Jon Meacham, *Franklin and Winston,* p. 314.

32. For numerous historical references see Burton Stevenson, *The Home Book of Proverbs, Maxims, and Famous Phrases* (New York: Macmillan, 1948), p. 1488.

33. For additional references see Wolfgang Mieder and George B. Bryan, *The Proverbial Winston S. Churchill,* pp. 43–46.

34. See Joseph Raymond, "Tensions in Proverbs: More Light on International Understanding," *Western Folklore,* 15 (1956), 153–158; also in Wolfgang Mieder and Alan Dundes (eds.), *The Wisdom of Many: Essays on the Proverb* (New York: Garland Publishing, 1981), pp. 300–308.

35. See James Obelkevich, "Proverbs and Social History," in Peter Burke and Roy Portere (eds.), *The Social History of Language* (Cambridge: Cambridge University Press, 1987), pp. 43–72; also in Wolfgang Mieder (ed.), *Wise Words: Essays on the Proverb* (New York: Garland Publishing, 1994), pp. 211–252; and W. Mieder and Janet Sobieski, *Proverbs and the Social Sciences. An Annotated International Bibliography* (Baltmannsweiler, Germany: Schneider Verlag Hohengehren, 2003).

8. Good Fences Make Good Neighbors

A somewhat shorter version of this chapter appeared in *Folklore* (London), 114 (2003), 155–179.

1. See Arvo Krikmann, *On Denotative Indefiniteness of Proverbs* (Tallinn, Estonia: Academy of Sciences of the Estonian SSR, Institute of Language and Literature, 1974); also in *Proverbium,* 1 (1984), 46–91; and Wolfgang Mieder, *American Proverbs. A Study of Texts and Contexts* (Bern: Peter Lang, 1989), pp. 20–22.

2. Kenneth Burke, "Literature [i.e., Proverbs] as Equipment for Living," in K. Burke, *The Philosophy of Literary Form: Studies in Symbolic Action* (Baton Rouge, Louisiana: Louisiana State University Press, 1941), p. 256.

3. For a discussion of proverbs as social strategies see Paul D. Goodwin and Joseph W. Wenzel, "Proverbs and Practical Reasoning: A Study in Socio-Logic," *Quarterly Journal of Speech,* 65 (1979), 289–302; also in Wolfgang Mieder and Alan Dundes (eds.), *The Wisdom of Many: Essays on the Proverb* (New York: Garland Publishing, 1981), pp. 140–160.

4. See Michael D. Lieber, "Analogic Ambiguity: A Paradox of Proverb Usage," *Journal of American Folklore,* 97 (1984), 423–441; also in Wolfgang Mieder (ed.), *Wise Words: Essays on the Proverb* (New York: Garland Publishing, 1994), pp. 99–126.

5. Caroline A. Westerhoff, *Good Fences. The Boundaries of Hospitality* (Cambridge, Massachusetts: Cowley, 1999), p. 157.

6. I would like to thank my colleagues Jake Barickman and Hope Greenberg as well as my work-study student Erin Regan for their invaluable help in locating some of the texts by way of electronic databases.

7. Wolfgang Mieder, *Encyclopedia of World Proverbs* (Englewood Cliffs, New Jersey: Prentice-Hall, 1986), pp. 155–156 and 346.

8. Samuel Singer, and Ricarda Liver (eds.), *Thesaurus proverbiorum medii aevi. Lexikon der Sprichwörter des romanisch-germanischen Mittelalters* (Berlin: Walter de Gruyter, 1995–2002), vol. 13, p. 355.

9. George Herbert, *Outlandish Proverbs* (London: Humphrey Blunden, 1640); cited from Sir John Mennes (ed.), *Musarium Deliciae* (London: John Camden Hotten, 1847), vol. 2, p. 488.

10. Van Wyck Brooks (ed.), *Benjamin Franklin. Poor Richard's Almanacks for the Years 1733–1758* (New York: Bonanza Books, 1979), p. 228; see also Frances M. Barbour, *Concordance to the Sayings in Franklin's "Poor Richard"* (Detroit, Michigan: Gale Research Company, 1974), p. 146.

11. Robb Sagendorph (ed.), *The Old Farmer's Almanac Sampler* (New York: Ives Washburn, 1957), p. 51.

12. Arthur Murphy, *The Citizen. A Farce* (London: Chiswick, 1815), p. 15.

13. Margaret Oliphant, *Neighbors on the Green* (London: Macmillan, 1889), p. 2.

14. Karl Friedrich Wilhelm Wander, *Deutsches Sprichwörter-Lexikon*, 5 vols. (Leipzig: F. A. Brockhaus, 1867–1880), vol. 3, col. 828; F. Edward Hulme, *Proverb Lore* (London: Elliot Stock, 1902; rpt. Detroit, Michigan: Gale Research Company, 1968), p. 105; and Horst and Annelies Beyer, *Sprichwörterlexikon* (München: C. H. Beck, 1985), p. 691.

15. Richard Hofstadter, "*A Benjamin Franklin Reader* [review]," *The New York Times* (April 17, 1946), p. 143.

16. For references see Alan B. Cheales, *Proverbial Folk-Lore* (London: Simpkin, Marshall & Co., 1875; rpt. Darby, Pennsylvania: Folcroft Library Editions, 1976), p. 93; G. L. Apperson, *English Proverbs and Proverbial Phrases*

(London: J. M. Dent, 1929; rpt. Detroit, Michigan: Gale Research Company, 1969), p. 387; William George Smith (ed.), *The Oxford Dictionary of English Proverbs* (Oxford: Clarendon Press, 1935), p. 280; Burton Stevenson, *The Home Book of Proverbs, Maxims and Famous Phrases* (New York: Macmillan, 1948), p. 1674; Morris Palmer Tilley, *A Dictionary of the Proverbs in England in the Sixteenth and Seventeenth Centuries* (Ann Arbor, Michigan: University of Michigan Press, 1950), pp. 494–495; F. P. Wilson (ed.), *The Oxford Dictionary of English Proverbs,* 3rd ed. (Oxford: Clarendon Press, 1970), p. 494; Bartlett Jere Whiting, *Early American Proverbs and Proverbial Phrases* (Cambridge, Massachusetts: Harvard University Press, 1977), p. 309; and Charles Panati, *Words to Live By. The Origins of Conventional Wisdom and Commonsense Advice* (New York: Penguin Books, 1999), p. 167).

17. See Wolfgang Mieder, Stewart A. Kingsbury, and Kelsie B. Harder (eds.), *A Dictionary of American Proverbs* (New York: Oxford University Press, 1992), p. 427.

18. John Mapletoft, *Select Proverbs. Italian, Spanish, French, English, Scottish, British, etc.* (London: Monckton, 1707), p. 47.

19. Cited from Wolfgang Mieder, *American Proverbs,* p. 160. For studies on the use of proverbs by Emerson and other authors, see Wolfgang Mieder and George B. Bryan, *Proverbs in World Literature. A Bibliography* (New York: Peter Lang, 1996).

20. See Alan Cheales, *Proverbial Folk-Lore,* p. 93; G. L. Apperson, *English Proverbs,* p. 296; William Smith, *Oxford Dictionary of English Proverbs,* p. 14; Burton Stevenson, *The Home Book of Proverbs,* p. 1675; Frances M. Barbour (ed.), *Proverbs and Proverbial Phrases of Illinois* (Carbondale, Illinois: Southern Illinois Press, 1965), p. 88; F. P. Wilson, *The Oxford Dictionary of English Proverbs,* p. 366; Wolfgang Mieder et al., *A Dictionary of American Proverbs,* p. 295; and Charles Panati, *Words to Live By,* p. 167.

21. W. Carew Hazlitt, *English Proverbs and Proverbial Phrases* (London: Reeves and Turner, 1869; rpt. Detroit, Michigan: Gale Research Company, 1969), p. 171; and William Smith, *The Oxford Dictionary of English Proverbs,* p. 124.

22. G. L. Apperson, *English Proverbs,* pp. 257, 259, 264.

23. William Smith, *The Oxford Dictionary of English Proverbs,* p. 123.

24. W. Carew Hazlitt, *English Proverbs,* p. 169; and G. L. Apperson, *English Proverbs,* p. 257.

25. G. L. Apperson, *English Proverbs,* pp. 259, 260, 264.

26. Randle Cotgrave, *A Dictionarie of the French and English Tongue* (London: A. Islip, 1611), under "Avocat" (no pages); see also G. L. Apperson, *English Proverbs,* p. 353; William Smith, *The Oxford Dictionary of English Proverbs,* p. 12; Burton Stevenson, *The Home Book of Proverbs,* p. 1370; Bartlett Jere

Whiting, *Early American Proverbs,* p. 255; and Mieder et al., *A Dictionary of American Proverbs,* p. 365.

27. Van Wyck Brooks, *Benjamin Franklin,* p. 50; Frances Barbour, *A Concordance to the Sayings in Franklin's "Poor Richard,"* p. 116; and Bartlett Jere Whiting, *Early American Proverbs,* p. 255.

28. David Pickering, *Dictionary of Proverbs* (London: Cassell, 1997), p. 156.

29. For the review see *Folklore* (London), 113 (2002), 112–114; and for the proverb see Fionnuala Williams (ed.), *Irish Proverbs: Traditional Wit and Wisdom* (New York: Sterling, 2000), p. 83.

30. Énrí Ó Muirgheasa, *Seanfhocail Uladh* (Dublin: Connrad na Gaedilge, 1907), pp. 38–39.

31. Patrick S. Dinneen, *An Irish-English Dictionary* (Dublin: Irish Text Society, 1927), p. 1203.

32. Tomás S. Ó Máille, *Sean-fhocla Chonnacht* (Dublin: Oifig an tSolárthair, 1948–1952), vol. 2, p. 88.

33. I would like to express my appreciation to my colleague and friend Fionnuala Williams (Belfast) for her superb help in gathering Irish materials and transliterating as well as translating them for me. Her husband Brian Williams was also of help, especially in providing me with the variant "Good mearns make good neighbors" that he recorded in oral use in the year 1990. See now also Fionnuala Williams and Wolfgang Mieder, "The Proverb 'Good Fences Make Good Neighbours' in Ireland," *Folklore* (London), 115 (2004), 332–337.

34. Cited from *Winthrop Papers* (Boston: Massachusetts Historical Society, 1929–1947), vol. 4, p. 282.

35. Robb Sagendorph (ed.), *The Old Farmer's Almanac Sampler,* p. 49.

36. Hugh Henry Brackenridge, *Modern Chivalry,* ed. Claude M. Newlin (New York: American Book Company, 1937), p. 787.

37. Samuel Hemenway, *The Vermont Anti-Masonic Almanac for the Year of Our Lord 1831* (Woodstock, Vermont: Hemenway & Holbrook, 1830), no pp. (month of May 1831).

38. I owe these two invaluable references to Fred Shapiro of the Yale Law Library, who found them by means of an electronic database search. The second reference is part of a "Farmer's Calendar" (p. 44).

39. Addison Barker, "'Good Fences Make Good Neighbors'," *Journal of American Folklore,* 64 (1951), 421. The proverb appears on p. 13 (1850) and p. 11 (1861) of the two issues of *Blum's Farmer's and Planter's Alamancs.*

40. Wolfgang Mieder, *Proverbs Are Never Out of Season. Popular Wisdom in the Modern Age* (New York: Oxford University Press, 1993), p. 180.

41. Oliver Loud and Lyman Wilmarth, *Western Agricultural Almanac* (Rochester, New York: E. Peck, 1822), no pp. (month of April).

42. Blake McKelvey, "Early Almanacs of Rochester," *Rochester History,* 3 (1941), 1–24 (here p. 10).

43. James Veech, *Mason and Dixon's Line. A History. Including an Outline of the Boundary Controversy Between Pennsylvania and Virginia* (Pittsburgh, Pennsylvania: W. S. Haven, 1857), p. 45.

44. S. H. Preston, Milo Soule, and Alex. Gordon, "Farms and Gardens," in *Transactions of the State Agricultural Society of Michigan; with Reports of County Agricultural Socieites, for the Year 1859* (Lansing, Michigan: John A. Kerr, 1861), vol. 11, pp. 341–343 (here p. 342).

45. Excerpted by Timothy Hudson from the *Home Advocate* (April 3, 1885), p. 3. http://ftp.rootsweb.com/pub/usgenweb/la/union/newspaper/1885/4ha1885april.txt

46. *The New York Times* (June 16, 1901), p. SM24.

47. Nigel Rees, *Brewer's Quotations. A Phrase and Fable Dictionary* (London: Cassell, 1994), p. 148.

48. See Kate Louise Roberts (ed.), *Hoyt's New Cyclopedia of Practical Quotations* (New York: Funk & Wagnalls, 1922), p. 615; John Bartlett, *Familiar Quotations,* ed. Christopher Morley. 11th ed. (Boston: Little, Brown and Company, 1941), p. 837; Mary Alice Smyth (ed.), *The Oxford Dictionary of Quotations* (Oxford: Oxford University Press, 1941), p. 157; D. C. Browning (ed.), *Dictionary of Quotations and Proverbs* (London: Chancellor Press, 1988 (1st ed. 1951), p. 102; J. M. and M. J. Cohen, *The Penguin Dictionary of Quotations* (Middlesex, England: Penguin Books, 1960), p. 163; Gorton Carruth and Eugene Ehrlich, *The Harper Book of American Quotations* (New York: Harper & Row, 1988), p. 293; John Daintith et al. (eds.), *The Macmillan Dictionary of Quotations* (New York: Macmillan, 1989), p. 385; Tony Augards (ed.), *The Oxford Dictionary of Modern Quotations* (Oxford: Oxford University Press, 1991), p. 86; Stephen Donadio et al. (eds.), *The New York Public Library Book of Twentieth-Century American Quotations* (New York: Warner Books, 1992), p. 260; John Bartlett, *Familiar Quotations,* ed. Justin Kaplan. 16th ed. (Boston: Little, Brown and Company, 1992), p. 622; A. Norman Jeffares and Martin Gray (eds.), *A Dictionary of Quotations* (New York: Barnes & Noble Books, 1995), p. 267; Elizabeth Knowles (ed.), *The Oxford Dictionary of Phrase, Saying, and Quotation* (Oxford: Oxford University Press, 1997), p. 89; Nigel Rees, *Cassell Companion to Quotations* (London: Cassell, 1997), p. 248; and Elizabeth Knowles (ed.), *The Oxford Dictionary of Quotations,* 5th ed. (Oxford: Oxford University Press, 1999), p. 326.

49. See Burton Stevenson, *The Home Book of Proverbs,* pp. 795 and 1675; David Kin (ed.), *Dictionary of American Maxims* (New York: Philosophical Library, 1955), p. 180; Lewis Copeland (ed.), *Popular Quotations for All Uses* (Garden City, New York: Doubleday, 1961), p. 327; Robert Andrews, *The Routledge*

Dictionary of Quotations (London: Routledge & Kegan Paul, 1987), p. 180; and R. Andrews, *The Columbia Dictionary of Quotations* (New York: Columbia University Press, 1993), p. 626.

50. See Elizabeth Knowles, *The Oxford Dictionary of Phrase, Saying, and Quotation,* pp. 89 and 164.

51. Tad Tuleja, *Book of Popular Americana* (New York: Macmillan, 1994), p. 249.

52. E. D. Hirsch, Joseph F. Kett, and James Trefil, *The Dictionary of Cultural Literacy* (Boston: Houghton Mifflin Company, 1988), p. 50.

53. Archer Taylor, *The Proverb* (Cambridge, Massachusetts: Harvard University Press, 1931; rpt. ed. Wolfgang Mieder. Bern: Peter Lang, 1985), p. 149.

54. Harold W. Thompson, *Body, Boots & Britches. Folktales, Ballads and Speech from Country New York* (Philadelphia, Pennsylvania: Lippincott, 1939; rpt. Syracuse, New York: Syracuse University Press, 1979), p. 491.

55. W. Edson Richmond, "The Collection of Proverbs in Indiana," *Hoosier Folklore,* 5 (1946), 150–156 (here p. 155.

56. John A. Simpson (ed.), *The Concise Oxford Dictionary of Proverbs* (Oxford: Oxford University Press, 1982), p. 98.

57. See Mac E. Barrick, "Proverbs and Sayings from Cumberland County [Pennsylvania]," *Keystone Folklore Quarterly,* 8 (1963), 139–203 (here p. 160); Frances M. Barbour, *Proverbs and Proverbial Phrases of Illinois,* p. 63; Bartlett Jere Whiting, *Early American Proverbs,* p. 149; John A. Simpson (ed.), *The Concise Oxford Dictionary of Proverbs,* p. 98; Rosalind Fergusson (ed.), *The Facts on File Dictionary of Proverbs* (New York: Facts on File Publications, 1983), p. 169; Wolfgang Mieder, *Encyclopedia of World Proverbs,* p. 19; W. Mieder, *Yankee Wisdom: New England Proverbs* (Shelburne, Vermont: The New England Press, 1989), p. 54; B. J. Whiting, *Modern Proverbs and Proverbial Sayings* (Cambridge, Massachusetts: Harvard University Press, 1989), p. 219; W. Mieder et al., *A Dictionary of American Proverbs,* p. 206; Anne Bertram and Richard A. Spears (eds.), *NTC's Dictionary of Proverbs and Clichés* (Lincolnwood, Illinois: National Textbook Company, 1993), p. 95; Gregory Titelman, *Random House Dictionary of Popular Proverbs & Sayings* (New York: Random House, 1996), p. 121; David Pickering, *Dictionary of Proverbs,* p. 115; John A. Simpson and Jennifer Speake (eds.), *The Concise Oxford Dictionary of Proverbs,* 3rd ed. (Oxford: Oxford University Press, 1998), p. 118; and W. Mieder and Anna Tóthné Litovkina, *Twisted Wisdom: Modern Anti-Proverbs* (Burlington, Vermont: The University of Vermont, 1999), p. 90.

58. I thank my friends Maria Teresa Agozzino and Alan Dundes from Berkeley for this information.

59. Muriel J. Hughes, "Vermont Proverbs and Proverbial Sayings," *Vermont History,* 28 (1960), 113–142 and 200–230 (here p. 131).

60. Robert Frost, *Complete Poems* (New York: Holt, Rinehart and Winston, 1949), pp. 47–48.

61. It is unnecessary to list all of these publications here. For those that deal especially with folkloristic or proverbial matters, see Wolfgang Mieder's *International Proverb Scholarship. An Annotated Bibliography,* 4 vols. (New York: Garland Publishing, 1982, 1990, 1993. New York: Peter Lang, 2001).

62. Lawrance Thompson (ed.), *Selected Letters of Robert Frost* (New York: Holt, Rinehart and Winston, 1964), p. 344.

63. See Dennis Vail, "Tree Imagery in Frost's 'Mending Wall'," *Notes on Contemporary Literature,* 3 (1973), 9–11 (here p. 10); and L. J. Morrissey, "'Mending Wall': The Structure of Gossip," *English Language Notes,* 25 (1988), 58–63 (here p. 59).

64. See Frank Lentricchia, "Experience as Meaning: Robert Frost's 'Mending Wall'," *CEA [College English Association] Critic,* 31 (1972), 8–12 (here p. 11).

65. See Mordecai Marcus, "Psychoanalytic Approaches to 'Mending Wall'," in Kathryn Gibbs Harris (ed.), *Robert Frost. Studies of the Poetry* (Boston: G. K. Hall, 1979), pp. 179–190 (here p. 186.

66. Zev Trachtenberg, "Good Neighbors Make Good Fences: Frost's 'Mending Wall'," *Philosophy and Literature,* 21 (1997), 114–122 (here p. 115).

67. George Monteiro, "Robert Frost's Linked Analogies," *New England Quarterly,* 46 (1973), 463–468 (here p. 467).

68. George Monteiro, "Robert Frost's Linked Analogies," p. 468. See also G. Monteiro, "'Good fences Make Good Neighbors': A Proverb and a Poem," *Revista de Etnografia,* 16 (1972), 83–88.

69. Fritz Oehlschlaeger, "Fences Make Neighbors: Process, Identity, and Ego in Robert Frost's 'Mending Wall'," *Arizona Quarterly,* 40 (1984), 242–254 (here p. 253).

70. See Edward Jayne, "Up Against the 'Mending Wall': The Psychoanlaysis of a Poem by Frost," *College English,* 34 (1973), 934–951 (here p. 959); and Zev Trachtenberg, "Good Neighbors Make Good Fences," p. 118.

71. Hubert Zapf, "Gaps in the Wall: Determinacy and Indeterminacy in Robert Frost's 'Mending Wall'," *Zeitschrift für Anglistik und Amerikanistik,* 39 (1991), 250–253 (here p. 253).

72. Robert Francis, *Pot Shots at Poetry* (Ann Arbor, Michigan: University of Michigan Press, 1980), p. 30.

73. Raymond Souster, *Collected Poems 1940–1955* (Ottawa, Canada: Oberon Press, 1980), p. 308.

74. Walter Hard, *Vermont Neighbors* (Middlebury, Vermont: Vermont Books, 1960), pp. 40–41.

75. Richard Eberhart, *Collected Poems 1930–1986* (New York: Oxford Univesity Press, 1988), p. 400.

76. Eric Linklater, *A Year of Space. A Chapter in Autobiography* (London: Macmillan, 1953), p. 19.

77. Alfred Duggan, *The King of Athelney* (London: Faber and Faber, 1961), p. 239.

78. John O'Hara, *The Lockwood Concern* (New York: Random House, 1965), p. 20. See also Mac E. Barrick, "Proverbs and Sayings from Gibbsville, Pennsylvania. John O'Hara's Use of Proverbial Materials," *Keystone Folklore Quarterly,* 12 (1967), 55–80 (here p. 68).

79. Dudley Lunt, *Taylors Gut in the Delaware State* (New York: Alfred Knopf, 1968), p. 270.

80. David Walker, *The Lord's Pink Ocean* (London: Collins, 1972), p. 17.

81. Erika Ellis, *Good Fences. A Novel* (New York: Random House, 1977), p. 17.

82. Tom Sharpe, *The Throwback* (London: Secker & Warburg, 1978), p. 98.

83. *The New York Times* (June 26, 1955), p. X45.

84. *The New York Times* (June 26, 1977), p. 21.

85. *The New York Times* (December 2, 1979), p. 88.

86. *Washington Post* (July 13, 1989), p. T20.

87. *Belfast Telegraph* (April 29, 1994), p.12.

88. *Burlington Free Press* (September 2, 1995), p. C1.

89. *Denver Post* (July 17, 2001), p. B7.

90. Josephine von Miklos, *Good Fences Make Good Neighbors* (New York: Charles Scribner's Sons, 1972), pp. vii–viii.

91. *St. Petersburg Times* (June 15, 1987), p. 1.

92. *Baltimore Sun* (March 8, 1995), p. B3.

93. *Daily News* (May 1, 1998), p. 2.

94. *Plain Dealer* (July 19, 1999), p. B1.

95. *Milwaukee Journal Sentinel* (April 5, 2002), p. B1.

96. Anthony G. Wilhelm, "Good Fences and Good Neighbors: John Locke's Positive Doctrine of Toleration," *Political Research Quarterly,* 52 (1999), 145–166 (here p. 158).

97. Anthony G. Wilhelm, "Good Fences and Good Neighbors," p. 145.

98. *Los Angeles Times* (April 23, 1989), p. A3.

99. *Washington Post* (July 13, 1989), p. T20.

100. See William Siebenschuh, "'Good Fences Make Good Neighbors': The Importance of Maintaining the Boundary Between Factual and Fictional Narrative," *Studies in Eighteenth Century Culture,* 13 (1984), 205–215.

101. *Washington Post* (September 10, 1978), p. M1.

102. See also Lizette Peterson, "Do Good Fences Really Make Good Neighbors? Challenges and Solutions for Behavioral Therapy from Nonbehavioral Arenas," *Behavior Therapy,* 24 (1973), 7–10.

103. *Los Angeles Times* (July 31, 1993), p. B7.

104. *Toronto Star* (April 29, 1995), p. F1.

105. *Sunday Telegraph* (January 19, 1997), p. 4.

106. *Christian Science Monitor* (August 16, 2000), p. 24.

107. *Baltimore Sun* (June 25, 2001), p. B3.

108. *The New York Times* (February 8, 1942), p. SM31. See also *The New York Times* (July 30, 1978), p. CN9.

109. The case was Illinois ex rel. McCollum v. Board of Education of School District No. 71, Champaign County, Illinois, et al. No. 90. Supreme Court of the United States. 333 U.S. 203; 68 S. Ct. 461; 92 L. Ed. 649; 1948 U.S. Lexis 2451; 2 A.L.R. 2d 1338. December 8, 1947, argued; March 8, 1948, decided.

110. See David S. Glenwick, "'Good Fences Make Good Neighbors': A Community-Oriented Course in Psychology and Criminal Justice," *College Student Journal*, 12 (1978), 197–201; Hubert Rottleuthner, "Borders Without Flaw: Do Good Fences Make Good Neighbors?" *Journal of Institutional and Theoretical Economics*, 150 (1994), 114–116; and Philip Weinberg, "Congress, the Courts, and Solid Waste Transport: Good Fences Don't Always Make Good Neighbors," *Environmental Law*, 25 (1995), 57–72.

111. F. A. Hayek, *Law, Legislation and Liberty* (Chicago: University of Chicago Press, 1973), vol. 1, p. 107.

112. Richard Epstein, *Transaction Costs and Property Rights: Or Do Good Fences Make Good Neighbors?* The Coase Lecture, Winter 1996 (Chicago, Illinois: Law School, University of Chicago, 1996), pp. 1–2.

113. *The New York Times* (November 3, 1991), section 10,5.

114. *Los Angeles Times* (May 17, 1994), p. 4.

115. *The Times* (May 14, 1997), no page.

116. *The Times* (July 15, 1997), no page.

117. *Christian Science Monitor* (May 31, 2001), p. 2.

118. *The New York Times* (November 9, 1989), p. C13.

119. *The New York Times* (June 18, 1941), p. 17.

120. See Joseph Barker, *Good Fences Make Good Neighbors. Why the United States Provokes Canadians* (Toronto: McClelland and Stewart, 1958).

121. *Toronto Star* (January 22, 1990), no page. See also Lesley B. Cormack. "'Good Fences Makes Good Neighbors': Geography as Self-Definition in Early Modern England," *Isis*, 82 (1991), 639–661.

122. *Toronto Star* (October 3, 2000), no page.

123. *Atlanta Journal and Constitution* (October 15, 2001), p. A10.

124. *Sunday Times* (February 20, 1994), no page.

125. See Clark W. Reynolds, *Do Good Fences Make Good Neighbors? Recent and Prospective U.S.–Mexican Relations* (Austin, Texas: University of Texas Press, 1973).

126. *San Francisco Chronicle* (December 8, 1991), p. 8.

127. *Los Angeles Times* (October 13, 1993), p. B6.

128. *Newsday* (August 25, 2000), p. A7.

129. *Los Angeles Times* (December 2, 1985), no page.

130. *The New York Times* (June 8, 1986), p. 15.

131. *Herald* (Glasgow), (August 5, 1983), p. 12.

132. *Washington Post* (November 13, 1994), p. C1.

133. *New Straits Times* (Malaysia), (September 19, 1996), p. 26.

134. *Independent* (London), (February 20, 2000), p. 3.

135. William Safire, *Political Dictionary* (New York: Random House, 1978), pp. 223–224.

136. *Christian Science Monitor* (April 19, 1989), p. 19.

137. *Jerusalem Post* (February 11, 1994), p. A5.

138. *The Gazette* (Montreal), (January 25, 1995, p. A9.

139. *Jerusalem Post* (October 22, 1999), p. A2.

140. *Newhouse News Service* (April 10, 2002), no page.

141. *Time* (June 17, 2002), pp. 38–39.

142. *The Times* (August 17, 2002), p. 22.

143. Laura Z. Eisenberg, "Do Good Fences Make Good Neighbors? Israel and Lebanon after the Withdrawal," *Middle East Review of International Affairs,* 4 (2000), 17–31 (here p. 28).

144. *Columbus Dispatch* (January 10, 2001), p. A8.

145. *The New York Times* (October 7, 1979), p. 88.

146. *Toronto Star* (August 2, 1998), p. A7.

147. *Washington Post* (June 1, 1996), p. H1.

Bibliography

This bibliography contains only those publications which deal with proverbial matters. The endnotes to the individual chapters register numerous additional references concerning specific studies on the subject matter at hand. For easy reference the present bibliography is divided into four parts: bibliographies, proverb journals, collections of proverbs and quotations, and scholarly studies of the proverb.

BIBLIOGRAPHIES

Bonser, Wilfrid. 1930. *Proverb Literature. A Bibliography of Works Relating to Proverbs.* London: William Glaisher; rpt. Nendeln/Liechtenstein: Kraus reprint, 1967.

de Caro, Francis, and William K. McNeil. 1971. *American Proverb Literature. A Bibliography.* Bloomington, Indiana: Folklore Forum, Indiana University.

Mieder, Wolfgang. 1977. *International Bibliography of Explanatory Essays on Individual Proverbs and Proverbial Expressions.* Bern: Peter Lang.

Mieder, Wolfgang. 1982, 1990, 1993, 2001. *International Proverb Scholarship. An Annotated Bibliography.* 4 vols. New York: Garland and Peter Lang.

Mieder, Wolfgang. 1984ff. "International Bibliography of New and Reprinted Proverb Collections." Annual bibliography in *Proverbium: Yearbook of International Proverb Scholarship.*

Mieder, Wolfgang. 1984ff. "International Proverb Scholarship: An Updated Bibliography." Annual bibliography in *Proverbium: Yearbook of International Proverb Scholarship.*

Mieder, Wolfgang. 1984. *Investigations of Proverbs, Proverbial Expressions, Quotations and Clichés: A Bibliography of Explanatory Essays which Appeared in "Notes and Queries" (1849–1983).* Bern: Peter Lang.

Mieder, Wolfgang, and George B. Bryan. 1996. *Proverbs in World Literature. A Bibliography.* New York: Peter Lang.

Mieder, Wolfgang, and Janet Sobieski. 2003. *Proverbs and the Social Sciences. An Annotated International Bibliography.* Baltmannsweiler, Germany: Schneider Verlag Hohengehren.

Moll, Otto. 1958. *Sprichwörterbibliographie.* Frankfurt am Main: Vittorio Klostermann.

Urdang, Laurence, and Frank R. Abate. 1983. *Idioms and Phrases Index.* 3 vols. Detroit, Michigan: Gale Research Co.

PROVERB JOURNALS

De Proverbio: An Electronic Journal of International Proverb Studies, 1995ff. [htpp:// info.utas.edu.au/docs/flonta/] Ed. Teodor Flonta et al. (Hobart/Tasmania, Australia).

Paremia: Boletin de Investigaciones Paremiológicas, 1993ff. Ed. Julia Sevilla Muñoz et al. (Madrid).

Proverbium: Bulletin d'information sur les recherches parémiologiques, 1–25 (1965–1975), 1–1008. Ed. Matti Kuusi et al. (Helsinki). Reprint (2 volks). Ed. Wolfgang Mieder. Bern: Peter Lang, 1987.

Proverbium Paratum: Bulletin d'information sur les recherches parémiologiques, 1–4 (1980–1989), 1–460. Ed. Vilmos Voigt et al. (Budapest).

Proverbium: Yearbook of International Proverb Scholarship, 1984ff. Ed. Wolfgang Mieder et al. (Burlington, Vermont).

COLLECTIONS OF PROVERBS AND QUOTATIONS

Andrews, Robert. 1987. *The Routledge Dictionary of Quotations.* London: Routledge & Kegan Paul.

Andrews, Robert. 1993. *The Columbia Dictionary of Quotations.* New York: Columbia University Press.

Apperson, G. L. 1929. *English Proverbs and Proverbial Phrases.* London: J. M. Dent; rpt. Detroit, Michigan: Gale Research Company, 1969.

Augarde, Tony (ed.). 1991. *The Oxford Dictionary of Modern Quotations.* Oxford: Oxford University Press.

Ayres, Alex (ed.). 1996. *The Wit and Wisdom of Eleanor Roosevelt.* New York: Meridian.

Barbour, Frances M. (ed.). 1965. *Proverbs and Proverbial Phrases of Illinois.* Carbondale, Illinois: Southern Illinois University Press.

Barrick, Mac E. 1963. "Proverbs and Sayings from Cumberland County [Pennsylvania]." *Keystone Folklore Quarterly* 8: 139–203.

Barrick, Mac E. 1967. "Proverbs and Sayings from Gibbsville, Pennsylvania. John O'Hara's Use of Proverbial Materials." *Keystone Folklore Quarterly* 12: 55–80.

Bartlett, John. 1941. *Familiar Quotations.* Ed. Christopher Morley. 11th ed. Boston: Little, Brown and Company.

Bartlett, John. 1980. *Familiar Quotations.* Ed. Emily Morison Beck. 15th ed. Boston: Little, Brown and Company.

Bartlett, John. 1992. *Familiar Quotations*. Ed. Justin Kaplan. 16th ed. Boston: Little, Brown and Company.

Bertram, Anne, and Richard A. Spears (eds.). 1993. *NTC's Dictionary of Proverbs and Clichés*. Lincolnwood, Illinois: National Textbook Company.

Beyer, Horst and Annelies. 1985. *Sprichwörterlexikon*. München: C. H. Beck.

Bilgrav, Jens Aa. Stabell. 1985. *20,000 Proverbs and Their Equivalents in German, French, Swedish, Danish*. Copenhagen: Hans Heide.

Boritt, Gabor S. (ed.). 1996. *Of the People, by the People, for the People, and Other Quotations by Abraham Lincoln*. New York: Columbia University Press.

Browning, D. C. (ed.). 1988. *Dictionary of Quotations and Proverbs*. London: Chancellor Press (1st ed. 1951).

Büchmann, Georg. 1995. *Geflügelte Worte*. Ed. Winfried Hofmann. 40th ed. Berlin: Ullstein.

Burnam, Tom. 1975. *The Dictionary of Misinformation*. New York: Thomas Y. Crowell.

Burrell, Brian. 1997. *The Words We Live By: The Creeds, Mottoes, and Pledges that Have Shaped America*. New York: The Free Press.

Carruth, Gorton, and Eugene Ehrlich. 1988. *The Harper Book of American Quotations*. New York: Harper & Row.

Carstensen, Broder, and Ulrich Busse. 1993–1996. *Anglizismen-Wörterbuch. Der Einfluß des Englischen auf den deutschen Wortschatz nach 1945*. 3 vols. Berlin: Walter de Gruyter.

Cassell, Clark (ed.). 1984. *President Reagan's Quotations*. Washington, D.C.: Braddock Publications.

Champion, Selwyn Gurney. 1938. *Racial Proverbs. A Selection of the World's Proverbs Arranged Linguistically*. London: George Routledge.

Champion, Selwyn Gurney. 1945. *The Eleven Religions and Their Proverbial Lore*. New York: E. P. Dutton.

Cohen, J. M. and M. J. 1960. *The Penguin Dictionary of Quotations*. Middlesex, England: Penguin Books.

Copeland, Lewis (ed.). 1961. *Popular Quotations for All Uses*. Garden City, New York: Doubleday.

Cordry, Harold V. 1997. *The Multicultural Dictionary of Proverbs. Over 20,000 Adages from More Than 120 Languages, Nationalities and Ethnic Groups*. Jefferson, North Carolina: McFarland & Company.

Cotgrave, Randle. 1611. *A Dictionarie of the French and English Tongue*. London: A. Islip; rpt. Hildesheim: Georg Olms, 1970.

Daintith, John et al. (eds.). 1989. *The Macmillan Dictionary of Quotations*. New York: Macmillan.

Dent, Robert W. 1981. *Shakespeare's Proverbial Language. An Index* (Berkeley, California: University of California Press.

Donadio, Stephen et al. (eds.). 1992. *The New York Public Library Book of Twentieth-Century American Quotations*. New York: Warner Books.

Fergusson, Rosalind (ed.). 1983. *The Facts on File Dictionary of Proverbs*. New York: Facts on File Publications.

Flonta, Teodor. 2001. *A Dictionary of English and Romance Languages Equivalent Proverbs*. Hobart, Tasmania: DeProverbio.com.

Frost, Elizabeth (ed.). 1988. *The Bully Pulpit: Quotations from America's Presidents*. New York: Facts on File Publications.

Gluski, Jerzy. 1971. *Proverbs: A Comparative Book of English, French, German, Italian, Spanish and Russian Proverbs with a Latin Appendix*. New York: Elsevier Publishing.

Griffin, Albert Kirby. 1991. *Religious Proverbs. Over 1600 Adages from 18 Faiths Worldwide*. Jefferson, North Carolina: McFarland.

Grigas, Kazys. 1976. *Lietuvių patarlės. Lyginamasis tyrinėjimas*. Vilnius, Lithuania: Vaga.

Grigas, Kazys. 1987. *Patarlių paralelės. Lietuvių patarlės su latvių, baltarusių, rusų, lenkų, vokiečių, anglų, lotynų, prancūzų, ispanų atitikmenimis*. Vilnius, Lithuania: Vaga.

Grigas, Kazys et al. 2000. *Lietuvių patarlės ir priežodžiai*. Vilnius, Lithuania: Lietuvių Literatūros ir Tautosakos Institutas.

Harnsberger, Caroline Thomas (ed.). 1964. *Treasury of Presidential Quotations*. Chicago: Follett.

Hazlitt, W. Carew. 1869. *English Proverbs and Proverbial Phrases*. London: Reeves and Turner; rpt. Detroit, Michigan: Gale Research Company, 1969.

Herbert, George. *Outlandish Proverbs*. London: Humphrey Blunden, 1640; rpt. in Sir John Mennes (ed.), *Musarium Deliciae*. London: John Camden Hotten, 1847, vol. 2, pp. 483–525.

Hirsch, E. D., Joseph F. Kett, and James Trefil. 1988. *The Dictionary of Cultural Literacy*. Boston: Houghton Mifflin Company.

Hughes, Muriel J. 1960. "Vermont Proverbs and Proverbial Sayings." *Vermont History* 28: 113–142 and 200–230.

Iscla, Luis. 1995. *English Proverbs and Their Near Equivalents in Spanish, French, Italian and Latin*. New York: Peter Lang.

Jay, Antony. 1996. *The Oxford Dictionary of Political Quotations*. Oxford: Oxford University Press.

Jeffares, A. Norman, and Martin Gray (eds.). 1995. *A Dictionary of Quotations*. New York: Barnes & Noble Books.

Kin, David (ed.). 1955a. *Dictionary of American Maxims*. New York: Philosophical Library.

Kin, David (ed.). 1955b. *Dictionary of American Proverbs*. New York: Philosophical Library.

Kirchberger, J. H. 1977. *Das große Krüger Zitaten Buch.* Frankfurt am Main: Wolfgang Krüger.

Knowles, Elizabeth (ed.) 1997. *The Oxford Dictionary of Phrase, Saying, and Quotation.* Oxford: Oxford University Press.

Knowles, Elizabeth (ed.). 1999. *The Oxford Dictionary of Quotations.* 5th ed. Oxford: Oxford University Press.

Kuusi, Matti. 1985. *Proverbia septentrionalia. 900 Balto-Finnic Proverb Types with Russian, Baltic, German and Scandinavian Parallels.* Helsinki: Suomalainen Tiedeakatemia.

Lean, Vincent Stuckey. 1903. *Collectanea: Proverbs, Folk-Lore, and Superstitions.* 5 vols. Bristol: J. W. Arrowsmith; rpt. Detroit, Michigan: Gale Research Company, 1969.

Lewis, Edward, and Richard Rhodes (eds.). 1967. *John F. Kennedy: Words to Remember.* Kansas City, Missouri: Hallmark Cards.

Ley, Gerd de. 1998. *International Dictionary of Proverbs.* New York: Hippocrene Books.

Mapletoft, John. 1707. *Select Proverbs. Italian, Spanish, French, English, Scottish, British, etc.* London: Monckton.

Mieder, Wolfgang. 1986a. *Encyclopedia of World Proverbs.* Englewood Cliffs, New Jersey: Prentice-Hall.

Mieder, Wolfgang. 1986b. *Talk Less and Say More: Vermont Proverbs.* Shelburne, Vermont: The New England Press.

Mieder, Wolfgang. 1989. *Yankee Wisdom: New England Proverbs.* Shelburne, Vermont: The New England Press.

Mieder, Wolfgang. 1990. *Not by Bread Alone. Proverbs of the Bible.* Shelburne, Vermont: The New England Press.

Mieder, Wolfgang, Stewart A. Kingsbury, and Kelsie B. Harder (eds.). 1992. *A Dictionary of American Proverbs.* New York: Oxford University Press.

Mieder, Wolfgang, and Anna Tóthné Litovkina. 1999. *Twisted Wisdom. Modern Anti-Proverbs.* Burlington, Vermont: The University of Vermont.

Miller, Donald L. (ed.). 1989. *From George ... to George: 200 Years of Presidential Quotations.* Washington, D.C.: Braddock Communications.

Ó Máille, Tomás S. (ed.). 1948–1952. *Sean-fhocla Chonnacht.* 2 vols. Dublin: Oifig an tSolárthair.

Ó Muirgheasa, Énrí (ed.). 1907. *Seanfhocail Uladh.* Dublin: Connrad na Gaedilge.

Paczolay, Gyula. 1997. *European Proverbs in 55 Languages with Equivalents in Arabic, Persian, Sanskrit, Chinese and Japanese.* Veszprém: Veszprémi Nyomda.

Panati, Charles. 1999. *Words to Live By. The Origins of Conventional Wisdom and Commonsense Advice.* New York: Penguin Books.

Pickering, David. 1997. *Dictionary of Proverbs.* London: Cassell.

Rees, Nigel. 1984. *Sayings of the Century.* London: George Allen & Unwin.

Rees, Nigel. 1994. *Brewer's Quotations. A Phrase and Fable Dictionary.* London: Cassell.

Rees, Nigel. 1995. *Phrases & Sayings.* London: Bloomsbury.

Rees, Nigel. 1997. *Cassell Companion to Quotations.* London: Cassell.

Richmond, W. Edson. 1946. "The Collection of Proverbs in Indiana." *Hoosier Folklore* 5: 150–156.

Roberts, Kate Louise (ed.). 1922. *Hoyt's New Cyclopedia of Practical Quotations.* New York: Funk & Wagnalls.

Safire, William. 1978. *Political Dictionary.* New York: Random House.

Schulze, Carl. 1860. *Die biblischen Sprichwörter der deutschen Sprache.* Göttingen: Vandenhoeck und Ruprecht; rpt. ed. by Wolfgang Mieder. Bern: Peter Lang, 1987.

Simpson, John A. (ed.). 1982. *The Concise Oxford Dictionary of Proverbs.* Oxford: Oxford University Press.

Simpson, John, and Jennifer Speake (eds.). 1998. *The Concise Oxford Dictionary of Proverbs.* Oxford: Oxford University Press.

Singer, Samuel, and Ricarda Liver (eds.). 1995–2002. *Thesaurus proverbiorum medii aevi. Lexikon der Sprichwörter des romanisch-germanischen Mittelalters.* 13 vols. Berlin: Walter de Gruyter.

Smith, William George (ed.). 1935. *The Oxford Dictionary of English Proverbs.* Oxford: Clarendon Press.

Smyth, Mary Alice (ed.). 1941. *The Oxford Dictionary of Quotations.* Oxford: Oxford University Press.

Snapp, Emma Louise. 1933. "Proverbial Lore from Nebraska." *University of Nebraska Studies in Language, Literature, and Criticism* 13: 51–112.

Stevenson, Burton. 1948. *The Home Book of Proverbs, Maxims, and Famous Phrases.* New York: Macmillan.

Stevenson, Burton. 1949. *The Home Book of Bible Quotations.* New York: Harper & Brothers.

Strauss, Emanuel. 1994. *Dictionary of European Proverbs.* 3 vols. London: Routledge.

Taylor, Archer and Bartlett Jere Whiting. 1958. *A Dictionary of American Proverbs and Proverbial Phrases, 1820–1880.* Cambridge, Massachusetts: Harvard University Press.

Taylor, E., and Lois F. Parks (eds.). 1965. *Memorable Quotations of Franklin D. Roosevelt.* New York: Thomas Y. Crowell.

Tilley, Morris Palmer. 1950. *A Dictionary of the Proverbs in England in the Sixteenth and Seventeenth Centuries.* Ann Arbor, Michigan: University of Michigan Press.

Titelman, Gregory. 1996. *Random House Dictionary of Popular Proverbs & Sayings.* New York: Random House.

Tuleja, Tad. 1994. *Book of Popular Americana*. New York: Macmillan.

Wander, Karl Friedrich Wilhelm. 1867–1880. *Deutsches Sprichwörter-Lexikon*. 5 vols. Leipzig: F. A. Brockhaus; rpt. Darmstadt: Wissenschaftliche Buchgesellschaft, 1964.

Whiting, Bartlett Jere. 1977. *Early American Proverbs and Proverbial Phrases*. Cambridge, Massachusetts: Harvard University Press.

Whiting, Bartlett Jere. 1989. *Modern Proverbs and Proverbial Sayings*. Cambridge, Massachusetts: Harvard University Press.

Wilkinson, P. R. 1992. *Thesaurus of Traditional English Metaphors*. London: George Routledge.

Williams, Fionnuala (ed.). 2000. *Irish Proverbs: Traditional Wit and Wisdom*. New York: Sterling.

Wilson, F. P. 1970. *The Oxford Dictionary of English Proverbs*. Third edition. Oxford: Oxford University Press.

Woods, Henry F. 1945. *American Sayings. Famous Phrases, Slogans, and Aphorisms*. New York: Duell, Sloan and Pearce.

Studies on the Proverb

Arora. Shirley L. 1984. "The Perception of Proverbiality." *Proverbium* 1: 1–38; also in Mieder 1994, 3–29.

Barbour, Frances M. 1974. *A Concordance to the Sayings in Franklin's "Poor Richard."* Detroit, Michigan: Gale Research Company.

Barker, Addison. 1951. "'Good Fences Make Good Neighbors.'" *Journal of American Folklore* 64: 421.

Barnes-Harden, Alene Leett. 1980. "Proverbs, Folk Expressions and Superstitions." In: A. L. Barnes-Harden, *African American Verbal Art: Their Nature and Communicative Interpretation: A Thematic Analysis*. Diss. State University of New York at Buffalo, 57–80.

Boller, Paul F. 1967. *Quotemanship: The Use and Abuse of Quotations for Polemical and Other Purposes*. Dallas, Texas: Southern Methodist University Press.

Bryan, George B., and Wolfgang Mieder. 1997. *The Proverbial Charles Dickens. An Index to Proverbs in the Works of Charles Dickens*. New York: Peter Lang.

Bryan, George B., and Wolfgang Mieder. 2003. "The Proverbial Carl Sandburg (1878–1967). An Index of Folk Speech in His American Poetry." *Proverbium* 20: 15–49.

Burke, Kenneth. 1941. "Literature [i.e., Proverbs] as Equipment for Living." In: K. Burke, *The Philosophy of Literary Form. Studies in Symbolic Action*. Baton Rouge, Louisiana: Louisiana State University Press, 253–262.

Cheales, Alan B. 1875. *Proverbial Folk-Lore*. London: Simpkin, Marshall & Co.; rpt. Darby, Pennsylvania: Folcroft Library Editions, 1976.

Crum, Richard Henry. 1947. "'Blood, Sweat and Tears.'" *Classical Journal* 42: 299–300.

Daniel, Jack L. 1973. "Towards an Ethnography of Afroamerican Proverbial Usage." *Black Lines* 2: 3–12.

Daniel, Jack L. 1979. *The Wisdom of Sixth Mount Zion [Baptist Church] from The Members of Sixth Mount Zion and Those Who Begot Them.* Pittsburgh, Pennsylvania: University of Pittburgh, College of Arts and Sciences.

Daniel, Jack L., Geneva Smitherman-Donaldson, and Milford A. Jeremiah. 1987. "Makin' a Way Outa no Way: The Proverb Tradition in the Black Experience." *Journal of Black Studies* 17: 482–508.

Donskov, Andrew. 1975. "Tolstoy's Use of Proverbs in The Power of Darkness." *Russian Literature* 9: 67–80; also in McKenna 1998, 61–74.

Doyle, Charles Clay. 1996. "On 'New' Proverbs and the Conservativeness of Proverb Collections." *Proverbium* 13: 69–84; also in Mieder 2003a, 85–98.

Dundes, Alan. 1969. "Thinking Ahead: A Folkloristic Reflection of the Future Orientation in American Worldview." *Anthropological Quarterly* 42: 53–72.

Dundes, Alan. 1972. "Folk Ideas as Units of Worldview." In: Américo Paredes and Richard Bauman (eds.), *Toward New Perspectives in Folklore.* Austin, Texas: University of Texas Press, 93–103.

Dundes, Lauren, Michael B. Streiff, and Alan Dundes. 1999. "'When You Hear Hoofbeats, Think Horses, Not Zebras': A Folk Medical Diagnostic Proverb." *Proverbium* 16: 95–103; also in Mieder 2003a, 99–107.

Gallacher, Stuart A. 1949. "Franklin's *Way to Wealth:* A Florilegium of Proverbs and Wise Sayings." *Journal of English and Germanic Philology* 48: 229–251.

Goodwin, Paul D., and Joseph W. Wenzel. 1979. "Proverbs and Practical Reasoning: A Study in Socio-Logic." *The Quarterly Journal of Speech* 65: 289–302; also in Mieder and Dundes 1981, 140–160.

Gossen, Gary. 1973. "Chamula Tzotzil [Mayan Indians from southern Mexico] Proverbs: 'Neither Fish nor Fowl.'" In: Munro S. Edmonson (ed.), *Meaning in Mayan Languages: Ethnolinguistic Studies.* The Hague: Mouton, 205–233; also in Mieder 1994, 351–392.

Grigas, Kazys. 1995. "The Motif of the Mote in Someone's Eye and the Comparative Study of a Proverb." *Arv: Nordic Yearbook of Folklore* 51: 155–159.

Grigas, Kazys. 1996. "Problems of the Type in the Comparative Study of Proverbs." *Journal of the Baltic Institute of Folklore* 1: 106–127.

Grigas, Kazys. 1998. "Das Sprichwort 'Man soll den Tag nicht vor dem Abend loben' in der Geschichte der europäischen Kulturen." *Proverbium* 15: 105–136.

Grigas, Kazys. 2000. "Einige Probleme der modernen Parömiographie und Parömiologie." *Acta Ethnographia Hungarica* 45: 365–369.

Grzybek, Peter. 1987. "Foundations of Semiotic Proverb Study." *Proverbium* 4: 39–85; also in Mieder 1994, 31–71.

Hakamies, Pekka. 2002. "Proverbs and Mentality." In: Anna-Leena Siikala (ed.), *Myth and Mentality. Studies in Folklore and Popular Thought.* Helsinki: Finnish Literature Society, 222–230.

Hertzler, Joyce O. 1933–1934. "On Golden Rules." *The International Journal of Ethics* 44: 418–436.

Hulme, F. Edward. 1902. *Proverb Lore.* London: Elliot Stock, 1902; rpt. Detroit, Michigan: Gale Research Company, 1968.

Jente, Richard. 1931–1932. "The American Proverb." *American Speech* 7: 342–348.

Jente, Richard. 1945. "The Untilled Field of Proverbs." In: George R. Coffman (ed.), *Studies in Language and Literature.* Chapel Hill, North Carolina: University of North Carolina Press, 112–119.

Krikmann, Arvo. 1974. *On Denotative Indefiniteness of Proverbs.* Tallinn: Academy of Sciences of the Estonian SSR, Institute of Language and Literature, 1974; also in *Proverbium* 1 (1984): 47–91.

Kuusi, Matti. 1957. *Parömiologische Betrachtungen.* Helsinki: Suomalainen Tiedeakatemia.

La Rosa, Ralph Charles. 1969. *Emerson's Proverbial Rhetoric: 1818–1838.* Diss. University of Wisconsin.

La Rosa, Ralph Charles. 1976. "Necessary Truths: The Poetics of Emerson's Proverbs." In: Eric Rothstein (ed.), *George Eliot, De Quincey, and Emerson.* Madison, Wisconsin: University of Wisconsin Press, 129–192.

Lau, Kimberly J. 1996. "'It's about Time': The Ten Proverbs Most Frequently Used in Newspapers and Their Relation to American Values." *Proverbium* 13: 135–159; also in Mieder 2003a, 231–254.

Lieber, Michael D. 1984. "Analogic Ambiguity: A Paradox of Proverb Usage." *Journal of American Folklore* 97: 423–441; also in Mieder 1994, 99–126.

Massing, Jean Michel. 1995. "From Greek Proverb to Soap Advert [*sic*]: Washing the Ethiopian." *Journal of the Warburg and Courtauld Institutes* 58: 180–201.

McKenna, Kevin J. (ed.). 1998. *Proverbs in Russian Literature: From Catherine the Great to Alexander Solzhenitsyn.* Burlington, Vermont: The University of Vermont.

McKenna, Kevin J. 2003. "A Nation Adrift: The Russian 'Ship of State' in *Pravda* Political Cartoons During the Decade of the 1990's." *Proverbium* 20: 237–258.

McKenzie, Alyce M. 1996a. "'Different Strokes for Different Folks': America's Quintessential Postmodern Proverb." *Theology Today* 53: 201–212; also in Mieder 2003a, 311–324.

McKenzie, Alyce M. 1996b. *Preaching Proverbs: Wisdom for the Pulpit.* Louisville, Kentucky: Westminster John Knox Press.

Meichsner, Irene. 1983. *Die Logik von Gemeinplätzen. Vorgeführt an Steuermannstopos und Schiffsmetapher.* Bonn: Bouvier.

Mieder, Wolfgang. 1971. "'Behold the Proverbs of a People': A Florilegium of Proverbs in Carl Sandburg's Poem *Good Morning, America.*" *Southern Folklore Quarterly* 35: 160–168.

Mieder, Wolfgang. 1973. "Proverbs in Carl Sandburg's Poem *The People, Yes.*" *Southern Folklore Quarterly* 37: 15–36.

Mieder, Wolfgang. 1985a. "Popular Views of the Proverb." *Proverbium* 2: 109–143.

Mieder, Wolfgang. 1985b. *Sprichwort, Redensart, Zitat. Tradierte Formelsprache in der Moderne.* Bern: Peter Lang.

Mieder, Wolfgang. 1987. *Tradition and Innovation in Folk Literature.* Hanover, New Hampshire: University Press of New England.

Mieder, Wolfgang. 1989a. *American Proverbs: A Study of Texts and Contexts.* Bern: Peter Lang.

Mieder, Wolfgang. 1989b. "'Ein Bild sagt mehr als tausend Worte': Ursprung und Überlieferung eines amerikanischen Lehnsprichworts." *Proverbium* 6: 25–37.

Mieder, Wolfgang. 1990. "Prolegomena to Prospective Paremiography." *Proverbium* 7: 133–144.

Mieder, Wolfgang. 1992. *Sprichwort—Wahrwort!? Studien zur Geschichte, Bedeutung und Funktion deutscher Sprichwörter.* Frankfurt am Main: Peter Lang.

Mieder, Wolfgang. 1993. *Proverbs Are Never Out of Season: Popular Wisdom in the Modern Age.* New York: Oxford University Press.

Mieder, Wolfgang (ed.). 1994. *Wise Words. Essays on the Proverb.* New York: Garland.

Mieder, Wolfgang. 1995a. *Deutsche Redensarten, Sprichwörter und Zitate. Studien zu ihrer Herkunft, Überlieferung und Verwendung.* Wien: Edition Praesens.

Mieder, Wolfgang. 1995b. *Sprichwörtliches und Geflügeltes. Sprachstudien von Martin Luther bis Karl Marx.* Bochum: Norbert Brockmeyer.

Mieder, Wolfgang. 1997a. *"Morgenstunde hat Gold im Munde": Studien und Belege zum populärsten deutschsprachigen Sprichwort.* Wien: Edition Praesens.

Mieder, Wolfgang. 1997b. *The Politics of Proverbs. From Traditional Wisdom to Proverbial Stereotypes.* Madison, Wisconsin: University of Wisconsin Press.

Mieder, Wolfgang. 1998. *"A House Divided": From Biblical Proverb to Lincoln and Beyond.* Burlington, Vermont: The University of Vermont.

Mieder, Wolfgang. 2000a. *Strategies of Wisdom. Anglo-American and German Proverb Studies.* Baltmannsweiler, Germany: Schneider Verlag Hohengehren.

Mieder, Wolfgang. 2000b. "The History and Future of Common Proverbs in Europe." In: Ilona Nagy and Kincső Verebélyi (eds.), *Folklore in 2000. Voces amicorum Guilhelmo Voigt sexagenario.* Budapest: Universitas Scientiarum de Rolando Eötvös nominata, 300–314.

Mieder, Wolfgang. 2000c. *The Proverbial Abraham Lincoln. An Index to Proverbs in the Works of Abraham Lincoln.* New York: Peter Lang.

Mieder, Wolfgang. 2001. *"No Struggle, No Progress" Frederick Douglass and His Proverbial Rhetoric for Civil Rights*. New York: Peter Lang.

Mieder, Wolfgang. 2002a. *"Call a Spade a Spade": From Classical Phrase to Racial Slur. A Case Study.* New York: Peter Lang.

Mieder, Wolfgang. 2002b. "Narrative History as Proverbial Narrative: David McCullough's Best-Selling *John Adams* [2001] Biography." *Proverbium* 19: 279–322.

Mieder, Wolfgang (ed.). 2003a. *Cognition, Comprehension, and Communication. A Decade of North American Proverb Studies (1990–2000)*. Baltmannsweiler, Germany: Schneider Verlag Hohengehren.

Mieder, Wolfgang. 2003b. *"Die großen Fische fressen die kleinen": Ein Sprichwort über die menschliche Natur in Literatur, Medien und Karikaturen*. Wien: Edition Praesens.

Mieder, Wolfgang. 2003c. "'Good Fences Make Good Neighbours': History and Significance of an Ambiguous Proverb." *Folklore* (London) 114: 155–179.

Mieder, Wolfgang. 2004a. "Der frühe Vogel und die goldene Morgenstunde: Zu einer deutschen Sprichwortentlehnung aus dem Angloamerikanischen." In: Irma Hyvärinen, Petri Kallio, and Jarmo Korhonen (eds.), *Etymologie, Entlehnungen und Entwicklungen. Festschrift für Jorma Koivulehto*. Helsinki: Societé Néophilologique, 193–206.

Mieder, Wolfgang. 2004b. "'Ein Apfel pro Tag hält den Arzt fern': Zu einigen amerikanischen Lehnsprichwörtern im Deutschen." *Revista de Filologia Alemana* 12: 143–157.

Mieder, Wolfgang. 2004c. "'Man soll nicht alle Eier in einen Korb legen': Zur deutschsprachigen Entlehnung eines angloamerikanischen Sprichwortes." *Nauchnyi vestnik. Seriia: Sovremennye lingvisticheskie is metodiko-didakticheskie issledovaniia* (Woronesh, Russia), no volume given, no. 1: 21–31.

Mieder, Wolfgang. 2004d. *Proverbs. A Handbook*. Westport, Connecticut: Greenwood Press.

Mieder, Wolfgang, and George B. Bryan. 1995. *The Proverbial Winston S. Churchill. An Index to Proverbs in the Works of Sir Winston Churchill*. Westport, Connecticut: Greenwood Press.

Mieder, Wolfgang, and George B. Bryan. 1997. *The Proverbial Harry S. Truman. An Index to Proverbs in the Works of Harry S. Truman*. New York: Peter Lang.

Mieder, Wolfgang, and Alan Dundes (eds.). 1981. *The Wisdom of Many: Essays on the Proverb*. New York: Garland; rpt. Madison, Wisconsin: University of Wisconsin Press, 1994.

Miller, Edd, and Jesse J. Villarreal. 1945. "The Use of Clichés by Four Contemporary Speakers [Winston S. Churchill, Anthony Eden, Franklin D. Roosevelt, and Henry Wallace]." *Quarterly Journal of Speech* 31: 151–155.

Monteiro, George. 1972. "'Good Fences Make Good Neighbors': A Proverb and a Poem." *Revista de Etnografia* 16: 83–88.

Nichols, Ray. 1996. "Maxims, 'Practical Wisdom,' and the Language of Action." *Political Theory* 24: 687–705.

Nikoláeva, Julia. 1999. "Vicisitudes ideológicas de la paremiología soviética." *Paremia* 8: 359–364.

Nussbaum, Stan. 1998. *The ABC of American Culture. First Steps toward Understanding the American People through Their Common Sayings and Proverbs.* Colorado Springs, Colorado: Global Mapping International.

Obelkevich, James. 1987. "Proverbs and Social History." In: Peter Burke and Roy Porter (eds.), *The Social History of Language.* Cambridge: Cambridge University Press, 43–72; also in Mieder 1994, 211–252.

Pfeffer, J. Alan. 1975. "Das biblische Zitat im Volksmund der Germanen und Romanen." In: Beda Allemann and Erwin Koppen (eds.), *Teilnahme und Spiegelung. Festschrift für Horst Rüdiger.* Berlin: Walter de Gruyter, 99–111.

Prager, Carolyn. 1987. "'If I Be Devil': English Renaissance Response to the Proverbial and Ecumenical Ethiopian." *Journal of Medieval and Renaissance Studies* 17: 257–279.

Prahlad, Sw. Anand. 1996. *African-American Proverbs in Context.* Jackson, Mississippi: University of Mississippi Press.

Profantová, Zuzana. 1998. "Proverbial Tradition as Cultural-Historical and Social Phenomenon." In: Peter Ďurčo (ed.), *Europhras '97. Phraseology and Paremiology.* Bratislava: Akadémia PZ, 302–307.

Raymond, Joseph. 1956. "Tensions in Proverbs: More Light on International Understanding." *Western Folklore* 15: 153–158; also in Mieder and Dundes 1981, 300–308.

Reaver, J. Russell. 1967. "Thoreau's Ways with Proverbs." *American Transcendental Quarterly* 1: 2–7

Reiner, Hans. 1948. "Die 'Goldene Regel': Die Bedeutung einer sittlichen Grundformel der Menschheit." *Zeitschrift für philosophische Forschung* 3: 74–105.

Roberts, John W. 1978. "Slave Proverbs: A Perspective." *Callaloo* 1: 129–140.

Röhrich, Lutz, and Wolfgang Mieder. 1977. *Sprichwort.* Stuttgart: Metzler.

Seitel, Peter. 1969. "Proverbs: A Social Use of Metaphor." *Genre* 2: 143–161; also in Mieder and Dundes 1981, 122–139.

Smitherman, Geneva. 1986. *Talkin and Testifyin: The Language of Black America.* Detroit, Michigan: Wayne State University Press.

Smitherman, Geneva. 1994. *Black Talk: Words and Phrases from the Hood to the Amen Corner.* New York: Houghton Mifflin.

Soliva, Claudio. 1964. "Ein Bibelwort [die 'Goldene Regel'] in Geschichte und Recht." *Unser Weg: Werkblatt der Schweizerischen Weggefährtinnen,* no volume given, nos. 6–7: 51–57.

Taylor, Archer. 1931. *The Proverb.* Cambridge, Massachusetts: Harvard University Press; rpt. with an introduction and bibliography by Wolfgang Mieder. 1985. Bern: Peter Lang.

Templeton, John Marks. 1997. *Worldwide Laws of Life. 200 Eternal Spiritual Principles.* Philadelphia, Pennsylvania: Templeton Foundation Press.

Tóthné Litovkina, Anna. 1996. "A Few Aspects of a Semiotic Approach to Proverbs, with Special Reference to Two Important American Publications [W. Mieder, *American Proverbs: A Study of Texts and Contexts* (1989) and W. Mieder et al., *A Dictionary of American Proverbs* (1992)]." *Semiotica* 108: 307–380.

Voigt, Vilmos. 2001. "Lithuanian Proverbs and Their Place in European Paremiology." *Tautosakos Darbai / Folklore Studies* 15 (22): 11–16.

White, Geoffrey M. 1987. "Proverbs and Cultural Models. An American Psychology of Problem Solving." In: Dorothy Holland and Naomi Quinn (eds.), *Cultural Models in Language and Thought.* Cambridge: Cambridge University Press, 152–172.

Williams, Fionnuala, and Wolfgang Mieder. 2004. "The Proverb 'Good Fences Make Good Neighbors' in Ireland." *Folklore* (London) 115: 332–337.

Name Index

Subject Index

Key Word Index of Proverbs